Rick Steves'
Mona Winks

Rick Steves'

Mona Winks

Self-Guided Tours of Europe's Top Museums

FIFTH EDITION

Rick Steves and Gene Openshaw

AVALON
TRAVEL

Other ATP travel guidebooks by Rick Steves
  Rick Steves' Best of Europe
  Rick Steves' Europe 101: History & Art for the Traveler (with Gene Openshaw)
  Rick Steves' Europe Through the Back Door
  Rick Steves' Postcards from Europe
  Rick Steves' France, Belgium & the Netherlands (with Steve Smith)
  Rick Steves' Germany, Austria & Switzerland
  Rick Steves' Great Britain
  Rick Steves' Ireland (with Pat O'Connor)
  Rick Steves' Italy
  Rick Steves' Scandinavia
  Rick Steves' Spain & Portugal
  Rick Steves' London (with Gene Openshaw)
  Rick Steves' Florence (with Gene Openshaw)
  Rick Steves' Paris (with Steve Smith and Gene Openshaw)
  Rick Steves' Rome (with Gene Openshaw)
  Rick Steves' Venice (with Gene Openshaw)
  Rick Steves' Phrase Books: French, Italian, German, Spanish and Portuguese,
    and French/Italian/German

Thanks to:
Elizabeth Openshaw and Shirley Openshaw for maternal support
and Anne Steves for athletic support.

Avalon Travel Publishing, 5855 Beaudry Street, Emeryville, CA 94608

Fifth edition. First printing October 2001.
Printed in the United States of America by R. R. Donnelley.

Library of Congress Cataloging-in-Publication Data
Steves, Rick, 1955–
  Rick Steves' Mona Winks: Self-Guided Tours of Europe's Top Museums/
  Rick Steves & Gene Openshaw—fifth ed.
      p.   cm.
  Includes index.
  ISBN 1-56691-345-4 (pbk.)
  1. Art museums—Europe—Guidebooks. I. Openshaw, Gene. II. Title.
  N1010.S7 2000
  708.94—dc21   20010 34127
                                                        CIP

Europe Through the Back Door Editor: Risa Laib
Avalon Travel Publishing Editor: Kate Willis
Research Assistance: Lisa Friend and Ben Cameron (London), Susan Minich
    (Madrid), Lisa Anderson (Venice and Florence), and Lynn Nicholas (Amsterdam)
Copy editor: Donna Leverenz
Production and Design: Kathleen Sparkes, White Hart Design, Albuquerque, NM
Cover Design: Kathleen Sparkes, Rhonda Pelikan
Maps: David C. Hoerlein
Photography: Rick Steves, Dominic Arizona Bonuccelli, David C. Hoerlein, and others

Distributed to the book trade by Publishers Group West, Berkeley, California

❀

To
all the artists
whose works hang
in no museums—
and
to those
who appreciate them.

❀

❧ CONTENTS ❧

INTRODUCTION

Even at its best, museum-going is hard work. This book attempts to tame Europe's "required" museums, making them meaningful, fun, fast, and painless. Here are some tips on how to use this book to get the most out of your museum visits.

Beforehand

Do some background reading. The more you know, the more you'll appreciate the art. Before your trip, take a class or read a book on art.

Rip up this book. Before your trip, rip out, staple bind, and pack just the individual chapters you'll use. (If this really bugs you, send all the pieces and $5 to Europe Through the Back Door, 130 4th Avenue North, Edmonds, WA 98020, and we'll send you a new copy. Really.)

Note that the modern art chapter in this book offers good background information for a visit to any modern art museum. Remember to bring this chapter along, regardless of your destination.

Read ahead. Scan the chapter the night before you visit the museum. Get a feel for the kind of art and artists you'll see.

Check the introductory material. This is included on the first page of each chapter. It lists the museum hours, cost, availability of information, and so forth. Avoid tactical problems by planning ahead.

In the Museum

Get oriented. Use the overview map to understand the museum's layout, location of art, and the basic tour route.

Use the maps and written directions. All featured art appears on the room maps. Maps are usually oriented so you enter from the bottom (look for the "start" arrow). Written directions reinforce the maps.

Keep the big picture. As you enter each room, get the general feel. Scan for the common characteristics of the art. Next, study the specific example mentioned in the text. Then browse, trying out what you have learned.

Partners, take turns acting as guide. It's easier if one looks while the other reads.

Use the index. Use the index to find supplemental information on artists and styles.

For more information: This book covers the highlights of museums. Serious art lovers might want to supplement *Mona* with an audioguide or guided tour at the museum.

Audioguides, available at many museums, are handheld devices you carry as you walk through a museum. When you see a piece of art that interests you, you dial a code number (listed next to the art), then listen to a description in English of the work. Audioguides are affordable (about $5) and usually dry, but worthwhile.

Some museums offer **guided tours** (sometimes free but usually at a cost of $6 or more). In France, Italy, and Spain, tours in English are most likely to occur during peak season. The quality of a tour depends on the guide's knowledge, fluency, and enthusiasm.

Watch For Changes

Museums change. Paintings can be on tour, on loan, out sick, or shifted at the whim of the curator. Even museum walls are often moved. To adapt:

(1) Pick up any available free floor plans as you enter.
(2) Let the museum's information person glance at this book's maps to confirm locations of paintings.
(3) If you can't find a particular painting, ask any museum worker where it is. Just point to the photograph in this book and ask, "Where?": in Italian, *"Dove?"* (DOH-vay); in French, *"Où est?"* (oo ay); in Spanish, *"Dónde?"* (DOHN-day).

Museum hours change. Museums change their entrance hours, especially in Italy and off-season. Confirm by telephone or at the city tourist office upon arrival.

Currencies change. Note that 2002 is the year the euro (€) appears as bills and coins in 12 European countries. We've listed prices in euros in this book for the "Euro" countries of France, Italy, Spain, and the Netherlands. (Britain is sticking with pounds.) Because it's a transition year for the euro, the prices we list are approximate. But regardless, Europe's great museums are a bargain.

General Museum Policies

Last entry: Many museums have "last entry" 30 to 60 minutes before closing. Guards usher people out before the official closing time.

Photography: Cameras are normally allowed, but no flashes or tripods (without special permission). Flashes damage oil paintings and distract others in the room. Even without a flash, a handheld camera with ASA-400 film and an F-2 aperture will take a fine picture (or buy slides at the museum bookstore). Video cameras are usually allowed.

Baggage check: For security reasons, you're often required to check even small bags. Every museum has a free checkroom at the entrance. They're safe. Check everything (except *Mona Winks*) and enjoy the museum. Or, to avoid checking your bag, try carrying it like a purse throughout your museum visit. (What scares officials is not just the backpack itself but the possibility of your bumping into priceless art with your pack on your back.)

Toilets: WCs are free and better and cleaner than the European average.

Food: Museum-going stokes appetites. Most museums have cafeterias with reasonable prices and decent food. Check the information at the beginning of each chapter for evaluations and recommendations.

Museum bookstores: These sell cards, prints, posters, slides, and guidebooks. Thumb through a museum's biggest guidebook (or scan its index) to be sure you haven't overlooked something that is of particular interest to you.

No Apologies

This book drives art snobs nuts. Its gross generalizations, sketchy dates, oversimplifications, and shoot-from-the-hip opinions will likely tweeze art highbrows. *Rick Steves' Mona Winks* isn't an art history text; it's a quick taste of Europe's fascinating but difficult museums. Use it as an introduction—not the final word. From this point on, "we" (your co-authors) will shed our respective egos and become "I." Enjoy.

A victim of the Louvre.

ART HISTORY
FIVE MILLENNIA IN SEVEN PAGES

Egypt: 3000–1000 B.C.

Tombs and mummies preserved corpses and possessions for the afterlife. Statues of pharaohs were political propaganda. Figures in paintings and statuary were stiff and unrealistic, perpetually standing to attention. Little changed in 2,000 years.

You'll find examples in the:
- British Museum (statues, mummies, and Rosetta Stone)
- Vatican Museum
- Louvre

Greece: 700 B.C.–A.D. 1

Greece provided the foundation of our "Western" civilization—science, democracy, art, and the faith that the universe is orderly and rational.

Archaic (700–500 B.C.)

In a time of wars the creative Greek spirit was beginning to show itself. Stiff statues reflect their search for stability and order amid chaos. Sculptors showed keen interest in, but no mastery of, the human body.

- "Kouros" statues (in Louvre and British Museum)

Golden Age (500–325 B.C.)

Athens rules a coalition of city-states in the days of Socrates, Pericles, Plato, and Aristotle. The Greek gods were portrayed as idealized human beings. Statues look natural, but their balanced poses show the order found in nature. Nothing in extreme.
- *Apollo Belvedere* (Vatican Museum, see photo)
- Elgin Marbles from the Parthenon (British Museum)
- *Venus de Milo* (Louvre)
- *Venus de' Medici* (Uffizi)

Hellenism (325 B.C.–A.D. 1)

Alexander the Great conquers Greece and spreads Greek culture around the Mediterranean. A time of individualism produces restless statues of people in motion—struggling against other people, animals, and themselves. Everything in extreme.

- *Laocoön* (Vatican Museum, see photo)
- *Winged Victory* (Louvre)

Rome: 500 B.C.–A.D. 500

The Romans conquered Greek lands and absorbed their culture and gods. The result: Greek style, with a "bigger is better" attitude. Romans were engineers, not artists. Using the arch and concrete, they built unprecedented grand structures, decorated with Greek columns and statues. Realistic portrait busts of the emperors reminded subjects who was in charge.

- Colosseum, Forum, and Pantheon (Rome)
- Greek-style statues (Vatican Museum, Louvre, British Museum)
- Portrait busts (Vatican Museum and Louvre)

Medieval Europe: A.D. 500–1400

Rome falls, plunging Europe into "dark" centuries of poverty, war, famine, and hand-me-down leotards. The church is the people's refuge, and Heaven is their hope. Art serves the church— Bible scenes, crucifixes, saints, and Madonnas (Mary, the mother of Jesus) decorate churches

and inspire the illiterate masses. Gothic architects used the pointed arch to build tall, spired churches with walls of stained glass.

Art is symbolic, not realistic. Saints float in a golden, heavenly realm, far removed from life on earth. Humans are scrawny sinners living in a flat, two-dimensional world.

- Altarpieces in many museums and churches
- Notre Dame and Sainte-Chapelle
- Illuminated manuscripts (British Museum)

Byzantine: A.D. 300–1450

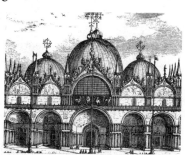

The Eastern half of the Roman Empire, centered in Constantinople (Istanbul), lived on after Rome fell. Byzantium preserved the classical arts and learning through the Dark Ages. These ideas reentered Europe via Venice.

- St. Mark's Church—mosaics, domes, and treasures (Venice)
- Icon-style gold-leafed paintings (many museums)

Italian Renaissance: 1400–1600

The Renaissance is the "rebirth" of the arts and learning of ancient Greece and Rome—democracy, science, and humanism. Architects built balanced structures with Greek columns and Roman domes and arches. Sculptors used 3-D realism to glorify human beings like Greek nudes. Artists, using mathematical laws of perspective to capture the 3-D world on a 2-D canvas, saw God in the orderliness of nature and the beauty of the human body. Art is no longer tied to the church. Art for art's sake is OK.

Florence (1400–1520)

In this city, the birthplace of the Renaissance, Greek-style sculpture and Roman-style architecture were revived. Pioneering 3-D painting, artists placed statuelike people in spacious settings.

- Michelangelo's *David* (Florence's Accademia)
- Botticelli's *Birth of Venus* (Uffizi, see photo above)
- Brunelleschi's dome (Florence)
- Donatello's sculpture (Bargello)
- Leonardo da Vinci, Giotto, Raphael (Uffizi and other museums)

High (or Roman) Renaissance (1500–1550)

The city of Rome was grandly rebuilt by energetic, secular-minded Renaissance popes.

- Sistine Chapel, Michelangelo (Vatican Museum, see photo)
- The dome of St. Peter's Basilica, by Michelangelo (Vatican City)
- Raphael (Vatican Museum)

Venetian Renaissance (1500–1600)

Big, colorful, sensual paintings celebrate the Venetian good life, funded by trade with the East. Whereas Florentine painters drew their figures with heavy outlines, Venetians "built" figures out of patches of color.

- Titian (see photo), Veronese, Tintoretto (many museums)
- Best museums: Venice's Accademia, Madrid's Prado
- Doge's Palace (Venice)

Northern Protestant Art: 1500–1700

Art was bought by middle-class merchants, not popes and kings. Everyday things were painted on small canvases in a simple, realistic, unemotional style, with loving attention to detail. Common subjects were portraits, landscapes, still lifes, and wacky slice-of-life scenes.

- Rembrandt (many museums)
- Vermeer (see photo, Amsterdam's Rijksmuseum)
- Dürer (National Gallery, Uffizi)
- Bosch (Prado)
- Best museums: Rijksmuseum, Prado

Baroque: 1600–1700

This style of divine-right kings (Louis XIV) and the Counter-Reformation Catholic Church was meant to overpower the common man. Baroque is big, colorful, and ornamented, though based on Renaissance balance. Featuring exaggerated beauty and violence, Baroque specializes in Greek gods, angels, nudes, and pudgy, winged babies.

- Palace of Versailles
- St. Peter's Basilica
- Rubens (many museums, see photo)

Rococo: 1700–1800

Baroque's frilly little sister is smaller, lighter, and even more ornamented, with pastel colors, rosy cheeks, and pudgier winged babies. In architecture, the oval replaces the circle as the basic pattern. Aristocratic tastes were growing more refined and more out of touch with the everyday world.

- Versailles' interior decoration
- Boucher (see photo), Watteau and Fragonard (Louvre)

Neoclassical: 1750–1850

With the French Revolution, rococo became politically incorrect. Neoclassical is yet another rebirth of the Greek and Roman world. It's simpler and more austere than Renaissance and Baroque versions of the classical style. Reflecting its era, neoclassical is the art of democracy and the "Age of Reason."

- J. L. David (Louvre)
- Ingres (Louvre and Orsay, see photo)
- Paris' Pantheon, Helsinki's Lutheran Cathedral

Romanticism: 1800–1850

Reacting against the overly rational neoclassical and Industrial Age, Romanticism is a return to Nature and Man's primitive roots. Dramatic, colorful art expresses the most intense inner emotions. Both individuals and nations struggle to be free.

- Goya (Prado, see photo)
- Delacroix (Louvre)
- Blake and Turner
  (Tate Britain)

Impressionism and Post-Impressionism: 1850–1900

Quick "impressions" of everyday scenes (landscapes, cafés) are captured with a fast and messy style. The thick brush strokes of bright colors laid side by side on the canvas blend at a distance, leaving the impression of shimmering light.

- Monet, Manet, Degas, and Renoir (see photo, Orsay)
- Van Gogh (Van Gogh Museum, Orsay)
- Gauguin, Cézanne, Rodin (Orsay)
- Best museums: Paris' Orsay, London's National Gallery

Modern Art: 20th Century and Beyond

In our no-holds-barred modern world, the artist's task is to show life in a fresh, new way. There are two basic strains of modern art: Artists continue to paint real things, but distort them to give us a new perspective (surrealism, Expressionism, pop art). Artists use the building blocks of painting—color and line—to create new and interesting patterns that hint at the nonvisual aspects of the world (abstract art, abstract expressionism). Most modern art mixes the two strains.

But what does it *mean*? Modern art offers an alternative to our normal, orderly, programmed McLives. It's a wild, chaotic jungle that you'll have to explore and tame on your own. *Grrr.*

- Picasso (Cubism and many other styles, see photo)
- Dali (surrealism)
- Mondrian (abstract)
- Warhol (pop art)
- Pollock (abstract expressionism)
- Chagall (mix of various styles)
- Museums: London's Tate Modern, Paris' Pompidou Center, Venice's Peggy Guggenheim, and more.

Additional Information

If you'd like to read an entire book on art, history, and culture, let me humbly recommend *Rick Steves' Europe 101: History and Art for the Traveler,* by my two favorite authors, Rick Steves and Gene Openshaw. While *Mona Winks* is your on-the-spot museum manual, *Europe 101* has the necessary background information. Written in the same fun and practical style, with many of the very same jokes, *Europe 101* brings Europe's churches, palaces, and statues to life.

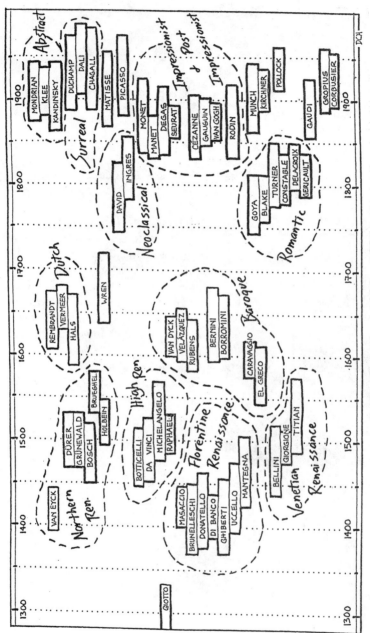

Artist Timeline: 1300 – 1985

ARTISTS & DATES

Avercamp, Hendrick (pron: AH-vehr-kahmp), 1585–1634: Dutch slice-of-life scenes.

Baldung Grien, Hans (BAHL-dung green), 1484–1545: Northern student of Italian Renaissance techniques.

Bellini, Giovanni (bel-LEE-nee), 1430–1516: Colorful soft-focus madonnas.

Bernini (ber-NEE-nee), 1598–1680: Baroque grandeur, exuberance, emotion, and flesh.

Blake, William, 1757–1827: Mystical visions.

Bosch, Hieronymous (bosh), 1450–1516: Crowded, bizarre scenes.

Botticelli, Sandro (bot-i-CHEL-lee), 1445–1510: Delicate Renaissance beauty.

Boucher, François (boo-shay), 1703–1770: Sensual rococo scenes for French aristocrats.

Brancusi, Constantin (brahn-KOO-zee), 1876–1957: Smooth, shiny, abstract statues.

Braque, Georges (brock), 1882–1963: Cubist pioneer.

Brueghel, Pieter (BROY-gull), c. 1525–1569: Netherlands, peasant scenes.

Brunelleschi, Filippo (broon-uh-LES-key), 1377–1446: First great Renaissance architect.

Calder, Alexander, 1898–1976: Abstract mobiles.

Canaletto (kah-nah-LET-toh), 1697–1768; Misty Venetian overviews.

Caravaggio (kar-ah-VAH-jee-oh), 1573–1610: Shocking ultrarealism.

Cellini, Benvenuto (chel-LEE-nee), 1500–1571: Renaissance metal statues.

Cézanne, Paul (say-zahn), 1839–1906: Bridged Impressionism and Cubism.

Chagall, Marc (shah-gahl), 1887–1985: Fiddlers on roofs, magical realism.

Cimabue (chee-MAH-bway), c. 1240–1302: Experimented with Renaissance techniques and influenced Giotto.

Claudel, Camille (cloh-del), 1864–1943: Rodin's protégée.

Constable, John, 1776–1837: Rustic English country scenes.

Courbet, Gustave (coor-bay), 1819–1877: Unglamorized realism.

Cranach, Lucas (KRAH-nakh), 1472–1553: Northern Renaissance plus sensuality.

da Vinci, Leonardo (dah VINCH-ee), 1452–1519: A well-rounded Renaissance genius who also painted.

Dalí, Salvador (DAH-lee), 1904–1989: Surrealist showman.

Daumier, Honoré (dohm-yay), 1808–1879: Caricatures of pomposity.

David, Jacques-Louis (dah-veed), 1748–1825: Chronicler of heroic Napoleonic era (neoclassicism).

Degas, Edgar (day-gah), 1834–1917: Impressionist snapshots, dancers.

Delacroix, Eugène (del-ah-kwah), 1798–1863: Colorful, emotional, exotic Romanticism.

Donatello, (doh-na-TEL-oh), c. 1386–1466: Early Renaissance sculptor.

Dürer, Albrecht (DEWR-er), 1471–1528: Renaissance symmetry with German detail; "the Leonardo of the north."

El Greco (el GREK-oh), 1541–1614: Spiritual scenes, elongated bodies.

Fabriano, Gentile da (fah-bree-AH-noh), 1370–1427: Medieval master of colorful detail.

Fra Angelico (frah ahn-JEL-lee-koh), 1387–1455: Renaissance techniques, medieval piety.

Fragonard, Jean-Honoré (frah-goh-nar), 1732–1806: Rococo candy.

Gainsborough, Thomas, 1727–1788: Relaxed portraits of English upper crust.

Gauguin, Paul (go-GAN), 1848–1903: Primitivism, native scenes, bright colors.

Géricault, Théodore (zher-ee-koh), 1791–1824: Dramatic Romantic.

Ghiberti, Lorenzo (gee-BEHR-tee, hard *g*), 1378–1455: Pioneer of Renaissance 3-D in bronze relief.

Giacometti, Alberto (jah-koh-MET-tee), 1901–1966: Stick-figure sculptures, modern art.

Giorgione (jor-JONE-ee), 1477–1510: Venetian Renaissance, mysterious beauty.

Giotto (JOT-oh), 1266–1337: Proto-Renaissance painter (3-D) in medieval times.

Goya, Francisco (GOY-ah), 1746–1828: Three stages: frilly court painter, political rebel, dark stage.

Guardi, Francesco (GWAHR-dee), 1712–1793: Postcards of Venice.

Hals, Frans (halls), 1581–1666: Snapshot portraits of Dutch merchants.

Hogarth, William, 1697–1764: Stage sets of English life.

Ingres, Jean Auguste Dominique (ang-gruh), 1780–1867: Neoclassical.

Kandinsky, Wassily (kahn-DIN-skee), 1866–1944: Colorful, abstract squiggles and shapes.

Kirchner, Ernest Ludwig (KIRSH-ner), 1880–1938: Expressionist critic of society in jagged shapes and lurid colors.

Klee, Paul (klay), 1879–1940: Simplified, playful, childlike forms.

Lorrain, Claude (loh-ran), 1602–1682: Glorious sunsets over classical architecture.

Leger, Fernand (leh-zhay), 1881–1955: Cylinder-shaped Cubism ("tubism").

Leonardo; see da Vinci.

Lippi, Fra Filippo (LIP-pee), 1406–1469: Young, pretty virgins.

Manet, Edouard (mah-nay), 1823–1883: Forerunner of Impressionist rebels.

Mantegna, Andrea (mahn-TAYN-yah), 1431–1506: Renaissance 3-D and "sculptural" painting.

Martini, Simone, 1284–1344: Sienese medieval altarpieces.

Matisse, Henri (mah-TEES), 1869–1954: Decorative "wallpaper," bright colors.

Michelangelo (mee-kel-AHN-jel-oh), 1475–1564: Earth's greatest sculptor and one of its greatest painters.

Millet, Jean-François (mee-yay), 1814–1875: Realist painter in Academic society.

Miró, Joan (mee-ROH), 1893–1983: Childlike, simplified forms.

Mondrian, Piet (MAHN-dree-ahn), 1872–1944: Abstract, geometrical canvases.

Monet, Claude (moh-nay), 1840–1926: Father of Impressionism.

Murillo, Bartolomé Esteban (moo-REE-yoh), 1617–1682: Sugar-coated Catholic images.

Newman, Barnett, 1905–1970: Big, empty, abstract canvases.

Parmigianino (par-mee-jah-NEE-noh), 1503–1540: Mannerist exaggeration, elongated bodies.

Picasso, Pablo (pee-KAHS-soh), 1881–1973: Master of many modern styles, especially Cubism.

Pissarro, Camile (pee-SAHR-roh), 1830–1903: Grainy Impressionism.

Pollaiolo, Antonio (pohl-eye-OH-loh), 1432–1498: Influential studies of human anatomy.

Pollock, Jackson (PAHL-luck), 1912–1956: Wild drips of paint.

Poussin, Nicolas (poo-san), 1594–1665: Calm, balanced, classical themes.

Raphael (roff-eye-ELL), 1483–1520: Epitome of the Renaissance—balance, realism, beauty.

Rembrandt (REM-brant), 1606–1669: Greatest Dutch painter, brown canvases, dramatic lighting.

Renoir, Auguste (ren-wah), 1841–1919: Impressionist style, idealized beauty, pastels.

Reynolds, Sir Joshua, 1723–1792: English academic in classical style.

Robert, Hubert, 1733–1808: Classical ruins.

Rodin, Auguste (roh-dan), 1840–1917: Classical statues with rough "Impressionist" finish.

Rossetti, Dante Gabriel (roh-SET-tee), 1828–1882: Pre-Raphaelite earnestness.

Rothko, Mark (RAWTH-koh), 1903–1970: Blurry, two-tone rectangles.

Rousseau, Henri (roo-soh), 1844–1910: Exotic scenes in children's-book style.

Rouault, Georges (roo-ohlt), 1871–1958: Stained glass–style paintings.

Rubens, Peter Paul (ROO-buns), 1577–1640: Baroque, fleshy women, violent scenes.

Seurat, Georges-Pierre (suh-rah), 1859–1891: Bright works made with dots of color (pointillism).

Steen, Jan (stain), 1626–1679: Slice-of-life everyday Dutch scenes.

Stubbs, George, 1724–1806: Horses.

Tiepolo, Giovanni Battista (tee-EP-oh-loh), 1696–1770: 3-D illusions on ceilings.

Tintoretto (tin-toh-RET-oh), 1518–1594: Venetian Renaissance plus drama.

Titian (TEESH-un), 1485–1576: Greatest Venetian Renaissance painter.

Toulouse-Lautrec, Henri de (too-loose-loh-trek), 1864–1901: Posters and scenes from seedy French nightclubs.

Turner, Joseph Mallord William, 1775–1851: Messy "proto-Impressionist" scenes of nature.

Uccello, Paolo (oo-CHEL-oh), 1396–1475: Early 3-D experiments.

Van der Weyden, Rogier (van dehr WAY-den), 1400–1464: Northern master of detailed altarpieces.

Van Dyck, Sir Anthony (van dike), 1599–1641: Flemish portraitist of Europe's aristocrats.

Van Eyck, Jan (van ike), 1390–1441: Northern detail.

Van Gogh, Vincent (van GO, or, more correctly, van HOCK), 1853–1890: Impressionist style plus emotion.

Velázquez, Diego (vel-LAHS-kes), 1599–1660: Objective Spanish court portraits.

Vermeer, Jan (vehr-MEER), 1632–1675: Quiet Dutch art, highlighting everyday details.

Veronese, Paolo (vehr-oh-NAY-zee), 1528–1588: Huge, colorful scenes with Venetian Renaissance backgrounds.

Verrochio, Andrea del (vehr-ROH-kee-oh), 1435–1388: Leonardo's teacher in painting and sculptures.

Watteau, Jean-Antoine (wah-toh), 1684–1721: Scenes of Louis XIV's court.

LONDON

*I*n the 19th century, the British flag flew over one-fourth of the world. And England collected art as fast as it collected colonies. In London you'll see much of the world's greatest art, from ancient Egypt, Greece, and Rome (the British Museum) to medieval and Renaissance painting (National Gallery). Study Britain's finest artists (Tate Britain) and read the manuscripts that shaped our age (British Library). Stroll through historic Westminster in the company of Big Ben, with a stop at its illustrious abbey.

BRITISH MUSEUM

The British Museum is *the* chronicle of Western civilization. History is a modern invention. Three hundred years ago people didn't care about crumbling statues and dusty columns. Nowadays, we value a look at past civilizations, knowing that "those who don't learn from history are condemned to repeat it."

The British Museum is the only place I know where you can follow the rise and fall of three great civilizations in a few hours with a coffee break in the middle. And, while the sun never set on the British Empire, it will on you, so on this tour we'll see just the most exciting two hours.

ORIENTATION

Cost: Free, but £2 donation requested.

Hours: The **British Museum** is open Mon–Sat 10:00–17:00, Sun 12:00–18:00; some galleries may be open until 20:30 on Thu and Fri. Closed on Good Friday, Dec 24–26, and Jan 1. Rainy days and Sundays always get me down because they're most crowded (the museum is least crowded on late afternoons on weekdays).

The **Great Court**—the grand entrance with eateries, gift shops, an exhibit gallery, and the Reading Room—has longer opening hours than the museum. The Court opens daily at 9:00 and closes Mon–Wed at 21:00, Thu–Sat at 23:00, and Sun at 18:00. The **Reading Room**, located within the Great Court, is free and open to the quiet public; it's open

BRITISH MUSEUM—OVERVIEW

daily 10:00–17:30, Thu–Fri until 20:30 (computer terminals within the Reading Room offer COMPASS; see Information, below).

Getting there: The main entrance is on Great Russell Street. Tube to Tottenham Court Road or Holborn, and a four-block walk. Buses: #7, #8, #10, #19, #24, #25, #29, #38, #55, #68, #73, #91, #98, #134, #188, or #242. Taxis are reasonable if you buddy up.

Information: The information desks just inside the Great Court sell museum plans for £2.50. To find out the schedule of the museum's frequent tours (see Tours, below), ask at the desk or call the museum (tel. 020/7323-8000, for recorded information tel. 020/7388-2227, on the Web at www.thebritishmuseum.ac.uk). The main bookstore is behind the Reading Room.

To take a virtual tour or plot the shortest route to the particular sights you want to see, study ahead at www.thebritishmuseum.ac.uk /compass or access this site online at the terminals in the Reading Room (free). For an educational Web site with some kid appeal, try the museum's www.ancientegypt.co.uk.

Tours: There are three types of guided tours: Highlights tours (£7, 2/day,

90 min), Focus tours (£5, 1/day, 60 min), and eyeOpeners (free, nearly hrly, 50 min). Two audioguide tours are available: one features the museum's top 50 highlights (£2.50, available at information desks in Great Court, to the left and right as you enter) and the other covers only the Elgin Marbles (£3, 60 min, pick up at entrance of Parthenon Galleries). **Length of our tour:** 2 hours.

Cloakroom: Baggage check costs £1 per item. You can carry a day bag in the galleries, but big backpacks are not allowed. If the line is long and not moving, the cloakroom may be full.

Photography: Photos allowed without a flash. No tripods.

No-nos: No eating, drinking, smoking, or gum chewing in the galleries.

Cuisine art: You have three choices inside the complex. In the Great Court, you'll find the Court Café (on the main level) as well as the more expensive Court Restaurant (on the upper floor). Within the museum, the Gallery Café is located off room 12 (the Greek section). There are lots of fast, cheap, and colorful cafés, pubs, and markets along Great Russell Street. No picnicking is allowed inside the Great Court or the museum. Marx snacked on the benches near the entrance and in Russell Square.

Starring: Rosetta Stone, Egyptian mummies, Assyrian lions, and the Elgin Marbles.

THE TOUR BEGINS

Enter through the main entrance on Great Russell Street. Ahead is the Great Court (with the round Reading Room in the center), providing access to all wings. To the right is the King's Library (containing exhibits on Asia, Africa, and the Americas). To the left (here on the ground floor) are Egypt, Assyria, and Greece—our tour.

From the entrance, turn left if you want to check your bag at the cloakroom. Then head toward the magnificent Great Court. The glass-domed roof is a huge umbrella, sheltering this people place. Just inside the Court, you'll find information desks that sell floor plans and rent audioguide tours.

• *The Egyptian Gallery is in the west wing to the left of the Reading Room. Enter the Egyptian Gallery and immediately turn left. The Rosetta Stone is 50 meters away, at the far end of the gallery.*

EGYPT (3000 B.C.–A.D. 1)

Egypt was one of the world's first "civilizations," that is, a group of people with a government, religion, art, free time, and a written language. The Egypt we think of—pyramids, mummies, pharaohs, and guys who walk

-------------------------------- EGYPT --------------------------------

1 - Rosetta Stone

2 - Limestone false door

3 - Painted limestone statue of Nenkheftka

4 - Red granite head from colossal figure

5 - Painted limestone funerary stela of Sapair

6 - Four black granite figures of Sakhmet

7 - Rameses II head

8 - Egyptian animal gods

9 - Upstairs to mummies and gilded wooden inner coffin

10 - Monumental granite scarab

GREAT COURT + READING ROOM

ASSYRIA

WINGED LIONS

CLOAKROOM

DCH

funny—lasted from 3000 to 1000 B.C. with hardly any change in the government, religion, or arts. Imagine two millennia of Eisenhower.

The Rosetta Stone (196 B.C.)

When this rock was unearthed in the Egyptian desert in 1799, it caused a sensation in Europe. Picture a pack of scientists (I think of the apes in that scene from *2001: A Space Odyssey*) screeching with amazement, dancing around it, and poking curiously with their fingers. This black slab caused a quantum leap in the evolution of history. Finally, Egyptian writing could be decoded.

The writing in the upper part of the stone is known as hieroglyphics. For a thousand years no one knew how to read this mysterious ancient language. Did a picture of a bird mean "bird"? Or was it a sound, forming part of a larger word, like "burden"? As it turned out, hieroglyphics are a complex combination of the two, surprisingly more phonetic than symbolic.

The Rosetta Stone allowed scientists to break the code. It contains a single inscription repeated in three languages. The bottom third is plain old Greek (find your favorite frat or sorority), while the middle is more modern Egyptian. By comparing the two known languages with the one they didn't know, they figured it out.

The breakthrough came from the large oval in the sixth line from the top. They discovered that the bird symbol represented the sound "a," part of the name Cleo-pa-tra. Simple.

• *On the wall opposite the Rosetta Stone, you'll find the...*

Limestone False Door (c. 2400 B.C.)

In ancient Egypt, you could take it with you. They believed that after you died, your soul lived on, enjoying its earthly possessions. This small statue represents the soul of a dead man.

It decorated his tomb, which contained all that he'd need in the next life: his mummified body, a résumé of his accomplishments on earth, and his possessions—sometimes including his servants, who might be buried alive with their master. The great pyramids, besides being psychic UFO power stations, were also elaborate tombs for the rich and powerful. But most tombs were small rectangular rooms of brick or stone.

"False doors" like this were slapped on the outside of the tomb. The soul of the deceased, like the statue, could come and go through the "door" as it pleased—grave robbers couldn't. The deceased's relatives placed food outside the door to nourish such spirits who woke up in the middle of eternity with the munchies.

• *Just a few steps farther down the gallery, in a glass case on the right, look for the...*

Painted Limestone Statue of Nenkheftka (2400 B.C.)

After a snack, the soul might wander through the nether lands (somewhere north of Belgium) searching for paradise, meeting strange beings and weird situations. If things got too hairy, the soul could always find temporary refuge in statues like this one. It was helpful to have as many statues of yourself as possible to scatter around the earth, in case your soul needed a safe resting place.

THE ANCIENT WORLD

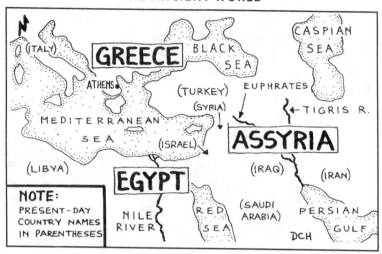

N

(ITALY) **GREECE** BLACK SEA

ATHENS (TURKEY) EUPHRATES

(SYRIA) ←TIGRIS R.

MEDITERRANEAN SEA (ISRAEL) **ASSYRIA**

(LIBYA) **EGYPT** (IRAQ) (IRAN)

NOTE:
PRESENT-DAY
COUNTRY NAMES
IN PARENTHESES

NILE RIVER RED SEA (SAUDI ARABIA) PERSIAN GULF

CASPIAN SEA

DCH

This statue, like most Egyptian art, is not terribly lifelike—the figure is stiff, hands at the sides, left leg forward, masklike face, stylized anatomy, and an out-of-date skirt. And talk about uptight—he's got a column down his back! But it does have all the essential features, like the simplified human figures on international traffic signs. To a soul caught in the fast lane of astral travel, this symbolic statue would be easier to spot than a detailed one.

You'll see the same rigid features on almost all the statues in the gallery.

• *Head past two tall columns that give a sense of the grandeur of the Egyptian temples. Find a huge head with a broken bowling-pin hat.*

Red Granite Head from a Colossal Figure of a King

Art also served as propaganda for the pharaohs, kings who called themselves gods on earth. Put this head on top of an enormous body (which still stands in Egypt) and you have the intimidating image of an omnipotent ruler who demands servile obedience. Next to the head is, appropriately, the pharaoh's powerful fist—the long arm of the law.

The crown is also symbolic. It's actually two crowns in one. The pointed upper half is the royal cap of Upper Egypt. This rests on the flat fezlike crown symbolizing Lower Egypt. A pharaoh wearing both crowns together is bragging that he rules a united Egypt.

• *On the wall to the right of the Red Granite Head, you'll see three painted stelas. The biggest of these is the . . .*

Painted Limestone Funerary Stela of Sapair

These people walk like Egyptian statues look—stiff. The two dimensional man in the lower right looks like he was just run over by a pyramid. We see his torso from the front and everything else—arms, legs, and face—in profile, creating the funny walk that has become an Egyptian cliché. (Like an early version of Cubism, we see various perspectives at once.)

But the stiffness is softened by a human touch. It's a family scrapbook; snapshots of loved ones from a happy time to be remembered for all eternity. In the upper half, Mr. Sapair worships the god Osiris (with pointed hat). Below, tanned Sapair relaxes with his pale wife while their children prepare a picnic. Their tiny son sniffs a giant flower, and their daughter crouches beneath her parents—a symbol of protection. When Sapair's winged spirit finally left his body (very top of stela), he could look at this painting on the tomb wall and think of his wife just like this . . . with her arms around him and a smile on her face.

• *On the opposite wall are four black lion-headed statues.*

Four Black Granite Figures of the Goddess Sakhmet (1400 B.C.)

This goddess was a good one to have on your side. She looks pretty sedate here, but this lion-headed woman could spring into a fierce crouch when crossed. Gods were often seen as part animal, admired for being stronger, swifter, or more fierce than puny *Homo sapiens*.

The gods ruled the Egyptian cosmos like a big banana republic (or the American Congress). To get a favor, Egyptians bribed their gods with offerings of food, animals, or money, or by erecting statues like these to them.

Notice the ankh that Sakhmet is holding. This key-shaped cross was the hieroglyph meaning "life" and was a symbol of eternal life.

Later, it was adopted as a Christian symbol because of its cross shape and religious overtones.
• *Continue on to the 2.5-meter-tall (8 foot) granite head and torso.*

Upper Half of Colossal Statue of Rameses II of Granite (1270 B.C.)

When Moses told the king of Egypt, "Let my people go!" this was the stony-faced look he got. Rameses II (reigned c. 1290–1223 B.C.) was likely in power when Moses led the Israelites out of captivity in Egypt to their homeland in Israel. According to the Bible, Moses, a former Egyptian prince himself, appealed to the pharaoh to let them go peacefully. When the pharaoh refused, Moses cursed the land with a series of plagues. Finally, the Israelites just bolted with the help of their God, Yahweh, who drowned the Egyptian armies in the Red Sea. Egyptian records don't exactly corroborate the tale, but this

Rameses here looks enough like Yul Brynner in *The Ten Commandments* to make me a believer.

This statue, made from two different colors of granite, is a fragment from a temple in Thebes. Rameses was a great builder of temples, palaces, tombs, and statues of himself. There are probably more statues of him in the world than there are cheesy fake *Davids*. He was so concerned about achieving immortality that he even chiseled his own name on other people's statues. Very cheeky.

Imagine, for a second, what the archaeologists saw when they came upon this: a colossal head and torso separated from the enormous legs and toppled into the sand—all that remained of the works of a once-great pharaoh. Kings, megalomaniacs, and workaholics, take note.
• *Say, "Ooh, heavy," and climb the ramp behind Rameses, looking for animals.*

Various Egyptian Gods as Animals

Before technology made humans the alpha animal on earth, it was easier to appreciate our fellow creatures. The Egyptians saw the superiority of animals and worshiped them as incarnations of the gods. The lioness was stronger, so she portrayed (as we saw earlier) the fierce goddess Sakhmet.

The powerful ram is the god Amun (King of the Gods), protecting a puny pharaoh under his powerful head. The clever baboon is Thoth, the god of wisdom. Horus, the god of the living, has a falcon's head. The standing hippo is Theoris, protectress of childbirth. Her stylized breasts and pregnant belly are supported by ankhs, symbols of life.

• *You can't call Egypt a wrap until you visit the mummies upstairs. If you can handle four flights of stairs (if not, return to Rosetta Stone and start the Assyria section—below), continue to the end of the gallery past the giant stone scarab (beetle) and up the stairs lined with Roman mosaics. At the top, take a left (into room 61), then a right into room 62. Snap a death-mask photo of your partner framed by an open coffin.*

Mummies

To mummify a body, disembowel it, fill its cavities with pitch or other substances, and dry it with natron, a natural form of sodium carbonate

(and, I believe, the active ingredient in Twinkies). Then carefully bandage it head to toe with fine linen strips. Place in a coffin, wait 2,000 years, and . . . voilà! Or just dump the corpse in the desert and let the hot, dry Egyptian sand do the work—you'll get the same results.

The mummies in the glass cases here are from the time of the Roman occupation. The X-ray photos on the cases tell us more about these people. On the walls are murals showing the Egyptian burial rites as outlined in the *Book of the Dead*. In Roman times, Egyptians painted a fine portrait in wax on the wrapping. Don't miss the animal mummies.

• *Linger in room 62, but remember that eternity is about the amount of time it takes to see this entire museum. Enter room 63 and you'll come face to face with a golden coffin.*

Gilded Wooden Inner Coffin of the Chantress of Amen-Ra Henutmehyt (1290 B.C.)

Look into the eyes of the deceased, a well-known singer, painted on the coffin. The Egyptians tried to cheat death by preserving their corpses. In the next life, the spirit was homeless without its body. They'd mummify the body, place it in a wooden coffin like this one, and, often, put that coffin inside a larger stone one. The result is that we now have Egyptian bodies that are as well preserved as Dick Clark.

The coffin is decorated with scenes of the deceased praising the gods, as well as magical spells to protect the body from evil and to act as crib notes for the confused soul in the netherworld.

• *In room 64, in a glass case, you'll find . . .*

"Ginger"

Nearly 5,500 years ago—a thousand years before the pyramids—this man died. His people buried him in the fetal position, where he could "sleep" for eternity. The hot sand naturally dehydrated and preserved the body. With him are a few of his possessions—vases, beads, and the flint blade next to his arm. The wisp of red hair gives him his name to scientists, and makes this man from a distant time seem very human.

• *Head back down the stairs to the Egyptian Gallery, returning to the huge stone beetle in the center of the room near the foot of the stairs.*

Monumental Granite Scarab (200 B.C.)

This species of beetle would burrow into the ground, then reappear—like dying and rebirth, a symbol of resurrection.

Like the scarab, Egyptian culture was buried—first by Greece, then by Rome. Knowledge of the ancient writing died, condemning the culture to obscurity. But since the discovery of the Rosetta Stone, Egyptology is booming and Egypt has come back to life.

• *Backtrack to the Rosetta Stone. Next to the stone are two huge winged Assyrian lions (with bearded human heads), standing guard over the exhibit halls. Grab a seat on a bench in their shadow. (We'll rendezvous here after strolling through Assyria.)*

ASSYRIA (1000–600 B.C.)

Assyria was the lion, the king of beasts of early civilizations. From its base in northern Mesopotamia (northern Iraq), it conquered and dominated the Middle East—from Israel to Iran—for more than three centuries. The Assyrians were a nation of warriors—hardy, disciplined, and often cruel conquistadores—whose livelihood depended on booty and slash-and-burn expansion.

ASSYRIA

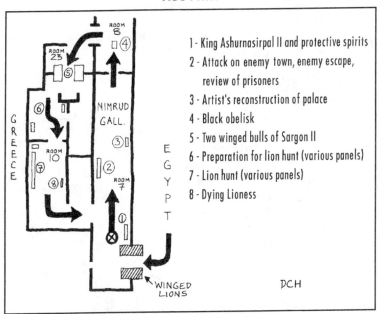

1 - King Ashurnasirpal II and protective spirits
2 - Attack on enemy town, enemy escape, review of prisoners
3 - Artist's reconstruction of palace
4 - Black obelisk
5 - Two winged bulls of Sargon II
6 - Preparation for lion hunt (various panels)
7 - Lion hunt (various panels)
8 - Dying Lioness

Two Winged Lions with Human Heads (c. 870 B.C.)

These lions stood guard at key points in Assyrian palaces to intimidate enemies and defeated peoples. With lion body, eagle wings, and human head, these magical beasts—and therefore the Assyrian people—had the strength of a lion, the speed of an eagle, the brain of a man, and the beard of ZZ Top. They protected the palace from evil spirits and they scared the heck out of foreign ambassadors and left-wing newspaper reporters. (What has five legs and flies? Take a close look. These quintupeds appear complete from both the front and the side.)

Carved into the stone between the bearded lions' loins, you can see one of civilization's most impressive achievements—writing. This wedge-shaped ("cuneiform") script is the world's first

written language, invented 5,000 years ago by the Sumerians and passed down to their less-civilized descendants, the Assyrians.

• *Walk between the lions, glance at the large reconstructed wooden gates from an Assyrian palace, and turn right into the narrow red gallery (room 7) lined with brown relief panels.*

Nimrud Gallery
(9th century B.C.)

This gallery is a mini version of the main hall of Ashurnasirpal II's palace. It was decorated with these pleasant sand-colored gypsum relief panels (which were, however, originally painted).

That's Ashurnasirpal himself in the first panel on your right, with braided beard and fezlike crown, flanked by his supernatural hawk-headed henchman. The bulging muscles tell us that Ashurnasirpal was a conqueror's conqueror who enjoyed his reputation as a merciless warrior who tortured and humiliated the vanquished. The room's panels chronicle his bloody career.

The cuneiform inscription running through the center of the panel is Ashurnasirpal's résumé: "The king who has enslaved all mankind, the mighty warrior who steps on the necks of his enemies, tramples all foes and shatters the enemy; the weapon of the gods, the mighty king, the King of Assyria, the king of the world, B.A., M.B.A., Ph.D., etc..."

• *Ten meters farther down, on your left, you'll find an upper panel labeled...*

Attack on an Enemy Town

Many "nations" conquered by the Assyrians consisted of little more than a single walled city. Here, the Assyrians lay siege with a crude "tank" that shields them as they advance to the city walls to smash down the gate with a battering ram. The king stands a safe distance away behind the juggernaut and bravely shoots arrows.

• *Next, to the right of the panel, you'll find...*

Enemy Escape

Soldiers flee the slings and arrows of outrageous Assyrians by swimming across the Euphrates, using inflated animal bladders as life preservers. Their friends in the castle downstream applaud their ingenuity.

• *Below, you'll see...*

Review of Prisoners

The Assyrian economy depended on booty. Here a conquered nation is paraded before the Assyrian king, who is shaded by a parasol. Ashurnasirpal sneers and tells the captured chief: "Drop and give me 50."

Above the prisoners' heads we see the rich spoils of war—elephant tusks, metal pots, and so on.

• *Notice the painted reconstruction of the palace on the opposite wall, then find the black obelisk in the next room (room 8).*

Black Obelisk of Shalmaneser III (c. 840 B.C.)

The cruel Assyrians demanded that the vanquished people pay tribute once every year (on April 15, I believe). The obelisk shows people bringing tribute to Shalmaneser from all corners of the empire. The second band from the top shows the Israelites carrying their offerings to the king, where they prostrate before him. Parts of Israel were under Assyrian domination from the ninth century B.C. on. Old Testament prophets like Elijah and Elisha constantly warned their people of the corrupting influence of the Assyrian gods.

Also check out the third band with its parade of exotic animals, especially the missing-link monkeys.

• *Hang a U-turn left through room 23 (Greek) and pause at the entrance of room 10 (Assyria) to see...*

Two Winged Bulls from the Khorsabad Palace of Sargon II (c. 710 B.C.)

These 16-ton bulls guarded the palace of Sargon II. And, speaking of large amounts of bull, "Sargon" wasn't his real name. It's obvious to savvy historians that Sargon must have been an insecure usurper to the throne, since the name meant "true king."

• *Sneak between these bulls and veer right (into room 10) where horses are being readied for the big hunt.*

Royal Lion Hunts

Lion hunting was Assyria's sport of kings. On the right wall we see horses being read- ied for the hunt. On the left wall, hunting dogs. And next to them are beautiful lions. They rest peacefully in their idyllic garden, unaware that they will shortly be rousted, stampeded, and slaughtered.

Lions lived in Mesopotamia up until modern times, and it had long been the duty of kings to keep the lion population down to protect farmers and herdsmen. This duty soon became sport, as the kings of men proved their power by taking on the king of beasts. They actually bred lions to stage hunts. As we'll see, these "hunts" were as sporting as shooting fish in a barrel. The last Assyrian kings had grown soft and decadent, hardly the raging warriors of Ashurnasirpal's time.

• *Enter the larger lion-hunt room. Reading the panels like a comic strip, start on the right and gallop counterclockwise.*

The Lion-Hunt Room (c. 650 B.C.)

They release the lions from their cages, while soldiers on horseback herd them into an enclosed arena. The king has them cornered. Let the slaughter begin. The chariot carries decrepit King Ashurbani- pal. The last of Assyria's great kings, he's ruled now for 50 years. He shoots the wrong way while spearmen hold off lions attacking from the rear.

• *At about the middle of the long wall...*

The fleeing lions, cornered by hounds, shot through with arrows and weighed down with fatigue, begin to fall, tragically. The lead lion carries on valiantly even while vomiting blood.

This, perhaps the low point of Assyrian cruelty, is the high point of their artistic achievement. It's a curious coincidence that civilizations often produce their greatest art in their declining years. Hmm.

Dying Lioness

• *On the wall opposite the vomiting lion…*

A dying lioness roars in pain and frustration. She tries to run but her body is too heavy. Her muscular hind legs, once the source of her power, are now paralyzed.

Did the sculptor sense the coming death of his own civilization? Like these brave, fierce lions, Assyria's once-great warrior nation was slain. Shortly after Ashurbanipal's death, Assyria was conquered, sacked, and looted by an ascendant Babylon. The mood of tragedy, of dignity, of proud struggle in a hopeless cause makes this *Dying Lioness* simply one of the most beautiful of all human creations.

• *Return to the huge winged Assyrian lions (near the Rosetta Stone) by exiting the lion-hunt room at the far end. To reach the Greek section, pass between the winged lions and turn right, then right again, into room 11.*

You'll walk past early Greek Barbie and Ken dolls from the Cycladic period (2500 B.C.). Continue into room 12 (the hungry can go straight to the Gallery Café) and turn right, into room 13. Continue to room 15, then relax on a bench and read, surrounded by vases and statues.

GREECE (600 B.C.—A.D. 1)

The history of ancient Greece could be subtitled "making order out of chaos." While Assyria was dominating the Middle Eastern world, "Greece"—a gaggle of warring tribes roaming the Greek peninsula—was floundering in darkness. But by around 700 B.C. these tribes began settling down, experimenting with democracy, forming self-governing city-states, and making ties with other city-states. Scarcely two centuries later, they would be a united community and the center of the civilized world.

During its "Golden Age" (500–430 B.C.), Greece set the tone for all of Western civilization to follow. Modern democracy, theater, literature, mathematics, philosophy, science, art, and architecture, as we know them, were all virtually invented by a single generation of Greeks in a small town of maybe 80,000 citizens.

Map of Greek World (500–430 B.C.)

Athens was the most powerful of the city-states and the center of the Greek world. Golden Age Greece was never really a full-fledged empire,

EARLY GREECE

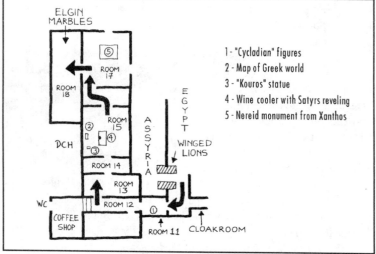

1 - "Cycladian" figures
2 - Map of Greek world
3 - "Kouros" statue
4 - Wine cooler with Satyrs reveling
5 - Nereid monument from Xanthos

but more a common feeling of unity among Greek-speaking peoples on the peninsula.

A century after the Golden Age, Greek culture was spread still further by Alexander the Great, who conquered the Mediterranean world and beyond. By 300 B.C. the "Greek" world stretched from Italy to India to Egypt (including most of what used to be the Assyrian Empire). Two hundred years later this Greek-speaking "Hellenistic Empire" was conquered by the Romans.

• *There's a nude male to the left of the map.*

Kouros (*Boy*) (490 B.C.)

The Greeks saw the human body as a perfect example of the divine orderliness of the universe. For the Greeks, even the gods themselves had human forms. The ideal man was geometrically perfect, a balance of opposites, the "Golden Mean." In a statue, that meant finding the right balance between motion and stillness, between realistic human anatomy (with human flaws) and the perfection of a Greek god. This *Boy* is still a bit uptight, stiff as the rock from which he's carved. But—as we'll see—in just a few short

decades, the Greeks would cut loose and create realistic statues that seemed to move like real humans.

• *Look in the glass case by the map, filled with decorated vases. One in the center is marked...*

Red-Figured Psykter (Wine Cooler) with Satyrs Reveling (490 B.C.)

This clay wine cooler, designed to float in a bowl of cooling water, is decorated with satyrs holding a symposium, or drinking party. These half-

man/half-animal creatures (notice their tails) had a reputation for lewd behavior, reminding the balanced and moderate Greeks of their rude roots.

The reveling figures painted on this jar are more realistic, more three-dimensional, and suggest more natural movements than even the literally three-dimension-

al but quite stiff *Kouros* statue. The Greeks are beginning to conquer the natural world in art. The art, like life, is more in balance. And, speaking of "balance," if that's a Greek sobriety test, revel on.

• *Carry on into room 17 and sit facing the Greek temple at the far end.*

Nereid Monument from Xanthos (c. 400 B.C.)

Greek temples (like this recon-struction of a temple-shaped tomb) housed a statue of a god or god-dess. Unlike Christian churches, which serve as meeting places, Greek temples were the gods' homes. Worshipers gathered out-side, so the most impressive part of the temple was its exterior. Tem-ples were rectangular buildings

surrounded by rows of columns and topped by slanted roofs.

The triangle-shaped roof, filled in with sculpture (reliefs or stat-ues), is called the "pediment." The cross beams that support the roof are called "metopes" (MET-o-pees). Now look through the columns to the building itself. Above the doorway is another set of relief panels running around the building (under the "eaves") called the "frieze."

Next, we'll see pediment, frieze, and metope decorations from Greece's greatest temple.

• *Leave the British Museum. Take the Tube to Heathrow and fly to Athens. In the center of the old city, on top of the high, flat hill known as the Acropolis, you'll find...*

The Parthenon

The Parthenon—the temple dedicated to Athena, goddess of wisdom and the patroness of Athens—was the crowning glory of an enormous urban renewal plan during Greece's Golden Age. After Athens was ruined in a war with Persia, the city—under the bold leadership of Pericles—

constructed the greatest building of its day. The Parthenon was a model of balance, simplicity, and harmonious elegance, the symbol of the Golden Age. Phidias, the greatest Greek sculptor, decorated the exterior with statues and relief panels.

While the building itself remains in Athens, many of the Parthenon's best sculptures are right here in the British Museum—the so-called Elgin Marbles (pronounced with a hard "g"), named for the shrewd British ambassador who acquired them in the early 1800s. Though the Greek government complains about losing its marbles, the Brits feel they rescued and preserved the sculptures.

• *Enter through the glass doors labeled "The Parthenon Galleries."*

THE ELGIN MARBLES (450 B.C.)

The marble panels you see lining the walls of this large hall are part of the frieze that originally ran around the exterior of the Parthenon. The statues at either end of the hall once filled the Parthenon's triangular-shaped pediments. Near the pediment sculptures, we'll also find the relief panels known as metopes. Let's start with the frieze.

The Frieze

These 56 relief panels show Athens' "Fourth of July" parade, celebrating the birth of their city. On this day, citizens marched up the Acropolis to symbolically present a new robe to the 12-meter-tall (40 feet) gold and ivory statue of Athena housed in the Parthenon.

ELGIN MARBLES

```
                                          ┌──┐┌──┐
      ┌──┐┌──┐                             │METOPES
                  ┌─────────────────┐      ┌─┐
                  │     FRIEZE      │      │P│
      ┌─┐                                  │E│
      │ │     ROOM          ↰↱            │D│
      │ │      18          ↲↰  ┌────────┐ │I│
      │ │                   ↳ │ FRIEZE │ │M│
                               └────────┘ │E│
                                          │N│
      ┌──┐┌──┐                            │T│
                                          └─┘
                              ┌──┐        ┌──┐

            ┌────────┐    ↑        ┌──────┐  TO LATER
            │        │    │        │      │   GREECE
            │ ROOM   │   ⊗ │      ┌─┴──┐   ↱
            │  17    │    │      │    │  │
   DCH      │        │    ↓      │NEREID│
            └────────┘           │MONUMENT
                     TO EGYPT    └──────┘
```

• *Start at the panels to your right (#136) and work counterclockwise.*

Men on horseback, chariots, musicians, animals for sacrifice, and young maidens with offerings are all part of the grand parade, all heading in the same direction. Prance on.

Notice the muscles and veins in the horses' legs (#130) and the intricate folds in the cloaks and dresses. Some panels (#113) have holes drilled in them, where gleaming bronze reins were fitted to heighten the festive look. Of course, all these panels were originally painted in realistic colors. Despite the bustle of figures posed every which way, the frieze has one unifying element—all the heads are at the same level, creating a single ribbon around the Parthenon.

• *Cross to the opposite wall.*

A three-horse chariot (#67) cut out of only a few centimeters of marble is more lifelike and three-dimensional than anything the Egyptians achieved in a freestanding statue.

Enter the girls (#61), the heart of the procession. Dressed in pleated robes, they shuffle past the parade marshals, carrying jugs of wine and bowls to pour out an offering to the thirsty gods.

The procession culminates (#35) in the presentation of the robe to Athena. A man and a child fold the robe for the goddess while the rest of

the gods look on. There are Zeus and Hera (#29), the king and queen of the gods, seated, enjoying the fashion show and wondering what length hemlines will be this year.

• *Head for the set of pediment sculptures at the right end of the hall.*

The Pediment Sculptures

These statues nestled nicely in the triangular pediment above the columns at the Parthenon's east entrance. The missing statues at the peak of the triangle once showed the birth of Athena. Zeus had his head split open, allowing Athena, the goddess of wisdom, to rise from his brain fully grown and fully armed.

The other gods at this Olympian banquet slowly become aware of the amazing event. The first to notice is the one closest to them, Hebe, the cup bearer of the gods (tallest surviving fragment). Frightened, she runs to tell the others, her dress whipping behind her. A startled Demeter (just left of Hebe) turns toward Hebe.

The only one that hasn't lost his head is laid-back Dionysus (the cool guy on the far left). He just raises another glass of wine to his lips. Over on the right, Aphrodite, goddess of love, leans back into her mother's lap, too busy admiring her own bare shoulder to even notice the hubbub. A horse screams, "These people are nuts—let me out of here!"

The scene had a message. Just as wise Athena rose above the lesser gods who are scared, drunk, or vain, so would her city, Athens, rise above her lesser rivals.

This is amazing workmanship. Compare Dionysus, with his natural, relaxed, reclining pose, to all those stiff Egyptian statues standing eternal-

ly at attention. The realism of the muscles is an improvement even over the *Kouros* we saw, sculpted only 50 years earlier.

Appreciate the folds of the clothes on the female figures (on the right half), especially Aphrodite's clinging, rumpled robe. Some sculptors would build a model of their figure first, put real clothes on it, and study how the cloth hung down before actually sculpting in marble. Others found inspiration at the tavern on wet T-shirt night.

Even without their heads, these statues with their detailed anatomy and expressive poses speak volumes.

Wander behind. The statues originally sat 12 meters above the ground. The backs of the statues, which were never intended to be seen, are almost as detailed as the fronts. That's quality control.

• *The metopes are the panels on the walls to either side. Start with "South Metope XXXI" on the right wall, center.*

The Metopes

In #XXXI, a centaur grabs a man by the throat while the man pulls his hair. The human Lapiths have invited some centaurs—wild half-man/half-horse creatures—to a wedding feast. All goes well until the brutish centaurs, the original party animals, get too drunk and try to carry off the Lapith women. A battle ensues.

The Greeks prided themselves on creating order out of chaos. Within just a few generations, they went from nomadic barbarism to the pinnacle of early Western civilization. These metopes tell the story of this struggle between the forces of civilization (Lapiths) and barbarism (centaurs).

In #XXVIII (opposite wall, center), the centaurs start to get the upper hand as one rears triumphant over a fallen man. The leopard skin draped over the centaur's arm roars a taunt at the prone man. The humans lose face.

In #XXVII (to the left), the humans finally rally and drive off the brutish centaurs. A centaur, wounded in the back, tries to run, but the man grabs him by the neck and raises his right hand (missing) to finish him off. Notice how the Lapith's cloak drapes a rough-textured background that highlights the smooth skin of this graceful, ideal man. The centaurs have been defeated. Civilization has triumphed over barbarism, order over chaos, and rational man over his half-animal alter ego.

Why are the Elgin Marbles so treasured? The British of the 19th century saw themselves as the new "civilized" race subduing "barbarians" in their far-flung empire. Maybe these rocks made them stop and wonder—will our great civilization also turn to rubble?

Centaurs slain around the world. Dateline 500 B.C.—Greece, China, India: Man no longer considers himself an animal. Bold new ideas are exploding simultaneously around the world. Socrates, Confucius, Buddha, and others are independently discovering a nonmaterial, unseen order in nature and in man. They say man has a rational mind or soul. He's separate from nature and different from the other animals.

The Rest of the British Museum

You've toured only the foundations of Western civilization on the ground floor, west wing. Upstairs you'll find still more artifacts from these lands, plus Rome and the civilization that sprang from it. Some highlights: the Lindow Man, a.k.a. "Bog Man," a victim of human sacrifice (room 50); the Sutton Hoo burial ship (room 41); and a Michelangelo cartoon (room 90).

But, of course, history doesn't begin and end in Europe. Look for remnants of the sophisticated, exotic cultures of Asia and the Americas (both in north wing, ground floor) and Africa (downstairs)—all part of the totem pole of the human family.

❧ 2 ❧
NATIONAL GALLERY TOUR

The National Gallery lets you tour Europe's art without ever crossing the Channel. With so many exciting artists and styles, it's a fine overture to art if you're just starting a European trip and a pleasant reprise if you're just finishing. The "National Gal" is always a welcome interlude from the bustle of London sightseeing.

ORIENTATION
Cost: Free.

Hours: Daily 10:00–18:00, Wed until 21:00, closed on Good Friday, Dec 24–26, and Jan 1.

Getting there: It's central as can be, overlooking Trafalgar Square, a 15-minute walk from Big Ben, 10 minutes from Piccadilly. Tube: Charing Cross or Leicester Square. Buses: #3, #6, #9, #11, #12, #13, #15, #23, #24, #29, #53, #88, #91, #94, or #109.

Information: The information desk in the lobby offers a free, handy floor plan. Find the latest events schedule and a listing of free lunch lectures in the free "National Gallery News" flier. Drop by the Micro Gallery, a computer room even your dad could have fun in (closes 30 min earlier than museum); you can study any artist, style, or topic in the museum and even print out a tailor-made tour map (tel. 020/7839-3321, recorded information tel. 020/7747-2885, www.nationalgallery.org.uk).

NATIONAL GALLERY HIGHLIGHTS

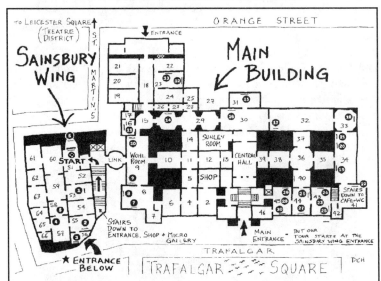

Medieval and Early Renaissance
1. Wilton Diptych
2. UCCELLO—Battle of San Romano
3. VAN EYCK—Arnolfini Marriage
4. CRIVELLI—Annunciation with St. Emidius
5. BOTTICELLI—Venus and Mars

High Renaissance
6. LEONARDO DA VINCI— Virgin and Child (painting and cartoon)
7. MICHELANGELO—Entombment
8. RAPHAEL—Pope Julius II

Venetian Renaissance
9. TITIAN—Bacchus and Ariadne
10. TINTORETTO —Origin of the Milky Way

Northern Protestant Art
11. VERMEER—Young Woman
12. REMBRANDT—Belshazzar's Feast
13. REMBRANDT—Self-Portrait

Baroque and Rococo
14. RUBENS—The Judgment of Paris
15. VAN DYCK—Charles I on Horseback

16. VELÁZQUEZ—The Rokeby Venus
17. CARAVAGGIO—Supper at Emmaus
18. BOUCHER—Pan and Syrinx

British
19. CONSTABLE—The Hay Wain
20. TURNER—The Fighting Téméraire
21. TURNER—Rain, Steam, Speed
22. DELAROCHE—The Execution of Lady Jane Grey

Impressionism and Beyond
23. MONET—Gare St. Lazare
24. MONET—The Water Lily Pond
25. MANET—The Waitress (La Servante de Bocks)
26. RENOIR—Boating on the Seine
27. SEURAT—Bathers at Asnières
28. DEGAS—Miss La La at the Cirque Fernando
29. VAN GOGH—Sunflowers
30. CÉZANNE—Bathers

Tours: Free one-hour overview tours are offered daily at 11:30 and 14:30 (also Wed at 18:30). Excellent audioguide tours (suggested £4 donation) let you dial up info on any painting in the museum.
Length of our tour: 90 minutes.
Cloakroom: Free cloakrooms at each entrance welcome your coat and umbrella but maybe not your bag. You can take in a bag.
Photography: Strictly forbidden.
Cuisine art: The Crivelli's Garden Café (first floor, Sainsbury Wing) is classy with reasonable prices and a petite menu. The Prêt à Manger Café (in basement, near end of this tour, just before the Impressionists) is a bustling, inexpensive, self-service cafeteria with realistic salads, Rubens sandwiches, and Gauguin juices. A block away there's a good cafeteria in the crypt of St. Martin-in-the-Fields church (facing Trafalgar Square). For pub grub, walk a block toward Big Ben and dip into the Clarence.
Starring: You name it—Leonardo, Van Eyck, Raphael, Titian, Caravaggio, Rembrandt, Rubens, Velázquez, Monet, Renoir, and van Gogh.

THE TOUR BEGINS
Of the two entrances that face Trafalgar Square, enter through the smaller building (50 meters left of the main entrance as you face it). Pick up the free map and climb the stairs. At the top, turn left and grab a seat in room 51, facing Leonardo's *Virgin of the Rocks*.

The National Gallery offers a quick overview of European art history. We'll stay on one floor, and after a brief preview of Leonardo, we'll work chronologically through medieval holiness, Renaissance realism, Dutch detail, Baroque excess, British restraint, and the colorful French Impressionism that leads to the modern world. Cruise like an eagle with wide eyes for the big picture, seeing how each style progresses into the next.

THE ITALIAN RENAISSANCE
(1400–1550)

Leonardo da Vinci—*The Virgin of the Rocks*
Mary, the mother of Jesus, plays with her son and little Johnny the Baptist (with cross, at left) while John's mother looks on. Leonardo brings this holy scene right down to earth, sitting among rocks, stalactites, water, and plants. But looking closer we see that Leonardo has deliberately posed his people into a pyramid shape, with Mary's head at the peak, creating an oasis of maternal stability and serenity amid the hard rock of the earth. Leonardo, who was illegitimate, may have sought the young mother he never knew in his art. Freud thought so.

The Renaissance—or "rebirth"— of the culture of ancient Greece and Rome was a cultural boom that changed people's thinking about every aspect of life. In politics, it meant democracy. In religion, it meant a move away from Church dominance and toward the assertion of man (humanism) and a more personal faith. Science and secular learning were revived after centuries of superstition and ignorance. In architecture, it was a return to the balanced columns and domes of Greece and Rome.

In painting, the Renaissance meant realism. Artists rediscovered the beauty of nature and the human body. With pictures of beautiful people in harmonious surroundings, they expressed the optimism and confidence of this new age.

• *We'll circle back around to Leonardo in a couple hundred years. But first, turn your back on the Renaissance and cruise through the medieval world in rooms 52, 53, and 54.*

Medieval and Early Renaissance (1260–1510)

Shiny gold paintings of saints, angels, Madonnas, and crucifixions. One thing is very clear: the art of the Middle Ages was religious, dominated by the Church. The illiterate faithful could meditate on an altarpiece and visualize heaven.

Medieval heaven was different from medieval earth. The holy wore gold plates on their heads. Faces were serene and generic. People posed stiffly, facing directly out or to the side, never in between. Saints are recognized by the symbols they carry (a key, a sword, a book), rather than their human features. They floated in an ethereal nowhere of gold leaf. In other words, medieval artists had no need to master the techniques of portraying the "real" world of rocks, trees, and distinguished noses, because their world was...otherworldly.

• *One of the finest medieval altarpieces is in a glass case in room 53.*

Anonymous—*The Wilton Diptych* (c. 1395)

In this two-paneled altarpiece, a glimmer of human realism peeks through the gold leaf. The kings on the left have distinct, down-to-earth faces as they adore Mary and the baby on the right. And the back side shows not a saint, not a god, not a symbol, but a real-life deer lying down in the grass of this earth.

Still, the anonymous artist is struggling with reality. Look at the panel with the kings—John the Baptist is holding a "lamb of God" that looks more like a chihuahua. Nice try. In the right panel, the angels with their flamelike wings and cloned faces bunch together single

file across the back rather than receding realistically into the distance. Mary's exquisite fingers hold an anatomically impossible little foot. The figures are flat, scrawny, and sinless with cartoon features—far from flesh-and-blood human beings.

• *Walking straight through room 54 into room 55, you'll leave this gold-leaf peace and you'll find...*

Uccello—*Battle of San Romano* (c. 1450)

This colorful battle scene shows the victory of Florence over Siena— and the battle for literal realism on the canvas. It's an early Renaissance attempt at a realistic, nonreligious, three-dimensional scene.

Uccello challenges his ability by posing the horses and soldiers at every conceivable angle. The background of farmyards, receding

hedges, and tiny soldiers creates a 3-D illusion of distance. In the foreground, Uccello actually constructs a 3-D grid out of fallen lances, then places the horses and warriors within it. Still, Uccello hasn't quite worked out the bugs— the figures in the distance are

far too big and the fallen soldier on the left isn't much bigger than the fallen shield on the right.

• *In room 56, you'll find...*

Van Eyck—*The Arnolfini Marriage* (1434)

Called by some "The Shotgun Wedding," this painting of a simple ceremony (set in Bruges, Belgium) is a masterpiece of down-to-earth details. Van Eyck has built us a medieval dollhouse and invites us to linger over the finely crafted details. Feel the texture of the fabrics, count the terrier's hairs, trace the shadows generated by the window. In fact, each object is painted at an ideal angle, with the details you'd

see if you were standing right in front of it. So the strings of beads hanging on the back wall are as crystal clear as the bracelets on the bride.

And, to top it off, look into the round mirror on the far wall—the whole scene is reflected backward in miniature, showing the loving couple and two mysterious visitors. Is it the concerned parents? The minister? Van Eyck himself at his easel? Or has the artist painted you, the home viewer, into the scene?

In medieval times (this was painted only a generation after *The Wilton Diptych*), everyone could read the hidden meaning of certain symbols—the chandelier with its one lit candle (love), the fruit on the windowsill (fertility), the dangling whisk broom (the bride's domestic responsibilities), and the terrier (Fido—fidelity).

By the way, she may not be pregnant. The fashion of the day was to wear a pillow to look pregnant in hopes you'd soon get that way. At least, that's what they told their parents.

The surface detail is extraordinary, but the painting lacks true Renaissance depth. The tiny room looks unnaturally narrow, cramped, and claustrophobic, making us wonder: Where will the mother-in-law sleep?
• *Return to room 55, then turn left into room 57.*

Crivelli—*The Annunciation with Saint Emidius*
Mary, in green, is visited by the dove of the Holy Ghost who beams down from the distant heavens in a shaft of light.

Like Van Eyck's wedding, this is a brilliant collection of realistic details. Notice the hanging rug, the peacock, the architectural minutia that lead you way, way back, then, bam, you've got a giant pickle in your face.

It combines meticulous detail with Italian spaciousness. The floor tiles and building bricks recede into the distance. We're sucked right in, accelerating through the alleyway, under the arch, and off into space. The Holy Ghost spans the entire distance, connecting heavenly background with earthly foreground. Crivelli creates an Escher-esque labyrinth of rooms and walkways that we want to walk through, around, and into—or is that just a male thing?

Renaissance Italians were interested in—even obsessed with—portraying 3-D space. Perhaps they focused their spiritual passion away from heaven and toward the physical world. With such restless energy, they needed lots of elbowroom. Space, the final frontier.
• *In room 58...*

Botticelli—*Venus and Mars*

Mars takes a break from war, succumbing to the delights of Love (Venus), while impish satyrs play innocently with the discarded tools of death. In the early spring of the Renaissance, there was an optimistic mood in the air, the feeling that enlightened Man could solve all problems, narrowing the gap between mortals and the Greek gods. Artists felt free to use the pagan Greek gods as symbols of human traits, virtues, and vices. Venus has sapped man's medieval stiffness, inviting him to come out of the darkness and into the Renaissance.
• *Walk through rooms 59 and 60 to return to the Leonardo in room 51, where we started.*

The High Renaissance (1500)

With the "Big Three" of the High Renaissance—Leonardo, Michelangelo, and Raphael—painters had finally conquered realism. But these three Florentine artists weren't content just to copy nature, cranking out photographs on canvas. Like Renaissance architects (which they also were), they carefully composed their figures on the canvas, "building" them into geometrical patterns that reflected the balance and order they saw in nature.
• *Enter the small dark cave behind the rocks.*

Leonardo da Vinci—
Virgin and Child with
St. John the Baptist and St. Anne

At first glance, this chalk drawing, or cartoon, looks like a simple snapshot of two loving moms and two playful kids. The two children play—

oblivious to the violent deaths they'll both suffer—beneath their mothers' *Mona Lisa* smiles.

But follow the eyes: Shadowy-eyed Anne turns toward Mary who looks tenderly down to Jesus who blesses John who gazes back dreamily. As your eyes follow theirs, you're led back to the literal and psychological center of the composition—Jesus—the alpha and omega. Without resorting to heavy-handed medieval symbolism, Leonardo drives home a theological concept in a natural, human way. Leonardo the perfectionist rarely finished paintings. This sketch gives us an inside peek at his genius.

• *Cross to the main building and enter the large room 9. We'll return to these big, colorful canvases, but first, turn right into room 8.*

Michelangelo—*Entombment* (unfinished)

Michelangelo, the greatest sculptor ever, proves it here in this "painted sculpture" of the crucified Jesus being carried to the tomb. The figures are

almost like chiseled statues of Greek gods, especially the musclehead in red rippling beneath his clothes. Christ's naked body, shocking to the medieval Church, was completely acceptable in the Renaissance world where classical nudes were admired as an expression of the divine.

In true Renaissance style, balance and symmetry reign. Christ is the center of the composition, flanked by two equally leaning people who support his body with strips of cloth. They in turn are flanked by two more.

Where Leonardo gave us expressive faces, Michelangelo lets the bodies do the talking. The two supporters strain to hold up Christ's body, and in their tension we, too, feel the great weight and tragedy of their dead god. Michelangelo expresses the divine through the human form.

Raphael—*Pope Julius II* (1511)

The new worldliness of the Renaissance even reached the Church. Pope Julius II, who was more a swaggering conquistador than a pious pope, set out to rebuild Rome in Renaissance style (including hiring Michelangelo to paint the ceiling of the Vatican's Sistine Chapel).

Raphael has captured this complex man with perfect realism and psychological insight. On the one hand, the pope is an imposing pyramid of power, with a velvet shawl, silk shirt, and fancy rings boasting of wealth and success. But at the same time he's a bent and broken man, his throne backed into a corner, with an expression that seems to say, "Is this all there is?"

In fact, the great era of Florence and Rome was coming to an end. With Raphael's death in 1520, the Renaissance shifted to Venice.

• *Return to the long room 9.*

Venetian Renaissance (1510–1600)

Big change. The canvases are bigger, the colors brighter. Madonnas and saints are being replaced by goddesses and heroes. And there are nudes—not Michelangelo's lumps of noble, knotted muscle, but smooth-skinned, sexy, golden centerfolds.

Venice got wealthy by trading with the luxurious and exotic East. Its happy-go-lucky art style shows a taste for the finer things in life. But, despite all the flashiness and fleshiness, Venetian art still keeps a sense of Renaissance balance.

Titian—*Bacchus and Ariadne* (1523)

In this Greek myth, Bacchus, the God of Wine, comes leaping into the

picture, his red cape blowing behind him, to cheer up Ariadne (far left), who has been jilted by her lover. Bacchus' motley entourage rattles cymbals, bangs on tambourines, and literally shakes a leg.

Man and animal mingle in this pre-Christian orgy, with leopards, a snake, a dog, and the severed head and leg of an ass ready for the barbecue. Man and animal also literally "mix" in the satyrs—part man, part goat. The fat, sleepy guy in the background has had too much.

Titian uses a pyramid composition to balance an otherwise unbalanced scene. Follow Ariadne's gaze up to the peak of Bacchus' flowing cape, then down along the snake handler's spine to the lower right corner. In addition he "balances" the picture with harmonious colors—blue on the left, green on the right, while the two main figures stand out with loud splotches of red.

Tintoretto—*The Origin of the Milky Way*

In another classical myth, the god Jupiter places his illegitimate son, baby Hercules, at his wife's breast. Juno says, "Wait a minute. That's not

my baby!" Her milk spurts upward, becoming the Milky Way, and downward, becoming lilies.

Tintoretto places us right up in the clouds, among the gods who swirl around at every angle. An "X" composition unites it all—Juno slants one way while Jupiter slants the other. The result is more dramatic and complex than the stable pyramids of Leonardo and

Raphael. Also, notice how Jupiter appears to be flying almost right at us. Such shocking 3-D effects hint at the Baroque art we'll see later.

• *Exit room 9 (just to the right of the Milky Way painting) and turn left into room 16 for Dutch art.*

NORTHERN PROTESTANT ART (1600–1700)

We switch from CinemaScope to a tiny TV—smaller canvases, subdued colors, everyday scenes, and not even a bare shoulder.

Money shapes art. While Italy had wealthy aristocrats and the powerful Catholic church to purchase art, the North's patrons were middle-class, hardworking, Protestant merchants. They wanted simple, cheap, no-nonsense pictures to decorate their homes and offices. Greek gods and Virgin Marys were out, hometown folks and hometown places were in—portraits, landscapes, still lifes, and slice-of-life scenes. Painted with great attention to detail, this is art meant not to wow or preach at you, but to be enjoyed and lingered over. Sightsee.

Vermeer—*A Young Woman Standing at a Virginal*

Here we have a simple interior of a Dutch home with a prim virgin playing a "virginal." We've surprised her and she pauses to look up at

us. Contrast this quiet scene with, say, Titian's bombastic, orgiastic *Bacchus and Ariadne.*

The Dutch took (and still take) great pride in the orderliness of their small homes. Vermeer, by framing off such a small world to look at—from the blue chair in the foreground to the wall in back—forces us to appreciate the tiniest details, the beauty of everyday things. We can meditate on the shawl, the tiles lining the floor, the subtle shades of the white wall, and, most of all, the pale diffused light that soaks in from the window. The painting of a nude cupid on the back wall only strengthens this virgin's purity.

• *Zigzag from room 16 (through 15, 18, and 24) to room 23 for the next two paintings.*

Rembrandt—*Belshazzar's Feast*

The wicked king has been feasting with God's sacred dinnerware when the meal is interrupted. Belshazzar turns to see the finger of God, burning an ominous message into the wall that Belshazzar's number is up. As he turns, he knocks over a goblet of wine. We see the jewels and riches of his decadent life.

Rembrandt captures the scene at the most ironic moment. Belshazzar is about to be ruined. We know it, his guests know it, and, judging by the look on his face, he's coming to the same conclusion.

Rembrandt's flair for the dramatic is accentuated by the strong contrast between light and dark. Most of his canvases are a rich, dark brown, with a few crucial details highlighted by a bright light.

Rembrandt—*Self-Portrait Aged 63*

Rembrandt throws the light of truth on . . . himself. This craggy self-portrait was done the year he died. Contrast it with one done three decades earlier (hanging nearby). Rembrandt, the greatest Dutch painter, started out as the successful, wealthy young genius of the art world. But he refused to crank out commercial works. Rembrandt painted things that he believed in but no one would invest in—family members, down-to-earth Bible scenes, and self-portraits like these.

Here, Rembrandt surveys the wreckage of his independent life. He was bankrupt, his mistress had just died, and he had also buried several of his children. We see a disillusioned, well-worn, but proud old genius.

• *Head to the long room 29 with mint-green wallpaper.*

BAROQUE (1600–1700)

Rubens

This room is full of big, colorful, emotional works by Peter Paul Rubens and others from Catholic Flanders (Belgium). While Protestant and democratic Europe painted simple scenes, Catholic and aristocratic countries turned to the style called "Baroque." Baroque art took what was flashy in Venetian art and made it flashier,  gaudy and made it gaudier, dramatic and made it shocking.

Rubens painted anything that would raise your pulse—battles, miracles, hunts, and, especially, fleshy women with dimples on all four cheeks. *The Judgment of Paris*, for instance, is little more than an excuse for a study of the female nude, showing front, back, and profile all on one canvas.

• *Exit room 29 at the far end. To the left, in room 31, you'll see the large canvas of . . .*

Van Dyck—*Charles I on Horseback*

Kings and bishops used the grandiose Baroque style to impress the masses with their power. This portrait of England's Catholic, French-educated, divine-right king portrays him as genteel and refined, yet very much in command. Charles is placed on a huge horse to accentuate his power. The horse's small head makes sure that little Charles isn't dwarfed. Charles ruled firmly as a Catholic king in a Protestant country until England's Civil War (1648), when his genteel head was separated from his refined body by Cromwell and company.

Van Dyck's portrait style set the tone for all the stuffy, boring portraits of British aristocrats who wished to be portrayed as sophisticated gentlemen—whether they were or not.

• *For the complete opposite of a stuffy portrait bust, backpedal into room 30 for...*

Velázquez—*The Rokeby Venus*

Though horny Spanish kings bought Titian-esque centerfolds by the gross, this work by the king's personal court painter is the first (and,

for over a century, the only) Spanish nude. Like a Venetian model, she's posed diagonally across the canvas with flaring red, white, and gray fabrics to highlight her rosy-white skin and inflame our passion. About the only concession to Spanish modesty is the false reflection in the mirror—if it really showed what the angle should show, Velázquez would have needed two mirrors... and a new job.

• *Turning your left cheek to hers, tango into room 32.*

Michelangelo Merisi de Caravaggio— *The Supper at Emmaus*

After Jesus was crucified, he rose from the dead and appeared without warning to some of his followers. Jesus just wants a quiet meal, but the man in green, suddenly realizing who he's eating with, is about to jump

out of his chair in shock. To the right, a man spreads his hands in amazement, bridging the distance between Christ and us by sticking his hand in our face.

Baroque took reality and exaggerated it. Most artists amplified the prettiness, but Caravaggio exaggerated the grittiness. He shocked the public by using real, ugly, unhaloed people in Bible scenes. Caravaggio's paintings look like a wet dog smells. Reality.

We've come a long way since the first medieval altarpieces that wrapped holy people in a golden foil. From the torn shirts to the five o'clock shadows to the uneven part in Jesus' hair, we are witnessing a very human miracle.

• *Leave the Caravaggio room under the sign reading "East Wing, painting from 1700–1900," and enter room 33.*

FRENCH ROCOCO (1700–1800)

As Europe's political and economic center shifted from Italy to France, Louis XIV's court at Versailles became its cultural hub. Every aristocrat spoke French, dressed French, and bought French paintings. The rococo art of Louis' successors was as frilly, sensual, and suggestive as the decadent French court at Versailles. We see their rosy-cheeked portraits and their fantasies: lords and ladies at play in classical gardens where mortals and gods cavort together.

• *One of the finest examples is the tiny...*

Boucher—*Pan and Syrinx* (1739)

Rococo art is like a Rubens that got shrunk in the wash—smaller, lighter pastel colors, frillier, and more delicate than the Baroque style. Same dimples, though.

• *Enter room 34 (the Sackler Room).*

BRITISH (1800–1850)

Constable—*The Hay Wain*

The more reserved British were more comfortable cavorting with nature than with the lofty gods. Come-as-you-are poets like Wordsworth found the same ecstasy just being outside.

Constable spent hours in the out-of-doors, capturing the simple majesty of billowing clouds, billowing trees, and everyday human activities. Even British portraits (by Thomas Gainsborough and others)

placed refined lords and ladies
amid idealized greenery.

This simple style—believe it
or not—was considered shocking in its day. The rough, thick
paint and crude country settings
scandalized art lovers used to
the highfalutin, prettified sheen
of Baroque and rococo.

• *Take a hike and enjoy the English-country-garden ambience of this room.*

Turner—*The Fighting Téméraire*

Constable's landscape was about to be paved over by the Industrial Revolution. Soon, machines began to replace humans, factories belched
smoke over Constable's hay cart, and cloud gazers had to punch the

clock. Romantics tried to resist
it, lauding the forces of nature
and natural human emotions in
the face of technological "progress." But, alas, here a modern
steamboat symbolically drags a
famous but obsolete sailing bat-
tleship off into the sunset to
be destroyed.

Turner—*Rain, Steam, and Speed*

A train emerges from the depths of fog, rushing across a bridge toward
us. The red-orange glow of the engine's furnace burns like embers of
a fire. (Turner was fascinated by how light penetrates haze.) Through the
blur of paints, the outline of a bridge is visible, while in the center shad-

owy figures (spirits?) head down
to the river.

Turner's messy, colorful style
gives us our first glimpse into the
modern art world—he influenced
the Impressionists. Turner takes
an ordinary scene (like Constable), captures the play of light
with messy paints (like Impressionists), and charges it with
mystery (like wow).

• *London's Tate Britain (see page 62) has an enormous collection of Turner's work. For now, enter room 41.*

Paul Delaroche—
The Execution of Lady Jane Grey

The teenage queen's nine-day reign has reached its curfew. This simple girl, manipulated into power politics by cunning advisors, is now sent to the execution site in the Tower of London. As her friends swoon with grief, she's blindfolded and forced to kneel at the block. Legend has it that the confused, humiliated girl was left kneeling on the scaffold. She crawled around, groping for the chopping block, crying out, "Where is it? What am I supposed to do?" The executioner in scarlet looks on with as much compassion as he can muster.

Britain's distinct contribution to art history is this Pre-Raphaelite style, showing medieval scenes in luminous realism with a mood of understated tragedy.

• *Exit room 41, pass the door that leads downstairs to the café and WC, and enter room 43. The Impressionist paintings are scattered throughout rooms 43 through 46.*

IMPRESSIONISM AND BEYOND
(1850–1910)

For 500 years, a great artist was someone who could paint the real world with perfect accuracy. Then along came the camera and, click, the artist was replaced by a machine. But unemployed artists refused to go the way of the *Fighting Téméraire*.

They couldn't match the camera for painstaking detail, but they could match it—even beat it—in capturing the fleeting moment, the candid pose, the play of light and shadow, the quick impression a scene makes on you. A new breed of artists burst out of the stuffy confines of the studio. They set up their canvases in the open air or carried their notebooks into a crowded café, dashing off quick sketches in order to catch a momentary . . . impression.

• *Start with the misty Monet train station.*

Monet—*Gare St. Lazare* (1877)

Claude Monet, the father of Impressionism, was more interested in the play of light off his subject than the subject itself. Here, the sun filters through the glass roof of the train station and is refiltered through the clouds of steam.

Monet—*The Water Lily Pond* (1916)

We've traveled from medieval spirituality to Renaissance realism to Baroque elegance and Impressionist colors. Before you spill out into the 21st-century hubbub of busy London, relax for a second in Monet's garden at Giverny near Paris. Monet planned an artificial garden, rechanneled a stream, built a bridge, and planted these water lilies—a living work of art, a small section of order and calm in a hectic world.

Manet—*The Waitress (Corner of a Café-Concert)* (1878–80)

Imagine how mundane (and therefore shocking) Manet's quick "impression" of this café must have been to a public that was raised on Greek gods, luscious nudes, and glowing Madonnas.
• *In room 44 . . .*

Renoir—*Boating on the Seine* (1879-80)

View this from about 15 feet away. It's a nice scene of boats on sun-dappled water. Now move in close. The "scene" breaks up into almost random patches of bright colors. The "blue" water is actually separate brushstrokes of blue, green, pink, purple, gray, white, etc. The rower's hat is a blob of green, white, and blue. Up close it looks like a mess, but when you back up to a proper distance, voilà! It shimmers. This kind of rough, coarse brushwork (where you can actually see the brushstrokes) is one of the telltale signs of Impressionism. Renoir was not trying to paint the water itself but the reflection of sky, shore, and boats off its surface.

Seurat—*Bathers at Asnières* (1883)

Seurat took the Impressionist color technique to its logical extreme. These figures—a bather, a hat, a river—are "built," dot by dot, like newspaper photos, using small points of different colors. Only at a distance do green, orange, lavender, and white blend together to make a patch of "green" grass.

• *In room 45 . . .*

Degas—*Miss La La at the Cirque Fernando* (1879)

Degas, the master of the candid snapshot, enjoyed catching everyday scenes at odd angles.

Van Gogh—*Sunflowers* (1888)

In military terms, van Gogh was the point man of his culture. He went ahead of his cohorts, explored the unknown, and caught a bullet young. He added emotion to Impressionism, infusing his love of life even into inanimate objects. These sunflowers, painted with characteristic swirling brushstrokes, shimmer and writhe in either agony or ecstasy—depending on your own mood.

Van Gogh painted these during his stay in southern France, a time of frenzied painting when he himself hovered between agony and ecstasy, bliss and madness. Within two years of painting this, he shot himself.

In his day, van Gogh was a penniless nobody, selling only one painting in his whole career. Today, a *Sunflowers* (he did a half dozen versions) sells for $40 million (a salary of about $2,500 a day for 45 years), and it's not even his highest-priced painting. Hmm.

Cézanne—*Bathers*
(*Les Grandes Baigneuses*) (1900–1906)

These bathers are arranged in strict triangles *à la* Leonardo—the five nudes on the left form one triangle, the seated nude on the right forms another, and even the background trees and clouds are triangular patterns of paint.

Cézanne uses the Impressionist technique of building a figure with dabs of paint (though his "dabs" are often larger-sized "cube" shapes) to make solid, 3-D geometrical figures in the style of the Renaissance. In the process, his cube shapes helped inspire a radical new art style, "cube"-ism, bringing art into the 20th century and beyond.

❧ 3 ❧
TATE BRITAIN TOUR

The Tate Britain has the world's best collection of British art. This is people's art, with realistic paintings rooted in the people, landscape, and stories of the British Isles. You'll see Hogarth's stage sets, Gainsborough's ladies, Blake's angels, Constable's clouds, Turner's tempests, the swooning realism of the Pre-Raphaelites, and the camera-eye portraits of Hockney and Freud. Even if these names are new to you, don't worry. Guaranteed you'll exit the Tate Britain with at least one new favorite.

ORIENTATION
Cost: Free.
Hours: Daily 10:00–17:50, closed Dec 24–26.
Getting there: It's on Millbank, on the Thames River, just north of Vauxhall Bridge. Subway to Pimlico (and 7-min walk); or take bus #88 (from Oxford Circus) or #77A (from National Gallery) directly to museum; or walk 25 minutes along the Thames from Big Ben. A ferry service on the Thames shuttles visitors between the Tate Britain and Tate Modern (May–Sept).
Information: Free map at information desk (tel. 020/7887-8000, recorded information 0171/7887-8008, www.tate.org.uk). The bookshop is great.
Tours: Free tours offered (normally 11:30—Turner, 14:30 and 15:30—

TATE BRITAIN—OVERVIEW

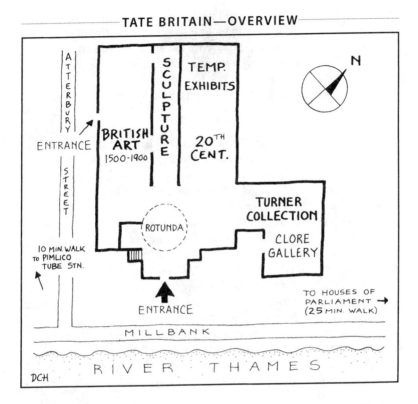

British Highlights, call to confirm schedule, tel. 020/7887-8000). Audioguide tours cost £3.

Length of our tour: One hour.

Cloakroom: Free.

Photography: Not allowed.

Cuisine art: Coffee shop (affordable gourmet buffet line) and restaurant (expensive, but delightful atmosphere).

Starring: Hogarth, Gainsborough, Reynolds, Blake, Constable, Pre-Raphaelites, and Turner.

THE TWO TATES

There are two separate Tate museums: The Tate Britain, which this tour is based on, features British art. The Tate Modern (at Bankside, on the south bank of the Thames across from St. Paul's) features modern art (for more information, see page 459).

The Tate Britain is completing a major expansion with a new

entrance (on Atterbury Street) and new galleries. Until the collection settles down, a painting-by-painting tour is impossible. In this chapter we'll cover the big picture, seeing the essence of each artist and style, then let the Tate Britain surprise us with its ever-changing wardrobe of paintings.

EARLY BRITISH ART
(1500–1800)

British artists painted people, horses, countrysides, and scenes from daily life, all done realistically and without the artist passing judgment (substance over style). What you won't see here is the kind of religious art so popular elsewhere. The largely Protestant English abhorred the "graven images" of Catholic saints and the Virgin Mary. Many were even destroyed during the 16th-century Reformation. They preferred landscapes of the quaint English countryside and flesh-and-blood English folk.

Portrait of Lord and Lady Whoevertheyare

These stuffy portraits of a beef-fed society try to make uncultured people look delicate and refined. English country houses often had a long hall built specially to hang family portraits. You  could stroll along and see your noble forebears looking down their noses at you. Britain's upper crust in the 1600s had little interest in art other than as a record of themselves along with their possessions—their wives, children, jewels, furs, ruffled collars, swords, and guns. You'll see plenty more portraits in the Tate Britain, right up to modern times. Each era had its own style— some, like these, were stern and dignified; others were more relaxed and elegant.

George Stubbs—Various pictures of horses

In the 1700s, as British art came into its own, painters started doing more than just portraits. Stubbs was the Michelangelo of horse painters. He understood these creatures from the inside out, having dissected them in his studio. He even used machinery to prop the corpses up into lifelike poses. He'd often paint the horses first on a blank canvas, then fill in the background landscape around them (notice the heavy outlines that make them stand out clearly from the countryside). The result is both incredibly natural—from the veins in their noses to the freshly brushed coats—and geometrically posed.

William Hogarth (1697–1764)

Hogarth loved the theater. "My picture is my stage," he said, "and my men and women my players." The curtain goes up and we see one scene that tells a whole story, often satirizing English high society. Hogarth often painted series based on popular novels or plays of the time.

William Hogarth reveled in the darker side of "merry olde England." Hogarth, an 18th-century Charles Dickens, showed slices of real England in his best paintings. Not content to paint just pretty portraits, he chose models from real life and put them into real-life scenes.

A born Londoner, Hogarth loved every gritty aspect of the big city. You could find him in seedy pubs and brothels, at the half-price ticket booth in Leicester Square, at prize-fights, cockfights, duels, and public executions—sketchbook in hand. With biting satire, he exposed the hypocrisy of the upper class...and exposed the upper classes to the hidden poverty of society's underbelly.

Thomas Gainsborough (1727–1788)

Portraits were still the bread and butter for painters, and Thomas Gainsborough was one of the best portaitists. His specialty was showcasing the elegant, educated women of his generation. The results were always natural and never stuffy. The cheeks get rosier, the poses more relaxed, the colors brighter and more pastel, showing the influence of the refined French culture of the court at Versailles. His models' clear, Ivory-soap complexions stand out from the swirling greenery of English gardens.

Sir Joshua Reynolds and the "Grand Style" (1750–1800)

Real life wasn't worthy of a painting. So said Britain's Royal Academy. People, places, and things had to be gussied up with Greek columns, symbolism, and great historic moments, ideally from classical Greece.

Sir Joshua Reynolds, the pillar of England's art establishment, stood for all that was noble, upright, tasteful, rational, brave, clean, reverent, and boring. According to Reynolds, art was meant to elevate the viewer, to appeal to his rational nature and fill him with noble sentiment.

By combining history and portraits, he could turn Lord Milquetoast into a heroic Greek patriot or Lady Bagbody into the Venus de Milo. Combining the Grand Style with landscapes, you get Versailles-type settings of classical monuments amid manicured greenery. Inspired by Rembrandt, he used dense paint to give his works the look of the Old Masters.

Since so much of the art we'll see from here on was painted in the looming shadow of Reynolds, and since his technique and morals are flawless, let's dedicate a minute's silence to his painting. Fifty-nine... fifty-eight... I'll be in the next room.

Constable's Landscapes (1776–1837)
While the Royal Academy thought Nature needed makeup, Constable thought she was just fine. He painted the English landscape just as it is, realistically, without idealizing it.

Constable's style became more "Impressionistic" near the end of his life—messier brushwork. He often painted full-scale "sketches" of works he'd perfect later (such as the Salisbury cathedral).

It's rare to find a Constable (or any British) landscape that doesn't have the mark of man in it—a cottage, hay cart, country lane, or field hand. For him, the English countryside and its people were one.

Cloudy skies are one of Constable's trademarks. Appreciate the effort involved in sketching ever-changing cloud patterns for hours on end—the mix of dark clouds and white clouds, cumuli and strati, the colors of the sunset. His subtle genius wasn't fully recognized in his lifetime, and he was forced to paint portraits for his keep. The neglect caused him to ask a friend: "Can it therefore be wondered at that I paint continual storms?"

Other Landscapes

Compare Constable's unpretentious landscapes with the others in the Tate Britain. Some artists mixed landscapes with intense human emotion to produce huge, colorful canvases of storms, burning sunsets, towering clouds, and crashing waves, all dwarfing puny humans. Others made supernatural, religious fantasy-scapes. Artists in the "Romantic" style saw the most intense human emotions reflected in the drama and mystery in nature. God is found within nature, and nature is charged with the grandeur and power of God.

THE INDUSTRIAL REVOLUTION (1800–1900)

Think of England around 1850. Newfangled inventions were everywhere. Railroads laced the land. You could fall asleep in Edinburgh and wake up in London, a trip that used to take days or weeks. But along with technology came factories coating towns with soot, urban poverty, regimentation, and clock punching. Machines replaced honest laborers, and once-noble Man was viewed as a naked ape.

Strangely, you'll see little of the modern world in paintings of the time—except in reaction to it. Many artists rebelled against "progress" and the modern world. They looked back to ancient Greece as a happier, more enlightened time (neoclassicism of Reynolds). Or to the Middle Ages (Pre-Raphaelites). Or they escaped the dirty cities to commune with nature (Romantics). Or they found a new spirituality in intense human emotions (dramatic scenes from history or literature). Or they left our world altogether. (Which brings us to . . .)

William Blake

At the age of four, Blake saw the face of God. A few years later he ran across a flock of angels swinging in a tree. Twenty years later he was living in a run-down London flat with an illiterate wife, scratching out a thin existence as an engraver. But even in this squalor, ignored by all but a few fellow artists, he still had his heavenly visions, and he described them in poems and paintings.

One of the original space cowboys, Blake was also a unique painter who is often classed with the "Romantics" because he painted in a fit of ecstatic inspiration rather than by studied technique. He painted angels, archangels, thrones, and dominions rather than the dull material world. While Britain was conquering the world with guns, and nature with machines, and while his fellow Londoners were growing rich, fat, and self-important, Blake turned his gaze inward, painting the glorious visions of the soul.

Blake's works hang in a darkened room to protect the watercolors. Enter his mysterious world and let your pupils dilate opium wide.

His pen and watercolor sketches glow with an unearthly aura. In visions of heaven and hell, his figures have superhero musculature. The colors are almost translucent.

Blake saw the material world as bad, trapping the divine spark inside each of our bodies and keeping us from true communion with God. Blake's prints illustrate his views on the ultimate weakness of material, scientific man. Despite their Greek-god anatomy, his men look noble but tragically lost.

A famous poet as well as painter, Blake summed up his distrust of the material world in a poem addressed to "The God of this World," that is, Satan:

> *Though thou art worshiped by the names divine*
> *Of Jesus and Jehovah, thou art still*
> *The son of morn in weary night's decline,*
> *The lost traveler's dream under the hill.*

PRE-RAPHAELITES
(1850–1880)

Millais, Rossetti, Waterhouse, Hunt, Burne-Jones, etc.

You'll see medieval damsels in dresses and knights in tights, legendary lovers from poetry, and even a very human Virgin Mary as a delicate young woman. The women, wearing flowing dresses, have long, wavy hair and delicate, elongated, curving bodies. Beautiful.

You won't find Pre-Raphaelites selling flowers at the airport, but this "Brotherhood" of young British artists had a cultic intensity. (You may see the initials P.R.B.—Pre-Raphaelite Brotherhood—by the artist's signature in some paintings.) After generations of the pompous Grand Style art, the Pre-Raphaelites finally said, "Enough's enough." They focused on: 1) nature, 2) sincere human feelings, 3) medieval subjects, and 4) expressive symbolism.

They returned to a style "Pre-Raphael." The art was intended to be

"medieval" in its simple style, in the melancholy mood, and often in subject matter. "Truth to Nature" was their slogan. Like the Impressionists who followed, they donned their scarves, barged out of the stuffy studio, and set up outdoors, painting trees, streams, and people as they really were. Still, they often captured nature with such a close-up clarity that it's downright unnatural.

And despite the Pre-Raphaelite claim to paint life just as it is, this is so beautiful it hurts. Be prepared to suffer, unless your heart is made of stone.

This is art from the cult of femininity, worshiping Woman's haunting beauty, compassion, and depth of soul. (Proto-feminism or retro-chauvinism?) The artists' wives and lovers were their models and muses, and the art echoed their love lives. The people are surrounded by nature at its most beautiful, with every detail painted crystal clear. Even without the people, there is a mood of melancholy.

The Pre-Raphaelites hated gushy sentimentality and overacting. Their subjects—even in the face of great tragedy, high passions, and moral dilemmas—barely raise an eyebrow. Outwardly, they're reflective, accepting their fate. But subtle gestures and sinuous postures speak volumes.

These volumes were footnoted by the small objects with symbolic importance placed around them: red flowers denoting passion, lilies for purity, pets for fidelity, and so on.

The colors—greens, blues, and reds—are bright and clear, with everything evenly lit so we see every detail. To get the luminous color, they painted a thin layer of bright paint over a pure white, still-wet undercoat, which subtly "shines" through. These canvases radiate a pure spirituality, like stained-glass windows.

VICTORIAN (1837–1901)

Middle-class Brits loved to see Norman Rockwell–style scenes from everyday life. The style has Pre-Raphaelite realism but is too sentimental for Pre-Raphaelite tastes.

We see families and ordinary people eating, working, and relaxing. Some works tug at the heartstrings, with scenes of parting couples, the grief of death, or the joy of families reuniting. Dramatic scenes from popular literature get the heart beating. There's the occasional touching look at the plight of the honest poor, reminiscent of Dickens. And many paintings warn us to be good little boys and girls by showing the consequences of a life of sin. Then there are the puppy dogs with sad eyes.

Stand for a while and enjoy the exquisite realism and human emotions of these Victorian works...real people painted realistically. Get your fill, because beloved Queen Victoria is about to check out, the modern world is coming, and, with it, new art to express modern attitudes.
• *To help ease the transition...*

The Turner Collection

J. M. W. Turner (1775–1851)

The Tate Britain has the world's best collection of Turners. Walking through his life's work, you can trace his progression from a painter of realistic historical scenes, through his wandering years, to "Impressionist" paintings of color-and-light patterns.
• *The Turner Collection is in the Clore Gallery, the wing that juts out the side of the Tate Britain.*

Youth
See his self-portrait as a young man, in a full-frontal pose, ready to take on the world.

High Art, History, and the Sublime
Trained in the Reynolds school of grandiose epics, Turner painted the obligatory big canvases of great moments in history—*The Battle of Waterloo, Hannibal in the Alps, Destruction of Sodom, The Lost Traveler's Checks, Jason and the Argonauts*, and various shipwrecks. Not content to crank them out in the traditional staid manner, he sets them in expansive

landscapes. Nature's stormy mood mirrors the human events but is so grandiose it dwarfs them.

This is a theme we'll see throughout his works: The forces of nature—the burning sun, swirling clouds, churning waves, gathering storms, and the weathering of time—overwhelm men and wear down the civilizations they build.

Travels with Turner

Turner's true love was nature. And he was a born hobo. Oblivious to the wealth and fame that his early paintings gave him, he set out traveling—mostly on foot—throughout England and the Continent, with a rucksack full of sketch pads and painting gear.

He found the "Sublime" not in the studio or in church, but in the overwhelming power of nature. The landscapes throb with life and motion.

Italy: Landscape and Antiquity

Rick Steves' guidebook in hand, Turner visited the great museums of Italy, drawing inspiration from the Renaissance masters. He painted the classical monuments and Renaissance architecture. He copied masterpieces and learned, assimilated, and fused a great variety of styles—a true pan-European vision.

Stand close to a big canvas of Roman ruins, close enough to where it fills your whole field of vision. Notice how the buildings seem to wrap around you. Turner was a master of using multiple perspectives to draw the viewer in. On the one hand, you're right in the thick of things, looking "up" at the tall buildings. Then again, you're looking "down" on the distant horizon, as though standing on a mountaintop.

Venice

I know what color the palazzo is. But what color is it at sunset? Or after filtering through the watery haze that hangs over Venice? Can I paint the glowing haze itself? Maybe if I combine two different colors and smudge the paint on....

Venice titillated Turner's lust for reflected light. This room contains both finished works and unfinished sketches... uh, which is which?

Marine and Coastal Subjects

Seascapes were his specialty, with waves, clouds, mist, and sky churning and mixing together, all driven by the same forces.

Turner used oils like many painters use watercolors. First he'd lay down a background (a "wash") of large patches of color, then he'd add a few dabs of paint to suggest a figure. The final product lacked photographic clarity but showed the power and constant change in the forces of nature. He was perhaps the most prolific painter ever, with some 2,000 finished paintings and 20,000 sketches and watercolors.

Late Works

The older he got, the messier both he and his paintings became. He was wealthy, but he died in a run-down dive where he'd set up house with a prostitute. Yet the colors  here are brighter and the subjects less pessimistic than in the dark and brooding early canvases. His last works—whether landscape, religious, or classical scenes—are a blur and swirl of colors in motion, lit by the sun or a lamp burning through the mist. Even Turner's own creations are finally dissolved by the swirling forces of nature.

These paintings are "modern" in that the subject is less important than the style. You'll have to read the title to "get" it. You could argue that an Englishman helped invent Impressionism a generation before Monet and his ilk boxed the artistic ears of Paris in the 1880s. Turner's messy use of paint to portray reflected light "chunneled" its way to France to inspire the Impressionists.

20TH-CENTURY BRITISH ARTISTS

Through the many trends and -isms of the 20th century, British artists continued the British tradition of realistic paintings of people and landscape. (Note: You'll find these artists' work both here in the Tate Britain and in the Tate Modern.)

David Hockney

The "British Andy Warhol"—bleach-blonde, horn-rimmed, gay, and famous—paints popular culture with photographic realism. Large, airy canvases of L.A. swimming pools or double-portraits of his friends in their stylish homes capture the superficial materialism of the '70s and '80s. (Is he satirizing or glorifying it by painting it on a monumental scale with painstaking detail?)

Hockney saturates the canvas with bright paint, eliminating any haze, making distant objects as clear and bright as close-up ones. This, combined with his slightly simplified "cut-out" figures, gives the canvas the flat look of a billboard.

Lucian Freud

Sigmund's grandson (who emigrated from Nazi Germany as a boy) puts every detail on the couch for analysis, then reassembles them into works that are still surprisingly realistic. His subjects look you right in the eye, slightly on edge. Even the plants create an ominous mood. Every detail is in sharp focus (unlike real life where you concentrate on one thing while your peripheral vision is blurred). Thick brushwork is especially good at capturing the pallor of British flesh.

Bridget Riley

The pioneer of op art paints patterns of lines and alternating colors that make the eye vibrate (the way a spiral will "spin") when you stare at it. These obscure, scientific experiments in human optics suddenly became trendy in the psychedelic, cannabis-fueled sixties. Like wow.

Francis Bacon

With a stiff upper lip, Britain survived the Blitz, the War, and the loss of hundreds of thousands of men—but at war's end, the bottled-up horror came rushing out. Bacon's 1945 exhibition stunned London with its unmitigated ugliness.

His deformed half-humans—caged in a claustrophobic room, with twisted, hunk-of-meat bodies and quadriplegic helplessness—can do nothing but scream in anguish and frustration. The scream becomes a blur, as though it goes on forever.

Bacon, largely self-taught, uses "traditional" figurativism to express the existential human predicament of being caught in a world not of your making, where you're isolated and helpless to change it. (Or is it the scream of undying shame from someone caught trying on his mom's underpants—as I read somewhere about Bacon.)

Henry Moore

Twice a week, young Henry Moore went to the British Museum to sketch ancient statues, especially reclining ones (like in the Parthenon pediment or the Mayan Chac Mool he saw in a photo). His statues—mostly female, mostly reclining—catch the primitive power of carved stone. Moore almost always carved with his own hands (unlike, say, Rodin, who modeled a small clay figure and let assistants chisel the real thing), capturing the human body in a few simple curves, with minimal changes to the rock itself.

The statues do look vaguely like what their titles say, but it's the stones themselves that are really interesting. Notice the texture and graininess of these mini-Stonehenges; feel the weight, the space they take up, and how the rock forms intermingle.

During World War II, Moore passed time in the bomb shelters sketching mothers with babes in arms, a theme found in later works.

Moore carves the human body with the epic scale and restless poses of Michelangelo but with the crude rocks and simple lines of the primitives.

Barbara Hepworth

Hepworth's small-scale carvings in stone and wood—like "mini-Moores"—make even holes look interesting. Though they're not exactly realistic, it isn't hard to imagine their being inspired by, say, a man embracing a woman, or the shoreline of her Cornwall-coast home encircling a bay, or a cliff penetrated by a cave—that is, two forms intermingling.

Jacob Epstein

Simplified, primitive-looking statues are polished to gleam like modern machines.

Gilbert and George

The Siegfried and Roy of art satirize the "Me Generation" by portraying their nerdy selves on the monumental scale normally dedicated to kings, popes, and saints.

Stanley Spencer

Spencer paints unromanticized landscapes, portraits, and hometown scenes. Even the miraculous Resurrection of the Dead is portrayed absolutely literally, with the dead climbing out of their Glasgow graves. In fully modern times, Spencer carries on the British tradition of sober realism.

❧ 4 ❧
BRITISH LIBRARY TOUR

The British Empire built its greatest monuments out of paper. It's in literature that England has made her lasting contribution to history and the arts. Opened in 1998 in a fine new building, this national archive of Britain has more than 12 million books, 300 kilometers of shelving, and the deepest basement in London. We'll concentrate on a handful of documents—literary and historical—that changed the course of history. Start with the top 12 stops (described in this tour), then stray according to your interests.

ORIENTATION

Cost: Free.

Hours: Mon–Fri 9:30–18:00 (until 20:00 on Tue), Sat 9:30–17:00, Sun 11:00–17:00.

Getting there: Take the tube to King's Cross. Leaving the station, turn right, and walk a block to 96 Euston Road. (Note that the British Library is no longer housed within the British Museum.)

Information: Tel. 020/7412-7000, www.bl.uk.

Tours: Sixty-minute tours are usually offered on Mon, Wed, Fri, Sat, and Sun at 15:00, plus Sat at 10:30, Sun at 11:30, and Tue at 18:30 (£4; to confirm schedule and to reserve, call 020/7412-7332).

Length of our tour: One hour.

BRITISH LIBRARY WALKING TOUR

TURNING THE PAGES 11

GOSPEL FRAGMENTS   CODEX SIN.

PRINTING 4   DIAMOND SUTRA   GUTENBERG

ILLUM. MANUSCRIPTS 3

EARLY ENGLISH LITERATURE 7

BIBLES 2   LINDISFARNE GOSPELS

KING JAMES BIBLE

LEONARDO 5   FIRST FOLIO   EXIT

MAGNA CARTA 6

SHAKE-SPEARE 8   BEOWULF   CHAUCER

HAMLET

MAPS 1

ENG. LIT 9   CARROLL   KIPLING

BEATLES   **MUSIC** 10

ELEV.   HANDEL

PEARSON GALLERY 12   DCH

1. Maps
2. Bibles
3. Lindisfarne Gospels and Illuminated Manuscripts
4. Printing
5. Leonardo
6. Magna Carta
7. Early English Literature
8. Shakespeare
9. English Literature
10. Music
11. Turning the Pages computer room
12. Pearson Gallery: Temporary exhibits

Cloakroom: Free.

No-nos: No photography, smoking, or chewing gum.

Cuisine art: A great cafeteria/restaurant is upstairs from the café. Inside, the 15-meter-tall wall of 65,000 books was given to the people by King George IV in 1823. This high-tech mother of all bookshelves is behind glass and has movable lifts.

Starring: Magna Carta, Bibles, Shakespeare, English Lit 101, and the Beatles.

THE TOUR BEGINS

Entering the library courtyard you'll see a big statue of a naked Isaac Newton bending forward with a compass to measure the universe. The statue symbolizes the library's purpose: to gather all knowledge and promote our endless search for truth.

Stepping inside you'll see the information desk. The cloakroom, WC, and café are to the right. The reading rooms upstairs are not open to the public. Our tour is in the tiny but exciting area to the left, under the sign marked "Exhibitions."

The priceless literary and historical treasures of the collection are in this one carefully designed and well-lit room. The "Turning the Pages" computer room (where you can "virtually" leaf through a few precious manuscripts) is in an adjoining room. Down a few steps you'll find the Pearson Gallery (which displays temporary—usually interesting—exhibits).

1. Maps

Navigate the wall of historic maps from left to right. "A Medieval Map of Britain," from 1250, puts medieval man in an unusual position—looking down on his homeland from 80 kilometers in the air. "The Christian World View" of 1260 has Jerusalem in the middle and God on top. The open book ("The World of Columbus"), from 1490, shows the best map Columbus could get—a map of everything in the world except... what was just off the page. And then a 1506 map ("America?") shows the first depiction of America... as part of Asia. By 1562 ("America!") North America had a New Yorker's perspective—detailed East Coast, sketchy California, and "Terra Incognita" in between. By 1570 you could plan your next trip with the map of "Mercator's Europe."

2. Bibles

My favorite excuse for not learning a foreign language is: "If English was good enough for Jesus Christ, it's good enough for me!" I don't know what that has to do with anything, but obviously Jesus didn't speak English—nor did Moses or Isaiah or Paul or any other Bible authors or characters. As a result, our present-day English Bible is not directly from the mouth and pen of these religious figures, but the fitful product of centuries of evolution and translation.

The Bible is not a single book; it's an anthology of books by many authors from different historical periods writing in different languages (usually Hebrew or Greek). So there are three things that editors must consider in compiling the most accurate Bible: 1) deciding which books actually belong, 2) finding the oldest and most accurate version of each book, and 3) translating it accurately.

Codex Sinaiticus (c. A.D. 350)

The oldest complete "Bible" in existence (along with one in the Vatican), this is one of the first attempts to collect various books together into one authoritative anthology. It's in Greek, the language in which most of the New Testament was written. The Old Testament portions are Greek translations from the original Hebrew. This particular Bible, and the nearby *Codex Alexandrus* (A.D. 425), contain some books not included in most modern English Bibles. (Even today Catholic Bibles contain books not found in Protestant Bibles.)

Gospel Fragments

Here are pieces—scraps of papyrus—of two such books that didn't make it into our modern Bible. The "Unknown Gospel" (an account of the life of Jesus of Nazareth) is as old a Christian manuscript as any in existence. Remember, the Gospels weren't written down for a full generation after Jesus died, and the oldest surviving manuscripts are from later than that. So why isn't this early version of Jesus' life part of our Bible right up there with Matthew, Mark, Luke, and John? Possibly because some early Bible editors didn't like the story it told about Jesus not found in the four accepted Gospels.

The "Gospel of Thomas" gives an even more radical picture of Jesus. This Jesus preaches enlightenment by mystical knowledge. He seems to be warning people against looking to gurus for the answers, a Christian version of "If you meet the Buddha on the road, kill him." This fragment dates from A.D. 150, more than a century after Jesus' death, but that's probably not the only reason why it's not in our Bible (after all, the Gospel of John is generally dated at A.D. 100). Rather, the message, which threatened established church leaders, may have been too scary to include in the Bible—whether Jesus said it or not.

The King James Bible (1611)

This Bible is in the same language you speak, but try reading it. The strange letters and archaic words clearly show how quickly languages have evolved.

Jesus spoke Aramaic, a form of Hebrew. His words were written down in Greek. Greek manuscripts were translated into Latin, the language of medieval monks and scholars. By 1400 there was still no English version of the Bible, though only a small percentage of the population understood Latin. A few brave reformers risked death to make translations into English and print them with Gutenberg's new invention. Within two centuries English translations were both legal and popular.

The King James version (done during his reign) has been the most widely used English translation. Fifty scholars worked for four years, borrowing heavily from previous translations, to produce the work. Its impact on the English language was enormous, making Elizabethan English something of the standard, even after all those "thees" and "thous" fell out of fashion in everyday speech.

Many of the most recent translations are both more accurate (based on better scholarship and original manuscripts) and more readable, using modern speech patterns.

3. Lindisfarne Gospels (A.D. 698) and Illuminated Manuscripts

Throughout the Middle Ages, Bibles had to be reproduced by hand. This was a painstaking process usually done by monks for a rich patron. This beautifully illustrated ("illuminated") collection of the four Gospels is the most magnificent of medieval British monk-u-scripts. The text is in Latin, the language of scholars ever since the Roman Empire, but the elaborate decoration mixes Irish, classical, and even Byzantine forms. (Read a virtual copy in the adjacent "Turning the Pages" computer room.)

These Gospels are a reminder that Christianity almost didn't make

it in Europe. After the fall of Rome (which had established Christianity as the official religion), much of Europe reverted to its pagan ways. This was the time of Beowulf, when people worshiped woodland spirits and terrible Teutonic gods. It took dedicated Irish missionaries 500 years to reestablish the faith on the Continent. Lindisfarne, an obscure monastery of Irish monks on an island off the east coast of England, was one of the few beacons of light after the fall of

Rome, tending the embers of civilization through the long night of the Dark Ages.

Browse through more illuminated manuscripts (in the cases behind the Lindisfarne Gospels). This is some of the finest art from what we call the "Dark Ages." The little intimate details offer a rare and fascinating peek into medieval life.

4. Printing

The *Diamond Sutra*, from 868, is the earliest dated printed document. Printing was common in Asia from the mid-700s—seven centuries before Gutenberg "invented" the printing press in Europe. Texts such as this "Buddhist Bible" were printed using

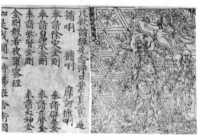

wooden blocks carved with Chinese characters that were dipped into paint or ink. Notice also the fine wood-block illustration of Buddha delivering his famous sermon. This was discovered in China in 1907.

The Gutenberg Bible—The First Book Printed in Europe (c. 1455)

It looks like just another monk-made Latin manuscript, but it's the first book printed in Europe. Printing is one of the most revolutionary inventions in history. Johann Gutenberg (c. 1397–1468), a German silversmith, devised a convenient way to reproduce written materials

quickly, neatly, and cheaply—by printing with movable type. You scratch each letter onto a separate metal block, then arrange them into words, ink them up, and press them onto paper. When one job was done you could reuse the same letters for a new one.

This simple idea had immediate and revolutionary consequences. Knowledge became cheap and accessible to a wide audience, not just the rich. Books became the "mass media" of Europe, linking people by a common set of ideas. And, like a drug, this increased knowledge only created demand for still more.

Suddenly the Bible was available for anyone to read. Church authorities, more interested in "protecting" than spreading the word of

God, passed laws prohibiting the printing of Bibles. As the Church feared, when people read the Bible they formed their own opinions of God's message, which was often different from the version spoon-fed to them by priests. In the resulting Reformation, Protestants broke away from the Catholic Church.

5. Leonardo da Vinci's Notebook

Books also spread secular knowledge. Renaissance men turned their attention away from heaven to the nuts and bolts of the material world around them. These pages from Leonardo's notebook show his powerful curiosity, his genius for invention, and his famous backward and inside-out handwriting.

One person's research inspired another's, and books allowed knowledge to accumulate. While Galileo championed the counter-commonsense notion that the earth spun around the sun, Isaac Newton perfected the mathematics of those moving bodies.

6. Magna Carta

How did Britain, a tiny island with a few million people, come to rule a quarter of the world? Not by force but by law. The Magna Carta was the basis for England's constitutional system of government. You'll find several different versions of the Magna Carta displayed in the glass case.

In the year 1215, England's barons rose in revolt against the slimy King John. After losing London, John was forced to negotiate. The barons presented him with a list of demands ("The Articles of the Barons"). John, whose rule was worthless without the support of the barons, had no choice but to fix his seal to it.

This was a turning point in the history of government. Kings had ruled by God-given authority. They were above the laws of men, acting however they pleased. Now, for the first time, there were limits— in writing—on how a king could treat his subjects. More generally, it established the idea of "due process"—that is, the government can't infringe on people's freedom without a legitimate legal reason. This small step became the basis for all constitutional governments, including yours.

A few days after John agreed to this original document, it was rewritten in legal form, and some 35 copies of this final version of the "Great Charter" were distributed around the kingdom ("Magna Carta" and "Burnt Magna Carta").

So what did this radical piece of paper actually say? Not much by today's standards. The specific demands had to do with things such as inheritance taxes, the king's duties to widows and orphans, and so on. It wasn't the specific articles that were important, but the simple fact that the king had to abide by them as law.

Around the corner there are many more historical documents in the library—letters by Queen Elizabeth I, Isaac Newton, Wellington, Gandhi, and so on. But for now, let's trace the evolution of...

7. Early English Literature

Four out of every five English words have been borrowed from other languages. The English language, like English culture (and London today), is a mix derived from foreign invaders. Some of the historic ingredients that make this cultural stew are:

1. The original Celtic tribesmen
2. Latin-speaking Romans (A.D. 1–500)
3. Germanic tribes called Angles and Saxons (making English a Germanic language and naming the island "Angle-land"— England)
4. Vikings from Denmark (A.D. 800)
5. French-speaking Normans under William the Conqueror (1066–1250)

Beowulf (c. 1000)

This Anglo-Saxon epic poem written in Old English, the early version of our language, almost makes the hieroglyphics on the Rosetta Stone look easy. The manuscript here is from A.D. 1000, although the poem itself dates to about 750. This is the only existing medieval manuscript of this first English literary masterpiece.

In the story, the young hero Beowulf defeats two half-human monsters threatening the kingdom. Beowulf symbolizes England's emergence from Dark Age chaos and barbarism.

The Canterbury Tales (c. 1410)

Six hundred years later, England was Christian but it was hardly the pious, predictable, Sunday-school world we might imagine. Geoffrey Chaucer's bawdy collection of stories, told by pilgrims on their way to Canterbury, gives us the full range of life's experiences—happy, sad, silly, sexy, and pious. (Late in life, Chaucer wrote an apology for those works of his "that tend toward sin.")

While most serious literature of the time was written in scholarly Latin, these tales were written in Middle English, which developed when the French invasion (1066) added a Norman twist to Old English.

8. Shakespeare

William Shakespeare (1564–1616) is the greatest author in any language. Period. He expanded and helped define modern English. In one fell swoop he made the language of everyday people as important as Latin. In the process, he gave us phrases like "one fell swoop" that we quote without knowing it's Shakespeare.

Perhaps as important was his insight into humanity. With his stock of great characters—Hamlet, Othello, Macbeth, Falstaff, Lear, Romeo and Juliet—he probed the psychology of human beings 300 years before Freud. Even today, his characters strike a familiar chord.

Shakespeare in Collaboration

Shakespeare co-wrote a play titled *The Booke of Sir Thomas More*. Some scholars have wondered if maybe Shakespeare had help on other plays as well. After all, they reasoned, how could a journeyman actor, with little education, have written so many masterpieces? Modern scholars, though, unanimously agree that Shakespeare did indeed write the plays ascribed to him. This particular manuscript is likely in Shakespeare's own handwriting. The crossed-out lines indicate that even geniuses need editing.

The Good and Bad Quarto of Hamlet

Shakespeare wrote his plays to be performed, not read. He published a few, but as his reputation grew, unauthorized "bootleg" versions also began to circulate. Some of these were written out by actors, trying (with faulty memories) to recreate a play they'd been in years before. Here are two different versions of *Hamlet*: "good" and "bad."

The Shakespeare First Folio (1623)

It wasn't until seven years after his death that this complete-works collection of his plays came out. The editors were friends and fellow actors.

The engraving of Shakespeare on the title page is one of only two portraits done during his lifetime. Is this what he really looked like? The best answer comes from his friend and fellow poet Ben Jonson in the introduction on the facing page. He concludes: "Reader, look not on his picture, but his book."

9. Other Greats in English Literature

The rest of the "Beowulf/Chaucer wall" is a greatest-hits sampling of British literature featuring the writing of Wordsworth, Blake, Dickens, James Joyce, and many others (a rotating collection). Especially interesting may be:

Coleridge—Xanadu, an Earthly Paradise from *Kubla Khan*

One day Samuel Taylor Coleridge took opium. He fell asleep while reading about the fantastic palace of the Mongol emperor, Kubla Khan. During his three-hour drug-induced sleep, he composed in his head a poem of "from two to three hundred lines." When he woke up, he grabbed a pen and paper and "instantly and eagerly wrote down the lines that are here preserved." But just then, a visitor on business knocked at the door and kept Coleridge busy for an hour. When Coleridge finally kicked him out, he discovered that he'd forgotten the rest! The poem *Kubla Khan* is only a fragment, but it's still one of literature's masterpieces.

Coleridge (aided by his muse in the medicine cabinet) was one of the Romantic poets. Check out his fellow Romantics—Keats, Shelley, and Wordsworth—nearby.

Dickens

In 1400, few people could read. By 1850 almost everyone in England could and did. Charles Dickens gave them their first taste of "literature." Periodicals serialized his books, and the increasingly educated masses read them avidly. Stories recount mobs of enthusiastic American fans waiting at the docks for the latest news of their favorite candidate.

Dickens also helped raise social concern for the underprivileged—of whom England had more than her share. When Dickens was 12 years old, his father was thrown into debtor's prison, and young Charles was put to work to support the family. The ordeal of poverty scarred him for life but gave depth to his books *Oliver Twist* and *David Copperfield*.

Lewis Carroll—The Original *Alice in Wonderland*

I don't know if Lewis Carroll ever dipped into Coleridge's medicine jar or not, but his series of children's books makes *Kubla Khan* read like the phone book. Carroll was a stammerer, which made him uncomfortable around everyone but children. For them he created a fantasy world where grown-up rules and logic were turned upside down.

10. Music

The Beatles

Future generations will have to judge whether this musical quartet ranks with artists such as Dickens and Keats, but no one can deny its historical significance. The Beatles burst onto the scene in the early 1960s to unheard-of popularity. With their long hair and loud music, they brought counterculture and revolutionary ideas to the middle class, affecting the values of a whole generation. Look for the photos of John Lennon, Paul McCartney, George Harrison, and Ringo Starr before and after their fame.

Most interesting are the manuscripts of song lyrics written by Lennon and McCartney, the two guiding lights of the group. "I Wanna Hold Your Hand" was the song that launched them to superstardom. John's song, "Help," was the quickly written title song for one of the Beatles' movies. Some call "A Ticket to Ride" the first heavy-metal song. "Yesterday," by Paul, was recorded with guitar and voice backed by a string quartet—a touch of sophistication by the producer George Martin. Also glance at the rambling, depressed, cynical, but humorous letter by John on the left. Is that a self-portrait at the bottom?

Music Manuscripts

Kind of an anticlimax after the Fab Four, I know, but here are manuscripts by Handel, Mozart, Beethoven, Schubert, and others.

11. Turning the Pages—Virtual-Reality Room

For a chance to virtually page through a few of the most precious books in the collection, drop by the "Turning the Pages" room. Grab a computer and let your fingers do the walking.

⚛ 5 ⚛

WESTMINSTER ABBEY

Westminster Abbey is the greatest church in the English-speaking world. England's kings and queens have been crowned and buried here since 1066. The histories of Westminster Abbey and England are almost the same. A thousand years of English history—3,000 tombs, the remains of 29 kings and queens, and hundreds of memorials—lie within its walls and under its stone slabs.

ORIENTATION

Cost: £5. Praying is free, thank God, but you must inform the marshal at the door of your purpose.

Hours: Mon–Fri 9:00–16:45, also Wed 18:00–19:45, Sat 9:00–14:45, closed Sun to sightseers but open for services, last admission 60 minutes before closing. Mornings are most crowded. On weekdays, 15:00 is less crowded; come then and stay for the 17:00 evensong (not held on Wed).

Getting there: Near Big Ben and Houses of Parliament (tube: Westminster or St. James' Park).

Information: Evensong is on Mon, Tue, Thu, and Fri at 17:00, Sat and Sun at 15:00; an organ recital is held Sun at 17:45 (confirm times, tel. 020/7222-7110). Special events and services can shut out sightseers.

Tours: Vergers, the church equivalent of docents, give entertaining

WESTMINSTER ABBEY

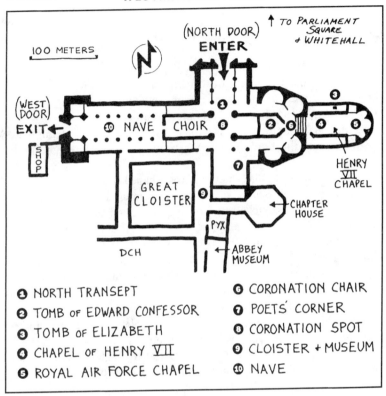

100 METERS

(NORTH DOOR)
ENTER

↑ *TO PARLIAMENT*
SQUARE
& WHITEHALL

(WEST)
(DOOR)
EXIT ←

SHOP

⑩ NAVE   CHOIR

①
⑧
② ⑥ ④ ⑤
⑦

③

HENRY
Ⅶ
CHAPEL

GREAT
CLOISTER   ⑨   ← CHAPTER
HOUSE

PYX

DCH   ← ABBEY
MUSEUM

❶ NORTH TRANSEPT
❷ TOMB OF EDWARD CONFESSOR
❸ TOMB OF ELIZABETH
❹ CHAPEL OF HENRY Ⅶ
❺ ROYAL AIR FORCE CHAPEL

❻ CORONATION CHAIR
❼ POETS' CORNER
❽ CORONATION SPOT
❾ CLOISTER + MUSEUM
❿ NAVE

guided tours for £3 (up to 6/day, 90 min, tel. 020/7222-7110 to get times). Tour themes are the historic church, the personalities buried here, and the great coronations. Informative audioguide tours cost £2 (offered until 15:00 weekdays or until 13:00 Sat).
Length of our tour: 90 minutes.
Photography: Prohibited.
Starring: Edwards, Elizabeths, Henrys, Annes, Richards, Marys, and the Poets' Corner.

THE TOUR BEGINS
You'll have no choice but to follow the steady flow of tourists in through the north transept, wandering among tombstones, circling behind the altar, into Poets' Corner in the south transept, detouring through the cloisters and finally back out through the west end of the

nave. It's all one-way and the crowds can be a real crush. Here are the abbey's top 10 stops:

• *Walk straight in, pick up the map flier that locates the most illustrious tombs, and belly up to the barricade in the center.*

1. North Transept

Look down the long and narrow center aisle of the church. Lined with the praying hands of the Gothic arches, glowing with light from the stained glass, it's clear that this is more than a museum. With saints in stained glass, heroes in carved stone, and the bodies of England's greatest under the floor stones, Westminster Abbey is the religious heart of England.

You're standing at the center of a cross-shaped church. The main altar (with cross and candlesticks) sits on the platform up the five stairs in front of you. To the right stretches the long, high-ceilinged nave. Nestled in the nave is the elaborately carved wooden seating of the choir (or "quire").

The abbey was built in 1065. Its name, Westminster, means Church in the West (west of St. Paul's). For the next 250 years the abbey was redone and remodeled to become essentially the church you see today, notwithstanding an extensive resurfacing in the 19th century. Thankfully, later architects—ignoring building trends of their generation—honored the vision of the original planner and the building was completed in one relatively harmonious style.

The abbey's 10-story nave is the tallest in England. The chandeliers, three meters tall, look small in comparison (16 were given to the abbey by the Guinness family).

The north transept (through which you entered) is nicknamed "Statesmen's Corner" and specializes in famous prime ministers. Find Gladstone and the novelist/politician Disraeli, who presided over England's peak of power under Queen Victoria.

• *Now turn left and follow the crowd. Walk under Robert Peel, the prime minister whose policemen were nicknamed "bobbies," and stroll a few meters into the land of dead kings and queens. Stop at the blocked wooden staircase on your right.*

2. Tomb of Edward the Confessor

The most holy part of the church is the raised area behind the altar (where the wooden staircase leads). Step back and peek over the dark coffin of Edward I to see the green and gold wedding-cake tomb of King Edward the Confessor—the man who built Westminster Abbey.

God had told pious Edward to visit St. Peter's Basilica in Rome. But with Normans thinking conquest, it was too dangerous for him to leave England. Instead he built this grand church and dedicated it to St. Peter. It was finished just in time to bury Edward (1065) and to crown his foreign rival, William the Conqueror (1066). After Edward's death, people prayed on his tomb and, after getting fine results, canonized him (he was the only English king ever to be sainted). This elevated, central tomb is surrounded by the tombs of eight kings and queens.

• *Continue on. At the top of the large staircase, detour left into the private burial chapel of Queen Elizabeth I.*

3. Tomb of Queen Elizabeth I and Mary I

Although there's only one effigy on the tomb (Elizabeth's), there are two queens buried beneath it, both daughters of Henry VIII (by different mothers). Bloody Mary—meek, pious, sickly, and Catholic—enforced Catholicism during her short reign (1553–1558) by burning "heretics" at the stake and executing young Lady Jane Grey, a rival to the throne.

Elizabeth—strong, clever, "virginal," and Protestant—steered England on an Anglican course. Her long reign (1559–1603) was one of the greatest in English history, a time when England ruled the seas and Shakespeare explored human emotions. The effigy, taken from Elizabeth's death mask, is considered a very accurate take on this virgin queen.

The two half sisters disliked each other in life—Mary even had Elizabeth locked up in the Tower of London. Now they lie side by side for eternity—with a prayer for Christians of all persuasions to live peacefully together.

• *Continue into the ornate room behind the main altar.*

4. Chapel of King Henry VII (a.k.a. the Lady Chapel)

The light from the stained-glass windows and the colorful banners overhead give the room the festive air of a medieval tournament. The prestigious Knights of Bath meet here, under the magnificent ceiling studded with gold pendants. Unless you're going to Cambridge's King's College Chapel, this ceiling is the finest English Perpendicular Gothic and fan vaulting you'll see. The brilliant stone ceiling was built in 1509, capping the Gothic period and signaling the vitality of the coming Renaissance.

The knights sit in the wooden stalls with churches on their heads, capped by their own insignia. When the queen worships here, she sits in the corner chair under the carved wooden throne.

Behind the small altar is an iron cage housing tombs of the old warrior Henry VII of Lancaster and his wife, Elizabeth of York. Their love and marriage finally settled the "War of the Roses" between the two clans. The combined red-and-white rose symbol decorates the iron-work. Henry VII was the first Tudor king, the father of Henry VIII, and the grandfather of Elizabeth I. This exuberant chapel heralds a new optimistic postwar era in English history.

• *Walk past Henry and Elizabeth to the far end of the chapel. Stand at the banister in front of the modern set of stained-glass windows.*

5. Royal Air Force Chapel

Saints in robes and halos mingle with pilots in bomber jackets and parachutes in this tribute to World War II flyers who earned their angel wings in the Battle of Britain. Hitler's air force ruled the skies in the early days of the war, bombing at will, threatening to snuff Britain out without a fight. These were the fighters about whom Churchill said, "Never has so much been owed by so many to so few."

The abbey survived the blitz virtually unscathed. As a memorial, a bit of bomb damage—the little glassed-over hole in the wall—is left below the windows in the lower left-hand corner. The book of remembrances lists each casualty of the Battle of Britain.

Hey. Look down at the floor. You're standing on the grave of Oliver Cromwell, leader of the rebel forces in England's Civil War. Or rather, Cromwell was buried here from 1658 to 1661. Then his corpse was exhumed, hanged, drawn, quartered, and decapitated, with the head displayed on a stake as a warning to future king-killers.

• *Exit the Chapel of Henry VII and step out of the flow of traffic. To your left is a door to a side chapel with the tomb of Mary Queen of Scots (beheaded by Elizabeth). Ahead of you, at the foot of the stairs, is the Coronation Chair. Behind the chair, again, is the tomb of the church's founder, Edward the Confessor.*

6. Coronation Chair

The gold-painted wooden chair waits here—with its back to the high altar—for the next coronation. For every English coronation since 1296, it's been moved to its spot before the high altar to receive the royal buttocks. The chair's legs rest on lions, England's symbol. The space below the chair originally held a big rock from Scotland called the Stone of Scone (pronounced "skoon"), symbolizing Scotland's unity with England's king. Recently, however, Britain gave Scotland more sovereignty, its own parliament, and the stone.

• *Continue on. Turn left into the south transept. You're in Poets' Corner.*

7. Poets' Corner

England's greatest contribution to art is the written word. Here lie buried the masters of arguably the world's most complex and expressive language. (Many writers are honored with plaques and monuments; relatively few are actually buried here.)

• *Start with Chaucer, buried in the wall under the blue windows. The plaques on the floor before Chaucer are memorials to other literary greats.*

Geoffrey Chaucer is often considered the father of English literature. Chaucer's *Canterbury Tales* told of earthy people speaking everyday English. He was buried here first. Later, Poets' Corner was built around his tomb.

Lord Byron, the great lover of women and adventure: "Though the night was made for loving, and the day returns too soon/Yet we'll go no more a-roving by the light of the moon."

Dylan Thomas, alcoholic master of modernism with a Romantic's heart: "Oh as I was young and easy in the mercy of his means/Time held me green and dying/Though I sang in my chains like the sea."

W. H. Auden: "May I, composed like them of Eros and of dust/Beleaguered by the same negation and despair/Show an affirming flame."

Lewis Carroll, creator of *Alice in Wonderland*: "'Twas brillig, and the slithy toves did gyre and gimble in the wabe...."

T. S. Eliot, the dry voice of modern society: "This is the way the world ends/Not with a bang but a whimper."

Alfred, Lord Tennyson, conscience of the Victorian Age: "'Tis better to have loved and lost/Than never to have loved at all."

Robert Browning: "Oh, to be in England/Now that April's there."

• *Farther out in the south transept, you'll find...*

William Shakespeare: Although he's not buried here, a fine statue of this greatest of English writers stands near the end of the transept, overlooking the others: "All the world's a stage/And all the men and women merely players./They have their exits and their entrances/And one man in his time plays many parts."

George Handel: High on the wall opposite Shakespeare is the man famous for composing "The Messiah": "Hallelujah, hallelujah, hallelujah." Musicians can read the vocal score in his hands for "I Know That My Redeemer Liveth." His actual tomb is on the floor next to...

Charles Dickens, whose serialized novels brought "literature" to the masses: "It was the best of times, it was the worst of times."

You'll also find tombs of Samuel Johnson (who wrote the first English dictionary) and the great English actor Lawrence Olivier. (Olivier disdained the "Method" style of experiencing intense emotions in order to portray them. When his co-star stayed up all night in order to appear haggard for a scene, Olivier said, "My dear boy, why don't you simply try acting?")

• *Walk to the center of the abbey in front of the high altar. You're standing directly under the central spire.*

8. The Coronation Spot

Here is where every English coronation since 1066 has taken place. The nobles in robes and powdered wigs look on from the carved wooden stalls of the choir. The archbishop stands at the high altar (table with candlesticks, up five steps). The coronation chair is placed in the center of the church, directly below the design-work cross on the ceiling high in the middle of the central tower. Surrounding the whole area are temporary bleachers for VIPs, creating a "theater." At Queen Elizabeth's 1953 coronation, 7,000 sat on bleachers going halfway up the rose windows of each transept.

Imagine the day when Prince William becomes king. Long silver trumpets hung with banners will sound a fanfare as the monarch-to-be enters the church. The congregation will sing, "I will go into the house of the Lord," as he parades slowly down the nave and up the steps to the altar. After a church service, he'll sit in the chair, facing the nobles in the choir. A royal scepter will be placed in his hands, and—dut, dutta dah—the archbishop will lower the Crown of St. Edward the Confessor onto his royal head. Finally, King William will stand up, descend the steps, and be presented to the people. The people will cry, "God save the king!"

• *Royalty are also given funerals here. Princess Diana's coffin lay here before her funeral service. She was then buried on her family estate. Exit the church (temporarily) at the south door, which leads to . . .*

9. Cloisters and Museum

The church is known as the "abbey" because it was the headquarters of Benedictine monks—until Henry VIII kicked them out in 1540. The buildings that adjoin the church housed the monks. Cloistered courtyards gave them a place to meditate on God's creations.

Look back at the church through the cloisters. Notice the flying buttresses—the stone bridges that push in on the church walls—that allowed Gothic architects to build so high.

Historians should pay £1 extra to cover admission to three more rooms (ask about free audioguide). The Chapter House, where the monks had daily meetings, features fine architecture with faded but well-described medieval art. The tiny Pyx Chamber has an exhibit about the King's Treasury. The Abbey Museum, formerly the monks' lounge with a cozy fireplace and snacks, now has fascinating exhibits on royal coronations, funerals, abbey history, and a close-up look at medieval stained glass.

• *Go back into the church for the last stop.*

10. Nave

On the floor near the west entrance of the abbey is the flower-lined Tomb of the Unknown Warrior, one ordinary WWI soldier buried in soil from France with lettering made from melted-down weapons from that war. Think about that million-man army from the Empire and Commonwealth and all those who gave their lives. Hanging on a column next to the tomb is the U.S. Congressional Medal of Honor, presented to England's WWI dead by General Pershing in 1921. Closer to the door is a memorial to Winston Churchill.

Look back down the nave of the abbey, filled with the remains of the people who made Britain great—saints, royalty, poets, musicians, soldiers, politicians. Now step back outside into a city filled with the same kind of people.

✤ 6 ✤
WESTMINSTER WALK
From Big Ben to Trafalgar Square

London is the N.Y., L.A., and D.C. of Britain. This walk starts with London's "star" attraction, continues to its "Capitol," passes its "White House," and ends at "Times Square"...all in about an hour.

Just about every visitor to London strolls the historic Whitehall Boulevard from Big Ben to Trafalgar Square. This quick eight-stop walk gives meaning to that touristy ramble. Under London's modern traffic and big-city bustle lie 2,000 fascinating years of history. You'll get a whirlwind tour as well as a practical orientation to London.

Start halfway across Westminster Bridge (tube: Westminster).

1. On Westminster Bridge
Views of Big Ben and the Parliament
• *First look south (upstream), toward the Parliament.*
Ding dong ding dong. Dong ding ding dong. Yes, indeed, you are in London. **Big Ben** is actually "not the clock, not the tower, but the bell that tolls the hour." However, since the 13-ton bell is not visible, everyone just calls the whole works Big Ben. Ben (named for a fat bureaucrat) is scarcely older than my great-grandmother, but it has quickly

94

WESTMINSTER WALK

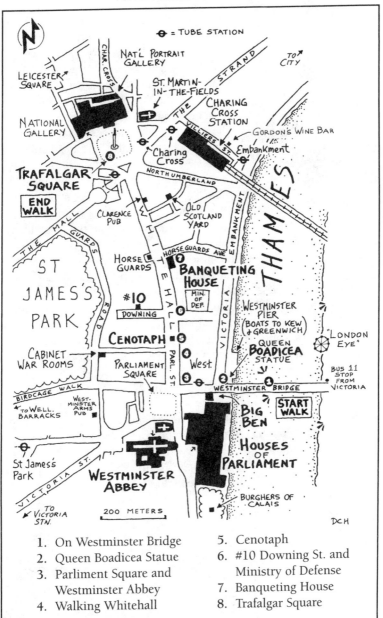

N = TUBE STATION

NAT'L PORTRAIT GALLERY

TO CITY

LEICESTER SQUARE

ST. MARTIN-IN-THE-FIELDS

CHARING CROSS STATION

NATIONAL GALLERY

GORDON'S WINE BAR

Embankment

Charing Cross

TRAFALGAR SQUARE

NORTHUMBERLAND

END WALK

CLARENCE PUB

OLD SCOTLAND YARD

THE MALL

HORSE GUARDS AVE

ST JAMES'S PARK

HORSE GUARDS

BANQUETING HOUSE

MIN. OF DEF.

#10 DOWNING

WESTMINSTER PIER (BOATS TO KEW & GREENWICH)

"LONDON EYE"

CENOTAPH

QUEEN BOADICEA STATUE

CABINET WAR ROOMS

PARLIAMENT SQUARE

West.

BUS 11 STOP FROM VICTORIA

BIRDCAGE WALK

WESTMINSTER ARMS PUB

TO WELL. BARRACKS

WESTMINSTER BRIDGE

START WALK

BIG BEN

HOUSES OF PARLIAMENT

St James's Park

WESTMINSTER ABBEY

TO VICTORIA STN.

BURGHERS OF CALAIS

200 METERS

DCH

1. On Westminster Bridge
2. Queen Boadicea Statue
3. Parliment Square and Westminster Abbey
4. Walking Whitehall
5. Cenotaph
6. #10 Downing St. and Ministry of Defense
7. Banqueting House
8. Trafalgar Square

become the city's symbol. The tower is 100 meters high (320 feet) and the clock faces are seven meters across. The four-meter-long minute hand sweeps the length of your body every five minutes.

Big Ben is the north tower of a long building, the **Houses of Parliament**, stretching along the Thames. Britain is ruled from this building. For five centuries it was the home of kings and queens. Then, as democracy was foisted on tyrants, a parliament of nobles was allowed to meet in some of the rooms. Soon, commoners were elected to office, the neighborhood was shot, and the royalty moved to Buckingham Palace. The current building, though it looks medieval, was built in the 1800s after a fire gutted old Westminster Palace.

Today, the **House of Commons**, which is more powerful than the queen and prime minister combined, meets in the north half of the building. The rubber-stamp **House of Lords** grumbles and snoozes in the south end of this 1,000-room complex and provides a tempering effect on extreme governmental changes. The two houses are very much separate: Notice the riverside tea terraces with the color-coded awnings—royal red for lords, common green for commoners.

Views of the Ferris Wheel and City

• *Now look north, toward the Ferris wheel.*

Aside from Big Ben and the Ferris wheel, London's skyline is not overwhelming; it's a city that wows from within.

Downstream and on the other side of the river stands the huge former city hall, now a hotel complex. Shut down a decade ago, this bastion of London liberals still seems to snarl across the river at the home of the national government. The building marks the start of London's vibrant gentrified arts and cultural zone along the South Bank of the Thames.

The **Jubilee Promenade**, hugging the South

Bank, makes a great one-hour walk. From Westminster Bridge (tube: Westminster), this pleasant riverside walking path runs all the way to Tower Bridge (tube: Tower Hill), leading you past the London Eye Ferris Wheel (which, at 140 meters, or 450 feet, gives you the highest public view in town); trendy restaurants, shops, and pubs; the National Theater; the Tate Modern (modern art museum); the Millennium Bridge (for pedestrians only); and Shakespeare's Globe Theater. Along the way are great views across the Thames of St. Paul's dome and the city.

On the other side of the river, notice the **Westminster Pier**; boats depart here for the Tower of London, Greenwich, and Kew. Beyond the pier are little green copper lions' heads with rings for tying up boats. Before the construction of the Thames Barrier (the world's largest movable flood barrier, downstream near Greenwich), floods were a recurring London problem. The police measured the river by these lions. "When the lions drink, the city's at risk."

London's history is tied to the Thames, the highway that links the interior of England with the North Sea. Until 1750 only London Bridge crossed the Thames. Then a bridge was built here. Early in the morning of September 3, 1803, William Wordsworth stood where you're standing and described what he saw:

"This city now doth like a garment wear
The beauty of the morning; silent, bare,
Ships, towers, domes, theaters, and temples lie
Open unto the fields, and to the sky;
All bright and glittering in the smokeless air."

• *Walk to Big Ben's side of the river. Near Westminster Pier is a big statue of a lady on a chariot (nicknamed "the first woman driver"... no reins).*

2. Boadicea, Queen of the Iceni

Riding in her two-horse chariot, daughters by her side, this Celtic Xena leads her people against Roman invaders. Julius Caesar had been the

first Roman to cross the Channel, but even he was weirded out by the island's strange inhabitants who worshiped trees, sacrificed virgins, and went to war painted blue. Later Romans subdued and civilized them, building roads and making this spot on the Thames—"Londinium"— into a major urban center.

But Boadicea refused to be Romanized. In A.D. 60, after Roman soldiers raped her daughters, she rallied her people, liberated London, and massacred 70,000 Romans. But the brief revolt was snuffed out, and she and her family took poison rather than surrender.

• *There's a civilized public toilet down the stairs behind Boadicea. Continue past Big Ben, one block inland to the busy intersection of Parliament Square.*

3. Parliament Square

To your left is the orange-hued Parliament. Ahead, the two white towers of Westminster Abbey rise above the trees. And broad Whitehall

(here called Parliament Street) stretches to your right up to Trafalgar Square.

This is the heart of what was once a suburb of London—the medieval City of Westminster. Like Buda and Pest, London is two cities which grew into one. The City of London, centered near St. Paul's Church and the Tower of London, was the place to live. But King Edward the Confessor decided to build an abbey (minster) here, west of the city walls—hence Westminster. And to oversee its construction, he moved his court here and built the **Palace of Westminster**. The palace gradually evolved into a meeting place for debating public policy, which is why to this day the Houses of Parliament are also known as the "Palace of Westminster."

Across from Parliament, the cute little church with the blue sundials, snuggling under the Abbey "like a baby lamb under a ewe," is **St. Margaret's Church**. Since 1480 this has been the place for politicians' weddings—such as Churchill's.

Parliament Square, the small park between Westminster Abbey and Big Ben, is filled with statues of famous Brits. The statue of **Winston Churchill**, the man who saved Britain from Hitler, is shown in the military coat he wore as he limped victoriously onto the beaches at Normandy after D-day. According to tour guides, the statue has a current of electricity running through it to honor Churchill's wish that if a statue is made of him, his head shouldn't be soiled by pigeons.

In 1868 the world's first traffic light was installed on the corner here where Whitehall now spills double-decker buses into the square. And speaking of lights, the little yellow lantern atop the concrete post on the street corner closest to Parliament says "Taxi." When a member of Parliament needs a taxi, this blinks to hail one.

• *If you have time, consider touring Westminster Abbey (see page 86). Otherwise, turn right, walk away from the Houses of Parliament and the abbey, and continue up Parliament Street, which becomes Whitehall.*

4. Walking along Whitehall

Today Whitehall is choked with traffic, but imagine the effect this broad street must have had on out-of-towners a century ago. In your horse-drawn carriage, you'd clop along a tree-lined boulevard past well-dressed lords and ladies; dodging street urchins, gazing left, then right, you'd try to take it all in, your eyes dazzled by the bone-white walls of this man-made marble canyon.

Today Whitehall is the most important street in Britain, lined with the ministries of finance, treasury, and so on. As you walk, notice the security measures. For example, iron grates seal off the concrete ditches between the buildings and sidewalks for protection against explosives. Why so much security? London is the N.Y./L.A./D.C. of Britain, yes, but it's also the Babylon of a former colonial empire that sometimes resents its lingering control.

Notice also the ornamental arrowhead tops of the iron fences. Originally these were colorfully painted. When Prince Albert died in 1861, Queen Victoria ordered them all painted black. Probably the world's most determined mourner, when her beloved Albert died ("the only one who called her Vickie"), she wore black for the standard 2.5 years of mourning for a Victorian widow—and added an extra 38 years.

• *Continue toward the tall, square, concrete monument in the middle of the road. On your right is a colorful pub, the Red Lion. Across the street a 225-meter detour down King Charles Street leads to the Cabinet War Rooms, the underground bunker of 21 rooms that was the nerve center for Britain's campaign against Hitler (admission £5, includes worthwhile audioguide, April–Oct daily 9:30–18:00, Nov–March 10:00–17:15).*

5. Cenotaph

This big white stone monument (in the middle of the boulevard) honors those who died in the two events that most shaped modern

Britain—World Wars I and II. The monumental devastation of these wars helped turn a colonial superpower into a cultural colony of an American superpower.

The actual cenotaph is the slab that sits atop the pillar—a tomb. You'll notice no religious symbols on this memorial. The dead honored here came from many creeds and all corners of Britain's empire. It looks lost in noisy traffic, but on each Remembrance Sunday (closest to November 18) Whitehall is closed off to traffic, the royal family fills the balcony overhead in the foreign ministry, and a memorial service is held around the cenotaph.

It's hard for an American to understand the impact of the Great War on Europe. It's said that if all the WWI dead from the British Empire were to march four abreast past the cenotaph, the sad parade would last for seven days.

Eternally pondering the cenotaph is an equestrian statue just up the street. Earl Haig, commander-in-chief of the British army from 1916 to 1918, was responsible for ordering so many brave and not-so-brave British boys out of the trenches and onto the killing fields of World War I.

• *Just past the cenotaph, on the other (west) side of Whitehall, is an iron security gate guarding the entrance to Downing Street.*

6. #10 Downing Street and the Ministry of Defense

Britain's version of the White House is where the current prime minister—Tony Blair—and his family live, at #10 (the black-brick building a

hundred meters down blocked-off street, on the right). It looks modest, but the entryway does open up into fairly impressive digs. Blair is a young Kennedy-esque politician who prefers persuasive charm to rigid dogma. There's not much to see here unless a VIP happens to drive up. Then the bobbies snap to and check credentials, the gates open, the traffic barrier midway down the street drops into its bat cave, the car drives in, and then...the bobbies go back to mugging with the tourists.

The huge bleak building across Whitehall from Downing Street is the **Ministry of Defense** (MOD). This place looks like a

Ministry of Defense should. When the building was being built, in the 1930s, they discovered and restored Henry VIII's wine cellar. English soldiers and politicians have drunk together here for 500 years. That's continuity.

One more security note: The drapes of the MOD are too long for good reason. They come with lead weights on the bottom. If a bomb blew out the windows, the drapes would billow in and contain the flying glass.

In front of the MOD are statues of illustrious defenders of Britain. "Monty" is **Field Marshal Montgomery**, the great British general of WWII fame. Monty beat the Nazis in North Africa (defeating "the Desert Fox" at El Alamein) and gave the Allies a jumping-off point to retake Europe. Along with Churchill, Monty breathed confidence back into a demoralized British army, persuading them they could ultimately beat Hitler.

Nearby, the statue of **Sir Walter Raleigh** marks the spot where he was presented in glory to Queen Elizabeth. Nothing marks the spot—a few hundred meters back toward Big Ben—where he was beheaded a few years later. He's buried in St. Margaret's Church.

You may be enjoying the shade of London's plane trees. They do well in polluted London: roots that work well in clay, waxy leaves that self-clean in the rain, and bark that sheds so the pollution doesn't get into its vascular system.

• *At the equestrian statue you'll be flanked by the Welsh and Scottish government offices. At the corner (same side as the MOD) you'll find the Banqueting House.*

7. Banqueting House

The Banqueting House is just about all that remains of what was once the biggest palace in Europe—Whitehall Palace, stretching from Trafalgar Square to Big Ben. Henry VIII started it when he moved out of the Palace of Westminster (now the Parliament) and into the residence of the archbishop of York. Queen Elizabeth I and other monarchs added on as England's worldwide prestige grew. Finally, in 1698, a roaring fire destroyed everything at Whitehall except the name and the Banqueting House.

The kings held their parties and feasts in the Banqueting House's grand ballroom on the first floor. At 34 meters wide by 17 meters tall and 17 meters deep, the Banqueting House is a perfect double cube. London's first Renaissance building must have been a wild contrast to the higgledy-piggledy sprawl of the Whitehall palace complex around it.

On January 27, 1649, a man dressed in black appeared at one of the Banqueting House's first-floor windows and looked out at a huge crowd that surrounded the building. He stepped out the window and onto a wooden platform. It was King Charles I. He gave a short speech to the crowd, framed by the magnificent backdrop of the Banqueting House. His final word was, "Remember." Then he knelt and laid his neck on a block as another man in black approached. It was the executioner—who cut off the King's head.

Plop—the concept of divine monarchy in Britain was decapitated. But there would still be kings after Cromwell. In fact, the royalty was soon restored and Charles' son, Charles II, got his revenge here in the Banqueting Hall... by living well. His elaborate parties under the chandeliers of the Banqueting House celebrated the Restoration of the monarchy. But from then on, every king would know that he rules by the grace of Parliament.

Charles I is remembered today with a statue at one end of Whitehall (in Trafalgar Square at the base of the tall column), while his killer, Oliver Cromwell, is given equal time with a statue at the other (at the Houses of Parliament).

• *Cross the street for a close look at the **Horse Guards** (11:00 changing of the guard Mon–Sat, 10:00 on Sun, dismounting ceremony daily at 16:00). Until the Ministry of Defense was created, the Horse Guards were the headquarters of the British army. It's still the home of the queen's private guard.*

*Continue up Whitehall, dipping into the guarded entry court of the next big building with the too-long Ionic columns. This holds the offices of the **Old Admiralty**, headquarters of the British Navy. Ponder the scheming that must have gone on behind these walls as the British Navy built the greatest empire the world has ever seen. Across the street, behind the old Clarence Pub (serves lunch only, no dinner), stood the original **Scotland Yard**, headquarters of London's crack police force in the days of Sherlock Holmes. Finally, Whitehall opens up into the grand, noisy, traffic-filled...*

8. Trafalgar Square

London's "Times Square" bustles around the monumental column with Admiral Horatio Nelson standing 52 meters tall (170 feet) in the crow's nest. Nelson saved England at a time as dark as World War II. In 1805 Napoleon (the Hitler of his day) was poised on the other side of the Channel, threatening to invade England. Meanwhile, more than 1,500 kilometers away, the one-armed, one-eyed, and one-minded Lord Nelson attacked the French fleet off the coast of Spain at Trafalgar. The French were routed, Britannia ruled the waves, and the once-invincible French army was slowly worn down, then defeated, at Waterloo.

Nelson, while victorious, was shot by a sniper in the battle. He died gasping, "Thank God, I have done my duty."

Surrounding the column are bronze reliefs cast from melted-down enemy cannons, and four huggable lions, dying to have their photo taken with you. The artist had never seen a lion before so he used his dog as a model. The legs look like doggie paws.

In front of the column (nearer you) stands the statue of Charles I on horseback (the oldest such statue in town). Directly behind Charles is a pavement stone marking the center of London.

In medieval times, Westminster was the seat of government, but the financial action was downstream in London. When people from "the City" and the government needed to meet halfway, it was here. Today Trafalgar is the center of modern London.

Trafalgar Square feels cohesive because of a banister that cuts from building to building right around the square. Follow it counterclockwise from the South Africa house on the right, past the steeple of St. Martin-in-the-Fields (built in 1722, inspiring the style of many town churches in New England), across the domed National Gallery, and, finally, along the Canada House on the left. Harmony.

You're smack-dab in the center of London, a thriving city atop thousands of years of history.

PARIS

*P*aris, the city of light, has been a beacon to cultured souls for centuries. It represents the finest and most beautiful products of our civilization—cuisine, fashion, literature, art, and escargot forks. It's a city fit for ultimates, from Venus de Milo and Mona Lisa to Louis XIV and Napoleon. Gazing at the wonders of this city, even presidents and dictators become mere tourists.

❦ 7 ❦
THE LOUVRE

Paris walks you through history in three world-class museums—the Louvre (ancient world to 1850), the Orsay (1850–1914, including Impressionism), and the Pompidou (20th century to today; see Modern Art chapter).

Start your art-yssey at the Louvre. The Louvre's collection—more than 30,000 works of art on display—is a full inventory of Western civilization. To cover the entire collection in one visit is in-Seine. We'll enjoy just three of the Louvre's specialties—Greek sculpture, Italian painting, and French painting.

ORIENTATION

Cost: €7.50, €4.75 after 15:00 and on Sun, free on first Sun of month and for those under 18. Tickets good all day; reentry allowed.

Paris Museum Pass: All major sightseeing admissions in Paris (including the Louvre and even Versailles) are covered by a pass sold at most participating museums (though the Louvre can run out), major Métro stations, and tourist information offices (1 day—€13.50, 3 consecutive days—€27, 5 consecutive days—€41, no discounts for kids). Summer lines can be an hour or two long. With a museum pass, you zip straight through.

Hours: Wed–Mon 9:00–18:00, closed Tue. Open Wed until 21:45. On Mon eve, part of the museum (the Richelieu wing) is open until 21:45.

Galleries start closing 30 minutes early. Closed Jan 1, Easter, May 1, Nov 1, and Dec 25. Crowds are worst on Sun, Mon, Wed, and mornings. Save money by visiting in the afternoon.

Getting there: The Métro stop Palais Royal/Musée du Louvre is closer to the entrance than the stop called Louvre Rivoli.

There is no grander entry than through the pyramid, but metal detectors create a long line at times. There are several ways to avoid the line. Museum-pass holders can use the group entrance in the pedestrian passageway between the pyramid and rue de Rivoli (facing the pyramid with your back to the Tuileries Gardens, go to your left, which is north; under the arches you'll find the entrance and escalator down). Otherwise, you can enter the Louvre underground from the Carrousel shopping mall, which is connected to the museum. Enter the mall at 99 rue de Rivoli (the door with the red awning) or directly from the Métro stop Palais Royal/Musée du Louvre (exit following signs to "Musée du Louvre").

A taxi stand is on rue de Rivoli next to the Palais Royal/Musée du Louvre Métro stop.

Information: Pick up the free *Louvre Handbook* in English at the information desk under the pyramid as you enter. Tel. 01 40 20 51 51, recorded info tel. 01 40 20 53 17, www.louvre.fr.

Tours: The 90-minute English-language tours leave six times daily except Sun (€6, tour tel. 01 40 20 52 09). Dull audioguides give you a directory of about 130 masterpieces, allowing you to dial a commentary on included works as you stumble upon them (costs €5;  get these at top of stairs after buying your entrance ticket). I recommend the free, self-guided tour described below.

Length of our tour: Two hours.

Checkrooms: The coat check does not take bags. The bag check is separate from the coat check and may have a much shorter line.

Photography: Photography without a flash is allowed.

Cuisine art: The underground shopping mall has a dizzying assortment of good-value eateries (up the escalator near the inverted pyramid). There's also a post office, handy tourist office, SNCF train office, glittering boutiques, and the Palais-Royal Métro entrance. Stairs at the far end take you right into the Tuileries Gardens, a perfect antidote to the stuffy, crowded rooms of the Louvre.

THE LOUVRE—A BIRD'S EYE VIEW

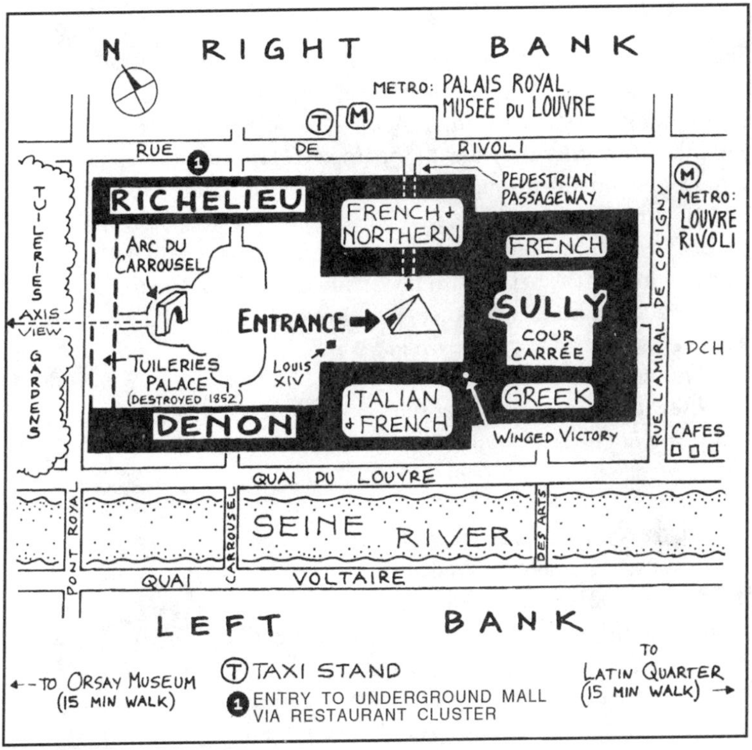

N   R I G H T   B A N K

METRO: PALAIS ROYAL
MUSÉE DU LOUVRE

RUE   DE   RIVOLI

RICHELIEU

FRENCH +
NORTHERN

PEDESTRIAN
PASSAGEWAY

FRENCH

METRO:
LOUVRE
RIVOLI

ARC DU
CARROUSEL

ENTRANCE →

SULLY
COUR
CARRÉE

DCH

AXIS
VIEW

TUILERIES GARDENS

← TUILERIES
PALACE
(DESTROYED 1852)

LOUIS
XIV

DENON

ITALIAN
+ FRENCH

GREEK

WINGED VICTORY

CAFES

QUAI   DU   LOUVRE

SEINE   RIVER

QUAI   VOLTAIRE

L E F T   B A N K

TO
LATIN QUARTER
(15 MIN WALK) →

← -TO ORSAY MUSEUM
(15 MIN WALK)

Ⓣ TAXI STAND
❶ ENTRY TO UNDERGROUND MALL
VIA RESTAURANT CLUSTER

Starring: *Venus de Milo, Winged Victory, Mona Lisa,* Raphael, Michelangelo, and the French painters.

SURVIVING THE LOUVRE

Pick up the map at the information desk under the pyramid as you enter. The Louvre, the largest museum in the Western world, fills three wings in this immense U-shaped palace. The north wing (Richelieu) houses French, Dutch, and Northern art. The east wing (Sully) houses the extensive French painting collection.

For this tour we'll concentrate on the Louvre's south wing (Denon), which houses the superstars: ancient Greek sculpture, Italian Renaissance painting, and French neoclassical and Romantic painting.

Expect changes. The Louvre is in flux for several years as they shuffle the deck. If you can't find a particular painting, ask a guard where it is. Point to the photo in your book and ask, *"Où est?"* (oo ay).

The Tour Begins
Greek Statues (600 b.c.—a.d. 1)

Every generation defines beauty differently. For Golden Age Greeks, beauty was balance, combining opposites in just the right proportions. They thought that the human body—especially the female form—embodied the order they saw in the universe. In the Louvre, we'll see a series of "Venuses" throughout history. Their different poses and gestures tell us about the people that made them. We'll see how the idea of beauty (as balance) began in ancient Greece, how it evolved into Hellenism (tipping the balance from stability to movement), and then how it resurfaced in the Renaissance, 2,000 years later.

• *From inside the big glass pyramid, you'll see signs to the three wings. Head for the Denon wing.*

Escalate up one floor. After showing your ticket, take the first left you can, climbing a set of stairs to the brick-ceilinged Salle (Room) 1: "La Grèce preclassique." Enter prehistory.

Pre-Classical Greece

These statues are noble but crude. The Greek Barbie dolls (3000 b.c.) are older than the pyramids, as old as writing itself. These pre-rational voodoo dolls whittle women down to their life-giving traits. Farther along, a woman (*Dame d'Auxerre*) pledges allegiance to stability. Another (*Core*) is essentially a column with breasts. A young naked man (*Couros*) seems to have a gun to his back—his hands at his sides, facing front, with sketchy

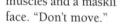

muscles and a masklike face. "Don't move."

The early Greeks who admired such statues found stability more attractive than movement. Like their legendary hero, Odysseus, the Greek people had spent generations wandering, war weary and longing for the comforts of a secure home. The noble strength and sturdiness of these works looked beautiful.

• *Exit Salle 1 at the far end and climb the stairs one flight. At the top, veer 10 o'clock left, where you'll soon see* Venus de Milo *rising above a sea*

GREEK STATUES

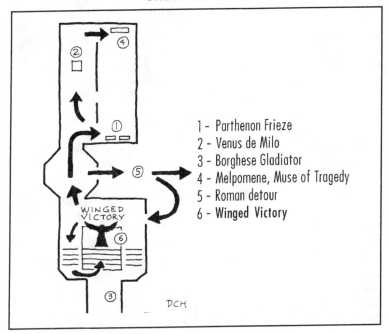

1 - Parthenon Frieze
2 - Venus de Milo
3 - Borghese Gladiator
4 - Melpomene, Muse of Tragedy
5 - Roman detour
6 - Winged Victory

of heads. As you approach her, pass the fancy Antiquités Romaines Hall (on right, we'll return here later) and turn right into Salle 7 (Salle du Parthénon), where you'll find two carved panels from the Parthenon on the wall.

Golden Age Greece

The great Greek cultural explosion that changed the course of history happened in a 50-year stretch (around 450 B.C.) in Athens, a Greek town smaller than Muncie, Indiana. They dominated the ancient world through brain, not brawn, and the art shows their love of rationality and order.

In a sense, we're all Greek. Democracy, mathematics, theater, philosophy, literature, and science were practically invented in ancient Greece. Most of the art that we'll see in the Louvre either came from Greece or was inspired by it.

Parthenon Frieze (Fragment de la Frise des Panathenées), c. 440 B.C.

These stone fragments once decorated the exterior of the greatest Athenian temple, the Parthenon. The right panel shows a half-man/half-horse creature sexually harassing a woman. It tells the story of how these rude centaurs crashed a party of humans. But the Greeks fought back and threw the brutes out, just as Athens (metaphorically) conquered its barbarian neighbors and became civilized.

The other relief shows the sacred procession of young girls who marched up the hill every four years with an embroidered veil for the 12-meter-high (40 feet) statue of Athena, the goddess of wisdom. The maidens, carved in only a few centimeters of stone, are amazingly realistic—more so than anything we saw in the pre-Classical period. They glide along horizontally (their belts and shoulders all in a line), while the folds of their dresses drape down vertically. The man in the center is relaxed and realistic. Notice the veins in his arm.

Greeks of the Golden Age valued the golden mean—that is, balance. The ideal person was well rounded—an athlete and a bookworm, a lover and a philosopher, a realtor who plays the piano, a warrior and a poet. In art, the balance between timeless stability and fleeting movement made beauty. The maidens' pleated dresses make them look as stable as fluted columns, but their arms and legs step out naturally—the human form is emerging from the stone.

• Now seek the Goddess of Love. You'll find her floating above a sea of worshiping tourists. It's been said that, among the warlike Greeks, this was the first statue to unilaterally disarm.

Venus de Milo (Aphrodite), c. 100 B.C.

The Venus de Milo (or Goddess of Love from the Greek island of Milos) created a sensation when it was discovered in 1820. Europe was already in the grip of a classical fad, and this statue seemed to sum up all that ancient Greece stood for. The Greeks pictured their gods in human form, telling us they had an optimistic view of the human race.

Most "Greek" statues are actually later Roman copies. This is a rare Greek original. This "epitome of the Golden Age" was actually sculpted three centuries later, though in the style of the earlier.

Venus de Milo is a harmonious balance of opposites. Venus is stable, resting her weight on one leg (called contrapposto, or "counterpose"), yet her other leg is slightly raised, ready to take a step. This slight movement sets her whole body in motion, though she remains perfectly still.

Split Venus down the middle (left and right) and see how the two

halves balance each other. As she lifts her left leg, her right shoulder droops down. And as her knee points one way, her head turns the other. The twisting pose gives an S curve to her body (especially noticeable from the back view) that the Greeks and succeeding generations found beautiful.

Other opposites balance as well, like the rough-cut texture of her dress (size 14) that sets off the smooth skin of her upper half. She's actually made from two different pieces of stone plugged together at the hips (the seam is visible). The face is realistic and anatomically accurate, but it's also idealized, a goddess, too generic and too perfect. This isn't any particular woman but Everywoman—all the idealized features that the Greeks found beautiful.

What were her missing arms doing? Some say her right arm held her dress while her left arm was raised. Others say she was hugging a man statue or leaning on a column. I say she was picking her navel.

• *This statue is interesting and different from every angle. Remember the view from the back—we'll see it again later. Orbit* Venus. *Make your reentry to Earth as you wander among Greek statues. Try to find even one that's not contrapposto. Now return to the Antiquités Romaines Hall.*

Roman Detour

The Romans were great conquerors but bad artists. Fortunately for us, they had a huge appetite for Greek statues and made countless copies. They took the Greek style and wrote it in capital letters—like the huge statue of Melpomene, holding the frowning mask of tragic plays.

One area the Romans excelled in was realistic portrait busts, especially of their emperors, who were worshiped as gods on earth. Stroll among the Caesars and try to see the man behind the public persona—Augustus, the first emperor, and his wily wife, Livia; Nero ("Neron"), who burned part of his own city; Hadrian, who popularized the beard;

crazy Caligula; the stoic Marcus Aurelius; Claudius of "I" fame; and the many faces of the ubiquitous Emperor Inconnu.

The Roman rooms also contain sarcophagi and an impressive mosaic floor. Weary? Relax with the statues in the Etruscan Lounge.

• *This Roman detour deposits you at the base of stairs leading up to the dramatic* Victory of Samothrace. *We'll be there momentarily, but first—to continue the evolution of Greek art from Golden Age balance to the more exuberant Hellenistic Age, find the...*

Borghese Gladiator (Guerrier Combattant, Dit Gladiateur Borghese)

We see a fighting gladiator at the peak of action. He blocks a blow with the shield that used to be attached to his left arm while his right hand, weighted with an early version of brass knuckles, prepares to deliver

the counterpunch. His striding motion makes a diagonal line from his left foot up his leg, along the body and out the extended arm. It's a dramatic, precariously balanced pose.

This is the motion and emotion of Greece's Hellenistic Age, the time after the culture of Athens was spread around the Mediterranean by Alexander the Great (c. 325 B.C.).

The earlier Golden Age Greeks might have considered this statue ugly. His rippling, knotted muscles are a far cry from the more restrained Parthenon sculptures and the soft-focus beauty of *Venus*. And the statue's off-balance pose leaves you hanging, like an unfinished melody. But Hellenistic Greeks loved these cliff-hanging scenes of real-life humans struggling to make their mark. The artist himself made his mark, signing the work proudly on the tree trunk: "Agasias of Ephesus, son of Dositheos, did this."

• *Now ascend the staircase, to the...*

Winged Victory of Samothrace (Victoire de Samothrace)

This woman with wings, poised on the prow of a ship, once stood on a hilltop to commemorate a great naval victory. Her clothes are wind-blown and sea sprayed, clinging to her body like the winner of a wet T-shirt contest. (Notice the detail in the folds of her dress around the navel, curving down to her hips.) Originally her right arm was

stretched high celebrating the victory like a
Super Bowl champion, waving a "we're-number-
one" finger.

This is the *Venus de Milo* gone Hellenistic—
a balance of opposites that produces excitement,
not grace. As *Victory* strides forward, the wind
blows her and her wings back. Her feet are firmly on the ground, but her wings (and missing
arms) stretch upward. She is a pillar of vertical
strength while the clothes curve and whip
around her. These opposing forces create a feeling of great energy, making her the lightest two-
ton piece of rock in captivity.

In the glass case nearby is *Victory's* open right hand, discovered in
1950, a century after the statue itself was unearthed. Also in the case is
Victory's finger. When the French discovered this was in Turkey, they
negotiated with the Turkish government for rights to it. Considering
all the other ancient treasures the French had looted from Turkey in
the past, the Turks thought it only appropriate to give France the finger.
• *Enter the octagonal room to the left as you face the* Winged Victory, *with*
Icarus bungee jumping from the ceiling. Bench yourself under a window
and look out toward the pyramid.

French History

The Louvre as a Palace

The Louvre, a former palace, was built in stages over several centuries.
On your right (the east wing) was the original medieval fortress. Next,
another palace, the Tuileries, was built 500 meters to the west—in the
open area past the pyramid and past the triumphal arch. Succeeding
kings tried to connect these two palaces, each one adding another section onto the long, skinny north and south wings. Finally, in 1852, after
three centuries of building, the two palaces were connected, creating a
rectangular Louvre. Soon after that, the Tuileries Palace burned down
during a riot, leaving the U-shaped Louvre we see today.

The glass pyramid was designed by the American architect I. M.
Pei. Many Parisians hated the pyramid, like they used to hate another
new and controversial structure 100 years ago—the Eiffel Tower.

The doorway leads to the Apollo Gallery, or Galerie d'Apollon (although the gallery is closed for renovation for several years, the jewels are
on display in the Sully wing). The plaque above the doorway explains

that France's Revolutionary National Assembly (the same people who brought you the guillotine) founded this museum in 1793. What could be more logical? You behead the king, inherit his palace and art collection, open the doors to the masses, and, Voilà! You've got Europe's first public museum. Major supporters of the museum are listed on the walls—notice all the Rothschilds.

• *The Italian collection ("Peintures Italiennes") is on the other side of the Winged Victory. Cross in front of the Victory to the other side and pause at the two fresco paintings on the wall to the left.*

ITALIAN RENAISSANCE

A thousand years after Rome fell, plunging Europe into the Dark Ages, the Greek ideal of beauty was "reborn" in 15th-century Italy. This was the Renaissance, the cultural revival of ancient art.

In these two frescoes by the Italian Renaissance artist Botticelli, we see echoes of ancient Greece. The maidens, with their poses, clear sculptural lines, and idealized beauty, are virtual *Venus de Milos* with clothes. The Renaissance was a time of great optimism, exploration, and liberation, and here we see it in its fresh-faced springtime.

The key to Renaissance painting was realism, and for the Italians "realism" was spelled "3-D." Painters were inspired by the realism and balanced beauty of Greek sculpture.

• *The Italian collection—including* Mona Lisa—*is scattered throughout the next few rooms (Salles 3 and 4), in the long Grand Gallery, and in adjoining rooms. To see the paintings in chronological order may require a little extra shoe leather. When in doubt, show the photo to a guard and ask, "Où est, s'il vous plaît?" (It rhymes.)*

Medieval and Early Italian Renaissance (1200–1500)

Painting a 3-D world on a 2-D surface is tough, and after a millennium of Dark Ages, artists were rusty. Living in a religious age, they painted mostly altarpieces full of saints, angels, Madonnas and bambinos, and crucifixes floating in an ethereal gold-leaf heaven. Gradually, though, they brought these otherworldly scenes down to earth.

THE GRAND GALLERY—ITALIAN AND FRENCH BIGGIES

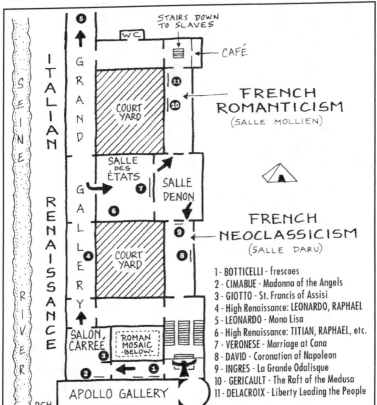

STAIRS DOWN TO SLAVES

CAFÉ

FRENCH ROMANTICISM (SALLE MOLLIEN)

FRENCH NEOCLASSICISM (SALLE DARU)

1 - BOTTICELLI - frescoes
2 - CIMABUE - Madonna of the Angels
3 - GIOTTO - St. Francis of Assisi
4 - High Renaissance: LEONARDO, RAPHAEL
5 - LEONARDO - Mona Lisa
6 - High Renaissance: TITIAN, RAPHAEL, etc.
7 - VERONESE - Marriage at Cana
8 - DAVID - Coronation of Napoleon
9 - INGRES - La Grande Odalisque
10 - GERICAULT - The Raft of the Medusa
11 - DELACROIX - Liberty Leading the People

Cimabue—*The Madonna of the Angels*

During the Age of Faith (1200s), most every church in Europe had a painting like this one. Mary was a cult figure—bigger than even the 20th-century Madonna—adored and prayed to by the faithful for bringing baby Jesus into the world.

And most every painting followed the same "Byzantine" style: somber iconic faces, stiff poses, elegant folds in the robes, and generic angels, all laid flat on a gold background like cardboard cutouts. Violating 3-D space, the angels at the "back" of Mary's throne are the same size as those holding the front.

Still, Cimabue (c. 1240–1302, pron. chee-MAH-bway) is considered the first painter to experiment with Renaissance techniques. He uses the

throne to give some sense of foreground and background, and puts shading ("modeling") around the edge of figures to make them look rounded. The work has Renaissance symmetry, three angels on each side, with the top ones bending in to frame the Virgin.

Cimabue was the first "name" artist in a world of anonymous craftsmen. His proud personality (Cimabue is a nickname meaning "bullheaded") was legendary. And the legend grew when, one day, he came across a shepherd boy sketching his sheep. Cimabue took young Giotto in, and raised him to shatter the icons of the medieval style.

Giotto—*St. Francis of Assisi Receiving the Stigmata* (and *Francis Preaching to the Birds*)

Francis of Assisi (1181–1226), a wandering Italian monk of renowned goodness, breathed the spirit of the Renaissance into medieval Europe. His humble love of man and nature inspired artists to portray real human beings with real emotions living in a physical world of beauty.

Here, Francis kneels on a rocky Italian hillside, pondering the pain of Christ's torture-execution. Suddenly he looks up, startled, to see Christ himself, with six wings, hovering above. Christ shoots lasers from his wounds to burn marks on the hands, feet, and side of the empathetic monk.

Like a good filmmaker, the artist Giotto (1266–1337, pron. JOT-toh) doesn't just *tell* us what happened in the past, he *shows* us in present tense, freezing the scene at the most dramatic moment. Though the perspective is crude—Francis' hut is smaller than he is, and Christ is somehow shooting at Francis while facing us—Giotto gives a glimpse of the 3-D world of the coming Renaissance.

In the *predella* (the panel of paintings at the bottom of the altarpiece), birds gather at Francis' feet to hear him talk about God. Giotto catches the late arrivals in midflight, an astonishing technical feat for an artist more than a century before the Renaissance. The simple gesture of

Francis' companion speaks volumes about his amazement. Breaking the stiff, iconic mold for saints, Francis bends forward at the waist to talk to his fellow creatures, while the tree bends down symmetrically to catch a few words from the beloved hippie of Assisi.

Painters such as Giotto, Fra Angelico, and Uccello broke Renaissance ground by learning to paint realistic, 3-D humans. They placed them in a painted scene with a definite foreground, background, and middle ground to create the illusion of depth. Composition was simple but symmetrically balanced in the Greek style. Art was a visual sermon, appreciated for its moral message, not its beauty.

• *The long Grand Gallery displays Italian Renaissance painting, some masterpieces, some not. Mona Lisa is at the far end. (Note that in 2003, Mona will have her own room, likely within the Salle des États, midway down the Grand Gallery to your right.)*

The Grand Gallery

The Grand Gallery was built in the late 1500s to connect the old palace with the Tuileries Palace. From the doorway, look to the far end—where Mona is waiting—and consider this challenge: I hold the world's record for the Grand Gallery Heel-Toe-Fun-Walk-Tourist-Slalom, going end to end in one minute, 58 seconds, two injured. Time yourself. Along the way, notice the following paintings and some of the . . .

Features of Italian Renaissance Painting

1. **Religious:** Lots of Madonnas, children, martyrs, and saints.
2. **Symmetrical:** The Madonnas are flanked by saints, two to the left, two to the right, and so on.
3. **Realistic:** Real-life human features are especially obvious in the occasional portrait.
4. **Three-Dimensional:** Every scene gets a spacious setting with a distant horizon.
5. **Classical:** You'll see some Greek gods and classical nudes, but even Christian saints pose like Greek statues, and Mary is a "Venus" whose face and gestures embody all that was good in the Christian world.

Mantegna—*St. Sebastian*

This isn't the patron saint of acupuncture. St. Sebastian was a Christian martyr, although here he looks more like a classical Greek statue. Notice the *contrapposto* stance (all of his weight resting on one leg) and the Greek ruins scattered around him. His executioners look like ignorant medieval brutes bewildered by this enlightened Renaissance man. Italian artists were beginning to learn how to create human realism and earthly beauty on the canvas. Let the Renaissance begin.

ITALIAN HIGH RENAISSANCE (1500–1600)

The two masters of Renaissance grace and balance were Raphael and Leonardo da Vinci.

Leonardo was the consummate Renaissance man. Musician, sculptor, engineer, scientist, and sometimes painter, he combined knowledge from all areas to create beauty. If he were alive today, he'd create a Unified Field theory in physics—and set it to music.

Leonardo da Vinci—*Virgin, Child, and St. Anne* (*La Vièrge, l'Enfant Jésus, et Sainte Anne*)

Three generations—grandmother, mother, and child—are arranged in a pyramid form with Anne's face as the peak and the lamb as the lower right corner. Within this balanced structure, Leonardo sets the figures in motion. Anne's legs are pointed to our left. (Is Anne *Mona*? Hmm.) Her daughter Mary, sitting on her lap, reaches to the right. Jesus looks at her playfully while turning away. The lamb pulls away from him. But even with all the twisting and turning, this is still a placid scene. It's as orderly as the geometrically perfect universe created by the Renaissance god.

There's a psychological kidney punch in this happy painting. Jesus, the picture of childish joy, is innocently playing with a lamb—the symbol of his inevitable sacrificial death.

The Louvre has the greatest collection of Leonardos in the world—

all five of them. Look for the neighboring *Madonna of the Rocks* and his androgynous *John the Baptist.*

Raphael—*La Belle Jardinière*

Raphael (roff-eye-ELL) perfected the style Leonardo pioneered. This Madonna, Child, and John the Baptist is also a balanced pyramid with hazy grace and beauty. Mary is a mountain of maternal tenderness (the title translates as "The Beautiful Kindergarten Teacher"), eyeing her son with a knowing look. Jesus looks up innocently, standing *contrapposto* like a chubby Greek statue.

With Raphael, the Greek ideal of beauty reborn in the Renaissance reached its peak. His work spawned so many imitators who cranked out sickly sweet generic Madonnas that we often take him for granted. Don't. This is the real thing.

While the *Jardinière* has an idealized beauty, Raphael could deliver photo-realism, too. See his portrait of black-hatted, clear-eyed Balthazar Castiglione.

• *The* Mona Lisa *is at the end of the Grand Gallery (until 2003, when she'll likely move into the Salle des États). Regardless, follow the signs and crowds.*

Leonardo da Vinci—*Mona Lisa*

Leonardo was already an old man when François I invited him to France. Determined to pack light, he took only a few paintings with him. One was a portrait of a Lisa del Giocondo, the wife of a wealthy Florentine merchant. When Leonardo arrived, François immediately fell in love with the painting, making it the centerpiece of the small collection of Italian masterpieces that would, in three centuries, become the Louvre museum. He called it *La Gioconda.* We know it as a contraction of the Italian for "my lady Lisa"—*Mona Lisa.*

Advance warning: *Mona* may disappoint you. She's smaller than you'd expect, darker, engulfed in a huge room, and hidden behind a glaring pane of glass. So, you ask, "Why all the hubbub?" Let's take a closer look. Like any lover, you've got to take her for what she is, not what you'd like her to be.

The famous smile attracts you first. Leonardo used a hazy technique called *sfumato,* blurring the edges of *Mona's* mysterious smile. Try as you

might, you can never quite see the corners of her mouth. Is she happy? Sad? Tender? Or is it a cynical supermodel's smirk? Every viewer reads it differently, projecting his own mood onto *Lisa's* enigmatic face. *Mona* is a Rorschach inkblot...so how are you feeling?

Now look past the smile and the eyes that really do follow you (most eyes in portraits do) to some of the subtle Renaissance elements that make this work work. The body is surprisingly massive and statuelike, a perfectly balanced pyramid turned at an angle so that we can see its mass. Her arm is resting lightly on the chair's armrest almost on the level of the frame itself, like she's sitting in a window looking out at us. The folds of her sleeves and her gently folded hands are remarkably realistic and relaxed. The typical Leonardo landscape shows distance by getting hazier and hazier.

The overall mood is one of balance and serenity, but there's also an element of mystery. Her smile and long-distance beauty are subtle and elusive, tempting but always just out of reach, like strands of a street singer's melody drifting through the Métro tunnel. *Mona* doesn't knock your socks off, but she winks at the patient viewer.

• *Backtrack through the Grand Gallery and take a left into the Salle des États...*

Titian—*Pastoral Symphony (Le Concert Champêtre)*

Venus enters the Renaissance in this colorful work by Titian the Venetian (they rhyme). The nymph turning toward the well at left is like a Titian reconstruction of the *Venus de Milo*, but what a difference! The Greek Venus was cold and virginal, but these babes are hot, voluptuous, sensual. The two couples are "making music," if you catch my drift.

The three figures on the grass form a pyramid, giving the scene a balanced, classical beauty, but this appeals more to the senses than to the mind. The golden glow of the skin, the ample flesh, and the hazy outlines became the standard of female nudes for centuries. French painters, especially, learned from Titian's rich colors and sensual beauty.

• *The huge canvas at the far end of the Salle des États is . . .*

Veronese—*Marriage at Cana*

Stand 10 steps away from this enormous canvas to where it just fills your field of vision, and suddenly. . . you're in a party! Pull up a glass of wine. This is the Renaissance love of beautiful things gone hog-wild. Venetian artists like Veronese painted the good life of rich, happy-go-lucky Venetian merchants.

In a spacious setting of Renaissance architecture we see colorful lords and ladies decked out in their fanciest duds, feasting on a great spread of food and drink while the musicians fuel the fires of good fun. Servants prepare and serve the food, jesters play, and animals roam. In the upper left, a dog and his master look on. A sturdy linebacker in yellow pours wine out of a jug, while nearby a ferocious cat battles a lion.  The man in white samples some wine and thinks, "Hmm, not bad." The wedding couple at the far left is almost forgotten.

Believe it or not, this is a religious work showing the wedding celebration where Jesus turned water into wine. And there's Jesus in the dead center of 130 frolicking figures, wondering if maybe wine coolers might not have been a better choice. With true Renaissance optimism, Venetians pictured Christ as a party animal, someone who loved the created world as much as they did.

Now, let's hear it for the band! On bass—the bad cat with the funny hat—Titian the Venetian! And joining him on viola—Crazy Veronese!

• *Exit behind the* Marriage at Cana *into the Salle Denon. The dramatic Romantic room is to your left, and the grand neoclassical room is to your right. They feature the most exciting French canvases in the Louvre. In the neoclassical room, kneel before the largest canvas in the Louvre.*

FRENCH PAINTING—
NEOCLASSICAL (1780–1850)

J. L. David—*The Coronation of Napoleon*

France's last kings lived in a fantasy world, far out of touch with the hard lives of their subjects. The people revolted, and this decadent world was decapitated—along with the head of state, Louis XVI. Then, after a decade of floundering under an inefficient revolutionary government, France was united by a charismatic, brilliant, temperamental upstart general who kept his feet on the ground, his eyes on the horizon, and his hand in his coat—Napoleon Bonaparte.

Napoleon quickly conquered most of Europe and insisted on being made emperor (not merely king) of this "New Rome." He staged an elaborate coronation ceremony in Paris. The painter David (dah-veed) recorded it for posterity.

We see Napoleon holding aloft the crown—the one we saw in the Apollo Gallery. He has just made his wife, Josephine, the empress, and she kneels at his feet. Seated behind Napoleon is the pope, who journeyed from Rome to place the imperial crown on his head. But Napoleon felt that no one was worthy of the task. At the last moment, he shrugged the pope aside, grabbed the crown, held it up for all to see . . . and crowned himself. The pope looks p.o.'d.

The radiant woman in the gallery in the background center wasn't actually there. Napoleon's mother couldn't make it to see her boy become the most powerful man in Europe, but he had her painted in anyway. (There's a key on the frame telling who's who in the picture.)

The traditional place of French coronations was the ultra-Gothic Notre-Dame cathedral. But Napoleon wanted a setting that would reflect the glories of Greece and the grandeur of Rome. So interior decorators erected stage sets of Greek columns and Roman arches to give the cathedral the architectural political correctness you see in this painting. (The *Pietà* statue on the right edge of the painting is still in Notre-Dame today.)

David was the new republic's official painter and propagandist, in charge of costumes, flags, and so on for all public ceremonies and spectacles. (Find his self-portrait with curly gray hair in the *Coronation*, way up in the second balcony, directly above Napoleon's crown.) His "neoclassical" style influenced French fashion. Take a look at his *Madame Juliet Récamier* portrait on the opposite wall, showing a modern Parisian woman in ancient garb and Pompeii hairstyle reclining on a Roman couch. Nearby paintings such as *The Death of Socrates* and the *Oath of the Horatii (Le Serment des Horaces)* are fine examples of neoclassicism, with Greek subjects, patriotic sentiment, and a clean, simple style.

Ingres—*La Grande Odalisque*

Take *Venus de Milo*, turn her around, lay her down, and stick a hash pipe next to her and you have the *Grande Odalisque*. OK, maybe you'd have to add a vertebra or two.

Using clean, polished, sculptural lines, Ingres (ang-gruh, with a soft "gruh") exaggerates the *S* curve of a standing Greek nude. As in the *Venus de Milo*, rough folds of cloth set off her smooth skin. The face, too, has a touch of *Venus*' idealized features (or like Raphael's kinder-

garten teacher), taking nature and improving on it. Contrast the cool colors of this statuelike nude with Titian's golden girls. Ingres preserves *Venus*' backside for posterior—I mean, posterity.

• *Cross back through the Salle Denon and into a room gushing with...*

ROMANTICISM (1800–1850)

Géricault—*The Raft of the Medusa* (*Le Radeau de la Méduse*)

Not every artist was content to copy the simple, unemotional style of the Golden Age Greeks. Like the ancient Hellenists, they wanted to express motion and emotion. In the artistic war between hearts and minds, the heart style was known as Romanticism. It was the complete flip side of neoclassicism, though they both flourished in the early 1800s.

What better setting for an emotional work than a shipwreck? This painting was based on the actual sinking of the ship *Medusa* off the coast of Africa. The survivors barely did, floating in open seas on a raft, suffering hardship and hunger, even resorting to cannibalism—all the exotic elements for a painter determined to shock the public and arouse their emotions.

That painter was young Géricault (zher-ee-ko). He'd honed his craft sketching dead bodies in the morgue and the twisted faces of lunatics in asylums. Here he paints a tangle of bodies and lunatics sprawled over each other. The scene writhes with agitated, ominous motion—the ripple of muscles, churning clouds, and choppy seas. On the right is a deathly green corpse sprawled overboard. In the face of the man at left cradling a dead body we see the despair of spending weeks stranded in the middle of nowhere.

But wait. There's a stir in the crowd. Someone has spotted something. The bodies rise up in a pyramid of hope culminating in a waving flag. They wave frantically trying to catch the attention of the tiny ship on the horizon, their last desperate hope... which did finally save them. Géricault uses rippling movement and powerful colors to catch us up in the excitement. If art affects your heartbeat, this is a masterpiece.

Delacroix—*Liberty Leading the People* (*La Liberté Guidant le Peuple*)

France is the symbol of modern democracy. They weren't the first (America was), nor are they the best working example of it, but they've had to work harder to achieve it than any other country. No sooner would they throw one king or dictator out than they'd get another. They're now working on their fifth republic.

In this painting, the year is 1830. The Parisians have taken to the streets once again to fight royalist oppressors. There's a hard-bitten proletarian with a sword (far left), an intellectual with a top hat and a

sawed-off shotgun, and even a little boy brandishing pistols.

Leading them on through the smoke and over the dead and dying is the figure of Liberty, a strong woman waving the French flag. Does this symbol of victory look familiar? It's the *Winged Victory*, wingless and topless.

To stir our emotions, Delacroix (del-ah-kwah) uses only three major colors—the red, white, and blue of the French flag.

This symbol of freedom is a fitting tribute to the Louvre, the first museum ever opened to the common rabble of humanity. The good things in life don't belong only to a small wealthy part of society, but to everyone. The motto of France is "Liberté, Egalité, Fraternité"—liberty, equality, and the brotherhood of all.

• *Exit the room at the far end (past the café) and go downstairs, where you'll bump into the bum of a large, twisting male nude looking like he's just waking up after a thousand-year nap.*

Michelangelo Buonarotti—*Slaves*, c. 1513

These two statues by earth's greatest sculptor are a fitting end to this museum—works that bridge the ancient and modern worlds. Michelangelo, like his fellow Renaissance artists, learned from the Greeks. The perfect anatomy, twisting poses, and idealized faces look like they could have been done 2,000 years earlier.

The so-called *Dying Slave* (also called the Sleeping Slave, who looks like he should be stretched out on a sofa) twists listlessly against his T-shirt-like bonds, revealing his smooth skin. Compare the polished detail of the rippling, bulging left arm with the sketchy details of the face and neck. With Michelangelo, the body does the talking. This is probably the most sensual nude ever done by the master of the male body.

The *Rebellious Slave* fights against his bondage. His shoulders turn one way while his head and leg turn the other, straining to get free. He even seems to be trying to free himself from the rock he's made of. Michelangelo said that his purpose was to carve away the marble to reveal the figures God put inside. This *Slave* shows the agony of that process and the ecstasy of the result.

• Finished? I am. *Où est la sortie?*

MORE FRENCH?
THE LOUVRE, PART DEUX

While you've seen the Louvre's greatest hits (as judged by postcards sold), the Louvre has the best collection of French paintings anywhere. And you've only seen a few of these.

French painting from the 14th through the 19th centuries is

displayed in the Richelieu and Sully wings (second floor). It's laid out chronologically; just follow the room numbers. If you go, plan on an hour to see it all.

• *From the pyramid, enter the Richelieu wing. Past the ticket taker, turn right and go up three escalators to the top. You're looking for Jean II le Bon (a small portrait in a glass case).*

Early French Painting (1300–1650)

Jean II le Bon

In an age when religious paintings were the norm, this was a breakthrough—the first easel portrait of a French king ever. Saints, angels, and Madonnas were headed out, real people were coming in.

• *Follow the rooms in order, and you'll see French art unfold. I've selected about one painting per room.*

Avignon Pietà (Quarton-Pietà de Villeneuve-les-Avignon)

This simple, poignant scene of Mary grieving over her crucified son is not realistic or exactly "beautiful"—but you can't deny its emotional power. In fact, it's the unrealistic distortion of Jesus' body that makes it so forceful. His corpse, suffering rigor mortis, has snapped in two like a broken stick. The

other figures melt in a sad arc around this rigid symbol of death.

Clouet— Portrait of Francois I

Thank this man for the Louvre's collection. He was the one who first bought great Italian art. He encouraged French painters and invited Leonardo da Vinci to visit France. He also fostered the Renaissance spirit of humanism.

École (School) de Fontainebleau— Diana the Huntress (Diane Chassereuse)

This was a portrait of the king's mistress as the Greek goddess Diana, with her bow and hunting dog. Not only is the subject Greek–influenced, but so is the beauty. Renaissance artists gloried in the natural beauty of the human body as an expression of the divine.

École de Fontainebleau—*Gabrielle d'Estree et une de ses Soeurs*

Two sisters are taking a bath together, the one twisting the other's nipple. This may be idealized beauty to some, but to others it's just plain smut. Some interpret this painting as an indictment of the loose morals of the French Renaissance court. In contrast to the two sisters in the foreground is a more domestic scene in the back—the way things should be—a woman fully clothed and industriously sewing

before a fire, oblivious to a man's open crotch.

Others say it's about an engaged woman (with ring), concerned about her fertility, being reassured by a friend. (Although every engaged woman I've reassured...)

• *Reach the Later French Painting by turning left into the Sully wing, Rooms 19–75.*

Later French Painting (1600–1850)

The French loved to paint beautiful things, nudes, scenes from Greek mythology, and historical events. Religious scenes are rare. I defy you to find even one crucifixion. This is colorful art designed to tickle the fancies of Louis XIV and his pleasure-seeking court at Versailles. As we move to the later Louises, it gets even frillier and prettier, as Renaissance turns to Baroque and rococo.

Alongside these idealized paintings, you'll see grittier, more realistic ones. France had two worlds existing side by side—dreamy Versailles and the reality of the working poor.

Nicolas Poussin—*Shepherds of Arcadia (Les Bergers d'Arcadie)*

The shepherds here are idealized humans, like Greek gods. They live in the Greek Paradise where everything's perfect. The colors are bright and the

atmosphere serene. However, they've stumbled upon a tomb and read the inscription and it worries them—there's Death even in Arcadia.

Claude de Lorrain (1600–1682)— *Port de Mer au Soleil Couchant*

In a typical Claude painting, the sun sets slowly on a harbor bordered by classical buildings. A boulevard of water stretches away from us,

melting into an infinite sky. The tiny humans are dwarfed by both the majestic buildings and the sea and sky. A soft, proto-Impressionist haze warms the whole scene, showing the harmony of man and nature. Claude's painted fantasies became real in the landscaped gardens and canals at Versailles.

Georges de la Tour—*St. Joseph in the Carpenter's Shop (Saint Joseph Charpentier)*

In this human look at a religious scene, the boy Jesus has joined his father in the carpentry shop and holds a candle for him while he works. Realism has been conquered here—notice the glow of the candle through Jesus' hand.

Louis le Nain—*Peasant Family (Famille de Paysans)*

When Marie-Antoinette said to France's poor, "Let them eat cake," this was the look she got. While lords and ladies feasted and frolicked in the rich French court, the common people continued to live the hard life. Most artists painted glorified visions of Greek gods, but this dark,

drab-colored "snapshot" shows the other side—the people whom Marie-Antoinette told to eat cake. The peasants look up from their activities, staring at us like we're rich kids who've just stumbled onto their turf.

Charles le Brun—*Chancellor Seguir* (*Le Chacelier Seguir*)

This portrait is a frilly contrast to le Nain's peasant family. Here a court official rides under a parasol, accompanied by wimpy servants with ribbons on their shoes. French aristocrats were the first in Europe to develop a refined taste in clothes, manners, and art. Soon feudal lords in other countries followed the French lead, leaving their farms, scraping the cow pies off their boots, and learning "cultchah."

Rigaud—*Portrait of Louis XIV* (1701)

Louis called himself the Sun King, whose radiance warmed all of France. In his youth, he was strong, handsome, witty, charming, and a pretty good hoofer—note the legs. He made France a world power and

the hub of culture by centralizing the government around himself as a cult figure. Anything he did—eating, dressing, even making love—was like a ritual of state.

Here, he goes through one of those rituals, re-enacting his coronation. Rigaud shows all the trappings of power: the huge fleur-de-lis robe, the canopied throne, the crown and sceptre. But he also gives us a peek-a-boo glimpse of the human Louis underneath the royal robe. Louis is a bit older now, a bit weary. He poses for the obligatory photo-op. But the face that peers out from the elaborate wig and pompous surroundings doesn't put on any airs. It's an honest face that seems to say, "Hey, it's my job."

Jean Antoine Watteau (1684–1721)— *Embarkation for Cythera* (*Pelerinage a l'Ile de Cythere*)

Louis and his successors kept the nobility from meddling in government affairs by entertaining them at the playground of Versailles. Here lords and ladies frolic in a mythical landcape with antigravity babies. This painting was the first of many showing these *"fêtes galantes,"*

where well-manicured aristocrats enjoy the delights of well-
manicured nature.

Watteau's warm, almost
phosphorescent, colors also set
a new artistic tone. Gone is the
majestic Baroque grandeur of
Louis XIV. Now French paint-
ings become smaller, lighter, frillier, more intimate, more sensual.

Watteau—*Gilles*

A clown, looking ridiculous dressed in an over-
sized suit, must perform for the amusement of the
rich. The crowd is jaded and indifferent. The look
on his face says, "Why am I here?" This may be a
portrait of Watteau himself.

Francois Boucher (1703–1770)—
The Forge of Vulcan
(*Les Forges de Vulcain*)

In the world at Versailles, Woman (like Venus in the painting) was to
rule over and civilize brutish Man (Vulcan), teaching him the indoor

arts. Men wore wigs, make-up, and
pantyhose, while women dictated government policy. Society was changing
fast, servants were challenging masters, and role-playing games were a
part of the gay life.

Boucher chronicled the cult of the
female body. Here, the man and wo-
man complement each other, forming part of a stable pyramid. But
there's more frill than form. Boucher's pastel pinks and blues must have
been popular at Versailles baby showers.

Honore Fragonard
(1732–1806)—
Women Bathing

Guess who was teacher's pet in Boucher's class? Fragonard takes us to the
pinnacle of French rococo. Compare
these puffy pastel goddesses with the

clean lines of the *Venus de Milo*, and you'll see how far we've come from the Greek ideal of beauty. This is sweet, cream-filled art that can only be taken, like French pastry, in small doses.

Hubert Robert—Various Scenes of Roman Ruins in France

These overgrown Roman ruins inspired Robert when he landscaped the gardens at Versailles with designer "ruins." The French were fascinated with earlier civilizations that had risen, dominated, and declined. They were becoming aware of their own cultural mortality.

19TH CENTURY NEOCLASSICAL AND ROMANTIC

J. L. David (1748–1825)—Various Portraits of Citizens (Including Citizen Bonaparte)

When the Revolution exploded, rococo became politically incorrect. The bourgeois middle class wielded power, simple dress became the fashion, and painters returned to clean and sober realism.

J. A. D. Ingres (1780–1867)—Nudes and Portraits

The great defender of the neoclassical tradition paints classical nudes. He also paints clothed Frenchmen with the clean lines and bulk of classical statues.

Eugene Delacroix (1797–1863)—*Portrait of Chopin*

Here we see the great pianist/composer with his face half in shadow. Romantics explored the hidden world of human emotion. Chopin expressed the turmoil of his soul in flurries of notes, while Delacroix used messy patches of color. Though their mediums were different, this reminds us that the various arts held hands as they walked from Renaissance, through Baroque, neoclassical, Romantic, and beyond.

❧ 8 ❧

ORSAY MUSEUM

The Musée d'Orsay (mew-zay dor-say) houses French art of the 1800s (specifically, art from 1848–1914), picking up where the Louvre leaves off. For us, that means Impressionism, the art of sun-dappled fields, bright colors, and crowded Parisian cafés. The Orsay houses the best collection of Manet, Monet, Renoir, Degas, van Gogh, Cézanne, and Gauguin anywhere. If you like Impressionism, visit this museum. If you don't like Impressionism, visit this museum. I find it a more enjoyable, rewarding place than the Louvre. Sure, ya gotta see *Mona* and *Venus de Milo*, but, after you get your gottas out of the way, enjoy the Orsay.

ORIENTATION
Cost: €7, €5.50 after 16:15 on Sun, and anytime for ages 18–25, free for youth under 18 and for anyone first Sun of month. Tickets are good all day. The Orsay is covered by the museum pass (as are all the Paris entries in this book), a great time- and money-saver. For specifics, see page 107 of the Louvre chapter. Museum-pass holders can enter to the left of the main entrance. While the main entrance is being renovated (until summer of 2002), use the temporary entrance on Quai Anatole France (marked on overview map).
Hours: June 20–Sept 20 Tue–Sun 9:00–18:00, Sept 21–June 19 Tue–Sat 10:00–18:00, Sun 9:00–18:00, closed Mon. Last entrance 45 minutes before closing. Galleries start closing 30 minutes early. Note: The Orsay is crowded on Tue, when the Louvre is closed.
Getting there: Directly at the RER-C stop called Musée d'Orsay. The

ORSAY GROUND FLOOR—OVERVIEW

nearest Métro stop is Solferino, three blocks south of the Orsay. From the Louvre, it's a lovely 15-minute walk: Go through the Tuileries Gardens and cross the Seine at the Pont Solferine pedestrian bridge.

Taxis wait in front of the museum on Quai Anatole France.

Information: The booth near the entrance gives free floor plans in English (tel. 01 40 49 48 48).

Tours: English-language tours usually run daily except Sunday at 11:30 (plus Impressionist tour Tue at 14:30 and Thu at 18:30). The 90-minute tours cost €6 and are available on audioguide for €5.

Length of our tour: Two hours.

Photography: Photography without a flash is allowed.

Cuisine art: The elegant second-floor restaurant has a buffet salad bar. A simple fourth-floor café is sandwiched between the Impressionists.

Starring: Manet, Monet, Renoir, Degas, van Gogh, Cézanne, and Gauguin.

GARE D'ORSAY: THE OLD TRAIN STATION

• *Pick up the free English map at the info desk, buy your ticket, and check bags to the right. Belly up to the stone balustrade overlooking the main floor and orient yourself.*

Trains used to run right under our feet down the center of the gallery. This former train station, or *gare*, barely escaped the wrecking ball in the 1970s when the French realized it'd be a great place to house their enormous collections of 19th-century art scattered throughout the city.

The main floor has early 19th-century art (as usual, conservative on the right, realism on the left). Upstairs (not visible from here) is the core of the collection—the Impressionist rooms. Finally, we'll end the tour with "the other Orsay" on the mezzanine level you see to the left. Clear as Seine water? *Bon.*

THE ORSAY'S 19TH "CENTURY" (1848–1914)

Einstein and Geronimo. Abraham Lincoln and Karl Marx. The train, the bicycle, the horse and buggy, the automobile, and the balloon. Freud and Dickens. Darwin's *Origin of Species* and the Church's Immaculate Conception. Louis Pasteur and Billy the Kid. V. I. Lenin and Ty Cobb.

The 19th century was a mix of old and new side by side. Europe was entering the modern Industrial Age, with cities, factories, rapid transit, instant communication, and global networks. At the same time, it clung to the past with traditional, rural—almost medieval—attitudes and morals.

According to the Orsay, the "19th century" began in 1848 with the socialist and democratic revolutions (Marx's *Communist Manifesto*). It ended in 1914 with the pull of an assassin's trigger, igniting World War I and ushering in the modern world.

The museum shows art that is also both old and new, conservative and revolutionary. We'll start with the Conservatives and early rebels on the ground floor, then head upstairs to see how a few visionary young artists bucked the system and revolutionized the art world, paving the way for the 20th century.

• *Walk down the steps to the main floor, a gallery filled with statues.*

CONSERVATIVE ART

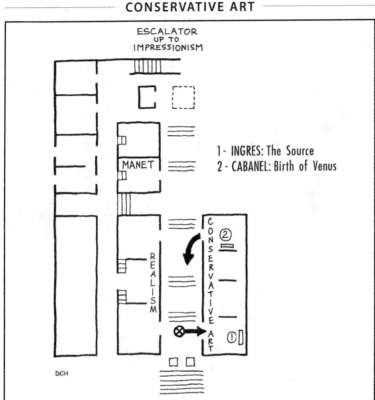

Conservative Art

No, this isn't ancient Greece. These statues are from the same century as the Theory of Relativity. It's the conservative art of the French schools that was so popular throughout the 19th century. It was popular because it's beautiful. The balanced poses, the perfect anatomy and sweet faces, the curving lines, the gleaming white stone—all this is very beautiful. (I'll be bad-mouthing it later, but for now appreciate the exquisite craftsmanship of this "perfect" art.)

• *Take your first right into the small Room 1, marked "Ingres." Look for a nude woman with a pitcher of water.*

Ingres—*The Source (La Source)*

Let's start where the Louvre left off. Ingres (ang-gruh, with a soft "gruh"), whose works help cap the Louvre collection, championed a

neoclassical style. *The Source* is virtually a Greek statue on canvas. Like *Venus de Milo*, she's a balance of opposite motions—her hips tilt one way, her breasts the other; one arm goes up, the other down; the fluid curve of her body is matched by the water falling from the pitcher.

Ingres worked on this over the course of 35 years and considered it his "image of perfection." Famous in its day, *The Source* influenced many artists whose classical statues and paintings are in the Orsay gallery.

In this and the next few rooms you'll see more of these visions of idealized beauty—nude women in languid poses, Greek myths, and so on. The "Romantics," like Delacroix, added bright colors, movement, and emotion to the classical coolness of Ingres.

• *Walk uphill (quickly, this is background stuff) to the last room, with a pastel blue-green painting.*

Cabanel—*Birth of Venus (Naissance de Venus)*

This goddess is a perfect fantasy, an orgasm of beauty. The Love Queen stretches back seductively, recently birthed from the ephemeral foam of the wave. This is art of a pre-Freudian society, when sex was dirty and

mysterious and had to be exalted into a more pure and divine form. The sex drive was channeled into an acute sense of beauty. French folk would literally swoon in ecstasy before these works of art.

Get a feel for the ideal beauty and refined emotion of these Greek-style works. You'll find a statue with a pose similar to Venus' back out in the gallery. Go ahead, swoon. If it feels good, enjoy it.

• *Now, take a mental cold shower, grab a bench in the main gallery of statues, and read on.*

Academy and Salon

Who liked this stuff? The art world was dominated by two conservative institutions: the Academy (the state art school) and the Salon, where works were exhibited to the buying public.

Now let's literally cross over to the "wrong side of the tracks," to the art of the early rebels.

• *Head back toward the entrance and turn right into Room 4, marked "Daumier" (opposite the Ingres room).*

REALISM—EARLY REBELS

Daumier—36 Caricature Busts (Ventre Legislatif)

This is a liberal's look at the stuffy bourgeois establishment that controlled the Academy and the Salon. In these 36 bustlets, Daumier, trained as a political cartoonist, exaggerates their most distinct characteristic to capture with vicious precision the pomposity and self-righteousness of these self-appointed arbiters of taste. The labels next to the busts give the name of the person being caricatured, his title or job (most were members of the French parliament), and an insulting nickname (like "gross, fat, and satisfied"

and Monsieur "Platehead"). Give a few nicknames yourself. Can you find Reagan, Clinton, Yeltsin, Thatcher, and Bush?

These people hated what you're about to see. Their prudish faces tightened as their fantasy world was shattered by the realists.

• *Go uphill four steps and through a few romantic and pastoral rooms to the final room, #6.*

Millet—*The Gleaners (Les Glaneuses)*

Millet (mee-yay) shows us three gleaners, the poor women who pick up the meager leavings after a field has already been harvested by the wealthy. Millet grew up on a humble farm. He didn't attend the Academy and hated the uppity Paris art scene. Instead of idealized gods, goddesses,

nymphs, and winged babies, he painted simple rural scenes. He was strongly affected by the Revolution of 1848, with its affirmation of the working class. Here he captures the innate dignity of these stocky, tanned women who work quietly in a large field for their small reward.

REALISM—EARLY REBELS

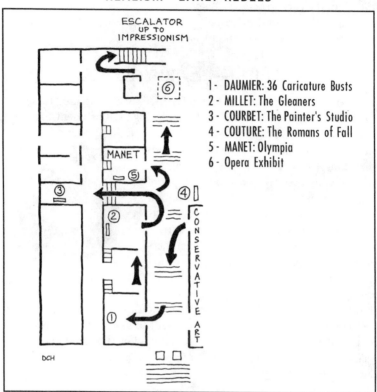

ESCALATOR
UP TO
IMPRESSIONISM

MANET

1 - DAUMIER: 36 Caricature Busts
2 - MILLET: The Gleaners
3 - COURBET: The Painter's Studio
4 - COUTURE: The Romans of Fall
5 - MANET: Olympia
6 - Opera Exhibit

CONSERVATIVE ART

DCH

This is "realism" in two senses. It's painted "real"-istically, unlike the prettified pastels of Cabanel's *Birth of Venus*. And it's the "real" world—not the fantasy world of Greek myth, but the harsh life of the working poor.

• *Swoon briefly back out into the main gallery and hang a U-turn left, climbing the steps to a large alcove with two huge canvases. On the left...*

Courbet—*The Painter's Studio* (*L'Atelier du Peintre*)

In an age when "realist painter" was equated with "bomb-throwing Socialist," it took great courage to buck the system. Rejected by the so-called experts, Courbet (coor-bay) held his own one-man exhibit. He built a shed in the middle of Paris, defiantly hung his art out, and basically "mooned" the shocked public.

Here we see Courbet himself in his studio, working diligently on a realistic landscape, oblivious to the confusion around him. Looking on are ordinary citizens (not Greek heroes), a nude model (not a goddess but a woman), and a little boy with an adoring look on his face. Perhaps

it's Courbet's inner child admiring the artist who sticks to his guns, whether it's popular or not.

• *Return to the main gallery. Back across the tracks, the huge canvas you see is...*

Couture—*The Romans of the Fall* (*Les Romains de la Décadence*)

We see a decadent society that's stuffed with too much luxury, too

much classical beauty, too much pleasure; it's wasted, burned out, and in decay. The old, backward-looking order was about to be slapped in the face.

• *Continue up the gallery, then left into Room 14 ("Manet, avant 1870"). Find the reclining nude.*

Manet—*Olympia*

"This brunette is thoroughly ugly. Her face is stupid, her skin cadaverous. All this clash of colors is stupefying." So wrote a critic when Edouard Manet's nude hung in the Salon. The public hated it, attacking Manet (man-nay) in print and literally attacking the canvas.

Think back on Cabanel's painting, *The Birth of Venus*—an idealized, pastel, Vaseline-on-the-lens beauty. Cabanel's nude was soft-core pornography, the kind you see selling lingerie and perfume. The public lapped it up (and Napoleon III purchased it).

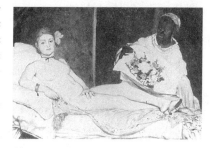

Manet's nude doesn't gloss over anything. The pose is classic, used by Titian, Goya, and countless others. But the sharp outlines and harsh contrasting colors are new and shocking. Her hand is a clamp, and her stare is shockingly defiant, with not a hint of the seductive, hey-sailor look of most nudes. This prostitute, ignoring the flowers sent by her last customer, looks out to us as if to say "next." Manet replaced soft-core porn with hard-core art.

Manet had an upper-class upbringing, some formal art training, and he had been accepted by the Salon. He could have cranked out pretty nudes and been a successful painter. Instead he surrounded himself with a group of young artists experimenting with new techniques. With his reputation and strong personality, he was their master, though he learned equally from them. Let the Impressionist revolution begin.

• Continue to the end of the gallery where you'll walk on a glass floor over a model of the city, ending up in front of a model of the Opera.

Opera Exhibit

Expand to 100 times your size and hover over a scale model section of the city. There's the 19th-century Garnier Opera House with its green roof in a diamond-shaped block in the center.

You'll also see a cross-section model of the Opera House. You'd enter from the right end, buy your ticket in the foyer, then move into the entrance hall with its grand staircase, where you could see and be seen by tout Paris. At curtain time, you'd find your seat in the golden auditorium, topped by a glorious painted ceiling. (The current ceiling, done by Marc Chagall, is even more wonderful than the model.) Notice that the stage is as big as the seating area, with elaborate riggings to raise and lower scenery. Nearby, there are models of set designs from some famous productions. These days, Parisians enjoy their Verdi and Gounod at the new opera house at place Bastille.

• Behind the Opera model (go left around model) a covered escalator leads to the often-crowded Impressionist rooms. To take a break and read ahead, consider wandering to the quiet far left corner of the ground floor where you'll find a huge painting of a hot-air-balloonist's eye view of pre-Eiffel Tower Paris (c. 1855).

Ride the escalator to the top floor. Take your first left for a commanding view of the Orsay. The second left takes you between a bookshop and a giant "backwards" clock to the art.

The Impressionist collection is scattered somewhat randomly through the next 10 or so rooms. Shadows dance and the displays mingle. You'll find nearly all of these paintings, but exactly where they're hung is a lot like their brushwork . . . delightfully sloppy. (If you don't see a described painting, move on. It's either hung farther down or on holiday.) Now, let there be light.

IMPRESSIONISM

The camera threatened to make artists obsolete. A painter's original function was to record reality faithfully like a journalist. Now a machine could capture a better likeness faster than you could say Etch-a-Sketch.

But true art is more than just painting reality. It gives us reality from the artist's point of view, putting a personal stamp on the work. It records not only the scene—a camera can do that—but the artist's impressions of the scene. Impressions are often fleeting, so you have to work quickly.

The Impressionist painters rejected cameralike detail for a quick style more suited to capturing the passing moment. Feeling stifled by the rigid rules and stuffy atmosphere of the Academy, the Impressionists' motto was "out of the studio, into the open air." They grabbed their berets and scarves and took excursions to the country, setting up their easels on riverbanks and hillsides or sketching in cafés and dance halls. Gods, goddesses, nymphs, and fantasy scenes were out; common people and rural landscapes were in.

The quick style and simple subjects were ridiculed and called childish by the "experts." Rejected by the Salon, the Impressionists staged their own exhibition in 1874. They brashly took their name from an insult thrown at them by a critic who laughed at Monet's "Impression" of a sunrise. During the next decade, they exhibited their own work independently. The public, opposed at first, was slowly drawn in by the simplicity, the color, and the vibrancy of Impressionist art.

Impressionism—Manet, Degas, Monet, Renoir

Light! Color! Vibrations! You don't hang an Impressionist canvas—you tether it. Impressionism features light colors, easygoing open-air scenes, spontaneity, broad brush strokes, and the play of light.

The Impressionists made their canvases shimmer by a simple but revolutionary technique. If you mix, say, red, yellow, and blue together you'll get brown, right? But Impressionists didn't bother to mix them. They'd slap a thick brush stroke of yellow down, then a stroke of green next to it, then red next to that. Up close all you see are the three messy strokes, but as you back up... *voilà*! Brown! The colors blend in the eye at a distance. But while your eye is saying "bland brown," your subconscious is shouting, "Red! Yellow! Blue! Yes!"

There are no lines in nature. Yet someone in the classical tradition (Ingres, for example) would draw an outline of his subject, then fill it in with color. But the Impressionists built a figure with dabs of paint... a snowman of color.

EARLY IMPRESSIONISM

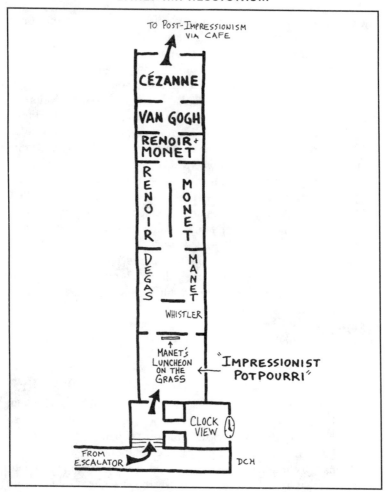

Manet—*Luncheon on the Grass*
(*Le Déjeuner sur l'Herbe*)

Manet really got a rise out of people with this one. Once again the public judged the painting on moral terms rather than artistic ones. What are these scantily clad women doing with these fully clothed men, they wondered? Or rather, what will they be doing after the last baguette is eaten?

A new revolutionary movement is budding: Impressionism. Notice the messy brushwork of the trees and leaves in the background, and the play of light on the pond in back and filtering through the trees onto the hazy woman stooping behind. And the strong contrasting colors (white skin, black clothes, green grass). And the fact that this is a true out-of-doors painting, not a studio production. The first shot had been fired.

Whistler—*Whistler's Mother* (*Portrait de la Mére de l'Auteur*)

Why so famous? I don't know either. It shouldn't be, of course, but it is. Perhaps because it's by an American, and we see in his mother some of the monumental solidity of our own ancestral moms made tough by pioneering the American wilderness.

Or perhaps because it was so starkly different in its day. In a roomful of golden goddesses, it'd stand out like a fish in a tree. The experts hated it and didn't understand it. (If music is the fear of silence, is art the fear of reality?) The subtitle is "Arrangement in Gray and Black," and the whole point is the subtle variations on dark shades softened by the rosy tint of her cheeks, but the critics kept waiting for it to come out in Colorization.

Degas—*The Dance Class* (*La Classe de Danse*)

Clearly, Degas loved dance and the theater. (Also catch his statue, *Tiny Dancer, 14 Years Old*, in the glass case.) The play of stage lights off his dancers, especially the halos of ballet skirts, is made to order for an Impressionist.

Edgar Degas (day-gah) was a rich kid from a family of bankers who got the best classical-style art training. Adoring Ingres' pure lines and cool colors, he painted in the conservative style. His work was exhibited in the Salon. He gained success and a good reputation, and then... he met the Impressionists.

Degas blends classical lines with Impressionist color and spontaneity. His dancers have outlines, and he's got them in a classic 3-D setting—with the floor lines slanting to the upper right.

So why is Degas an Impressionist? First off, he's captured a candid, fleeting moment, a momentary "impression"—the dancers are tired and bored, at the tail end of a long rehearsal. Look at the girl on the left scratching her back restlessly and the cuddly little bundle of

dog in the foreground. Degas loved the unposed "snapshot" effect, catching his models off guard.

Finally, he's got that Impressionistic "fury" of the brush. In *The Dance Class*, look at the bright green bow on the girl with her back to us. Not only are the outlines sketchy, but see how he slopped green paint onto her dress and didn't even say, "*Excusez-moi.*"

Degas—*The Glass of Absinthe* (*Au Café, dit L'Absinthe*)

Degas hung out with low-life Impressionists discussing art, love, and life in the cheap cafés and bars in Montmartre (the original Bohemia-ville). He painted Impressionistic snapshots of everyday people. Here a weary lady of the evening meets morning with a last lonely coffin-nail drink in the glaring light of a four-in-the-morning café. The pale-green drink forming the center of the composition is that toxic substance absinthe that fueled many artists and burned out many more.

Look across the room at some later works by Manet. The old dog was learning new tricks from his former disciples.
• *The next rooms feature works by two Impressionist masters at their peak, Monet and Renoir. You're looking at the quintessence of Impressionism.*

Monet—*La Gare St. Lazare*

Claude Monet (moh-nay) is the father of Impressionism. He learned from Manet (*a* before *o*) but quickly went beyond even Manet's shocking slabs of colors. Monet fully explored the possibilities of open-air painting and lighter, brighter colors.

He could even make this drab train station glow with reflected light.

The sun diffuses through the skylight and mingles with the steam from the engine. The yellow buildings in the background merge with the blue smoke in the foreground to illuminate an otherwise colorless scene.

Stand a good two meters (six feet) from the canvas and look at the tall building with the slanted Mansard roof behind the station. Looks fine? Now stand really close. It's a confusing pile of color blobs. And the smoke is truly "thick." Light on!

Monet—*The Cathedral of Rouen* (*La Cathédrale de Rouen*)

Monet went to Rouen, rented a room across from the cathedral, set up his easel...and waited. He wanted to catch "a series of differing impressions" of the cathedral facade at different times of day and year. He often had several canvases going at once. In all he did 30 canvases, and each is

unique. The time-lapse series shows the sun passing slowly across the sky, creating different colored light and shadows. These five are labeled: in the morning, in gray weather, morning sun, full view, full sunlight.

As Monet zeroes in on the play of colors and light, the physical subject—the cathedral—is dissolving. It has become only a rack upon which to hang the light and color. Later artists would boldly throw away the rack, leaving purely abstract modern art in its place.

Monet—Paintings from Monet's Garden at Giverny

One of Monet's favorite places to paint was the garden of his home in Giverny, west of Paris (and worth a visit if you like Monet more than you hate crowds). You'll find several different views of it along with the painter's self-portrait. The *Blue Water Lilies* is similar to the large

and famous water lily paintings in the nearby L'Orangerie Museum (across the river in the Tuileries Gardens, closed for renovation until the end of 2002).

Renoir—*Dance at the Moulin de la Galette* (*Bal du Moulin de la Galette*)

On Sunday afternoons, working-class folk would dress up and head for the fields on Butte Montmartre (near Sacré-Coeur Church) to dance, drink, and eat little cakes (*galettes*) till dark. Renoir (ren-wah) liked to go there to paint the common Parisians living and loving in the afternoon sun. The sunlight filtering through the trees creates a kaleidoscope of colors, like a 19th-century mirrored ball throwing darts of light on the dancers.

This dappled light is the "impression" that Renoir came away with. He captures it with quick blobs of yellow. Look at the sun-dappled straw hat (right of center) and the glasses (lower right). Smell the powder on the ladies' faces. The painting glows with bright colors. Even the shadows on the ground, which should be gray or black, are colored a warm blue. As if having a good time was required, even the shadows are caught up in the mood, dancing. Like a photographer who uses a slow shutter speed to show motion, Renoir paints a waltzing blur.

Renoir—*The City Dance/The Country Dance* (*La Danse à la Ville/La Danse à la Campagne*)

In contrast to Monet's haze of colors, Renoir clung to the more traditional technique of drawing a clear outline, then filling it in.

This two-panel "series" by Renoir shows us his exquisite draftsmanship, sense of beauty, and smoother brushwork. Like Degas, Renoir had classical training and exhibited at the Salon.

Renoir's work is lighthearted with light colors, almost pastels. He seems to be searching for an ideal, the pure beauty we saw on the ground floor. In later years he used more and more red tones as if trying for even more warmth.

• *On the divider in the center of the room, you'll find...*

Pissarro and Others

We've neglected many of the founders of the Impressionist style. Browse around and discover your own favorites. Pissarro is one of mine. His grainy landscapes are more subtle and subdued than the flashy Monet and Renoir, but, as someone said, "He did for the earth what Monet did for the water."

You may find the painting *Young Girl in the Garden* (*Jeune Fille en Jardin*) with a pastel style as pretty as Renoir's. It's by Mary Cassatt, an American who was attracted to the strong art magnet that was and still is Paris.

• *Take a break. Look at the Impressionist effect of the weather on the Paris skyline. Notice the skylight above you—these Impressionist rooms are appropriately lit by ever-changing natural light. Then carry on...*

POST-IMPRESSIONISM

Take a word, put "-ism" on the end, and you've become an intellectual. Commune-ism, sex-ism, cube-ism, computer-ism... Post-Impression-ism.

"Post-Impressionism" is an artificial and clumsy concept to describe those painters who used Impressionist techniques after Monet and Renoir. It might just as well be called something like "Pre-Modernism," because it bridged Impressionism with the 20th century... or you could call it bridge-ism.

• *The Orsay's Post-Impressionist collection (we'll see van Gogh, Cézanne, Gauguin, Rousseau, Seurat, and Toulouse-Lautrec) flip-flops back and forth between here and the end of this gallery. Be prepared to skip around.*

Van Gogh

Impressionists have been accused of being "light"-weights. The colorful style lends itself to bright country scenes, gardens, sunlight on the water, and happy crowds of simple people. It took a remarkable genius to add profound emotion to the Impressionist style.

Vincent van Gogh (van-go, or van-HOCK to the Dutch and the snooty) was the son of a Dutch minister. He too felt a religious calling, and he spread the gospel among the poorest of the poor—peasants and

POST-IMPRESSIONISTS

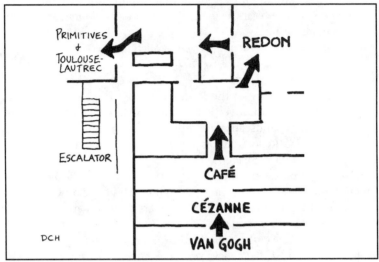

miners. When he turned to painting, he channeled this same spiritual intensity into his work. Like Michelangelo, Beethoven, Rembrandt, Wayne Newton, and a select handful of others, he put so much of himself into his work that art and life became one. In this room you'll see both van Gogh's painting style and his life unfold.

Van Gogh—*Peasant (Paysanne près de l'Atre)*
As a young man, van Gogh left his steady clerking job to work with poor working people in overcast Belgium and Holland. He painted these hardworking, dignified folks in a crude, dark style reflecting the oppressiveness of their lives... and the loneliness of his own as he roamed northern Europe in search of a calling.

Van Gogh—*Self-Portrait, Paris (Portraite de l'Artiste)*, 1887

Encouraged by his art-dealer brother, van Gogh moves to Paris and, *voilà!* The color! He meets Monet and hobnobs with Gauguin and Toulouse-Lautrec. He rents a room in Montmartre, learning the Impressionist style. (See how he builds a bristling brown beard using thick strokes of reds and greens side by side.)

At first he paints like the others, but soon he develops his own style. By using thick, swirling brush strokes, he infuses life into even inanimate objects. Van Gogh's brush strokes curve and thrash around like a garden hose pumped with wine.

Van Gogh—*Midday* (*La Méridienne*), 1890, based on a painting by Millet

The social life of Paris becomes too much for the solitary van Gogh. He moves to the south of France. At first, in the glow of the bright spring sunshine, he has a period of incredible creativity and happiness, overwhelmed by the bright colors—an Impressionist's dream. Here again we see his love of the common people taking a glowing siesta in the noon sun.

Van Gogh—*Van Gogh's Room at Arles* (*La Chambre de Van Gogh à Arles*), 1889

But being alone in a strange country begins to wear on him. An ugly man, he finds it hard to get a date. The distorted perspective of this painting makes his tiny rented room look even more cramped. He invites his friend Gauguin to join him, but after two months together arguing passionately about art, nerves get raw. Van Gogh  threatens Gauguin with a knife, driving him back to Paris. In crazed despair, van Gogh mutilates his own ear.

The people of Arles realize they have a madman on their hands and convince van Gogh to seek help. He enters a mental hospital.

Van Gogh—*The Church at Auvers-sur-Oise* (*L'Église d'Auvers-sur-Oise*), 1890

Van Gogh's paintings done in the peace of the mental hospital are more meditative—fewer bright landscapes, more closed-in scenes with deeper and almost surreal colors.

There's also a strong sense of mystery. What's behind this church? The sky is cobalt blue and the church's windows are also blue, like

we're looking right through the church to an infinite sky. There's something mysterious lurk-
ing on the other side. You can't see it, but you
feel its presence like the cold air from an approaching Métro train still hidden in the tunnel. There's a road that leads from us to the
church, then splits to go behind. A choice must
be made. Which way?

Van Gogh— Self-Portrait, St. Remy, 1889

Van Gogh wavered between happiness and
madness. He despaired of ever being sane
enough to continue painting.

This self-portrait shows a man engulfed
in a confused but beautiful world. The background brush strokes swirl and rave, setting in
motion the waves of the jacket. He's caught in
the current, out of control. But in the midst of
this rippling sea of mystery floats a still, detached island of a face with
probing, questioning, wise eyes.

Do his troubled eyes know that only a few months later he would
take a pistol and put a bullet through his chest?

Cézanne

Cézanne's art brought Impressionism into the 20th century. There's less
color here, less swirling brushwork, less passion. It's cleaner, chunkier,
more intellectual. Cézanne (say-zahn) can be difficult to appreciate
after the warmth of Renoir, and he won't give you the fireworks of van
Gogh. But he's worth the effort.

Cézanne—Self-Portrait (Portrait de l'Artiste)

Cézanne was virtually unknown and un-
appreciated in his lifetime. He worked
alone, lived alone, and died alone, ignored by all but a few revolutionary
young artists who understood his efforts.

And Cézanne couldn't draw. His
brush was a blunt instrument. With it,
he'd bludgeon reality into submission,

CÉZANNE

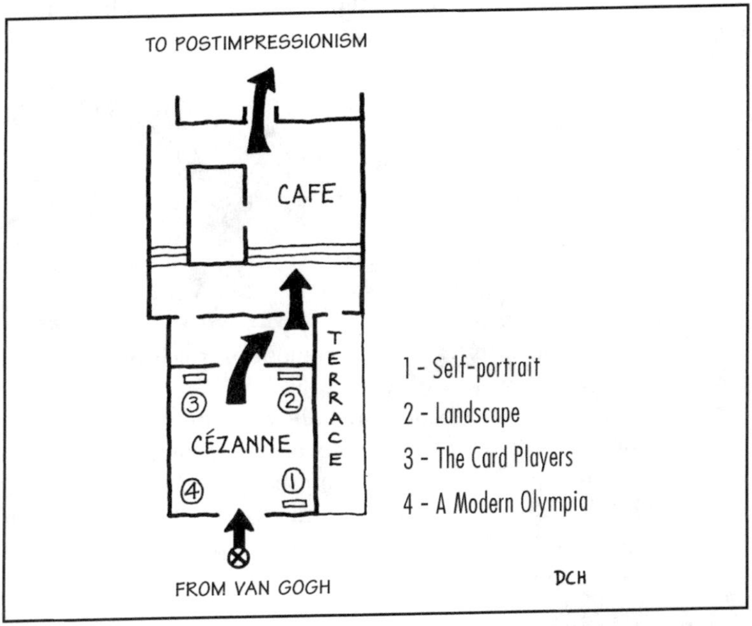

TO POSTIMPRESSIONISM

CAFE

TERRACE

CÉZANNE

FROM VAN GOGH

DCH

1 - Self-portrait
2 - Landscape
3 - The Card Players
4 - A Modern Olympia

drag it across a canvas, and leave it there to dry. But Cézanne the mediocre painter was a great innovator. His works are not perfected, finished products but revolutionary works-in-progress—gutter balls with wonderful spin. His work spoke for itself—which is good because, as you can see here, he had no mouth.

Cézanne—Landscape (Rochers près des Grottes au dessus de Château-Noir)

Cézanne used chunks of color as blocks to build three-dimensional forms. The rocky brown cliffs here consist of cubes of green, tan, and blue that blend at a distance to create a solid 3-D structure. It only makes sense from a distance. Try this: Stand a hand's length from the painting and fade back. At some point the messy slabs become reality on the rocks.

Why is this revolutionary? Past artists created the illusion of 3-D with lines (like when we draw receding lines to turn a square into a cube). The Impressionists pioneered the technique of using blobs of color, not lines, to capture a subject. But most Impressionist art is flat and two-dimensional, a wall of color like Monet's *Rouen Cathedral* series. Cézanne went 3-D with chunks.

These chunks are like little "cubes." No coincidence that his experiments in reducing forms to their geometric basics influenced the... cubists.

Cézanne—*The Card Players* (*Les Joueurs de Cartes*)

These aren't people. They're studies in color and pattern. The subject matter—two guys playing cards—is less important than the pleasingly balanced pattern they make on the canvas, two sloping forms framing a cylinder (a bottle) in the center. Later, abstract artists would focus solely on the shapes and colors.

Again, notice how the figures are built with chunks of color. The jacket of the player to the right consists of tans, greens, and browns. As one art scholar put it: "Cézanne confused intermingled forms and colors, achieving an extraordinarily luminous density in which lyricism is controlled by a rigorously constructed rhythm." Just what I said—chunks of color.

Cézanne— *A Modern Olympia* (*Une Moderne Olympia*)

Is this Cézanne himself paying homage to Manet? And dreaming up a new, more radical style of painting? We've come a long way since Manet's *Olympia*, which seems tame to us now.

• *Exit to the café and consider a well-deserved break. From the café, continue ahead, walking under the large green beam, following signs saying, "suite de la visite."*

A hallway leads past WCs to a dark room in the right corner...

Redon

Now flip out the lights and step into his mysterious world. If the Orsay's a zoo, this is the nocturnal house. Prowl around. This is wild, wild stuff. It's intense—imagine Richard Nixon on mushrooms playing sax.

• *Coming out of the darkness, pass into the gallery lined with metal columns containing the primitive art of Rousseau and Gauguin. Start in the first alcove to the left.*

PRIMITIVISM

Henri Rousseau—*War* (*La Guerre ou La Chevauchée de la Discorde*)

Some artists, rejecting the harried, scientific, and rational world, re-

membered a time before "-isms," when works of art weren't scholarly "studies in form and color" but voodoo dolls full of mystery and magic power. They learned from the art of primitive tribes in Africa and the South Seas, trying to recreate a primal Garden of Eden of peace and wholeness. In doing so, they created another "ism": primitivism.

One such artist was Rousseau, a man who painted like a child. He was an amateur artist who palled around with all the great painters, but they never took his naive style of art seriously.

This looks like a child's drawing of a nightmare. The images are primitive—flat and simple, with unreal colors—but the effect is both beautiful and terrifying. War in the form of a woman with a sword flies on horseback across the battlefield, leaving destruction in her wake—broken bare trees, burning clouds in the background, and heaps of corpses picked at by the birds.

Gauguin—*The Beautiful Angel* (*La Belle Angele*)

A woman in peasant dress sits in a bubble like the halos in a medieval religious painting. Next to it is a pagan idol. This isn't a scene but an

ordered collage of images with symbolic overtones. It's left to us to make the connection.

Paul Gauguin (go-gan) learned the bright clashing colors from the Impressionists but diverged from this path about the time van Gogh waved a knife in his face.

Gauguin simplifies. His figures are two-dimensional with thick dark outlines filled in with basic blocks of color. He turned his back on the entire Western tradition of realism begun in the Renaissance, which tried to recreate the 3-D world on a 2-D canvas. Instead he returns to an age where figures become symbols.

PRIMITIVISM

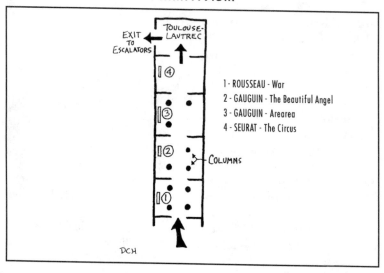

1 - ROUSSEAU - War
2 - GAUGUIN - The Beautiful Angel
3 - GAUGUIN - Arearea
4 - SEURAT - The Circus

Gauguin—*Arearea (Pleasantries)*

Gauguin got the travel bug early in childhood and grew up wanting to be a sailor. Instead he became a stockbroker. In his spare time he painted and was introduced to the Impressionist circle. At the age of 35, he got fed up with it all, quit his job, abandoned his family (see his wife's stern portrait bust), and took refuge in his art. He traveled to the South Seas in search of the exotic, finally settling on Tahiti.

In Tahiti, Gauguin found his Garden of Eden. He simplified his life to the routine of eating, sleeping, and painting. He simplified his painting still more to flat images with heavy black outlines filled in with bright, pure colors. He painted the native girls in their naked innocence (so different from Cabanel's seductive *Venus*). But this simple style had a deep undercurrent of symbolic meaning.

Arearea shows native women and a dog. In the "distance" (there's no attempt at traditional 3-D here), a procession goes by with a large pagan idol. What's the connection between the idol and the foreground figures who are apparently unaware of it? Gauguin makes us dig deep down into our medulla oblongata to make a mystical connection between the beautiful women, the dog, and religion. In primitive societies, religion permeates life. Idols, dogs, and women are holy.

Seurat—*The Circus* (*Le Cirque*)

With pointillism, Impressionism is brought to its logical conclusion—little dabs of different colors placed side by side to blend in the viewer's eye. Using only red, yellow, blue, and green points of paint, Seurat (sur-rah) creates a mosaic of colors that shimmers at a distance, capturing the wonder of the dawn of electric lights.

Toulouse-Lautrec—*The Clownesse Cha-U-Kao*

Henri de Toulouse-Lautrec was the black sheep of a noble family. At age

15 he broke both legs, which left him a cripple. Shunned by his family, a freak to society, he felt more at home in the underworld of other outcasts—prostitutes, drunks, thieves, dancers, and actors. He painted the nightlife lowlife in the bars, cafés, dance halls, and brothels he frequented. Toulose-Lautrec died young of alcoholism.

The Clownesse Cha-U-Kao is one of his fellow freaks, a fat lady clown who made her living being laughed at. She slumps wearily after a performance, indifferent to the applause, and adjusts her dress to prepare for the curtain call.

Toulouse-Lautrec was a true "impression"-ist, catching his models in candid poses. He worked spontaneously, never correcting his mistakes, as you can see from the blotches on her dark skirt and the unintentional yellow sash hanging down. Can you see a bit of Degas here, in the subject matter, snapshot pose, and colors?

Toulouse-Lautrec—*Jane Avril Dancing*

Toulouse-Lautrec hung out at the Moulin Rouge dance hall in Montmartre. One of the most popular dancers was this slim, graceful, elegant, and melancholy woman who stood out above the rabble of the Moulin Rouge. Her legs keep dancing while her mind is far away. Toulouse-Lautrec the aristocrat might have identified with her noble face—sad and tired of the nightlife, but stuck in it.

• *You've seen the essential Orsay and are permitted to cut out (the exit is straight below you). But there's an "Other Orsay" I think you'll find entertaining.*

To reach the mezzanine ("niveau median"), cross to the other side of the gallery at this level and go down three flights. In front of you is the restaurant, behind you (at the foot of the escalator) is a grand ballroom and the mezzanine (which overlooks the main floor).

Peek into the restaurant Le Salon de Thé du Musée (or enjoy the salad bar or a cup of coffee). This was part of the original hotel which adjoined the train station (built in 1900, abandoned after 1939, condemned, and restored to the elegance you see today). Then, find the palatial room of mirrors and chandeliers, marked "Salle des Fêtes" or "Arts et Dècors de la IIIème République" (Room 52).

THE "OTHER" ORSAY— MEZZANINE

The beauty of the Orsay is that it combines all the art of the 1800s (1848–1914), both modern and classical, in one building. The classical art, so popular in its own day, has been maligned and was forgotten in the 20th century. It's time for a reassessment. Is it as gaudy and gawd-awful as we've been led to believe? From our modern-day perspective, let's take a look at the opulent 19th-century French high society and its luxurious art.

The Grand Ballroom
(Arts et Dècors de la IIIème République)

This was one of France's most luxurious nightspots when the Orsay hotel was here. You can easily imagine gowned debutantes and white-gloved dandies waltzing the night away to the music of a chamber orchestra.

THE "OTHER" ORSAY—MEZZANINE

1 - Grand Ballroom
2 - Art worth a second look
3 - Art NOT worth a second look
4 - Art Nouveau
5 - RODIN - The Walking Man
6 - CLAUDEL - L'Age Mur
7 - RODIN - The Gates of Hell
8 - RODIN - Balzac

Notice:

1) The interior decorating: raspberry marble-ripple ice-cream columns, pastel ceiling painting, gold work, mirrors, and leafy strands of chandeliers.

2) The statue *Bacchante Couchée* sprawled in the middle of the room. Familiar pose? If not, you flunk this tour.

3) The statue *Aurore*, with her canopy of hair, hide-and-seek face, and silver-dollar nipples.

4) The large painting *The Birth of Venus* (*La Naissance de Venus*) by William Bouguereau. Van Gogh once said: "If I painted like Bouguereau, I could hope to make money. The public will never change—they love only sweet things."

5) *La Nature*, with the only see-through veil of marble I've ever seen through.

So here's the question: Is this stuff beautiful or merely gaudy? Divine or decadent?

• *Return to the mezzanine overlooking the main gallery. Head toward the far end. Enter the first room on the left (#55).*

Art Worth a Second Look

We've seen some great art; now let's see some not-so-great art—at least, that's what modern critics tell us. This is realistic art with a subconscious kick, art from a neurotic society before Freud articulated its demons.

• *Working clockwise, you'll see...*

Cain

The world's first murderer, with the murder weapon still in his belt, is exiled with his family. Archaeologists had recently discovered a Neanderthal skull, so the artist shows them as a prehistoric hunter/gatherer tribe.

The Dream (Le Rêve)

Soldiers sleep, while visions of Gatling guns dance in their heads.

Payday (La Paye des Moissonneurs)

Peasants getting paid, painted by the man called "the grandson of Courbet and Millet." The subtitle of the work should be, "Is this all there is to life?"

The Excommunication of Robert Le Pieux

The bishops exit after performing the rite. The king and queen are stunned, the scepter dropped. The ritual candle has been snuffed out; it falls, fuming, echoing through the huge hall.... Again, is this art or only cheap theatrics?

• *Return to the mezzanine. Skip the next room, then go left into Room 59, labeled "Symbolisme."*

Art Not Worth a Second Look

The Orsay's director said: "Certainly we have bad paintings. But we have only the greatest bad paintings." And here they are.

Serenity

An idyll in the woods. Three nymphs with harps waft off to the right. These people are stoned on something.

The School of Plato (L'École de Platon)

Subtitled "The Athens YMCA." A Christlike Plato surrounded by adoring, half-naked nubile youths gives new meaning to the term "Platonic relationship."

Will the pendulum shift so that one day art like *The School of Plato* becomes the new, radical avant-garde style?

• *Return to the mezzanine and continue to the far end. Enter the last room on the left (#65) and head for the far corner.*

ART NOUVEAU

The Industrial Age brought factories, row houses, machines, train stations, geometrical precision—and ugliness. At the turn of the century, some artists reacted against the unrelieved geometry of harsh, pragmatic, iron-and-steel Eiffel Tower art with a "new art"—Art Nouveau. Hmm. I think I had a driver's-ed teacher by that name.

Charpentier—Dining Room of Adrien Benard (Boiserie de la Salle à Mangé de la Propriété Benard)

Like nature, which also abhors a straight line, Art Nouveau artists used

the curves of flowers and vines as their pattern. They were convinced that "practical" didn't have to mean "ugly" as well. They turned everyday household objects into art.

This wood-paneled dining room, with its organic shapes, is one of the finest examples of the Art Nouveau style (called Jugendstil in Germanic countries). Another is the curvy wrought-iron work of Paris' early Métro entrances (some survive; one is between Notre-Dame and Sainte-Chapelle), built by the same man who commissioned this dining room for his home.

• *Browse through the Art Nouveau rooms to the left. You'll spill out back onto the mezzanine. Grab a seat in front of the Rodin statue of a man missing everything but his legs.*

Auguste Rodin

Rodin completes the tour—from classical sculpture to Impressionist painting to an artist who brought them both together. Rodin combined classical solidity with Impressionist surfaces to become the greatest sculptor since Michelangelo.

Rodin—*The Walking Man* (*L'Homme Qui Marche*)

This muscular, forcefully striding man could be a symbol of the Renaissance Man with his classical power. With no mouth or hands, he speaks with his body. But Rodin also learned a thing or two from the comparatively lightweight Impressionist painters. Get close and look at the statue's surface. This rough "unfinished" look reflects light like the rough Impressionist brushwork, making the statue come alive, never quite at rest in the viewer's eye.

• *Near the far end of the mezzanine, you'll see a small bronze couple (L'Âge Mur) by Camille Claudel, a student of Rodin's.*

Claudel—*Maturity* (*L'Âge Mur*)

Camille Claudel, Rodin's student and mistress, may have portrayed their doomed love affair here. A young girl desperately reaches out to an older man, who is led away reluctantly by an older woman. The center of the composition is the empty space left when their hands separate. In real life, Rodin refused to leave his wife, and Camille (see her head sticking up from a block of marble) ended up in an insane asylum.

Rodin—*The Gates of Hell* (*Porte de l'Enfer*)

Rodin worked for decades on these doors depicting Dante's Hell, and they contain some of his greatest hits, small statues that he later executed in full size. Find *The Thinker* squatting above the doorway, contemplating Man's fate. And in the lower left is the same kneeling man eating his children (*Ugolin*) you'll see in full size nearby. Well established in his career, Rodin paid models to run, squat, leap, and spin around his studio however they wanted. When he saw an interesting pose he'd yell "freeze" (or "statue maker") and get out his sketch pad.

Rodin—*Balzac*

The great French novelist is given a heroic, monumental ugliness. Wrapped in a long cloak, he thrusts his head out at a defiant angle, showing the strong individualism and egoism of the 19th-century Romantic movement. Balzac is proud and snooty—but his body forms a question mark, and underneath the twisted features we can see a touch of personal pain and self doubt. This is hardly camera-eye realism— Balzac wasn't that grotesque—but it captures a personality that strikes us even if we don't know the man.

From this perch, look over the main floor at all the classical statues between you and the big clock and realize how far we've come—not in years but in style changes. Many of the statues below—beautiful, smooth, balanced, and idealized—were done at the same time as Rodin's powerful, haunting works. Rodin is a good place to end the tour. With a stable base of 19th-century stone, he launched art into the 20th century.

❧ 9 ❧
RODIN MUSEUM

Auguste Rodin (1840–1917) was a modern Michelangelo, sculpting human figures on an epic scale, revealing through the body their deepest thoughts and feelings. Like many of Michelangelo's unfinished works, Rodin's statues rise from the raw stone around them, driven by the life force. With missing limbs and scarred skin, these are prefab classics, making ugliness noble. Rodin's people are always moving restlessly. Even the famous *Thinker* is moving. While he's plopped down solidly, his mind is a million miles away. The museum presents a full range of Rodin's work, housed in a historic mansion where he once lived and worked. The gardens are picnic perfect (BYO), but there's also a pleasant, if pricey, café.

ORIENTATION
Cost: €4.80, €3.10 on Sun and for students, free for youth under 18 and for anyone first Sun of month; €1 for garden only; all covered by museum pass.

Hours: April–Sept Tue–Sun 9:30–17:45, garden closes at 18:45. Oct–March Tue–Sun 9:30–17:00, garden closes at 17:00. Closed Mon. Last entrance 30 minutes before closing.

Getting there: The museum is near Napoleon's Tomb (77 rue de Varennes, Metro: Varenne).

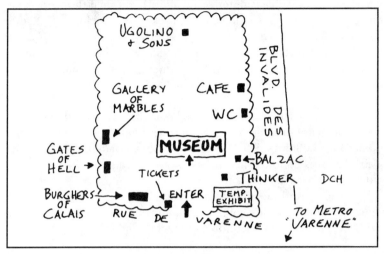

Information: Tel. 01 44 18 61 10, www.musee-rodin.fr.
Length of our tour: One hour.
Photography: Allowed without a flash.
Cuisine art: In the garden, try the snack bar or have a picnic.
Starring: Rodin's *Thinker, Kiss, Balzac, Burghers of Calais, Gates of Hell,* and more.

Entrance Hall

Two bronze men stride forward, as bold as the often-controversial Rodin. *The Walking Man* (*L'Homme Qui Marche*) plants his back foot forcefully as though he's about to step, while his front foot already has stepped. Rodin, who himself had one foot in the past, one in the future, captures two poses at once.

• *Pick up a museum plan with room numbers and walk left, through the shop, and to the far corner to start a circular tour of the ground floor.*

Room 1

Rodin's early works match the style of the time—pretty portrait busts and classical themes. Born of working-class roots, Rodin taught himself art by sketching statues at the Louvre and then sculpting copies.

 The Man with the Broken Nose (*L'homme au nez casse*)—a deliberately ugly work—was 23-year-old Rodin's first break from the norm.

He meticulously sculpted this deformed man (one of the few models the young, struggling sculptor could afford), but then the clay statue froze in his unheated studio, and the back of the head fell off. Rodin loved it! The Salon hated it. Rodin persevered.

See the painting of Rodin's future wife, Rose Beuret (*Portrait de Madame Rodin*), who suffered with him through obscurity and celebrity.

Room 2

To feed his new family, Rodin cranked out small works with his boss's name on them—portraits, ornamental vases, nymphs, and knickknacks to decorate buildings. Still, the series of mother-and-childs (Rose and baby Auguste?) allowed him to experiment on a small scale with the intertwined twosomes he'd do later.

His job gave him enough money to visit Italy, where he was inspired by Michelangelo's boldness, monumental scale, restless figures, and "unfinished" look. Rapidly approaching middle age, Rodin was ready to rock.

Room 3

He moved to Brussels, where his first major work, *The Bronze Age* (*L'âge d'airain*), brought controversy and the fame that surrounds it. This nude youth, perhaps inspired by Michelangelo's *Dying Slave* in the Louvre, awakens to a new world. It was so lifelike that Rodin was accused of not sculpting it himself but simply casting it directly from a live body. The boy's left hand looks like he should be leaning on a spear, but it's just that missing element that makes the pose more tenuous and interesting.

The art establishment still snubbed Rodin the outsider, and no wonder. Look at his ultraintense take on the symbol of France (*La Défense*)—this Marseillaise screams "Off with their heads" at the top of her lungs. Rodin was a slave to his muses, and some inspired monsters.

Room 4

Like the hand of a sculptor, *The Hand of God* (*La main de Dieu*) shapes Adam and Eve from the mud of the earth to which they will return. Rodin himself worked in "mud," using his hands to model clay figures, which were then reproduced in marble or bronze, usually by his assistants. Spin this masterpiece on its turntable. Rodin wants you to see it from every angle. He first worked from the front view, then checked the back and side profiles, then filled in the in-between.

Other works in this room show embracing couples who seem to emerge from the stone just long enough to love. Rodin left many works "unfinished," reminding us that all creating is a hard process of dragging a form out of chaos.

Room 5

The two hands that form the arch of *The Cathedral* (*La Cathèdrale*) are actually two right hands (a man's and a woman's?).

In *The Kiss*, a passionate woman twines around a solid man for their first, spontaneous kiss. In their bodies, we can almost read the thoughts, words, and movements that led up to this meeting of lips. *The Kiss* was the first Rodin work the public loved. Rodin despised it, thinking it simple and sentimental.

Rodin worked with many materials— he chiseled marble (*The Kiss*), used clay (the smaller, red-brown *Kiss*—opposite the big kiss), cast bronze, worked plaster, painted, and sketched. He often created a different version of the same subject in a different medium.

Room 6

This room displays works by Camille Claudel, mostly in the style of her master. The 44-year-old Rodin took 18-year-old Camille as his pupil, muse, colleague, and lover. We can follow the arc of their relationship:

Rodin was inspired by young Camille's beauty and spirit, and he often used her as a model. You'll see her head emerging from a block of marble.

As his student, "Mademoiselle C" learned from Rodin, doing portrait busts in his lumpy style. Her bronze bust of Rodin (by the door) shows the steely-eyed sculptor with strong front and side profiles, barely emerging from the materials he worked with.

Soon they were lovers. *The Waltz* (*La Valse*) captures the spinning exuberance the two must have felt as they embarked together on a new life. The couple twirls in a delicate balance.

But Rodin was devoted as well to his lifelong companion, Rose. *Maturity* (*L'Âge Mur*) shows the breakup. A young girl on her knees begs the man not to leave her, as he's led away reluctantly by an older woman. The center of the composition is the hole left when their hands drift apart.

Rodin did leave Camille. Overwhelmed by grief and jealousy, she went crazy and was institutionalized until she died. *The Wave* (*La*

Vague), carved in onyx in a very un-Rodin style, shows sensitive—perhaps fragile—women huddled under a wave about to engulf them.

Rooms 7 and 8
What did Rodin think of women? Here are many different images from which you can draw conclusions.

Eve buries her head in shame, hiding her nakedness. But she can't hide the consequences of that first sin—she's pregnant.

Rodin became famous, wealthy, and respected, and society ladies all wanted him to do their portraits. In Room 8, you'll also see his last mistress (*La Duchesse de Choiseul*), who lived with him here in this mansion.

Room 9
This dimly lit room is filled with Rodin's sketches. The first flash of inspiration for a huge statue might be a single line sketched on notepaper. Rodin wanted nude models in his studio at all times—walking, dancing, and squatting—in case they struck some new and interesting pose. Rodin thought of sculpture as simply "drawing in all dimensions."

• *Upstairs you'll find a glass display case that tries hard to explain how...* Rodin made his bronze statues by pouring molten bronze into the narrow space between an original clay model and the mold around it. Once you had a mold, you could produce other copies, which is why there are famous Rodin bronzes all over the world.

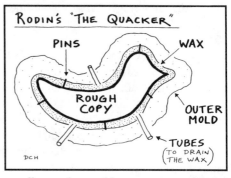

RODIN'S "THE QUACKER"

As the display case clearly fails to make clear, the classic "lost wax" technique works like this:
1) The artist sculpts a clay model.
2) It is covered with materials that harden to make a shell that's hard on the outside, flexible inside. The shell is removed by cutting it into two halves that can be pieced back together—this is your mold.
3) Cement is poured into the mold to make a durable, rough copy. The mold is removed.
4) The surface of the copy is sanded down slightly.

5) The mold is put back over it, using pins to keep a one-centimeter space between the mold and the rough copy. Hot wax is poured into the space, it cools, and the mold is removed. The artist touches up the wax "skin" of the rough copy into its final form.

6) The waxy piece of art is covered with materials that harden into a new mold. Ventilation tubes are added.

7) The whole contraption is coated with heat-resistant materials.

8) The wax is heated—it melts and drains away (gets "lost"), leaving one centimeter of open space between the rough copy and the mold. Molten bronze is poured in to fill the space. As the bronze cools, it takes the shape of the mold.

9) The mold and the tubing are removed, and the bronze halves are lifted off the rough copy. After the halves are soldered together, you have a hollow bronze statue ready to be polished and varnished.

Rooms 10 and 11

For decades, Rodin wrestled with a massive project—a doorway encrusted with characters from Dante's *Inferno*. These *Gates of Hell* were never completed (see unfinished piece in the garden), but his studies created some of Rodin's masterpieces—including *The Thinker*, who was to be the centerpiece.

Rodin's figures struggle to come into existence. Rodin was fascinated with the theory of evolution—not Darwin's version of the survival of the fittest but the Frenchman Lamarck's. His figures survive not by the good fortune of random mutation (Darwin), but by their own striving (Lamarck). They are driven by the life force, a restless energy that animates and shapes dead matter (Lamarck and Bergson). Rodin must have felt that force even as a child when he first squeezed soft clay and saw a worm emerge.

In Room 11 you'll see studies of the female body in all its aspects—open, closed, wrinkled.

Room 12

A virtual unknown until his mid-30s, Rodin slowly began receiving major commissions for public monuments. *The Burghers of Calais* depicts the actual event in 1347, when, in order to save their people, the city fathers surrender the keys of the city—and their own lives—to the enemy. Rodin portrays them not in some glorious pose drenched in pomp and allegory but as a simple example of men sacrificing their lives together. As they head to the gallows, with ropes already around their necks, each shows a distinct emotion: from courage to despair. Compare the small plaster model in the glass case with the final, life-size bronze group out the window in the garden (near the street behind the ticket booth).

Room 15
Rodin's feverish attempts to capture a portrait of the novelist Balzac ranged from a pot-bellied Bacchus to a headless nude cradling an erection. In a moment of inspiration, Rodin threw a plaster-soaked robe over the nude and watched it dry into what would become the final, definitive version.

Room 17
Legendary lovers kiss, embrace, and intertwine in yin-yang bliss.

Room 14
Rodin's portrait busts of celebrities and some paintings by (yawn, are we through yet?) van Gogh, Monet, and Renoir. Rodin enjoyed discussions with Monet and other artists, and incorporated their ideas in his work. Rodin is often considered an Impressionist because he captured spontaneous "impressions" of figures and created rough surfaces that catch reflected light.

Room 13
By the end of his life Rodin was more famous than his works. The museum's film clip shows Rodin making the marble chips fly. In fact, he rarely picked up a chisel, leaving that to assistants. Compare Rodin's small plaster "sketches" (in the glass case) with the final, large-scale marble versions executed by others.

The Gardens
Rodin lived and worked in this mansion, renting rooms alongside Matisse, the poet Rilke (Rodin's secretary), and the dancer Isadora Duncan. He loved placing his creations in the overgrown gardens. These are his greatest works, Rodin at his most expansive. The epic human figures are enhanced, not dwarfed, by nature.
• *Leaving the house, there are five more stops: two on the left and three on the right. Beyond these stops is a big breezy garden ornamented with statues, a cafeteria, and a WC.*

The Thinker

Leaning slightly forward, tense and compact, every muscle working toward producing that one great thought, Man contemplates his fate. No constipation jokes, please.

This is not an intellectual but a linebacker who's realizing there's more to life than frat parties. It's the first man evolving beyond his animal nature to think the first thought. It's anyone who's ever worked hard to reinvent himself or to make something new or better. Said Rodin: "It is a statue of myself."

There are 29 other authorized copies of this statue, arguably the most famous in the world.

• *To the left of* The Thinker *you'll find . . .*

Balzac

The iconoclastic novelist turns his nose up at the notion he should be honored with a statue. This final version also stands in the Musée d'Orsay and on a street median in Montparnasse. When the statue was unveiled, the crowd booed, a fitting tribute to both the defiant novelist and the bold man who sculpted him.

• *Along the street near the ticket booth are . . .*

The Burghers of Calais

The six city fathers trudge to their execution, and we can read in their faces and poses what their last thoughts are. They mill about, dazed, as each one deals with the decision he's made to sacrifice himself for his city.

• *Circling counterclockwise . . .*

The man carrying the key to the city tightens his lips in determination. The bearded man is weighed down with grief. Another buries his head in his hands. One turns, seeking reassurance from his friend, who turns away and gestures helplessly. The final key bearer (in back) has been stoic, but now he's raising his hand to his head.

Each is alone in his thoughts, but they're united by their mutual sacrifice, by the base they stand on, and by their weighty robes—gravity is already dragging them down to their graves.

Pity the poor souls, then salute King Edward III, who, at the last second, pardoned them.

• *Follow* The Thinker's *gaze to the opposite side of the house. Standing before a tall white backdrop is a big dark door—the* Gates of Hell.

The Gates of Hell

These doors (never meant to actually open) were never finished for a museum that was never built. But the vision of Dante's trip into hell gave Rodin a chance to explore the dark side of human experience. "Abandon hope all ye who enter in," was hell's motto. The Three Shades at the top of the door point down—that's where we're going. Beneath The Shades, pondering the whole scene from above, is Dante as The Thinker. Below him, the figures emerge from the darkness just long enough to tell their sad tale of depravity. There's Paolo and Francesca (in the center of the right door), who were driven into an illicit love affair that brought them here. Ugolino (left door, just below center) crouches in prison over his kids. This poor soul was so driven by hunger that he ate the corpses of his own children. On all fours like an animal, he is the dark side of natural selection. Finally, find what some say is Rodin himself (at the very bottom, inside the right doorjamb, where it just starts to jut out), crouching humbly.

You'll find some of these figures writ large in the garden. *The Thinker* is behind you, *The Shades* are 30 meters to the right, and *Ugolino* dines in the fountain at the far end.

It's appropriate that *The Gates*—Rodin's "cathedral"—remained unfinished. He was always a restless artist for whom the process of discovery was as important as the finished product.

• *To the right of the* Gates of Hell *is a glassed-in building, the...*

Gallery of Marbles

Unfinished, they show human features emerging from the rough stone. Imagine Rodin in his studio working to give them life.

Victor Hugo (at the far end of the Gallery), the great champion of Les Miz progress, leans back like Michelangelo's nude *Adam*, waiting for the spark of creation. He tenses his face and cups his ear, straining to hear the vague call from the blurry Muse above him. Once inspired, he can bring the idea to life (just as Rodin did) with the strength of his powerful arms. It's been said that all of Rodin's work shows the struggle of mind over matter, of brute creatures emerging from the mud and evolving into a species of thinkers.

❧ 10 ❧
HISTORIC PARIS WALK
From Notre-Dame to Sainte-Chapelle

Paris has been the capital of Europe for centuries. We'll start where it did, on the Île de la Cité, with forays onto both the Left and Right Banks, on a walk that laces together the story of Paris: Roman, medieval, the Revolution, café society, the literary scene of the '20s, and the modern world. Allow four hours to do justice to this five-kilometer (three-mile) walk.

ORIENTATION

All sights that charge admission are covered by the Paris museum pass, a great value (sold at many museums, major Métro stations, and tourist offices).

Notre-Dame: Free, daily 8:00–18:45; treasury costs €2.60, daily 9:30–17:30; Sunday Mass at 8:00, 8:45, 10:00, 11:30, 12:30, and 18:30. Leaflet with church schedule at booth inside entrance. Ask about free English tours, normally Wed and Thu at 12:00 and Sat at 14:30. The tower climb takes 400 steps and €6—worth it for the gargoyle's-eye view of the cathedral, Seine, and city (daily 9:00–17:30, closed during lunch and off-season).

Notre-Dame Archaeological Crypt: Costs €6, or €8.50 with Notre-Dame's tower, daily 10:00–18:00, closes at 17:00 October–April, entry 100 meters in front of the cathedral.

Deportation Memorial: Free, Mon–Fri 8:30–21:45, Sat–Sun and holidays from 9:00, sometimes closes 12:00–14:00, shorter hours off-season.

Sainte-Chapelle: Costs €6, daily 9:30–18:30, off-season 10:00–16:30.

Conciergerie: Costs €6, daily 9:30–18:30, off-season 10:00–17:00.

Starring: Our Lady, gargoyles, the Latin Quarter, glorious stained glass, Marie Antoinette, and great views.

ÎLE DE LA CITÉ

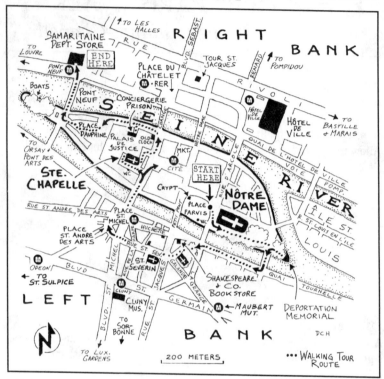

NOTRE-DAME

• *Start at the Notre-Dame Cathedral on the island in the River Seine, the physical and historic bull's-eye of your Paris map (closest Métro stops are Cité, Hôtel de Ville, and St. Michel, each requiring a short walk). On the square in front of the cathedral, stand far enough back to take in the whole facade. Look at the circular window in the center.*

For centuries, the main figure in the Christian "pantheon" has been the goddess Mary, the mother of Jesus. Common people pray to her directly in times of trouble to gain comfort and to ask her to convince God to be compassionate with them. The church is dedicated to "Our Lady" (Notre Dame), and there she is, cradling God, right in the heart of the facade, surrounded by the halo of the rose window. Though the church is massive and imposing, it has always stood for the grace and compassion of Mary, the "mother of God."

Imagine the faith of the people who built this. They broke ground in 1163 with the hope that someday their great-great-great-great-great-great grandchildren might attend the dedication mass two centuries later. Look up the bell towers, 65 meters tall (200 feet), and imagine a tiny medieval community mustering the money and energy to build this. Master masons supervised, but the people did much of the grunt work themselves for free—hauling the

huge stones from distant quarries, digging a 10-meter-deep trench to lay the foundations, and treading like rats on a wheel designed to lift the stones up, one by one. This kind of backbreaking, arduous manual labor created the real hunchbacks of Notre-Dame.

• *"Walk this way" toward the cathedral, and view it from the bronze plaque on the ground marked...*

Point Zero

You're standing at the very center of France, from which all distances are measured. The "Cité" started here in the third century B.C. In 52 B.C., the Romans booted out the Parisii tribe and built their government palace at the end of the square behind you and the Temple of Jupiter where the cathedral sits. Two thousand years of dirt and debris have raised the city's altitude. The archaeological crypt nearby offers a fascinating look at the remains of the earlier city and church below today's street level.

Still facing the church, on your right is a grand equestrian statue of Charlemagne ("Charles the Great"), whose reign marked the birth of modern Europe. Crowned in A.D. 800, he briefly united much of Europe during the Dark Ages. (Maybe even greater than Charles are nearby pay toilets—the cleanest you'll find in downtown Paris.)

Before renovation, 150 years ago, this square was much smaller, a characteristic medieval shambles facing a run-down church, surrounded by winding streets and countless buildings (look at the outlines marked in the pavement of the square, showing the medieval street plan). The huge church bell towers rose above this tangle of smaller buildings, inspiring Victor Hugo's story of a deaf, bell-ringing hunchback who could look down on all Paris.

• *Now turn your attention to the church facade. Look at the left doorway and, to the left of the door, find the statue with his head in his hands.*

NOTRE DAME FACADE

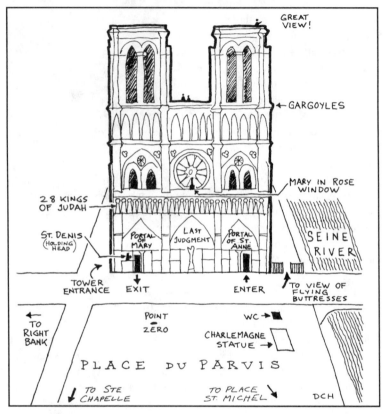

GREAT VIEW!

← GARGOYLES

MARY IN ROSE WINDOW

28 KINGS OF JUDAH →

ST. DENIS (HOLDING HEAD)

PORTAL OF MARY

LAST JUDGMENT

PORTAL OF ST. ANNE

SEINE RIVER

TOWER ENTRANCE

EXIT

ENTER

TO VIEW OF FLYING BUTTRESSES

← TO RIGHT BANK

POINT ZERO

WC →

CHARLEMAGNE STATUE →

PLACE DU PARVIS

TO STE CHAPELLE

TO PLACE ST. MICHEL

DCH

Notre-Dame Facade

When Christianity began making converts in Roman Paris, the Bishop of Paris was beheaded. But these early Christians were hard to keep down. St. Denis got up, tucked his head under his arm, headed north, paused at a fountain to wash it off,  and continued until he found just the right place to meet his maker. The Parisians were convinced of this miracle, Christianity gained ground, and a church soon replaced the pagan temple.

By the way, Christians think Montmartre (the one hill overlooking Paris) is named for this martyr (pagans think it was named after a

Roman temple of Mars—
Mount of Mars—which once
stood here). Denis eventually
died on the edge of town where
the church of St. Denis was
built (famous in history books
as the first Gothic church, but
not much to see today).
• *Now look above the central
doorway, where you'll find scenes
from the Last Judgment.*

Central Portal
It's the end of the world, and Christ sits on the throne of judgment (just
under the arches, holding his hands up). Below him, an angel and a
demon weigh souls in the balance. The good people stand to the left,
looking up to heaven. The naughty ones to the right are chained up
and led off to . . . a six-hour tour of the Louvre on a hot day. Notice the
crazy sculpted demons to the right, at the base of the arch.
• *Above the arches is a row of 28 statues, known as . . .*

The Kings of Judah
In the days of the French Revolution (1789–1793), these Biblical kings
were mistaken for the hated French kings, and Notre-Dame represented the oppressive Catholic hierarchy. The citizens stormed the church,
crying, "Off with their heads!" Plop, they lopped off the crowned heads
of these kings with glee, creating a row of St. Denises that wasn't repaired for decades.
   But the story doesn't end there. A schoolteacher who lived nearby
collected the heads and buried them in his backyard for safekeeping.
There they slept until 1977, when they were accidentally unearthed.
Today you can stare into the eyes of the original kings a few blocks
away in the Cluny Museum (€6, €4.50 on Sun, covered by museum
pass, Wed–Mon 9:15–17:45, closed Tue, 6 place Paul-Painlevé, near the
corner of boulevards St. Michel and St. Germain, tel. 01 53 73 78 00).
• *Enter the church and find a spot to view the long, high central aisle.*

Notre-Dame Interior
Remove your metaphorical hat and become a simple bareheaded peasant, entering the dim medieval light of the church. Take a minute to
let your pupils dilate, to take in the subtle, mysterious light show God

beams through the stained-glass windows. Follow the slender columns up to the praying-hands arches of the ceiling and contemplate the heavens. Let's say it's dedication day for this great stone wonder. The priest intones the words of the mass that echo through the hall: "*Terribilis est locus iste*"—"This place is *terribilis*," meaning awe inspiring or even terrifying. It's a huge, dark, earthly cavern lit with an unearthly light.

This is Gothic. Taller and filled with light, this was a major improvement over the earlier Romanesque style. Gothic architects needed only a few structural columns topped by pointed arches that crisscross the columns to support the weight of the roof. This let them build higher than ever, freeing up the walls for windows. The church is designed in the shape of a cross, with the altar where the cross beams intersect.

• *Walk up to the main altar.*

The Altar

This marks the spot where mass is said and the bread and wine of communion are prepared and distributed. In olden days, there were no chairs. The church can hold up to 10,000. Join the statue of Joan of Arc (*Jeanne d'Arc*, in the right transept) in gazing up to the rose-shaped window, the only one of the three with its original medieval glass.

This was the holy spot for Romans, Christians . . . and even atheists. When the Revolutionaries stormed the church, they gutted it and turned it into a "Temple for the Cult of Reason." A woman dressed up like the Statue of Liberty held court at the altar as a symbol of the divinity of Man. France today, while nominally Catholic, remains aloof from Vatican dogmatism. Instead of traditional wooden confessional booths, notice the open, glass-walled room where modern sinners seek counseling as much as forgiveness.

Just past the altar are the walls of the choir, where more intimate services can be held in this spacious building. The aisles are lined with chapels, each dedicated to a particular saint. The faithful can pause at their favorite, light a candle as an offering, and meditate in the cool light of the stained glass. (The nearby treasury, containing lavish robes and golden relic-holders, probably isn't worth the entry fee.)

• *Amble around the ambulatory, spill back outside, and make a U-turn left. Walk to the back end of the church along the side that faces the river.*

Notre-Dame Side View

Along the side of the church, you'll notice the flying buttresses. These 15-meter (50 feet) stone "beams" that stick out of the church were the

key to the complex architecture of
Gothic. The pointed arches we saw
inside caused the weight of the roof
to push outward rather than downward. The "flying" buttresses support
the roof by pushing back inward.
Gothic architects were masters at

playing architectural forces against each other to build loftier and loftier churches.

Picture Quasimodo running around along the railed balcony at the
base of the roof among the gargoyles. These grotesque beasts that stick

out from pillars and buttresses represent souls caught between heaven and
earth. They also function as rain
spouts when there are no evil spirits to
do battle with.

The neo-Gothic 90-meter spire is a
product of the 1860 reconstruction of
the dilapidated old church. Around its base are apostles and evange-
lists (the green men) as well as Viollet-le-Duc, the architect in charge of
the work. Notice how the apostles look outward, blessing the city, while
the architect (at top) looks up at the spire, marveling at his fine work.
• *Behind Notre-Dame, squeeze through the tourist buses, cross the street,
and enter the iron gate into the park at the tip of the island.*

Deportation Memorial
(Mémorial de la Déportation)

This memorial to the 200,000 French victims of the Nazi concentration
camps draws you into their experience. As you descend the steps, the city

around you disappears. Surrounded by walls, you have become a
prisoner. Your only freedom is
your view of the sky and the tiny
glimpse of the river below.

Enter the dark, single-file
chamber up ahead. Inside, the
circular plaque in the floor reads,
"They descended into the mouth
of the earth and they did not return."

The hallway stretching in front of you is lined with 200,000 lighted
crystals, one for each French citizen that died. Flickering at the far end is

the eternal flame of hope. The tomb of the unknown deportee lies at your feet. Above, the inscription reads, "Dedicated to the living memory of the 200,000 French Deportees sleeping in the night and the fog, exterminated in the Nazi concentration camps." Above the exit as you leave is the message you'll find at all Nazi sights: "Forgive, but never forget."

Île St. Louis
Back on street level, look across the river to the Île St. Louis. If the Île de la Cité is a tug laden with the history of Paris, it's towing this classy little residential dinghy laden only with boutiques, characteristic restaurants, and famous sorbet shops. This island wasn't developed until much later (18th century). What was a swampy mess is now harmonious Parisian architecture.

• *From the tip of the Île de la Cité, cross the bridge to the Left Bank and turn right. Walk along the river, toward the front end of Notre-Dame. Stairs detour down to the riverbank if you need a place to picnic. This side view of the church from across the river is one of Europe's great sights.*

LEFT BANK (RIVE GAUCHE)
The Left Bank of the Seine—"left" if you were floating downstream—still has many of the twisting lanes and narrow buildings of medieval times. The Right Bank is more modern and business oriented, with wide boulevards and stressed Parisians in suits. Here along the riverbank, the "big business" is books, displayed in the green metal stalls on the parapet. These literary entrepreneurs pride themselves on their easygoing business style. With flexible hours and literally no overhead, they run their businesses as they have since medieval times.

• *When you reach the bridge (pont au Double) that crosses over in front of Notre-Dame, veer to the left, across the street to a small park (square Viviani). Go through the park to the small rough-stone church of St. Julien-le-Pauvre. You'll pass Paris' oldest inhabitant, a false acacia tree ("Robinier") that may have once shaded the Sun King.*

Medieval Paris (1000–1400)
This church dates from the 12th century, and the area around it keeps the same feel. A half-timbered house stands to the right of the entrance. Many buildings in medieval times were built like this, with a wooden frame filled in with a plaster of mud, straw, and dung. Back then, the humble "half-timbered" structure would have been hidden by a veneer of upscale stucco.

Looking along nearby rue Galande, you'll see a few old houses built every which way. In medieval days, people were piled on top of each other, building at all angles, as they scrambled for this prime real estate near the main commercial artery of the day—the Seine. The smell of fish competed with the smell of neighbors in this knot of humanity.

These narrow streets would have been dirt (or mud). Originally the streets sloped from here down into the mucky Seine, until modern quays cleaned that up. Many Latin Quarter lanes were named for their businesses or crafts. The rue de la Bucherie (or "Butcher Street," just around the corner, in the direction of the river) was where butchers slaughtered livestock. The blood and guts drained into the Seine and out of town.

• *At #37 rue de la Bucherie is . . .*

Shakespeare & Company Bookstore

Along with butchers and fishmongers, the Left Bank has been home to scholars, philosophers, and poets since medieval times. This funky bookstore—a reincarnation of the original shop from the 1920s—has picked up the literary torch. In the '20s it was famous as a meeting place of Paris' literary expatriate elite. Ernest Hemingway, a struggling

American writer, strangled and cooked pigeons in the park and borrowed books from here to survive. Fitzgerald, Joyce, and Pound also got their English fix here.

Today it does its best to carry on that literary tradition. Struggling writers are given free accommodations upstairs in tiny, book-lined rooms with views of Notre-Dame. Downstairs, travelers enjoy the best selection of used English books in Paris. Pick up *Free Voice*, a newspaper published for today's American expatriates, and say hi to George.

• *Return to St. Julien-le-Pauvre, follow it to rue Galande, then turn right (west) on rue Galande, which immediately intersects with the busy rue St. Jacques (also called rue du Petit Pont). Way back in Roman times, the rue St. Jacques was the straight, wide, paved road that brought chariots racing in and out of the city. (Roman-iacs can see remains from the 3rd-century baths, along with a fine medieval collection, at the Cluny Museum, 2 blocks to the left.) Cross rue St. Jacques and walk straight, pausing at the small Gothic church of St. Severin, then continue straight, into the Latin Quarter.*

St. Severin

Don't ask me why, but it took a century longer to build this church than Notre-Dame. This is flamboyant, or "flamelike," Gothic, and you can see the short, prickly spires meant to make this building flicker in the eyes of the faithful. The church gives us a close-up look at gargoyles. This weird, winged species of flying mammal, now extinct, used to swoop down on unwary peasants, occasionally carrying off small children in their beaks. Today they're most impressive in thunderstorms, when they vomit rain.

The Latin Quarter

While it may look more like the Tunisian Quarter today, this area is the Latin Quarter, named for the language you'd hear on these streets if you walked them in the Middle Ages. The university, one of the leading universities of medieval Europe, was (and still is) nearby.

A thousand years ago, the "crude" or vernacular local languages were sophisticated enough to communicate basic human needs, but if you wanted to get philosophical, the language of choice was Latin. The educated elite of Dark Ages Europe was a class that transcended nations and borders. From Sicily to Sweden, they spoke and corresponded in Latin. The most Latin thing about this area now is the beat you may hear coming from some of the subterranean jazz clubs.

Along rue St. Severin you can still see the shadow of the medieval sewer system. (The street slopes into a central channel of bricks.) In the days before plumbing and toilets, when people still went to the river or neighborhood wells for their water, flushing meant throwing it out the window. Certain times of day were flushing times. Maids on the fourth floor would holler "Garde de l'eau!" ("Look out for the water!") and heave it into the streets, where it would eventually wash down into the Seine.

• At #22 rue St. Severin, you'll find the skinniest house in Paris, two windows wide. Continue along rue St. Severin to...

Boulevard St. Michel

Busy boulevard St. Michel (or "boul' Miche") is famous as the main artery for bohemian Paris, culminating a block away (to the left), where it intersects with boulevard St. Germain. Although nowadays you're more likely to find pantyhose at 30 percent off, there are still many cafés, boutiques, and bohemian haunts nearby.

The Sorbonne—the University of Paris' humanities department—is also close, if you want to make a detour. (Turn left on boulevard St.

Michel and walk two blocks. The entrance is at #47 rue des Écoles, or just gaze at the dome from the Place Sorbonne courtyard.) Founded as a theology school around the radical Peter Abelard, it became the alma mater for Thomas Aquinas, Loyola, Erasmus, and John Calvin. Children of kings and nobles were sent here to become priests, though many returned as heretics, having studied radical new secular ideas as well. Paris still is a world center for new intellectual trends.

• *Cross boulevard St. Michel. Just ahead is a tree-filled square lined with cafés and restaurants.*

Place Saint Andre des Arts

In Paris, most serious thinking goes on in cafés. For centuries, these have been social watering holes, where you could buy a warm place to sit and stimulating conversation for the price of a cup of coffee. Every great French writer—from Voltaire and Rousseau to Sartre and Derrida—had a favorite haunt.

Paris honors its writers. If you visit the Panthéon (a few blocks down boulevard St. Michel and to the left), you will find great French writers and scientists buried in a setting usually reserved for warriors and politicians.

• *Adjoining this square on the river side is the triangular place St. Michel, with a Métro stop and a statue of St. Michael killing a devil.*

Place St. Michel

You're standing at the traditional core of the Left Bank's artsy, liberal, hippie, bohemian district of poets, philosophers, and winos. You'll find international eateries, far-out bookshops, street singers, pale girls in black berets, jazz clubs, and—these days—tourists. Small cinemas show avant-garde films, almost always in the *version originale* (v.o.). For colorful wandering and café sitting, afternoons and evenings are best. In the morning, it feels sleepy. The Latin Quarter stays up late and sleeps in.

In less commercial times, place St. Michel was a gathering point for the city's malcontents and misfits. Here, in 1871, the citizens took the streets from the government troops, set up barricades "Les Miz" style, and established the Paris Commune. In World War II, the locals rose up against their Nazi oppressors (read the plaques by the St. Michel fountain).

And in the spring of 1968, a time of social upheaval all over the world, young students battled riot batons and tear gas, took over the square, and declared it an independent state. Factory workers followed their call to arms and went on strike, toppling the de Gaulle government and forcing change. Eventually the students were pacified, the university was reformed, and the Latin Quarter's original cobblestones were replaced with pavement, so future scholars could never again use them as weapons.

• *From place St. Michel, look across the river and find the spire of Sainte-Chapelle, with its weathervane angel. Cross the river on pont St. Michel and continue along boulevard du Palais.*

On your left you'll see the doorway to Sainte-Chapelle. But first, carry on another 30 meters and turn right at a wide pedestrian street, the rue de Lutece.

Cité "Metropolitain" Stop

Of the 141 original early-20th-century subway entrances, this is one of 17 survivors now preserved as a national art treasure. (New York's Museum of Modern Art even exhibits one.) The curvy, plantlike ironwork is a textbook example of Art Nouveau, the style that rebelled against the erector-set squareness of the Industrial Age.

The flower market on place Louis Lepine is a pleasant detour. On Sundays this square chirps with a busy bird market. And across the way is the Prefecture de Police, where Inspector Clouseau of Pink Panther fame used to work, and where the local resistance fighters took the first building from the Nazis in August of 1944, leading to the allied liberation of Paris a week later.

• *Pause here to admire the view. Sainte-Chapelle is a pearl in an ugly architectural oyster, part of a complex of buildings that includes the Palace of Justice (to the right of Sainte-Chapelle, behind the iron and bronze gates).*

Return to the entrance of Sainte-Chapelle. You'll need to pass through a metal detector to get into Sainte-Chapelle. (It's best to leave your Uzi at the hotel.) Walk through the security scanner. Toilets are ahead on the left. The line into the church may be long. (Museum passholders can go directly in.) Enter the humble ground floor...

SAINTE-CHAPELLE

Sainte-Chapelle, the triumph of Gothic church architecture, is a cathedral of glass like no other. It was built in 1248 for St. Louis IX (France's only canonized king) to house the supposed Crown of Thorns. Its

architectural harmony is due to the fact that it was completed under the direction of one architect and in only five years—unheard-of in Gothic times. Recall that Notre-Dame took over 200.

The exterior is ugly. But those fat buttresses are all the support needed to hold up the roof, opening up the walls for stained glass. The design clearly shows an Old Regime approach to worship. The basement was for staff and more common folks. Royal Christians worshiped upstairs. The paint job, a 19th-century restoration, helps you imagine how grand this small, painted, jeweled chapel was. (Imagine Notre-Dame painted like this....)

• *Climb the spiral staircase to the Haute Chapelle. Leave the rough stone of the earth and become enlightened.*

The Stained Glass

Fiat lux. "Let there be light." From the first page of the Bible, it's clear, light is important. Light shining through stained glass was a symbol of God's grace shining down to earth, and Gothic architects used their new technology to turn dark stone buildings into lanterns of light. For me, the glory of Gothic shines brighter here than in any other church.

There are 15 separate panels of stained glass, with more than 1,100 different scenes, mostly from the Bible. In medieval times, scenes like these helped teach Bible stories to the illiterate. These cover the entire

Christian history of the world, from the Creation in Genesis (first window on the left), to the coming of Christ (over the altar), to the end of the world (the round "rose"-shaped window at the rear of the church). Each individual scene is interesting, and the whole effect is overwhelming.

Let's look at a single scene. Head toward the altar to the fourth big window on the right. Look at the bottom circle, second from the left. It's a battle scene (the campaign of Holophernes) showing three soldiers with swords slaughtering three men. The background is blue. The men have

"Stained Glass Supreme"

- Melt one part sand with two parts wood ash to make glass.
- Mix in rusty metals to get different colors—iron makes red, cobalt makes blue, copper/green, manganese/purple, cadmium/yellow.
- Blow glass into a cylinder shape, cut lengthways, and lay flat.
- Cut into pieces with an iron tool, or by heating and cooling a select spot to make it crack.
- Fit pieces together to form a figure, using strips of lead to hold in place.
- Place masterpiece so high on a wall that no one can read it.

different colored clothes—red, blue, green, mauve, and white. Notice some of the details. You can see strands of hair and facial features. Look at the victim in the center—his head is splotched with blood! Details such as the folds in the robes (see the victim in white, lower left) came by either scratching on the glass or by baking in imperfections. It was a painstaking process of finding just the right colors, fitting the pieces together to

It takes 13 tourists to build a Gothic church: six columns, six buttresses, and one steeple.

make a scene...and then multiplying by 1,100. (The sun lights up different windows at different times of day. Overcast days give the most even light. On bright sunny days, some sections are glorious while others look like a sheet of lead.)

Other scenes worth a look:

1) Cain clubbing Abel (first window on the left, second row of circles, far right—Cain is in red).
2) The life of Moses (second window, the bottom row of diamond panels). First panel shows baby Moses in a basket, placed by his sister in the squiggly brown river. Next, he's found by the pharaoh's daughter. Then, he grows up. And finally, he's a man, a prince of Egypt on his royal throne.

3) In the next window (third on left) you'll see various scenes of Moses. He's often given "horns" because of a medieval mistranslation of the Biblical description of his "aura" of holiness.

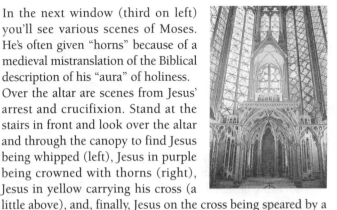

4) Over the altar are scenes from Jesus' arrest and crucifixion. Stand at the stairs in front and look over the altar and through the canopy to find Jesus being whipped (left), Jesus in purple being crowned with thorns (right), Jesus in yellow carrying his cross (a little above), and, finally, Jesus on the cross being speared by a soldier (above, left).

5) Helena, the mother of Constantine (the first Christian Roman emperor), travels to Jerusalem to find relics of Jesus' crucifixion (first window to the right, lowest level).

If you can't read much into the individual windows, you're not alone. As we've all read, stained glass was a way to teach Bible stories to the illiterate medieval masses . . . who apparently owned state-of-the-art binoculars. (In case you don't, a little book with color photos is on sale downstairs with the postcards.) Yes, the windows tell stories, but obviously, their main purpose was to light a dark church in a colorful and decorative way.

The altar was raised up high (notice the staircase for the priest) to better display the relic around which this chapel was built—the Crown of Thorns. This was the crown put on Jesus when the Romans were torturing and humiliating him before his execution. King Louis was convinced he'd found the real McCoy and paid three times as much money for it as was spent on this entire chapel. Today the supposed Crown of Thorns is kept in the Notre-Dame Treasury and shown only on Good Friday.

Notice the little private viewing window in the wall to the right of the altar. Louis was both saintly and shy. He liked to be able to go to

church without dealing with the rigors of public royal life. Here he could worship still dressed in his jammies.

Lay your camera on the ground and shoot the ceiling. Those pure and simple ribs growing out of the slender columns are the essence of Gothic structure.

Palais de Justice

As you walk around the church exterior, look down and notice how much Paris has risen in the 800 years since Sainte-Chapelle was built. You're in a huge complex of buildings that has housed the local government since ancient Roman times. It was the site of the original Gothic palace of the early kings of France. The only surviving medieval parts are Sainte-Chapelle and the Conciergerie prison.

Paris' City Palace in 1650, with Sainte-Chapelle, the Conciergerie, and Pont Neuf (then 30 years old) in the background.

Most of the site is now covered by the giant Palais de Justice, home of France's supreme court, built in 1776. *"Liberté, Egalité, Fraternité"* over the doors is a reminder that this was also the headquarters of the Revolutionary government. Here they doled out justice, condemning many to torture in the Conciergerie downstairs or to have their heads removed by "Monsieur de Paris"—the guillotine.

• *Now pass through the big iron gate to the noisy boulevard du Palais and turn left (toward the Right Bank).*

On the corner is the site of the city's oldest public clock (1334). While the present clock is Baroque, it still manages to keep accurate time.

Turn left onto quai d'Horologe and walk along the river. The round medieval tower just ahead marks the entrance to the Conciergerie. Even if you don't pay to see the Conciergerie, you can visit the courtyard and lobby. Step past the serious-looking guard into the courtyard.

Conciergerie

The Conciergerie, a former prison and place of torture, is a gloomy place. Kings used it to torture and execute failed assassins. The leaders of the Revolution put it to similar good use. The tower next to the entrance, called "the babbler," was named for the painful sounds that leaked from it.

Look at the stark printing above the doorways. This was a nononsense revolutionary time. Everything, including lettering, was subjected to the test of reason. No frills or we chop 'em off.

Marie-Antoinette was imprisoned here. During a busy eight-month period in the Revolution, she was one of 2,600 prisoners kept here on their way to the guillotine.

The interior (requires ticket), with its huge vaulted and pillared rooms, echoes with history but is pretty barren. You can see Marie-Antoinette's cell, with a collection of Marie-Antoinette mementos. In another room, a thought-provoking list of those made "a foot shorter at the top" by the guillotine includes ex-King Louis XVI, Charlotte Corday (who murdered Marat in his bathtub), and the chief Revolutionary who got a taste of his own medicine—Maximilien Robespierre.

• *Back outside, wink at the flak-vested guard, turn left, and continue your walk along the river. Across the river you can see the rooftop observatory of the Samaritaine department store, where we'll end this walk. At the first corner, veer left into a sleepy triangular square called "place Dauphine."*

Place Dauphine

It's amazing to find such coziness in the heart of Paris. This city of two million is still a city of neighborhoods, a collection of villages. The French Supreme Court building looms behind like a giant marble gavel. Enjoy the village-Paris feeling in the park. You may see lawyers on their lunch break playing *boules*.

• *Walk through the park to the statue of Henry IV, who in 1607 inaugurated the Pont Neuf. (If you need a romantic hideaway in the midst of this megacity, take the steps down into the park on the tip of the island and dangle your legs over the prow of this concrete island.) From the statue, turn right onto the old bridge. Walk to the little nook halfway across.*

Pont Neuf

The Pont Neuf, or "new bridge," is now Paris' oldest. Its 12 arches span the widest part of the river. The fine view includes the park on the tip of the island (note Seine boats), the Orsay, and the Louvre. These turrets were originally for vendors and street entertainers. In the days of Henry, who originated the promise of "a chicken in every pot," this would have been a lively scene.

• *The first building you'll hit on the Right Bank is the venerable old department store Samaritaine. Go through the door, veer left, and catch the elevator to the ninth floor. Climb two sets of stairs to the panorama. (Don't confuse the terrace level with the higher, better panorama. Light meals are served on the terrace. Public WCs on fifth and ninth floors.)*

THE REST OF PARIS

From the circular little crow's nest of the building, ponder the greatest skyline in Europe. Retrace the walk you just made, starting with Notre-Dame and Sainte-Chapelle. Then spin counterclockwise (or run down the stairs to hop on the Métro) and check out the rest of Paris:

The **Pompidou Center**, the wild and colorful rectangular tangle of blue and white pipes and tubes, is filled with art that makes this building's exterior look tame (for more information, see page 460).

Sacré-Coeur is a neo-Romanesque church topping Montmartre. This is an atmospheric quarter after dark, its streets filled with strolling tourists avoiding strolling artists.

The **Louvre** is the largest building in Paris, the largest palace in Europe, and the largest museum in the world (see tour on page 107).

Stretching away from the Louvre, the **Tuileries Gardens**, place de la Concorde, and the Champs-Élysées lead to the Arc de Triomphe. The gardens are Paris' "Central Park," filled with families at play, cellists in the shade, carousels, pony rides, and the ghost of Maurice Chevalier.

The gardens overlook the grand **place de la Concorde**, marked by an ancient obelisk, where all of France seems to converge. It was "guillotine central" during the Revolution and continues to be a place of much festivity.

Europe's grandest boulevard, the **Champs-Élysées**, runs uphill from place de la Concorde about 1.5 kilometers to the Arc de Triomphe. While pretty globalized, and with rich-and-single aristocrats more rare than ever, it's still the place you're most likely to see Sylvester Stallone.

Napoleon began constructing the magnificent **Arc de Triomphe** in 1806 to commemorate his victory at the battle of Austerlitz. It was finished in 1836, just in time for the emperor's funeral parade. Today it commemorates heroes of past wars. There's no triumphal arch bigger (50 meters high, 40 meters wide). And, with 12 converging boulevards, there's no traffic circle more thrilling, either behind the wheel or on foot (take the underpass).

Paris, the capital of Europe, is built on an appropriately monumental plan, with an axis that stretches from the Louvre, up the Champs-Élysées, past the Arc de Triomphe, all the way to the modern Grande Arche among the skyscrapers at **La Défense**. (Find the faint shadow of this arch, just above the Arc de Triomphe.)

The **Orsay**, the train-station-turned-art-museum, is just beyond the Louvre on the Left Bank.

The body of Napoleon lies under the gilded dome. The giant

building is **Les Invalides**, designed to house his wounded troops. Today it houses a fine military museum. The **Rodin Museum** is nearby (see tour on page 164).

The **Eiffel Tower** is a 300-meter-high exclamation point built as a temporary engineering stunt to celebrate the 100th anniversary of the French Revolution. Paris decided to let it be an exception to a downtown building code that allows the skyline to be broken only by a few prestigious domes and spires.

The 52-story **Montparnasse Tower**, a city in itself (5,000 workers, 215 meters high), reminds us that, while tourists look for hints of Louis and Napoleon, work-a-day Paris looks to the future.

✤ 11 ✤
VERSAILLES

If you've ever wondered why your American passport has French writing in it, you'll find the answer at Versailles (vehr-sigh). The powerful court of Louis XIV at Versailles set the standard of culture for all of Europe right up to modern times. Versailles was every king's dream palace. Today, if you're planning to visit just one palace in all of Europe, make it Versailles.

ORIENTATION

Cost: €8 (covered with museum pass); €6.20 after 15:30, on Sunday, and for those over 60 or ages 18–25; under 18 free. Admission is payable at entrances A, C, and D. Tours cost extra (see below). The Grand Trianon is €4.25 and the Petit Trianon is €2.60 (both covered with museum pass); one ticket for both is €5.20.

Hours: May–Sept Tue–Sun 9:00–18:30, Oct–April 9:00–17:30, closed Mon, last entry 30 minutes before closing. (Grand and Petit Trianon open at 10:00 year-round.) In summer, Versailles is especially crowded around 10:00 and 13:00, and all day Tue and Sun. Remember, the crowds gave Marie-Antoinette a pain in the neck too, so relax and let them eat cake. For fewer crowds, go early or late: Either arrive by 9:00 (when the palace opens, touring the palace first, then the gardens) or after 15:30 (you'll get a reduced entry ticket, but you'll miss the last guided tours of the day, which generally depart at 15:00). If you arrive midday, see the gardens first and the palace later, at 15:00. The gardens and palace are great late. On my last visit, at 18:00 I was the only tourist in the Hall of Mirrors... even on a Tuesday.

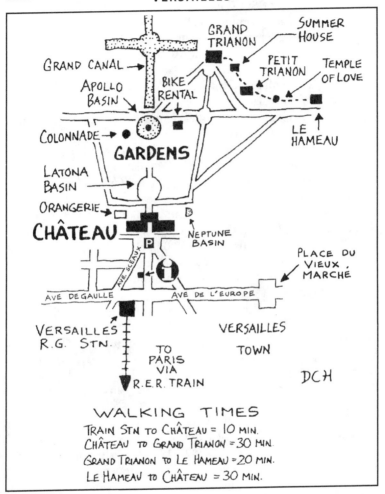

VERSAILLES

WALKING TIMES

TRAIN STN TO CHÂTEAU = 10 MIN.
CHÂTEAU TO GRAND TRIANON = 30 MIN.
GRAND TRIANON TO LE HAMEAU = 20 MIN.
LE HAMEAU TO CHÂTEAU = 30 MIN.

Fountain spectacles: Classical music fills the king's backyard and the garden's fountains are in full squirt on Sat July–Sept and on Sun early April–early Oct (schedule for both days: 11:00–12:00, 15:30–17:00, and 17:20–17:30). On these "spray days," the gardens cost €5.20 (not covered by museum pass). Louis had his engineers literally reroute a river to fuel these fountains. Even by today's standards they are impressive. For more information, pick up the map of the fountain show (*Les Grandes Eaux Musicales*) at any information booth.

Getting there: Take the **RER-C train** (€5 round-trip, 30 min one-way) to Versailles R.G. or "Rive Gauche" (not Versailles C.H., which is farther from the palace). Trains, usually named "Vick," leave about five times an hour for the palace. RER-C trains leave from these RER/Métro stops: Invalides, Champ de Mars, Musée d'Orsay, St. Michel, and Gare d'Austerlitz. Get off at Versailles Rive Gauche (the end of the line), turn right out of the station, and turn left at the first boulevard. It's a 10-minute walk to the palace.

When returning from Versailles, look through the windows past the turnstiles for the departure board. Any train leaving Versailles goes as far as downtown Paris (they're marked: *toutes gares jusqu'à Bibliothèque nationale*—all stations until the National Library).

Allow the local equivalent of €40 each way for a **taxi** from Paris to Versailles.

Information: A helpful tourist information office is just past the Sofitel Hôtel on your walk from the station to the palace (April–Oct daily 9:00–19:00, Nov–March daily 9:00–18:00, tel. 01 39 24 88 88). You'll also find information booths inside the château (doors A, B-2, and C). The useful brochure, "Versailles Orientation Guide," explains your sightseeing options.

Tours: Versailles' highlights are the State Apartments, the lavish King's Private Apartments, the Opera House, and the magnificent Hall of Mirrors. Most visitors are satisfied with a spin through the State Apartments (following my self-guided tour, below), the gardens, and the Trianons. Versailles aficionados should spend the time (and money) for the King's Private Apartments, which can be visited only with an audioguide or live guide (neither tour covered by museum pass).

Self-guided tour—For the basic self-guided tour, join the line at entrance A if you need to pay admission. Those with a museum pass are allowed in through entrance B-2 without a wait. Enter the palace and take a one-way walk through the State Apartments (follow my tour, below) from the "King's Wing," through the Hall of Mirrors, and out via the "Queen's Wing."

Audioguide tours—Two informative but dry audioguide tours are available (€5.20). One tour covers the State Apartments (includes Hall of Mirrors and Queen's Wing; this starts at entrance A or, if you have a museum pass, entrance B-2). The other tour includes more of the King's Private Apartments (Louis XIV) and a sampling of nobles' chambers (this tour starts at entrance C).

Guided tours—You may select a one-hour guided tour of lesser-known nobles' apartments, like those of the well-coiffed Madame

VERSAILLES' ENTRANCES

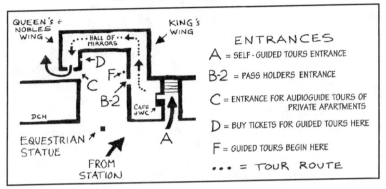

Pompadour (€4.20, several itineraries, join first English tour available). Or consider the 90-minute tour (€6.30) of the King's Private Apartments (Louis XV, Louis XVI, and Marie-Antoinette), chapel, and opera. This tour, which is the only way visitors can see the Opera House, can be long; the occasional dull guide stretches it to eternity. Make reservations for a live tour upon arrival, at entrance D, as tours can sell out by 13:00. Guided tours begin at entrance F.

If you think you might take a guided tour after you've seen the palace on your own, remember to keep your ticket to prove you've already paid for admission.

Length of our tour: Allow two hours for the palace and two for the gardens. Including two hours to cover your round-trip transit time, it's a six-hour day trip from Paris.

Cuisine art: The cafeteria is next to entrance A. You'll find restaurants on the street to the right of equestrian statue of Louis XIV, though the best places line the pleasant market square in the town center (turn right out of the train station, cross the avenue de Paris, and continue about 5 blocks to place du Marché). A handy McDonald's is immediately across from the train station (WC without crowds).

Starring: Louis XIV and the Old Regime.

KINGS AND QUEENS AND GUILLOTINES

• *Read this on the train ride out there. Relax, the palace is the last stop.*

Come the Revolution, when they line us up and make us stick out our hands, will you have enough calluses to keep them from shooting you? A grim thought, but Versailles raises questions like that. It's the symbol of the Old Regime, a time when society was divided into rulers and the ruled, when you were born to be rich or to be poor. To some it's the pinnacle of civilization, to others the sign of a civilization in decay. Either way it remains one of Europe's most impressive sights.

Versailles was the residence of the king and seat of France's government for a hundred years. Louis XIV (reigned 1643–1715) moved out of the Louvre in Paris, the previous royal residence, and built an elaborate palace in the forests and swamps of Versailles, 20 kilometers west. The reasons for the move were partly personal—Louis loved the outdoors and disliked the sniping environs of stuffy Paris—and partly political.

Louis was creating the first modern, centralized state. At Versailles he consolidated Paris' scattered ministries so he could personally control policy. More important, he invited to Versailles all of France's nobles so he could control them. Living a life of almost enforced idleness, the "domesticated" aristocracy couldn't interfere with the way Louis ran things. With 18 million people united under one king (England had only 5.5 million), a booming economy, and a powerful military, France was Europe's number-one power.

Versailles was also the cultural heartbeat of Europe. Every king wanted a palace like Versailles. Everyone learned French. French taste in clothes, hairstyles, table manners, theater, music, art, and kissing spread across the Continent. That cultural dominance has continued to some extent right up to modern times.

Louis XIV

At the center of all this was Europe's greatest king. He was a true Renaissance man, a century after the Renaissance—athletic, good-looking, a musician, dancer, horseman, statesman, art lover, lover. For all his grandeur, he was one of history's most polite and approachable kings, a good listener who could put even commoners at ease in his presence.

Louis called himself the Sun King because he gave life and warmth to all that he touched. He was also thought of as Apollo, the Greek god of the sun. Versailles became the personal temple of this god on earth, decorated with statues and symbols of Apollo, the sun, and Louis himself.

Louis was a hands-on king who personally ran affairs of state. All decisions were made by him. Nobles, whose counterparts in other countries were the center of power, became virtual slaves dependent on Louis' generosity. For 70 years he was the perfect embodiment of the absolute monarch. He summed it up best himself with his famous rhyme—"*L'état, c'est moi!*" ("The state, that's me!").

Only Two More Louises To Remember

Three kings lived in Versailles during its century of glory. Louis XIV built it and established French dominance. Louis XV, his great-grandson (Louis XIV reigned for 72 years), carried on the tradition and policies but without the Sun King's flair. During Louis XV's reign, France's power abroad was weakening and there were rumblings of rebellion from within.

France's monarchy was crumbling, and the time was ripe for a strong leader to reestablish the old feudal order. They didn't get one. Instead, they got Louis XVI, a shy, meek bookworm, the kind of guy who lost sleep over Revolutionary graffiti . . . because it was misspelled. Louis XVI married a sweet girl from the Austrian royal family, Marie-Antoinette, and together they retreated into the idyllic gardens of Versailles while revolutionary fires smoldered.

THE TOUR BEGINS

This tour covers the ceremonial center of the palace (the State Apartments) and the extensive grounds. It begins outside the palace at the equestrian statue of Louis XIV.

The central palace, the part we'll tour, forms a U around the courtyard in front of you. The right half (King's Wing) is separated from the left half (Queen's Wing) by the Hall of Mirrors ahead of you. Then two long wings shoot out to the right and left (north and south) of this U. In this  tour, we'll walk counterclockwise through the U-shaped part on the middle floor.

The Original Château

The part of the palace directly behind the horse statue, at the far end of the courtyard, is the original château. Louis XIV's dad used to come out to the forests of Versailles to escape the worries of kingship. Here he built this small hunting lodge. His son spent the happiest times of his boyhood at the lodge, hunting and riding. Louis XIV's three arched bedroom windows (beneath the clock) overlooked the courtyard. Naturally, it faced the rising sun. The palace and grounds are laid out on an east-west axis.

When he became king, Louis XIV spent more and more time here, away from the hubbub of Paris. He expanded the lodge, planted gardens, and entertained guests. The reputation spread about this "Enchanted Island," a kind of Disneyworld for dukes and duchesses. As visitors flocked here, Louis expanded around the original hunting château, attaching wings to create the present U shape. Then the long north and south wings were built. The total cost of the project has been estimated at half of France's entire GNP for one year.

Think how busy this courtyard must have been 300 years ago. There were as many as 5,000 nobles here at any one time, each with an entourage. They'd buzz from games to parties to amorous rendezvous in sedan-chair taxis. Servants ran about delivering secret messages and roast legs of lamb. Horse-drawn carriages arrived at the fancy gate with their finely dressed passengers, having driven up the broad boulevard that ran direct from Paris. (You can still see the horse stables lining the boulevard.) Incredible as it seems, both the grounds and most of the palace were public territory where even the lowliest peasant could come to gawk. Of course, this meant that there were, then as now, hordes of tourists, pickpockets, and dark-skinned men selling wind-up children's toys.

• *Enter at Entrance A (or at B-2 if you have a museum pass) and buy your ticket. After showing your ticket, pass through the 21 rooms of the history museum, with paintings on the background of Versailles and its kings.*

Our tour starts upstairs, in the room that overlooks the lavish Royal Chapel.

The State Apartments

Royal Chapel

In the vast pagan "temple" that is Versailles, built to glorify one man, Louis XIV, this Royal Chapel is a paltry tip of the hat to that "other" god, the Christian one. It's virtually the first, last, and only hint of Christianity you'll see in the entire complex. Versailles celebrates Man, not God, by raising Louis to almost godlike status, the personification of all good human qualities. In a way, Versailles is the last great flowering of Renaissance humanism and revival of the classical world.

Louis attended mass here every morning. While he sat on the upper level, the lowly nobles below would turn their backs to the altar and look up—worshiping Louis worshiping God. Important religious ceremonies took place here, including the marriage of young Louis XVI to Marie-Antoinette.

• *Take a seat in the next room, a large room with a fireplace and a colorful painting on the ceiling.*

Hercules Drawing Room

Pleasure ruled. The main suppers, balls, and receptions were held in this room. Picture elegant partygoers in fine silks, wigs, rouge, and lipstick (and that's just the men) dancing to the strains of Mozart played by a string quartet.

On the wall opposite the fireplace is an appropriate painting, showing Christ in the middle of a Venetian party. The work by Veronese, a gift from the Republic of Venice, was one of Louis' favorites, so they decorated the room around it.

The ceiling painting of Hercules being crowned a god gives the room its name. Hercules (with his club) rides up to heaven on a chariot, where the king of the gods is ready to give him his daughter in marriage. Louis XIV built the room for his own daughter's wedding reception.

• *The following rooms are listed in order. The names of the rooms generally come from the paintings on the ceilings. From here on it's a one-way tour—getting lost is not allowed. Follow the crowds into the small green room with a goddess in pink on the ceiling.*

The King's Wing

Cornucopia Room

If the party in the Hercules Room got too intense, you could always step in here for some refreshments. Silver trays were loaded up with liqueurs, coffee, juice, chocolates, and, on really special occasions, three-bean salad.

The ceiling painting shows the cornucopia of riches poured down on invited guests. Around the edges of the ceiling are painted versions of the king's actual dinnerware and treasures.

Louis himself might be here. He was a gracious host who enjoyed letting his hair down at night. If he took a liking to you, he might sneak you through those doors there (in the middle of the wall) and into his own private study, where he'd show off his collection of dishes, medals, jewels, or... the *Mona Lisa*, which hung on his wall.

Venus Room

Love ruled at Versailles. In this room, couples would cavort beneath a canopy of golden garlands (on the ceiling) sent down to earth by the goddess of love to ensnare mortals in love. Notice how a painted garland goes "out" the bottom of the central painting, becomes a gilded wood garland held by a satyr, and then turns back to a painting again. Baroque artists loved to mix their media to fool the eye. Another illusion is in the paintings at both ends of the room, which extend this grand room into mythical courtyards.

Don't let the statue of a confident Louis as a Roman emperor fool you. He started out as a poor little rich kid with a chip on his shoulder. His father had died before he was old enough to rule, and, during the regency period, the French Parliament treated little Louis and his mother like trash. They were virtual prisoners, humiliated in their home (the Louvre), surviving on bland meals, hand-me-down leotards, and pointed shoes. Once he attained power and wealth, there was one topic you never discussed in Louis' presence—poverty. Maybe Versailles was his way of saying, "Living well is the best revenge."

Diana Room

This was the billiards room. Men played on a table that stood in the center of the room, while ladies sat surrounding them on Persian-carpet cushions.

The famous bust of Louis by Bernini (now in the center) shows a handsome, dashing, 27-year-old playboy-king. His gaze is steady amid his windblown cloak and hair. Young Louis loved life. He hunted by day (notice Diana the Huntress on the ceiling) and partied by night.

Games were actually an important part of Louis' political strategy known as "the domestication of the nobility." By distracting the nobles with the pleasures of courtly life, he was free to run the government his way. Billiards, dancing, and concerts were popular, but the biggest distraction was gambling, usually a card game similar to blackjack. Louis lent money to the losers, making them even more indebted to him. The good life was an addiction, and Louis kept the medicine cabinet well stocked.

Mars Room

Decorated with a military flair, this was the room for Louis' Swiss bodyguards. On the ceiling there's Mars, the Greek god of war, in a chariot pulled by wolves. The bronze cupids in the corners are escalating from love arrows to heavier artillery. Notice the fat walls that hid thin servants who were to be at their master's constant call—but out of sight when not needed. Don't miss the view of the sculpted gardens out the window.

Mercury Room

Louis' life was a work of art, and Versailles was the display case. Everything he did was a public event designed to show his subjects how it should be done. This room served as Louis' official bedroom, where the Sun King would ritually rise each morning to warm his subjects.

The tapestry on the wall shows how this ceremony might have looked. From a canopied bed, Louis would rise, dress, and take a seat for morning prayer. Meanwhile, the nobles (on the left) stand behind a balustrade, in awe of his piety, nobility, and clean socks. When Louis went to bed at night, the nobles would fight over who got to hold the candle while he slipped into his royal jammies. Bedtime, wake up, and meals were all public rituals.

The two chests that furnish the room, with their curved legs, gilding, and heavy animal feet, are done in the "Louis the XIV" style. Later furniture found in other rooms is lighter, straighter, and less ornamented. The clock dates from Louis' time. When the cocks crowed at the top of the hour and the temple doors opened, guess who popped out?

Apollo Room

This was the grand throne room. Louis held court from a silver-canopied throne three meters high on a raised platform placed in the center of the room. (Notice the four metal bolts in the ceiling that once supported the canopy.)

Everything in here reminds us that Louis was not just any ruler, but the Sun King who lights the whole world with his presence. The ceiling shows Apollo in his chariot, dragging the sun across the heavens every day. Notice the ceiling's beautifully gilded frame and Goldfinger maidens.

In the corners are the four corners of the world—all, of course, warmed by the sun. Counterclockwise from above the exit door are: 1) Europe, with a sword; 2) Asia, with a lion; 3) Africa, with an elephant; and 4) good old America, an Indian maiden with a crocodile.

The famous portrait by Rigaud over the fireplace gives a more human look at Louis. He's shown in a dancer's pose, displaying the legs that made him one of the all-time dancing fools of kingery. At night, they often held parties in this room, actually dancing around the throne.

Louis (who was 63 when this was painted) had more than 300 wigs like this one, and he changed them many times a day. This fashion "first" started when his hairline began to recede, then sprouted all over Europe, spreading even to the American colonies in the time of George Washington.

Louis may have been treated like a god, but he was not an overly arrogant man. His subjects adored him because he was a symbol of everything a man could be, the fullest expression of the Renaissance Man.

The War Room

Versailles was good propaganda. It showed the rest of the world how rich and powerful Louis was. One look at this eye-saturating view of the gardens sent visitors reeling.

But France's success also made other countries jealous and nervous. The semicircles on the ceiling show Germany (with the double eagle), Holland (with its ships), and Spain (with a red flag and roaring lion) ganging up on Louis. Two guesses who won. Of course, these mere mortals were no match for the Sun King. The stucco relief on the wall shows Louis on horseback triumphing over his fallen enemies.

But Louis' greatest triumph may be the next room, the one that everybody wrote home about.

The Hall of Mirrors

No one had ever seen anything like this hall when it was opened. Mirrors were still a great luxury at the time, and the number and size of these monsters were astounding. The hall is 75 meters long (nearly 250 feet). There are 17 arched mirrors matched by 17 windows with that breathtaking view of the gardens. Lining the hall are 24 gilded candelabras, eight

busts of Roman emperors, and eight classical-style statues (seven of them ancient). The ceiling decoration chronicles Louis' military accomplishments, topped off by Louis himself in the central panel (with cupids playing cards at his divine feet), doing what he did best—triumphing.

This was where the grandest festivities were held for the most important ambassadors and guests. The throne could be moved from the Apollo Room and set up at the far end of the hall. Imagine this place filled with guests dressed in silks and powdered wigs, lit by the flames of thousands of candles. The mirrors are a reflection of an age when beautiful people loved to look at themselves. It was no longer a sin to be proud of good looks or fine clothes or to enjoy the good things in life: laughing, dancing, eating, drinking, flirting, and enjoying the view.

From the center of the hall, you can fully appreciate the epic scale of Versailles. The huge palace (by architect Le Vau), the fantasy interior (Le Brun), and the endless gardens (Le Notre) made Versailles *le* best.

In more recent times, the Hall of Mirrors is where the Treaty of Versailles was signed, ending World War I (and, some say, starting World War II).

• *Enter the small Peace Room and grab a bench.*

Peace Room

"Louis Quatorze was addicted to wars..." but, by the end of his life, he was tired of fighting. In this sequel to the War Room, peace is granted to Germany, Holland, and Spain as cupids play with the discarded cannons, armor, and swords.

The oval painting above the fireplace shows 19-year-old Louis bestowing an olive branch on Europe. Beside him is his wife, Marie Therese, cradling their two-year-old twin daughters. If being a father at 17 seems a bit young, remember that Louis was married when he was four.

The Peace Room marks the beginning of the queen's half of the palace. On Sundays the queen held chamber-music concerts here for family and friends.

• *Enter the first room of the Queen's Wing, with its canopied bed.*

The Queen's Wing

Queen's Bedchamber

This was the queen's official bedroom. It was here that she rendezvoused with her husband. Two queens died here. This is where 19 princes were born. The chandelier is where two of them were conceived. Just kidding.

True, Louis was not the most faithful husband. There was no attempt to hide the fact that the Sun King warmed more than one bed, for he was above the rules of mere mortals. Adultery became acceptable—even fashionable—in court circles. The secret-looking doors on either side of the bed were for Louis' late-night liaisons—they lead straight to his rooms.

Some of Louis' mistresses became more famous and powerful than his rather quiet queen, but he was faithful to the show of marriage and had genuine affection for his wife. Their private apartments were connected, and Louis made a point of sleeping with the queen as often as possible, regardless of whose tiara he tickled earlier in the evening.

This room looks just like it did in the days of the last queen, Marie-Antoinette. That's her bust over the fireplace, and the double eagle of her native Austria in the corners. The big chest to the left of the bed held her jewels.

The queen's canopied bed is a reconstruction. The bed, chair, and wall coverings switched with the seasons. This was the cheery summer pattern.

Drawing Room of the Nobles

The queen's circle of friends met here, seated on the stools. Discussions ranged from politics to gossip, food to literature, fashion to philosophy. The Versailles kings considered themselves enlightened monarchs who promoted the arts and new ideas. Folks such as Voltaire—a political radical—and the playwright Molière participated in the Versailles court. Ironically, these discussions planted the seeds of liberal thought that would grow into the Revolution.

Queen's Antechamber

This is where the Royal Family dined publicly while servants and nobles fluttered around them, admiring their table manners and laughing at the king's jokes like courtly Paul Shaeffers. A typical dinner consisted of four different soups, two whole birds stuffed with truffles, plus mutton, ham slices, fruit, pastry, compotes, and preserves.

The central portrait is of luxury-loving, "Let-them-eat-cake" Marie-Antoinette, who became a symbol of decadence to the peasants. The portrait at the far end is a public-relations attempt to soften her image, showing her with three of her nine children.

Queen's Guard Room

On October 6, 1789, a mob of revolutionaries—appalled by their queen's taste in wallpaper—stormed the palace. They were fed up with the life of luxury led by the ruling class in the countryside while they were starving in the grimy streets of Paris.

The king and queen locked themselves in. Some of the revolutionaries got access to this upper floor. They burst into this room, where Marie-Antoinette had taken refuge, then killed three of her bodyguards and dragged her and her husband off. (Some claim that, as they carried her away, she sang "Louis, Louis, oh-oh . . . we gotta go now.")

The enraged peasants then proceeded to ransack the place, taking revenge for the years of poverty and oppression they'd suffered. Marie-Antoinette and Louis XVI were later taken to the place de la Concorde in Paris, where they knelt under the guillotine and were made a foot shorter at the top.

Did the king and queen deserve it? Were the revolutionaries destroying civilization or clearing the decks for a new and better one? Was Versailles progress or decadence?

Coronation Room

No sooner did they throw out a king than they got an emperor. The Revolution established democracy, but it was shaky in a country that wasn't used to it. In the midst of the confusion, the upstart general Napoleon Bonaparte took control and soon held dictatorial powers. This room captures the glory of the Napoleon years, when he conquered most of Europe. In the huge canvas on the left-hand wall, we see him crowning himself emperor of a new, revived "Roman" Empire. (This is a lesser-quality copy of a version hanging in the Louvre.)

Catch the portrait of a dashing, young, charismatic Napoleon by the window on the right. This shows him in 1796, when he was just a general in command of the Revolution's army in Italy. Compare this with the portrait next to it from 10 years later—looking less like a revolutionary and more like a Louis. Above the young Napoleon is a portrait of Josephine, his wife and France's empress. In David's *Distribution of Eagles* (opposite the *Coronation*), the victorious general (in imperial garb) passes out emblems of victory to his loyal troops. In *The Battle of Aboukir* (opposite the window), Napoleon looks rather bored as he slashes through a tangle of dark-skinned warriors. His horse, though, has a look of "What are we doing in this mob? Let's get out of here!" Let's.

• *Pass through a couple of rooms to the exit staircase on your left. The long Battle Gallery ahead of you shows 130 meters of scenes from famous French battles, arranged chronologically clockwise around the gallery. The exit staircase puts you outside on the left (south) side of the palace.*

The Gardens—Controlling Nature

Louis was a divine-right ruler. One way he proved it was by controlling nature like a god. These lavish grounds, so elaborately planned out, pruned, and decorated, showed everyone that Louis was in total command.

• *Exiting the palace into the gardens, veer to the left toward the*

concrete railing about 75 meters away. You'll pass by horse carriages for hire and through flowers and cookie-cutter patterns of shrubs and green cones. Stand at the railing overlooking the courtyard below and the Louis-made lake in the distance.

The Orangerie

The warmth from the Sun King was so great that he could even grow orange trees in chilly France. Louis had a thousand of these to amaze his visitors. In winter they were kept in the greenhouses (beneath your feet) that surround the courtyard. On sunny days they were wheeled out in their silver planters and scattered around the grounds.

• From the stone railing, turn about-face and walk back toward the palace, veering left toward the two large pools of water. Sit on the top stair and look away from the palace.

View down the Royal Drive

This, to me, is the most impressive spot in all of Versailles. In one direction, the palace. Stretching out in the other, the endless grounds. Versailles was laid out along a 12-kilometer axis that included the grounds, the palace, and the town of Versailles itself, one of the first instances of urban planning since Roman times and a model for future capitals such as Washington, D.C., and Brasilia.

Looking down the Royal Drive (also known as "The Green Carpet"), you see the round Apollo fountain way in the distance. Just beyond that is the Grand Canal. The groves on either side of the Royal Drive were planted with trees from all over, laid out in an elaborate grid and dotted with statues and fountains. Of the original 1,500 fountains, 300 remain.

Looking back at the palace, you can see the Hall of Mirrors—it's the middle story, with the arched windows.

• Stroll down the steps to get a good look at the frogs and lizards that fill the round Latona Basin.

The Latona Basin

The theme of Versailles is Apollo, the god of the sun, associated with Louis. This round fountain tells the story of the birth of Apollo and his sister Diana. On top of the fountain are Apollo and Diana as little kids with their mother, Latona (they're facing toward the Apollo fountain). Latona, an unwed mother, was insulted by the local peasants. She called on the king of the gods, Zeus (the children's father), to avenge the insult. Zeus swooped down and turned all the peasants into the frogs and lizards that ring the fountain.

• *As you walk down past the basin toward the Royal Drive, you'll pass by "ancient" statues done by 17th-century French sculptors. The Colonnade is hidden in the woods on the left-hand side of the Royal Drive, about three-fourths of the way to the Apollo Basin.*

The Colonnade

Versailles had no prestigious ancient ruins, so Louis built his own. This prefab Roman ruin is a 33-meter (100 foot) circle of 64 marble columns supporting arches. Beneath the arches are small birdbath fountains. Nobles would picnic in the shade to the tunes of a string quartet, pretending they were the enlightened citizens of the ancient world.

The Apollo Basin

The fountains of Versailles were its most famous attraction, a marvel of both art and engineering. This one was the centerpiece, showing the Sun God—Louis—in his sunny chariot starting his journey across the sky. The horses are half submerged, giving the impression, when the fountains play, of the sun rising out of the mists of dawn. Most of the fountains were only turned on when the king walked by, but this one played constantly for the benefit of those watching from the palace.

All the fountains are gravity powered. They work on the same principle as when you block a hose with your finger to make it squirt. Underground streams feed into smaller pipes at the fountains that shoot the water high into the air.

Looking back at the palace from here, realize that the distance you just walked is only a fraction of this vast complex of buildings, gardens, and waterways. Be glad you don't have to mow the lawn.

The Grand Canal

Why visit Venice when you can just build your own? In an era before virtual reality, this was the next best thing to an actual trip. Couples in gondolas would pole along the waters accompanied by barges with orchestras playing "O Sole Mio." The canal is actually cross-shaped, this being the long arm, 1.5 kilometers from end to end. Of course, this too is a man-made body of water with no function other than pleasing.

The Trianon Area—Retreat from Reality

Versailles began as an escape from the pressures of kingship. In a short time, the palace was as busy as Paris ever was. Louis needed an escape from his escape and built a smaller palace out in the tules. Later, his successors retreated still farther into the garden, building a fantasy world of simple pleasures from which to ignore the real world, which was crumbling all around them.

• *You can rent a bike or catch the TGV tram (5/hr, 4 stops), but the walk is half the fun. It's about a 30-minute walk from here to the end of the tour, plus another 30 minutes to walk back to the palace.*

Grand Trianon

This was the king's private residence away from the main palace. Louis usually spent a couple nights a week here, but the two later Louises spent more and more time retreating.

The facade of this one-story building is a charming combination of pink, yellow, and white, a cheery contrast to the imposing Baroque facade of the main palace. Ahead you can see the gardens through the columns. The king's apartments were to the left of the columns.

The flower gardens were changed daily for the king's pleasure—for new color combinations and "nasal cocktails."

Walk around the palace (to the right) if you'd like, for a view of the gardens and rear facade.

• *Facing the front, do an about-face. The Summer House is not down the driveway but about 200 meters away, along the smaller pathway at about 10 o'clock.*

The Summer House of the French Garden

This small white building with four rooms fanning out from the center was one more step away from the modern world. Here the queen spent summer evenings with family and a few friends, listening to music or playing parlor games. All avenues of *la douceur de vivre*—"the sweetness of living"—were explored. To the left are the buildings of the Menagerie, where cows, goats, chickens, and ducks were bred.

• *Continue frolicking along the path until you run into...*

Petit Trianon

Louis XV developed an interest in botany. He wanted to spend more time near the French Gardens, but the Summer House just wasn't big enough. He built the Petit Trianon (the "small" Trianon), a masterpiece of neoclassical architecture. This gray, cubical building has four distinct facades, each a perfect and

harmonious combination of Greek-style columns, windows, and railings. Walk around it and find your favorite.

Louis XVI and his wife, Marie-Antoinette, made this their home base. Marie-Antoinette was a sweet girl from Vienna who never quite fit in with the fast, sophisticated crowd at Versailles. Here at the Petit Trianon she could get away and recreate the simple home life she remembered from her childhood. On the lawn outside she installed a merry-go-round.

• *Five minutes more will bring you to* . . .

The Temple of Love

A circle of 12 marble Corinthian columns supporting a dome decorates a path where lovers would stroll. Underneath, there's a statue of Cupid making a bow (to shoot arrows of love) out of the club of Hercules. It's a delightful monument to a society whose rich could afford that ultimate luxury, romantic love. When the Revolution came, I bet they wished they'd kept the club.

• *And finally you'll reach* . . .

Le Hameau—The Hamlet

Marie-Antoinette longed for the simple life of a peasant. Not the hard labor of real peasants—who sweated and starved around her—but the fairy-tale world of simple country pleasures. She built this complex of 12 buildings as her own private village.

This was an actual working farm with a dairy, a waterwheel mill, and domestic animals. The harvest was served at Marie's table. Marie didn't do much work herself, but she "supervised," dressed in a plain white muslin dress and a straw hat.

The Queen's House is the main building, actually two buildings connected by a wooden gallery. Like any typical peasant farmhouse, it had a billiard room, library, elegant dining hall, and two living rooms.

Nearby was the small theater. Here Marie and her friends acted out plays far from the rude intrusions of the real world . . .

• *The real world and the main palace are a 30-minute walk to the southeast. Along the way, stop at the Neptune Basin near the palace, an impressive miniature lake with fountains, and indulge your own favorite fantasy.*

AMSTERDAM

RIJKSMUSEUM

VAN GOGH MUSEUM

*A*msterdam today looks much as it did in its Golden Age, the 1600s. It's a retired sea captain of a city, still in love with life, with a broad outlook and a salty story to tell. The canvases that hang in the Rijksmuseum and the Van Gogh Museum tell that story vividly.

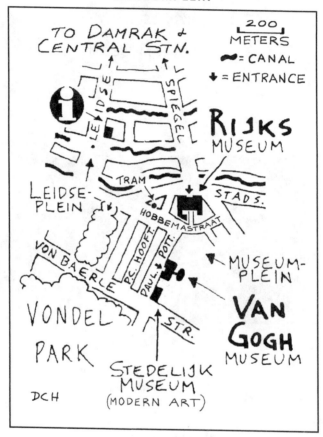

✤ 12 ✤
RIJKSMUSEUM

Holland: windmills, wooden shoes, tulips, cheese, and great artists. In its 17th-century glory days, tiny Holland was a world power—politically, economically, and culturally—with more great masters per kilometer than any other country.

At the Rijksmuseum ("Rijks" rhymes with "yikes"), Holland's Golden Age shines with the best collection around of Rembrandt, Vermeer, Hals, and Steen. And the art we'll see is a clog dance with Holland's past, from humble family meals to the Dutch Masters.

ORIENTATION

Cost: €7; free under age 18; tickets good all day.

Hours: Daily 10:00–17:00, closed only on Jan 1.

Getting there: It's at Stadhousderskade 42, near the Van Gogh Museum. From the train station, catch tram #2, #5, or #20. The trams stop at the rear of the Rijksmuseum on Hobbemastraat; to get to the front of the museum, backtrack to the last intersection and go right a half block.

Information: Helpful info booth has free maps and a good "Tour of the Golden Age" brochure (€0.50). Free 20-minute movies are sometimes shown in English; they are restful and informative but not necessary. The ARIA computer terminals in the room behind Rembrandt's *Night Watch* contain more information on much of the artwork (free to use, small fee only if you print out information). You can also access ARIA from anywhere through the museum's Web site: www.rijksmuseum.nl. Tel. 020/674-7047. WC and phones in basement.

Audioguide tour: The audioguides, which cost about €3.50, cover over 500 of the exhibits with dial-a-number convenience.

Length of our tour: 90 minutes.

Checkrooms: Leave your bag at the free checkrooms at either of the front entrances (East or West). The checkrooms look alike; remember which one you used so you know where to pick up your bag.

Photography: Without a flash is permitted.

Cuisine art: The cafeteria is fine but doesn't have free tap water. The Vondelpark (picnic-perfect park) and Leidseplein (a lively square with cafés) are a couple of blocks away, in different directions.

Starring: Rembrandt, Vermeer, Frans Hals, and Jan Steen.

MUSEUM OVERVIEW

• *The Rijksmuseum, which straddles a road, was built to show off Rembrandt's* Night Watch. *Check your bag at the checkrooms at either of the front entrances, then climb the stairs (or take the elevator). To get oriented, look down the long gallery to* The Night Watch.

Our tour is in about a dozen rooms on this floor to the left of *The Night Watch*. (The right half of the museum is an impressive, but normally ignored, collection of Golden Age hutches and their contents.)

We'll concentrate on only four painters—Rembrandt, Frans Hals, Vermeer, and Jan Steen. All of them lived during Holland's "Golden Age"—the 1600s—when foreign trade made it one of Europe's richest lands. But first, a couple of quick stops to get a feel for Dutch art before its ship came in.

Note: Most of the Rijksmuseum will close for renovation from the fall of 2003 until 2006. During the renovation, the south wing will function as a mini-Rijksmuseum, displaying a sampling of the museum's treasures.

DUTCH ART

Dutch art is meant to be enjoyed, not studied. It's straightforward, meat-and-potatoes art for the common man. The Dutch love the beauty of everyday things painted realistically and with exquisite detail. So set your cerebral cortex on "Low" and let this art pass straight from the eyes to the heart with minimal detours.

• *Start in room 201, located through the glass door (marked "Painting 15th–16th century") at the left end of the lobby. Start with the first painting on your right.*

DUTCH ART BEFORE THE GOLDEN AGE (PRE-1600)

Gelderland School—Eighteen Scenes from the Life of Christ (c. 1435)

In the days when 90 percent of Europe was illiterate, art was Sunday school. These first few rooms are filled with Bible scenes. This painting can be read "page by page," going left to right. "Page 1" is the Annunciation, where an angel tells Mary she'll give birth to Christ. "Page 2" is the birth, "Page 3" is Jesus being circumcised, then the visit of the Three Wise Men, and so on through Jesus' arrest, execution, and resurrection. I like the next-to-last scene of Jesus ascending into heaven. Holy toes.

• *Pass through the next room to reach room 203.*

Attributed to Jan Mostaert— *The Tree of Jesse* (c. 1520)

Here we see Jesus' family tree—literally. At the top is Mary with the baby Jesus. His ancestors are below—David (with the harp), Solomon (with

RIJKSMUSEUM TOUR

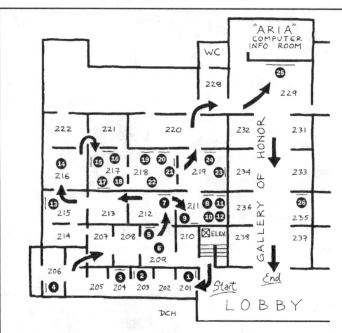

1. Eighteen Scenes from the Life of Christ
2. The Tree of Jesse
3. Feast of the Golden Calf
4. Christ in the House of Mary and Martha

5. HALS – The Merry Drinker
6. Various still lifes

7. AVERCAMP – Winter Scene

8. REMBRANDT – Self-Portrait, Age 22
9. REMBRANDT – The Musical Allegory
10. REMBRANDT – Portrait of Saskia
11. REMBRANDT – Jeremiah Lamenting the
        Destruction of Jerusalem
12. REMBRANDT – Portrait of Maria Trip

13. The Threatened Swan
14. Various landscapes and seascapes

15. REMBRANDT – St. Peter's Denial
16. REMBRANDT – The Jewish Bride
17. REMBRANDT – De Staalmeesters
18. REMBRANDT – Self-Portrait as the
        Apostle Paul

19. VERMEER – The Kitchen Maid
20. VERMEER – Young Woman Reading
        a Letter
21. VERMEER – The Love Letter
22. VERMEER – The Little Street

23. STEEN – The Feast of St. Nicholas
24. STEEN – The Merry Family

25. REMBRANDT – The Night Watch
26. HALS – Wedding Portrait of
        Isaac and Beatrix

the scepter), and others stacked like an early version of *Hollywood Squares.* Again, this is an instructional aid for the illiterate masses. But notice the care the artist has taken with the little details, especially the beautiful faces, clothes, and scepters. The painting is packed with pretty things to please the eye.

• *Walk through the next room of mostly religious scenes, stopping in room 205 at a colorful three-panel work.*

Lucas Van Leyden—*The Feast of the Golden Calf* (c. 1530)

The Dutch love to fill a picture with people having a good time. Here, folks in colorful robes are exchanging good food, wine, and conversation in an outdoor setting. It's a pleasant scene to look at.

Or is it? What are those people in the background dancing around? A golden idol. And who are the two tiny, faint figures in the dark distance at the foot of a smoking mountain? It's Moses (with tablets of stone) and Aaron.

Their leader's been away, and the children of Israel play. Everyone's partying, but nobody's smiling. They're trying desperately to enjoy themselves in Sinai's Red-Light District. Look at the couple making out in the right panel. She's kissing him, but he's thinking about what will happen when Moses gets back.

• *Now enter room 206 and find a large, appetizing painting.*

Joachim Bueckelaer—*Christ in the House of Mary and Martha* (1566)

Here we see the Dutch painters' favorite subject. While Italians painted saints, angels, and Madonnas, the Dutch painted...food. For the middle-class merchant, food was a religion, and he worshiped thrice daily. Notice the delicious realism—the skin of the martyred birds, the temptation of the melons, the artichokes in ecstasy. The sacred detail! You can practically count the hares' hairs.

But this too is a Bible scene. In the faint background someone is preaching. The title is *Christ in the House of Mary and Martha.*

Compare the sketchy, sloppy work on Christ with the painstaking detail of the food. Dutch priorities.

• *Leave the medieval world through the glass doors into the Golden Age. Scan the paintings as you pass through two rooms to reach room 209.*

THE GOLDEN AGE (1600S)

Who bought this art? Look around and you'll see—ordinary middle-class people, merchants, and traders. Even in their Sunday best, you can see that these are hardworking, businesslike, friendly, simple people (with a penchant for ruffled lace collars).

Dutch fishermen sold their surplus catch in distant areas of Europe, importing goods from these far lands. In time, fishermen became traders, and, by 1600, Holland's merchant fleets ruled the waves with colonies as far away as India, Indonesia, and America (New York was originally "New Amsterdam"). The Dutch slave trade—selling Africans to Americans—generated a lot of profit for luxuries such as the art you're looking at.

Look around again. Is there even one crucifixion? One saint? One Madonna? OK, maybe one. But this is people art, not church art. In most countries, Catholic bishops and rich kings supported the arts. But the Republic of the Netherlands, recently free of Spanish rule and Vatican domination, was independent, democratic, and largely Protestant, with no taste for saints and Madonnas.

Instead, Dutch burghers bought portraits of themselves, and pretty, unpreachy, unpretentious works for their homes. Even poor people bought smaller canvases by "no-name" artists designed to fit the budgets and lifestyles of this less-than-rich-and-famous crowd. We'll see examples of their four favorite subjects—still lifes (of food and everyday objects), landscapes, portraits (often of groups), and scenes from everyday life.

• *In room 209 . . .*

Frans Hals—*The Merry Drinker*

You're greeted by a jovial man in a black hat. Notice the details—the happy red face of the man offering us a glass of wine, the sparkle in his eyes, the lacy collar, the decorative belt buckle, and so on.

Now move in closer. All these meticulous details are accomplished with a few quick, thick, and messy brush strokes. The beard is a tangle of brown worms, the belt buckle a yellow blur. His hand is a study in smudges. Even the expressive face is done with a few well-chosen patches of color. Unlike the still-life scenes, this canvas is meant to be viewed from a distance where the colors and brush strokes blend together.

Frans Hals (c. 1580–1666) was the premier Golden Age portrait painter. Merchants hired him like we'd hire a wedding photographer. With a few quick strokes, Hals captured not only the features but the personality.

Rather than posing his subject, making him stand for hours saying "cheese," Hals tried to catch him at a candid moment. He often painted common people, fishermen, and barflies such as this one. He had to work quickly to capture the serendipity of the moment.

Two centuries later the Impressionists learned from Hals' messy brushwork. In the Van Gogh Museum, you'll see how van Gogh painted, say, a brown beard by using thick dabs of green, yellow, and red that blend at a distance to make brown.

• *Also in room 209, ponder the…*

Various Still Lifes (c. 1630)

The Dutch people love their homes, cultivating them like gardens until they're immaculate, decorative, and well ordered. This same sense of pride is reflected in Dutch still lifes such as these, where everyday objects are arranged in the most attractive way possible. They showed expensive delicacies, like lemons from the south, or those most rare and exotic of spices of the time…salt and pepper.

Pick one. Get so close that the guard joins you. Linger over the little things: the pewterware, the seafood, the lemon peels, the rolls, and the glowing goblets that cast a warm reflection on the tablecloth. You'd swear you can see yourself reflected in the pewter vessels. At least you can see the faint reflections of the food and even of the surrounding room. The closer you get, the better it looks.

• *Enter room 212.*

Avercamp—*Winter Scene*

A song or a play is revealed to the audience at the writer's pace. But in a painting, we set the tempo, choosing where to look and how long to linger.

Exercise your right to loiter at this winter scene by Hendrick Avercamp. Avercamp, who was deaf and mute and unfamiliar with the structure of music or theater, would never want to force your attention in any direction. But I will. Can you find the couple making out in the hay-tower silo? Also, there's a "bad moon on the rise" in the broken-down outhouse at left, and another nearby. The whole scene is viewed from a height (the horizon line is high), making it seem as if the fun goes on forever. Just skate among these Dutch people—rich, poor, lovers hand in hand, kids, and moms—and appreciate the silent beauty and this intimate look at old Holland.

• *Enter room 211.*

Rembrandt—Early Works

Rembrandt van Rijn (1606–1669) is the greatest Dutch painter. Whereas most painters specialized in one field—portraits, landscapes, still lifes—Rembrandt excelled in them all.

• *Look for the following Rembrandts in room 211.*

Rembrandt—*Self-Portrait, Age 22*

Rembrandt was a precocious kid. His father insisted he be a lawyer. His mother hoped he'd be a preacher (look for a portrait of her reading the Bible, nearby). Rembrandt combined the secular and religious worlds by becoming an artist, someone who can hint at the spiritual by showing us the beauty of the created world.

He moved to Amsterdam and entered the highly competitive art world. Amsterdam was a booming town and, like today, a hip and cosmopolitan city.

Here we see the young country boy about to launch himself into whatever life has to offer. But, even at this youthful age, he is something of a mystery. Rembrandt portrays himself divided—half in light, half hidden by hair and shadows—looking out but wary of an uncertain future.

Rembrandt—*Musical Allegory* (1626)

Rembrandt's paintings are, of course, highly sought after today. This rather crude, early work was lost for centuries, hidden unknown in some attic, discovered by accident and sold at auction for a small fortune. Painted when Rembrandt was 19, it's actually a portrait of his own family in funny costumes—his father (in turban), mother, grandmother, and himself standing in back.

By the way, of the 500 so-called Rembrandts in existence, 100 have been officially declared fakes by a panel of Dutch experts, with some 50 more under serious scrutiny.

Most of the fakes are not out-and-out forgeries but works executed by his adoring students. In this room and elsewhere, you'll see real Rembrandts, paintings by others that look like his, portraits of Rembrandt by his students, and one or two "Rembrandts" that may soon be "audited" by the Internal Rembrandt Service. So be careful the next time you plunk down $4 million for a "Rembrandt."

Rembrandt—*Portrait of Saskia* (1633)

It didn't take long for Amsterdam to recognize Rembrandt's great talent. Everyone wanted his or her portrait done by the young master. He became wealthy and famous. He fell in love with and married the rich, beautiful, and cultured Saskia. By all accounts, the two were enormously happy, entertaining friends, decorating their house with fine furniture, raising a family, and living the high life. In this wedding portrait (thought to be Saskia), her face literally glows. Barely 30 years old, Rembrandt was the most successful painter in Holland. He had it all.

Rembrandt—*Jeremiah Lamenting the Destruction of Jerusalem* (1630)

The Babylonians have sacked and burned Jerusalem. But what's important for Rembrandt isn't the pyrotechnics (in the murky background at left). That's for Spielberg and the big screen. Instead, Rembrandt tells us the whole story of Israel's destruction in the face of the prophet who predicted the disaster. Jeremiah is deep in thought, confused, and despondent, trying to understand why this evil had to happen. Rembrandt turns his floodlight of truth on the prophet's face.

Rembrandt wasn't satisfied cranking out portraits of fat merchants in frilled bibs, no matter what they paid him. He wanted to experiment, trying new techniques and more probing subjects. Many of his paintings weren't commissioned and were never even intended for sale. His subjects could be brooding and melancholy, a bit "dark" for the public's taste. So was his technique.

You can recognize a Rembrandt canvas by his play of light and dark. Most of his paintings are a deep brown tone, with only a few bright spots glowing from the darkness. This allows Rembrandt to "highlight" the details he thinks are most important.

Light has a primal appeal to humans. (Dig deep into your DNA and remember the time when fire, a sacred thing, was not tamed. Light! In the middle of the night! This miracle separated us from our fellow animals.) Rembrandt strikes us at that instinctive level.

Rembrandt—*Portrait of Maria Trip* (1639) ·

When he chose to, Rembrandt could dash off a commissioned portrait like nobody's business. The surface details are immaculate—the clothing, the pearls behind the veil, the subtle face and hands. But Rembrandt gives us not just a person but a personality. This debutante daughter of a wealthy citizen is shy and reserved, maybe a bit awkward in her new dress and adult role, but still self-assured.

Look at the rings around her eyes, a detail a lesser painter would have air-brushed out. Rembrandt takes this feature unique to her and uses it as a setting for her luminous, jewel-like eyes. Without being prettified, she's beautiful.
• *Backtrack to room 212 (which has Avercamp's* Winter Scene)*, and continue straight through 213 to reach 215.*

Shhh . . . Dutch Art
You can be sitting at home late one night and it's perfectly quiet. Not a sound, very peaceful. And then . . . the refrigerator motor turns off . . . and it's *really* quiet.

Dutch art is really quiet art. It silences our busy world so that every sound, every motion is noticed. You can hear sheep tearing off grass 50 meters away. Dutch art is still. It slows our fastlane world so we notice the motion of birds. We notice how the cold night air makes the stars

sharp. We notice that the undersides of leaves and of cats are always a lighter shade than the tops. Dutch art stills the world so we can hear our own heartbeat and reflect upon that most noble muscle that without thinking gives us life.

To see how subtle Dutch art is, realize that the most exciting, dramatic, emotional, and extravagant Dutch painting in this whole museum is probably *The Threatened Swan* on the wall in front of you. Quite a contrast to the rape scenes and visions of heaven of Italian Baroque from the same time period.

• *Continue to room 216.*

Various Landscapes, Seascapes and Church-scapes

The things that we think of as typically Dutch—windmills, flowers, wooden shoes—are products of the flat, wet Dutch countryside. The windmills used wind power to pump water out of the soil, reclaiming land that was once part of the sea. To walk on the marshy farmland, you needed wooden shoes. The sandy soil wasn't the best for farming, but tulips (originally from Turkey) flourished.

The seascapes remind us that this great art was financed by wealth from a far-flung trading empire. And the meticulous paintings of church interiors tell us of the meticulous, hardworking nature of the country's people, who made good with little to start with. As the saying goes: "God made the Dutch; the Dutch made Holland."

• *Enter room 217.*

Rembrandt—Later Works

In our last episode, we left Rembrandt at the height of fame, wealth, and happiness. He may have had it all, but not for long. The commissions came more slowly. The money ran out. His wife, Saskia, died. His mother died. One by one his sons died. He had to auction off his paintings and furniture to pay debts. He moved out of his fine house to humble lodgings. His bitter losses added a new wisdom to his work.

Rembrandt—*St. Peter's Denial* (1660)

Jesus has been arrested as a criminal. Here, his disciple Peter has followed him undercover to the prison to check on the proceedings. The young girl recognizes Peter and asks him, "Don't you know Jesus?" Peter, afraid of being arrested by the Romans, denies it.

Here we see Peter as he answers the girl's question. He must decide where his loyalties lie. With the Roman soldier who glares at him suspiciously from the left, not buying Peter's story at all? Or with his doomed master in the dark background on the right looking knowingly over his shoulder, understanding Peter's complicated situation? Peter must choose. The confusion and self-doubt are written all over his face. He has told his lie and now he's stuck with it.

The strong contrasts of light and dark heighten the drama of this psychologically tense scene. The soldier is a blotch of brown. Jesus is a distant shadowy figure, a lingering presence in Peter's conscience. The center of the picture is the light shining through the girl's translucent fingers, glowing like a lamp as she casts the light of truth on Peter. Peter's brokenhearted betrayal and sense of guilt could only have been portrayed by an older, wiser—and perhaps himself guilt-ridden—Rembrandt.

Rembrandt—*The Jewish Bride* (1662)

A melancholy though touching painting is the uncommissioned portrait

known as *The Jewish Bride*. This is a truly human look at the relationship between two people in love. The man gently draws the woman toward him. She's comfortable enough with him to sink into thought, but she still reaches up unconsciously to return the gentle touch. The touching hands form the center of this somewhat sad but yes-saying work. Van Gogh said: "Rembrandt alone has that tenderness—the heartbroken tenderness."

Rembrandt—*De Staalmeesters* (1662)

While commissions were rare, Rembrandt could still paint a portrait better than anyone. Here, in the painting made famous by Dutch Masters cigars, he catches the Draper's Guild in a natural but dignified pose (except, perhaps, for the guy who looks like he's sitting on his friend's lap). They've gathered around a table to examine the company's books. They look up spontaneously, as though we've just snapped our fingers to catch their attention. It's as natural as a snapshot, though radiographs show Rembrandt made many changes in posing them perfectly. Even in this simple portrait we feel we can read the guild members' personalities in their faces.

Rembrandt—*Self-Portrait as the Apostle Paul* (1661)

Perhaps Rembrandt's greatest legacy is his many self-portraits. They show us the evolution of a great painter's style as well as the progress of a genius' life. For Rembrandt, the two were intertwined.

Compare this later self-portrait with the youthful, curious Rembrandt of age 22 we saw earlier. This man has seen it all—success, love, money, fatherhood, loss, poverty, death. He took these experiences and wove them into his art. Rembrandt died poor and misunderstood, but he remained very much his own man to the end.

• *Continue to room 218. The only thing quiet and still about this often-crowded Vermeer room is its paintings.*

Vermeer (1632–1675)

Jan Vermeer is the master of quiet and stillness. He creates a clear and silent pool that is a world in itself. The Rijksmuseum has the best collection of Vermeers in the world—all four of them. (There are only 30 in captivity.) But each is a small jewel worth lingering over.

Vermeer—*The Kitchen Maid*

Shhh... This painting is so calm, you can practically hear the milk pouring into the bowl.

Vermeer brings out the beauty in everyday things. The subject is ordinary, a kitchen maid, but you could look for hours at the tiny details and rich color tones. These are common objects, but we see them as though for the very first time, glowing in a diffused light: the

crunchy crust, the hanging basket, even the nail in the wall with its tiny shadow. The maid is alive with radiant yellow, blue, and white. She is content, solid, and sturdy. Her full arms seem constructed by reflected light. Vermeer squares off a little world in itself (framed by the table in the foreground, the wall in back, the window to the left, and the foot stool at right), then fills this space with objects for our perusal.

Vermeer—*Young Woman Reading a Letter*

Vermeer's placid scenes also have an air of mystery. Something is being revealed to the girl, but we don't know what it is. She is reading a letter. From whom? A lover? A father away at sea? Not even taking time to sit down, she reads it intently, with parted lips and a bowed head. It must be important.

Again, Vermeer has framed off a moment of everyday life. But within this small world are hints of a wider, wilder world. The light coming from the left is obvious-

ly from a large window, giving us a whiff of a much broader world outside. The map hangs prominently, reminding us of travel to exotic lands, most likely where the sender of the letter is.

Vermeer—*The Love Letter*

There's a similar theme here. The curtain is parted, and we see through the doorway into one world, then through the seascape on the back wall to the wide ocean. The mysterious letter brought by the servant intrudes like a pebble dropped into the tide pool of Vermeer's quiet world.

Vermeer—*The Little Street*

Vermeer lived his whole life in the quiet, picturesque town of Delft. This is the view from his front door.

Here, the details actually aren't very detailed—the "cobblestone" street doesn't have a single individual stone in it. What Vermeer wants to show us is the beautiful interplay of colored rectangles on the buildings. Our eye moves back and forth from shutter to gable to window...and then from front to back as we notice the woman deep in the alleyway.

• *Continue to room 219.*

Jan Steen (1626–1679)

Not everyone could afford a masterpiece, but even the poorer people wanted works for their own homes (the way some people today put a Sears landscape over the sofa). Jan Steen, the Norman Rockwell of his day, painted humorous scenes from the lives of the lower classes.

Jan Steen—
The Feast of St. Nicholas

It's Christmastime, and the kids have been given their gifts. A little girl got a doll. The mother says, "Let me see it," but the girl turns away playfully.

Everyone is happy except... the boy who's crying. His Christmas present is only a rod in his shoe—like coal in your stocking, the gift for bad boys. His sister gloats and passes it around gleefully. The kids laugh at him. But wait, it turns out the family is just playing a trick. In the background, the grandmother is beckoning to him saying, "Look, I have your real present in here." Out of the limelight but smack in the middle sits the father providing ballast to this family scene.

Steen has frozen the moment, sliced off a piece, and laid it on a canvas. He's told a story with a past, present, and future. These are real people in a real scene.

Steen's fun art reminds us that museums aren't mausoleums.

• *In the same room . . .*

Jan Steen—*The Merry Family* (1668)

This family is eating, drinking, and singing like there's no tomorrow. The broken eggshells and scattered cookware are symbols of waste and extravagance. The neglected proverb tacked to the fireplace reminds us that children will follow the footsteps of their parents. The father in this jolly scene is very drunk—ready to topple over—while in the fore-

ground his mischievous daughter is feeding her brother wine straight from the flask. Mom and Grandma join the artist himself (playing the bagpipes) in a raucous singalong, but the child learning to smoke would rather follow dad's lead. Today, the Dutch describe such a family as a "Jan Steen household."

• *Pass through rooms 220, 227, and 228 to reach the Gallery of Honor and the museum's centerpiece.*

Rembrandt—*The Night Watch*

• *The best viewing spot is to the right of center. This is the angle Rembrandt had in mind when he designed it for its original location.*

This is Rembrandt's most famous—though not necessarily greatest— painting. Done in 1642 when he was 36, it was one of his most important commissions—a group portrait of a company of Amsterdam's civic guards to hang in their meeting hall.

This is an action shot. The guardsmen (who, by the 1640s, were really only an honorary militia of rich bigwigs) are spilling into the street from a large doorway in the back. It's all for one and one for all as they rush to the rescue of Amsterdam. Flags are flying, the drummer beats a march cadence, the soldiers grab lances and load their muskets. In the center, the commander steps forward energetically with a hand gesture that seems to say, "What are we waiting for? Let's move out!"

Why is *The Night Watch* so famous? Compare it with the less famous group portraits on either side of the room. Every face is visible. Everyone is well lit, flat, and flashbulb perfect. These people paid good money to have their mugs preserved for posterity, and they wanted it right up front. These colorful, dignified, and relaxed works are certainly the work of a master... but not quite masterpieces.

By contrast, Rembrandt rousted the Civic Guards off their fat duffs. He took posers and turned them into warriors. He turned a simple portrait into great art.

By adding movement and depth to an otherwise static scene, Rembrandt caught the optimistic spirit of Holland in the 1600s. Their war of independence from Spain was heading to victory, and their economy was booming. These guardsmen on the move epitomize the proud, independent, upwardly mobile Dutch.

The Night Watch. *Rembrandt makes this much more than a group portrait. It's an action scene, capturing the can-do spirit of the Golden Age.*

OK, some *Night Watch* scuttlebutt: First off, "The Night Watch" is a misnomer. It's a daytime scene, but, over the years, as the preserving varnish darkened and layers of dirt built up, the sun set on this painting, and it got its popular title. When the painting was moved to a smaller room, the sides were lopped off (and the pieces lost), putting the two main characters in the center and causing the work to become more static than intended. During World War II, the painting was rolled up and hidden for five years. More recently, a madman attacked the painting, slicing the captain's legs (now skillfully repaired).

The Night Watch, contrary to common myth, was a smashing success in its day. However, there are elements in it that show why Rembrandt soon fell out of favor as a portrait painter. He seemed to spend as much time painting the dwarf and the mysterious glowing girl with a chicken (the very appropriate mascot of this "militia" of shopkeepers) as he did the faces of his employers.

Rembrandt's life darkened long before his *Night Watch* did. This work marks the peak of Rembrandt's popularity... and the beginning of his fall from grace. He continued to paint masterpieces. Free from the dictates of employers whose taste was in their mouths, he painted what he wanted, how he wanted it. Rembrandt goes beyond mere craftsmanship to probe into and draw life from the deepest wells of the human soul.

• *As you walk down the Gallery of Honor to return to the entrance, stop at room 235.*

Frans Hals—*Wedding Portrait of Isaac Abrahamsz Massa and Beatrix van der Laen* (1622)

In this wedding portrait of a chubby, pleasant merchant and his bride, Hals sums up the story of the Golden Age. This overseas trader was away from home for years at a time on business. So Hals makes a special effort to point out his patron's commitment to marriage. Isaac has his hand over his heart as a pledge of fidelity.

Beatrix's wedding ring is prominently displayed, dead center between them (on her right-hand forefinger, Protestant style). The vine clinging to a tree is a symbol of man's support and woman's dependence. And in the distance at right, in the classical love garden, are other happy couples strolling arm in arm amid peacocks, a symbol of fertility.

Hals didn't need symbolism to tell us that these two are prepared for their long-distance relationship—they seem relaxed together, but they each look at us directly, with a strong, individual identity. Good as gold, these are the type of people that propelled this soggy little country into its glorious Golden Age.

VAN GOGH MUSEUM

The Van Gogh Museum (we say "van-GO," the Dutch say "van-HOCK") is a cultural high even to those "not into art." It's a short, well-organized, and user-friendly look at the art of one fascinating man. If you like bright-colored landscapes in the Impressionist style, you'll like this museum. If you enjoy finding deeper meaning in works of art, you'll really love it. The mix of van Gogh's creative genius, his tumultuous life, and the traveler's determination to find meaning in it makes this museum as much a walk with Vincent as with his art.

ORIENTATION

Cost: €7; free under age 13; €2 for ages 13–17 and for those with one ear. Exhibitions are held in the new wing. During the special Van Gogh/Gauguin exhibition, held from Feb. 9 to June 2 in 2002, the museum costs more (€13, includes audioguide), and it's open longer (9:00–21:00 except Mon and Thu 9:00–18:00). It also requires the advance purchase of a ticket with an entry time (see www.vangoghgauguin.com).

Hours: Daily 10:00–18:00, closed only on Jan 1.

Getting there: It's at Paulus Potterstraat 7. From the Central Station, catch tram #2, #5, or #20 to Hobbemastraat, behind the Rijksmuseum.

Information: The free floor plan contains a brief history of the artist's short life. The bookstore has posters (with tubes). Tel. 020/570-5200, www.vangoghmuseum.nl.

Audioguide tour: Audioguides rent for €4 at the "Acoustiguide" desk.

Length of our tour: One hour.
Checkroom: Free and mandatory.
Photography: No cameras allowed.
Starring: Take it, Vincent.

MUSEUM OVERVIEW

The core of the museum and this entire *Mona* tour is on the first floor (one flight up from the ground floor). The bookstore and pricey cafeteria are on the ground floor. The top two floors contain more van Goghs, including his drawings, and works by his friends and colleagues such as Gauguin and Toulouse-Lautrec. The new wing (accessed from the ground floor by going down the escalator) was built to showcase exhibitions. Each exhibition runs for a couple of months and focuses on an artistic theme (which may or may not involve van Gogh).

The paintings on the first floor are arranged chronologically, taking us through the changes in van Gogh's life and styles. Some background on Vincent's star-crossed life makes the museum even better, so I've included liberal doses of biographical material.

The paintings are divided into five periods of van Gogh's life—Netherlands, Paris, Arles, St. Remy, and Auvers-sur-Oise—proceeding clockwise around the floor. (Although the busy curators frequently move the paintings around, they *usually* keep them within the same room, so if you don't see, for example, a particular "Arles" painting at the position indicated on our map, look around the "Arles" room.)
• *Before heading upstairs to the paintings, find a seat to read about. . .*

The Artist

"I am a man of passions. . ."

You can see van Gogh's canvases as a series of suicide notes . . . or as the record of a life full of beauty—too full of beauty. He attacked life with a passion, experiencing life's highs and lows more intensely than the average person. The beauty of the world overwhelmed him, and its ugliness struck him as only another dimension of beauty. He tried to absorb all of life, good and bad, and channel it onto a canvas. The frustration of this overwhelming task drove him to madness. If all this is a bit overstated—and I guess it is—it's an attempt to show the emotional impact van Gogh's works have had on many people, myself included.

Van Gogh's life and art were one. His style changed with his circumstances and changing mood. For each painting, I'll give a little background material and let the work itself say the rest. Since the museum divides his life and art into distinct periods, let's do the same.

VAN GOGH MUSEUM—OVERVIEW 2ND FLOOR

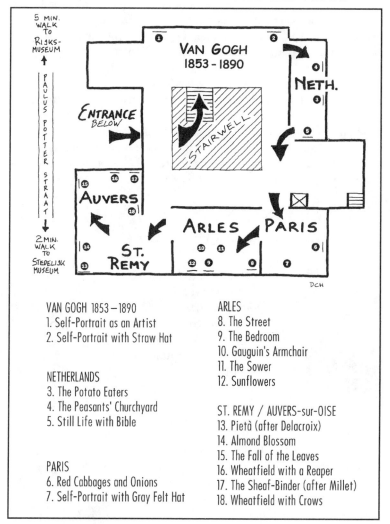

VAN GOGH 1853–1890
1. Self-Portrait as an Artist
2. Self-Portrait with Straw Hat

NETHERLANDS
3. The Potato Eaters
4. The Peasants' Churchyard
5. Still Life with Bible

PARIS
6. Red Cabbages and Onions
7. Self-Portrait with Gray Felt Hat

ARLES
8. The Street
9. The Bedroom
10. Gauguin's Armchair
11. The Sower
12. Sunflowers

ST. REMY / AUVERS-sur-OISE
13. Pietà (after Delacroix)
14. Almond Blossom
15. The Fall of the Leaves
16. Wheatfield with a Reaper
17. The Sheaf-Binder (after Millet)
18. Wheatfield with Crows

Early Years (1853–1880)—Wandering

Vincent was a pastor's son from a small Dutch town. At 16 he went to work as a clerk for an art dealership. But his two interests, art and religion, distracted him from his dreary work and, after several years, he was finally fired.

The next 10 years are a collage of dead ends as he travels northern

Europe pursuing one path after another. He'd launch into each project with incredible energy, then get disillusioned and move on to something else: teacher at a boarding school, assistant preacher, bookstore apprentice, preacher again, theology student, English student, literature student, art student. He bounces around England, France, Belgium, and the Netherlands. He falls in love but is rejected for someone more respectable. He quarrels with his family and is exiled. He lives with a prostitute and her daughter, offending the few friends he has. Finally, in his late twenties, worn out, flat broke, and in poor health, he returns to his family in Nuenen in the Netherlands and makes peace. He starts to paint.

• *Climb the stairs to the first floor. The first room is an introduction to van Gogh, illustrated with some self-portraits. He painted both of the following during his stay in Paris.*

VINCENT VAN GOGH
(1853–1890)

Self-Portrait in Front of the Easel (1888)

"I am now living with my brother Vincent who is studying the art of painting with indefatigable zeal."
    —Theo to a friend

Here Vincent proudly displays his new palette full of bright new colors, trying his hand at the Impressionist technique of building a scene using dabs of different colored paint. A whole new world of art—and life—opened up to him in Paris.

Self-Portrait with Straw Hat (1887)

"You wouldn't recognize Vincent, he has changed so much . . . The doctor says that he is now perfectly fit again. He is making tremendous strides with his work . . . He is also far livelier than he used to be and is popular with people."
    —Theo to their mother

The shimmering effect from Impressionist paintings comes from the technique of placing dabs of different colors side by side on the canvas. At a distance, the two colors blend in the eye of the viewer to become a third color. For example, here van Gogh uses separate strokes of blue, yellow, green, and red to create a brown beard—but a brown that throbs with excitement.

• *Let's go back in time to begin a chronological look at his art. For his stark, early work, enter the next room . . .*

The Netherlands (1880–1885)— Poverty and Religion

These dark gray canvases show us the hard, plain existence of the people and town of Nuenen in rural, southern Netherlands. We see simple buildings, bare or autumn trees, and overcast skies, a world where it seems spring will never arrive. What warmth there is comes from the sturdy, gentle people themselves.

The style is crude—van Gogh couldn't draw very well, nor would he ever be a great technician. The paint is laid on thick, as though painted with Nuenen mud. The main subject is almost always dead center, with little or no background, so there's a claustrophobic feeling. We are unable to see anything but the immediate surroundings.

The Potato Eaters (1885)

"Those that prefer to see the peasants in their Sunday best may do as they like. I personally am convinced I get better results by painting them in their roughness . . . If a peasant picture smells of bacon, smoke, potato steam—all right, that's healthy."

Van Gogh had dabbled as an artist during his wandering years, sketching things around him and taking a few art classes, but it wasn't until he was 30 that he threw himself into it with abandon.

He painted the poor working peasants. He had worked as a lay minister among the poorest of the poor, peasants and miners. He joined them at work in the mines, taught their children, and even gave away his own few possessions to help them. The church authorities finally dismissed him for "excessive zeal," but he came away understanding the poor's harsh existence and the dignity with which they bore it.

The Peasants' Churchyard (1885)

The crows circle above the local cemetery of Nuenen. Soon after his father's death, van Gogh—in poor health and depressed—moves briefly to Antwerp. He then decides to visit his brother Theo, an art dealer living in the art capital of the world. Theo's support—financial and emotional—allows Vincent to spend the rest of his short life painting.

Still Life with Bible (1885)

"I have a terrible need of—shall I say the word?— religion. Then I go out and paint the stars."

A Bible and a book titled *Lust for Life*—these two things dominated van

Gogh's life. In his art he tried to fuse his religious upbringing with his love of the world's beauty. He lusted after life with a religious fervor. The burned-out candle tells us of the recent death of his father.

Van Gogh moves from rural, religious, poor Holland to . . . Paris, the City of Light. Vincent van Gone.

• *Continue to the next room.*

Paris (1886–1888)—Impressionism

Whoa! Whip out the sunglasses! The colors! The sun begins to break through, lighting up everything he paints. His landscapes are more spacious, with plenty of open sky, giving a feeling of exhilaration after the closed, dark world of Nuenen.

In the cafés and bars of Paris' bohemian Montmarte district, van Gogh meets the revolutionary Impressionists. He rooms with Theo and becomes friends with other struggling young painters, such as Gauguin and Toulouse-Lautrec. His health improves, he becomes more sociable, has an affair with an older woman, and is generally happy.

He signs up to study under a well-known classical teacher but quits after only a few classes. He can't afford to hire models, so he roams the streets with sketch pad in hand and learns from his Impressionist friends.

The Impressionists emphasized getting out of the stuffy studio and setting up the canvas outside on the street or in the countryside to paint the play of sunlight off the trees, buildings, and water.

At first van Gogh copied from the Impressionist masters. In nearby paintings you'll see garden scenes like Monet's, café snapshots like Degas', "block prints" like the Japanese masters, and self-portraits... like nobody else's.

Still Lifes, such as *Red Cabbages and Onions* (1887)

He quickly develops his own style—thicker paint, broad, swirling brush strokes, and brighter clashing colors that make even inanimate objects seem to vibrate with life. The many different colors are supposed to blend together, but you'd have to back up to Belgium before these colors resolve.

Self-Portrait with Gray Felt Hat

"He has painted one or two portraits which have turned out well, but he insists on working for nothing. It is a pity that he shows no desire to earn some money because he could easily do so here. But you can't change people."

—Theo to their mother

Despite his new sociability, van Gogh never quite fit in with his Impressionist friends. He was developing into a good painter and was anxious to strike out on his own. Also, he thought the social life of the big city was distracting him from serious work. In this painting, his face screams out from a swirling background of molecular activity. Van Gogh wanted peace and quiet where he could throw himself into his work completely. He heads for the sunny south of France.

• *Travel to the next room to reach...*

Arles (1888–1889)— Sunlight, Beauty, and Madness

Winter was just turning to spring when he arrived in Arles near the French Riviera. After the dreary Paris winter, the colors of springtime overwhelmed him. The blossoming trees inspired him to paint canvas after canvas, pulsing with new life and drenched in sunlight.

The Street (1888)

"It is my intention . . . to go temporarily to the South, where there is even more color, even more sun."
He rents this house with the green shutters. Look at that blue sky! He paints in a frenzy, working feverishly to try and take it all in. He is happy and productive.

The Bedroom (1888)

"I am a man of passions, capable of and subject to doing more or less foolish things—which I happen to regret, more or less, afterwards."
But Vincent is alone, a stranger in Provence. And that has its downside. Vincent swings from flurries of ecstatic activity to bouts of great loneliness. Like anyone traveling alone, he experiences those high highs and

low lows. This narrow bedroom that's almost folding in on him must have seemed like a prison cell at times. (Psychologists point out that most everything in this painting comes in pairs—two chairs, two paintings, a double bed squeezed down to a single—indicating his desire for a mate. Hmm.)

He invites his friend Gauguin to join him, envisioning a sort of artists' colony in Arles. He spends months preparing a room upstairs for Gauguin's arrival.

Gauguin's Armchair (1888)

"Empty chairs—there are many of them, there will be even more, and sooner or later, there will be nothing but empty chairs."
Gauguin arrives. At first they get along great, painting and carousing. But then things go bad. They clash over art, life, and personalities. Van Gogh, enraged during an argument, pulls out a knife and waves it in Gauguin's face. Gauguin takes the hint and quickly leaves town. Vincent is horrified at himself. In a fit of remorse and madness, he mutilates his own ear.

• *The following painting may be in this room (the Arles room) but has also been sighted upstairs.*

The Sower (1888)

A dark, silhouetted figure sows seeds in the burning sun. It's late in the day. The heat from the sun, the source of all life, radiates out in thick swirls of paint. The sower must be a hopeful man, because the field looks slanted and barren. Someday, he thinks, the seeds he's planting will grow into something great, like the tree that slashes diagonally across the scene—tough and craggy, but with small optimistic blossoms.

Vincent had worked sowing the Christian gospel in a harsh environment (see Mark 4:1–9). Now in Arles, ignited by the sun, he flung his artistic seeds to the wind, hoping.

• *In the Arles room, pick some . . .*

Sunflowers (1889)

"The worse I get along with people the more I learn to have faith in Nature and concentrate on her."

The people of Arles realize they have a madman on their hands, and the local vicar talks him into admitting himself to a mental hospital. Vincent writes to Theo: "Temporarily I wish to remain shut up, as much for my own peace of mind as for other people's."

Even a simple work like these *Sunflowers* (one of a half dozen Vincent painted) bursts with life. Different people see different things in the *Sunflowers*. Is it a happy mood or a melancholy one? Take your own emotional temperature.

• *Continue into the next room.*

Saint-Remy (1890)—The Mental Hospital

In the mental hospital, van Gogh continues to paint whenever he's well enough. He can't go out as often, so he copies from books, making his own distinctive versions of works by Rembrandt, Delacroix, Millet, and others.

We see a change from bright, happy landscapes to more introspective subjects. The colors are less bright and more surreal, the brushwork even more furious. The strong outlines of figures are twisted and tortured.

Pietà (after Delacroix)

It's evening after a thunderstorm. Jesus has been crucified, and the corpse lies at the mouth of a tomb. Mary, whipped by the cold wind, holds her empty arms out in despair and confusion. She is the tender mother who receives us all in death as though saying, "My child, you've been away so long—rest in my arms."

At first the peace and quiet of the asylum do van Gogh good and his health improves. Occasionally he's allowed outside to paint the gardens and landscapes. Meanwhile, the paintings he has sent to Theo begin to attract attention in Paris for the first time. A woman in Brussels buys one of his canvases—the only painting he ever sold during his lifetime. Nowadays, a *Sunflowers* sells for $40 million.

Almond Blossom

Van Gogh moves north to Auvers, a small town near Paris where he can stay at a hotel under a doctor-friend's supervision. On the way

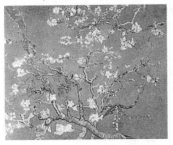

there, he visits Theo. Theo's wife had just had a baby, which they named Vincent. Van Gogh shows up with this painting under his arm as a birthday gift. Theo's wife later recalls: "I had expected a sick man, but here was a sturdy, broad-shouldered man with a healthy color, a smile on his face, and a very resolute appearance."

The Fall of the Leaves

"*. . . a traveler going to a destination that does not exist . . .*"

The stark brown trees are blown by the wind. A solitary figure (who?) winds along a narrow, snaky path as the wind blows leaves on him. The colors are surreal—blue, green, and red tree trunks with heavy black outlines. A road runs away from us, heading nowhere.

Wheatfield with a Reaper

"I have been working hard and fast in the last few days. This is how I try to express how desperately fast things pass in modern life."

The harvest is here. The time is short. There's much work to be done. A lone reaper works uphill, scything through a swirling wheatfield, cutting slender paths of calm.

The Sheaf-binder (after Millet)

"I want to paint men and women with that something of the eternal which the halo used to symbolize..."

Van Gogh's compassion for honest laborers remained constant since his work with Belgian miners. These sturdy folk with their curving bodies wrestle as one with their curving wheat. The world van Gogh sees is charged from within by spiritual fires, twisting and turning, matter turning into energy and vice versa.

The fits of madness return. During these spells, he loses all sense of his own actions. It means he can't paint, the one thing he feels driven to do. He writes to Theo: "My surroundings here begin to weigh on me more than I can say—I need air. I feel overwhelmed by boredom and grief."

Auvers (1890)—Flying Away

"The bird looks through the bars at the overcast sky where a thunderstorm is gathering, and inwardly he rebels against his fate. 'I am caged, I am caged, and you tell me I have everything I need! Oh! I beg you, give me liberty, that I may be a bird like other birds.' A certain idle man resembles this idle bird..."

In his new surroundings, he continues painting, interrupted by spells that swing from boredom to madness. His letters to Theo are generally optimistic, but he worries that he'll succumb completely to insanity and never paint again. The final landscapes are walls of bright, thick paint.

Wheatfield with Crows (1890)

"This new attack...came on me in the fields, on a windy day, when I was busy painting."

On July 27, Vincent leaves his hotel, walks out to a nearby field and puts a bullet through his chest.

This is the last painting Vincent finished. We can try to search the wreckage of his life for the black box explaining what happened, but there's not much there. His life was sad and tragic, but the record he left is one not of sadness but of beauty. Intense beauty.

The wind-blown wheatfield is a nest of restless energy. Scenes like this must have overwhelmed van Gogh with their incredible beauty—too much too fast with no release. The sky is dark blue, almost night-time, barely lit by two suns boiling through the deep ocean of blue. The road starts nowhere, leads nowhere, disappearing into the burning wheatfield. Above all of this swirling beauty fly the crows, the dark ghosts that had hovered over his life since the cemetery in Nuenen.

VENICE

ST. MARK'S CATHEDRAL

DOGE'S PALACE

ACCADEMIA

*E*choes of a time when Venice was Europe's economic superpower still bounce down the lush halls of the Doge's Palace, around the gilded domes of St. Mark's basilica, and through the rich paintings of the Accademia. With a huff and a puff from *Mona Winks*, Europe's best-preserved big city once again becomes that most serene (hedonistic, mysterious, and lavish) republic.

✤ 14 ✤
ST. MARK'S CATHEDRAL

Venice was once Europe's richest city. As middleman in the trade between Asia and Europe, it reaped wealth from both sides. In 1450, Venice had 150,000 citizens (far more than Paris), and a gross "national" product 50 percent greater than the entire country of France. The rich Venetians learned to love the good life—silks, spices, and jewels from the East, crafts from northern Europe, good food and wine, fine architecture, music, and gaiety. Venice was a vibrant city full of impressed visitors, palaces, and glittering canals. Five centuries after its "fall," Venice is all of these still, with the added charm of romantic decay. In this tour, we'll spend an hour in the religious heart of this Old World superpower.

ORIENTATION
Cost: The church is free. The treasury, altarpiece, and loggia with horses cost €1.70 apiece.

Dress code: Strict dress code enforced (no shorts or bare shoulders).

Hours: Mon–Sat 9:45–17:30, Sun 14:00–17:00. The interior is beautifully lit on Sun 14:00–17:00 (and sometimes on Sat 14:00–17:00, for Sat Mass at 18:45, and some middays 11:00–12:00).

Getting there: Signs all over town point to San Marco. It's on Piazza San Marco, near the Grand Canal. Vaporetto stop: San Marco.

Information: Guidebooks in church atrium bookstand. Public pay WC just beyond far end of square.

Tours: See the schedule board in the atrium listing free English guided tours (July–Aug Mon–Fri up to 4 tours/day, Sat 1/day, off-season 2/week, 30–90 minutes depending on guide and group).

Photography: Not allowed.

Cuisine art: Pricier cafés with live music on St. Mark's Square, cheaper bars just off the square.

Starring: St. Mark, Byzantium, mosaics, and ancient bronze horses.

PIAZZA SAN MARCO

• *Before touring the church, have a look at the grand square and the buildings that surround it. Sit on the steps at the far end of the square (away from the church).*

Bride of the Sea

Imagine this square full of water with gondolas floating where people are now sipping coffee at the café tables. That happens every so often at very high tides, a reminder that Venice and the sea are intertwined.

Venetian wealth came from sea trading. As middleman between Europe and the East (the Moslem world of Turkey and the Middle East), Venice became the wealthiest city in Europe. In St. Mark's Square, the exact center of this East-West axis, we see both the luxury and the mix of Eastern and Western influences.

Basilica San Marco dominates the square with its Byzantine-style domes and glowing mosaics. Mark Twain said it looked like "a warty bug taking a meditative walk." To the left and right stand the government offices that administered the Venetian Empire's vast network of trading outposts. On the left are the "Old" offices, built in 1530 in solid Renaissance style. The "New" offices on the right from a century later are a little heavier and more ornamented, mixing various arches, columns, and statues in the Baroque style.

• *Behind you, you'll find the public WC, post office, American Express office, and a tourist information office. Another office is on the lagoon. Given Venice's inconsistent opening hours, it's wise to confirm your sightseeing plans here.*

PIAZZA SAN MARCO

Walk to the center of the square—to the cool shadow of the tall brick bell tower (Campanile). Grab a seat on the bench at the foot of the tower, facing the square. Watch out for pigeon speckle.

The Piazza

The square is big, but it feels intimate. Napoleon called it "the most beautiful drawing room in Europe." We have Napoleon himself to thank for the intimate feel. He built the final wing, opposite the church.

For architecture buffs, here are three centuries of styles, bam, side by side, *uno due tre*, for easy comparison: (1) Old wing, Renaissance, (2) New wing, Baroque, (3) Napoleon's wing, neoclassical—a return to simpler, more austere classical columns and arches. Napoleon's architects tried to make his wing bridge the styles of the other two. But it turned out a little too high for one side and not enough for the other. Nice try.

The Clock Tower

Two bronze Moors (African Moslems), "rescued" from who knows where, stand atop the clock tower across the square. At the top of each hour they swing their giant clappers. The dial shows the 24 hours, the signs of the zodiac, and the phases of the moon. Above it is the world's first digital clock, which changes every five minutes. There are both Roman numerals and Arabic numerals. Look for the symbol of St. Mark, an alert winged lion, looking down on the crowded square.

The Campanile

The original Campanile (pron: camp-ah-NEE-lay), or bell tower, was a marvel of 10th-century architecture until the 20th century, when it toppled into the center of the piazza. It had groaned ominously the night before, sending people scurrying from the cafés. The next morning . . . crash!

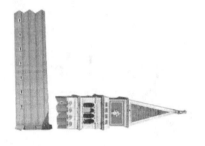

The Campanile fell in 1902 and was rebuilt 10 years later, complete with its golden angel on top facing the breeze. You can ride a lift to the top for the best view of Venice. Notice the photo of the crumpled tower on the wall just before you enter the elevator. The view on the top is glassed in, stuffy, and crowded at times, but worth it.

• *Take a seat on the other side of the Campanile, facing the water. The small square between the church and the water is . . .*

The Piazzetta

This "Little Square" is framed by the Doge's Palace on the left and the Old Library on the right. In former days it used to be closed off to the public for a few hours a day so that government officials and bigwigs could gather in the sun to strike shady deals.

The two large 12th-century

columns near the water were looted from Constantinople. These columns were used to string up and torture criminals so the public could learn its lessons vicariously. The winged lion on top of one of them represents St. Mark, Venice's patron saint. The other shows St. Theodore, the former patron saint who was replaced when they got hold of Mark. I guess stabbing crocodiles in the back isn't classy enough for an upwardly mobile world power.

Venice was the "Bride of the Sea" because she was dependent on sea trading for her livelihood. This "marriage" was celebrated annually by the people. The Doge, in full regalia, boarded a ritual boat here at the edge of the Piazzetta and sailed out into the canal. There a vow was made, and he dropped a jeweled ring into the water to seal the marriage.

In the distance, on an island across the Grand Canal, is one of the grandest scenes in the city, the Church of San Giorgio Maggiore. The church was designed by the late-Renaissance architect Palladio.

Speaking of architects, I will for the next second and a half: Sansovino. The Old Offices, the Old Library, and the delicate Loggetta you're sitting under (at the base of the Campanile) were all designed by him. Take 10 steps toward the Doge's Palace, turn around and you can see all three of these at once. More than any single man, he made Piazza San Marco what it is.

When Venice floods, the puddles appear first around round, white pavement stones like the one between the Loggetta and the Doge's Palace.

• *Meet you at the center flagpole in front of the church.*

BASILICA SAN MARCO

Exterior

St. Mark's Cathedral is a treasure chest of booty looted during Venice's glory days. That's only appropriate for a church built on the bones of a stolen saint.

St. Mark was the author of one of the four Bible books telling the story of Jesus' life (Matthew, Mark, Luke, and John). Seven centuries after his death, his holy body was in Moslem-occupied Alexandria, Egypt. Two visiting merchants of Venice "rescued" the body from the infidels and spirited it away to Venice, giving the fast-growing city

BASILICA SAN MARCO

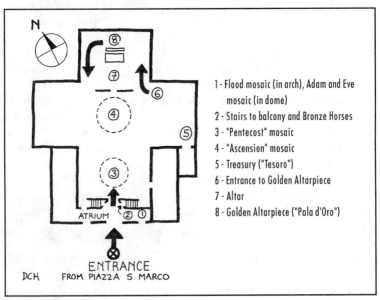

1 - Flood mosaic (in arch), Adam and Eve mosaic (in dome)
2 - Stairs to balcony and Bronze Horses
3 - "Pentecost" mosaic
4 - "Ascension" mosaic
5 - Treasury ("Tesoro")
6 - Entrance to Golden Altarpiece
7 - Altar
8 - Golden Altarpiece ("Pala d'Oro")

instant religious status. They made Mark the patron saint of the city, and you'll see his symbol, the winged lion, all over Venice. (Find four in 20 seconds.)

The original church, which was built (over Mark's dead body) in the ninth century, burned down in 976. The structure we see was begun in the 11th century. True to its founding, St. Mark's is built with materials looted from buildings throughout the Venetian empire. The style has been called "Early Ransack."

Above the door on the far left of the church is a mosaic of the theft that put Venice on the pilgrimage map. The *Transporting of St. Mark* shows two men in the center (with crooked staffs) entering the church bearing a coffin with the body. Mark looks grumpy from the long voyage. In this mosaic, one of the oldest, you can see the church as it looked in the 13th century—even with its famous bronze horses on the balcony.

Look up at the church balcony to see copies of the bronze horses (the impressive originals are housed inside the church museum). The

Venetians stole the horses from their fellow Christians during the looting of Constantinople and brought them here to the church. Napoleon stole the horses away to Paris—the French later returned them. (Copies also top the arch next to the Louvre in Paris.)

The facade of St. Mark's shows a crazy mix of East and West. The doorways are massive Romanesque (European) arches but lined with marble columns from Eastern buildings. The mosaics are mostly Venetian designs but executed by Greek craftsmen. There's sculpture from Constantinople, columns from Alexandria, and capitals from Sicily. The upper story has some pointed Gothic-style arches, while the whole affair is topped by Greek domes with their onion-shaped caps. What's amazing isn't so much the variety as the fact that the whole thing comes together in a bizarre sort of harmony. St. Mark's remains simply the most unique church in Europe, a church that, as Goethe said, "can only be compared with itself."

• *Enter through the central door—a sixth-century bronze-paneled Byzantine job. Turn right in the atrium (the entry hall) and drop anchor under the last dome.*

The Atrium Mosaics

St. Mark's is famous for its mosaics. Some of the oldest and finest are here in the atrium. Mosaics are made of small cubes of glass or stone pressed into wet plaster. Their popularity spread from ancient Rome to the Greek-speaking world through Constantinople. Byzantine churches perfected the gold background effect by baking gold leaf right into the tiny cubes of glass.

Medieval mosaics were teaching aids to tell Bible stories to the illiterate masses. Today's literate masses have trouble reading them, so let's look at two simple examples.

In the arch next to the dome is the story of Noah and the Great Flood. If you face the piazza you'll see (on top) Noah building the Ark. Below that are three scenes of Noah putting all species of animals into the Ark, two by two. Turning around and facing the church interior, you'll

see the Flood in full force, drowning the wicked. Noah sends out a dove twice to see if there's any dry land to dock at. He finds it, leaves the Ark with a gorgeous rainbow overhead, and offers a sacrifice of thanks to God. Easy, huh?

Now that our medieval literacy rate has risen, let's try the story that rings the bottom of the dome—Adam and Eve in the Garden of Eden. Stand right under the dome facing the church, crane your neck, and read clockwise around the dome:

(1) Adam names the animals; (2) God creates Eve from a spare rib, and (3) presents her to Adam; (4) Eve is tempted by the serpent; (5) she picks and gives the forbidden fruit to Adam; (6) they realize that they're naked and (7) in shame, try to hide from God; (8) God finds them and (9) lectures them; (10) He gives them clothes and (11) pushes them out into the real world where they have to work for a living.

• *Enter the church through the central door past the gaily dressed guard who makes sure all who enter have covered legs and shoulders. There are benches along the back wall to both sides of the entry, but wait a second.*

While your eyes adjust to the dark, get a feel for the church. Before reading on, walk up to the center of the church and back. Notice the floor plan of four equal arms radiating from the center. Meet you back here at the bench.

The Greek-Cross Floor Plan

Western Christianity focuses on the death of Jesus; Eastern Christianity focuses on his resurrection. That's why most Western European church-es have so many crucifixes, and even the shape of the church itself is often in the form of a crucifix. But look around St. Mark's—not many crucifixes. And the floor plan is not the Latin Cross symbolizing the crucifixion but the Greek Cross (+), symbolizing perfection.

Topping the Greek Cross are five domes—one large one in the center and one over each arm, or transept. These are decorated with golden mosaics in the Byzantine style, though many were designed by Italian Renaissance and later artists. The entire upper part is in mosaic (imagine paving a football field with contact lenses). The often-over-looked lower walls are in beautiful marble.

The overall effect is one of "mystical, golden luminosity." It's a subtle effect, one that grows on you, especially as the filtered light changes. There are more beautiful churches, bigger, more overwhelming, and even more holy, but none are as stately.

• *Find the chandelier near the central doorway (in the shape of a "Greek Cross" cathedral space station), and run your eyes up the support chain to the dome above.*

The Mosaics

This dome has one of the oldest mosaics in the church, from around 1125. The scene is the Pentecost. The Holy Spirit in the form of a dove sends out tongues of fire—the miracle of speaking in tongues, looking like a red horn on each head—to the 12 Apostles below. (As the poet Yeats described it: "O sages standing in God's holy fire as 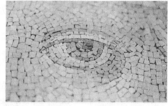 in the gold mosaic of a wall, come from the holy fire...and be the singing-masters of my soul.") While the mosaics in the Atrium were from the Old Testament, we've now entered the new age of the New Testament.

• *Walk up the aisle again to the central dome. Take a seat against a pillar. The corner seat is ideal.*

Central Dome Mosaic

You've probably noticed that the floor is also mosaics, mostly geometrical designs and animals. You've also noticed it rolls like the sea. Venice is sinking—and shifting—creating these cresting waves of stone.

Gape upwards. The mosaic in the central dome is, again, not the death of Jesus, but *The Ascension* into heaven after the Resurrection. This isn't the dead, crucified, mortal Jesus shown in most churches, but a powerful God, the Creator of All, seated on a crescent moon in the center of starry heaven solemnly giving us his blessing. Below him is Mary (with shiny golden Greek crosses on each shoulder and looking ready to play patty-cake) flanked by two winged angels and the 12 apostles.

Sailing to Byzantium

For centuries, Constantinople (modern Istanbul) was the greatest city in Europe. In A.D. 330, the Emperor Constantine moved the Roman

Empire's capital to the newly built city of Constantinople, taking with him Rome's best and brightest. While the city of Rome decayed and fell, the Eastern half of the Empire lived on, speaking the Greek language and adopting a more Oriental outlook. Venetian traders tapped the wealth of this culture during the Crusades, the series of military expeditions to "save" the holy city of Jerusalem from the Moslems. The Venetians would rent ships to the Crusaders in exchange for money, favors, and booty. During the Fourth Crusade (1202–1204), which went horribly awry, the Crusaders sacked Constantinople, a fellow Christian city. This was, at least until the advent of TV evangelism, perhaps the lowest point in Christian history. Among the looted treasures shipped back to Venice were the bronze horses and many of the artifacts in the Treasury.

Consider checking out the Treasury and the Golden Altarpiece (Pala d'Oro). This is your best chance outside of Istanbul or Ravenna to experience the glory of the Byzantine civilization. The Treasury entrance is in the right transept. The Altarpiece is in the apse, behind the high altar. Of the three separate admissions you'll encounter in this church, I'd prioritize in this order: Loggia and horses (see below), Golden Altarpiece, Treasury.

• *The Treasury (Tesoro) is at the far corner of the right transept (€1.70, daily 9:45-17:10, until 16:10 in winter).*

Treasury

You'll see Byzantine chalices, silver reliquaries, monstrous monstrances (for displaying the Communion wafer), the marble *Chair of St. Mark*, and icons done in gold, silver, enamels, agate, studded with precious gems, and so on. This is marvelous handiwork, but all the more marvelous because many were done in A.D. 500, when Western Europe was still rooting in the mud.

• *Exiting the Treasury, cross the right transept to the Golden Altarpiece entrance (€1.70, open daily 9:45–17:10, until 16:10 in winter). On the way, notice the door under the rose window at the end of the transept. This was the Doge's private entrance direct from the Doge's Palace. Follow the crowds behind the altar. Read as you shuffle on.*

Golden Altarpiece (Pala d'Oro)

The first thing you see after showing your ticket is the high altar itself (under the stone canopy). Beneath this lies the body of Mark, the Gospel writer (the tomb, through the grate under the altar, says "Marxus"). Legend has it that before he died he visited Venice, where an angel promised him he could rest his weary bones when he died. Hmm. Shhh.

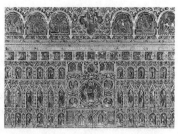

Above the altar is a marble canopy. The four supporting columns are wonderful and mysterious—scholars don't even know whether they're from fifth-century Byzantium or 13th-century Venice! I spent as much time looking at the funny New Testament scenes carved in them as at the Golden Altarpiece with its crowds and glaring lights. (On the right-hand pillar closest to the Altarpiece, fourth row from the bottom—is that a genie escaping from a bottle while someone tries to stuff him back in?)

The Golden Altarpiece is a stunning golden wall made of 80 Byzantine enamels decorated with religious scenes set in gold and studded with rubies, emeralds, sapphires, pearls, amethysts, and topaz. Byzantine craftsmen made this for the Doges over the course of several centuries (976–1345). It's a bit much to take in all at once, but one figure you might recognize is in the center of the lower half—Jesus as Creator of All, similar to the mosaic in the main dome—with Matthew, Mark, Luke, and John around him. Once you've looked at some of the individual scenes, back up as far as this small room will let you, and just let yourself be dazzled by the "whole picture"—this "mosaic" of Byzantine greatness.

The Bronze Horses and View of the Piazza

• *The staircase up to the bronze horses is in the atrium near the main entrance. The sign says "Loggia dei Cavalli, Museo" (€1.70, daily 9:45–16:00, sometimes until 17:00).*

Your ticket gives you admission to:

1. A small museum with fragments of mosaics that you can examine up close.
2. An upstairs gallery with an impressive top-side view of the church interior with its mosaic wallpaper.
3. The Loggia, the balcony overlooking Piazza San Marco. Nice view, fun pigeon and people watching.
4. The Bronze Horses. You can walk among the copies on the Loggia with their "1978" date on the hoof. Then go inside to a room with the real things. Stepping lively in pairs with smiles on their faces, they exude energy and exuberance. Originally gilded bronze, you can still see some streaks of gold.

These horses have done some traveling in their day. Made in the time of Alexander the Great, they were taken by Nero to Rome. Constantine took them to his new capital in Constantinople. The Venetians then stole them from their fellow  Christians during the looting of noble Constantinople and brought them to St. Mark's.

What goes around comes around, and Napoleon came around and took the horses when he conquered Venice in 1797. They stood atop a triumphal arch in the Louvre courtyard until Napoleon's empire was "blown-aparte" and they were returned to their "rightful" home.

The horses were again removed from their spot when attacked by their most dangerous enemy yet—modern man. The threat of oxidation from pollution sent them galloping for cover inside the church.

❀ 15 ❀
DOGE'S PALACE

Venice is a city of beautiful facades—palaces, churches, carnival masks—that can cover darker interiors of intrigue and decay. The Doge's Palace, or Palazzo Ducale, with its frilly pink exterior hides the fact that "the Most Serene Republic" (as it called itself) was far from serene in its heyday.

The Doge's Palace housed the fascinating government of this rich and powerful Empire. It also served as the home for the Venetian ruler known as the Doge (pron: DOJE-eh), or Duke. For four centuries (about 1150–1550) this was the most powerful half acre in Europe. The Doges wanted it to reflect the wealth of the Republic, impressing visitors and serving as a reminder that the Venetians were number one in Europe.

ORIENTATION

Cost: €10. Admission includes entry to a number of lesser museums, including the Correr Museum (on city history, entry on square opposite St. Mark's Basilica).

Hours: April–Oct daily 9:00–19:00, Nov–March 9:00–17:00, last entry 90 minutes before closing. Closed Jan 1, May 1, Dec 25.

Getting there: It's next to St. Mark's Basilica, on the Grand Canal, and just off St. Mark's Square. Vaporetto stop: San Marco.

Information: There are no English descriptions. Guidebooks are on sale in the bookshop. Tel. 041-522-4951. WC in courtyard near palace exit.

Tours: Audioguide tours of the palace cost €4.

DOGE'S PALACE—OVERVIEW

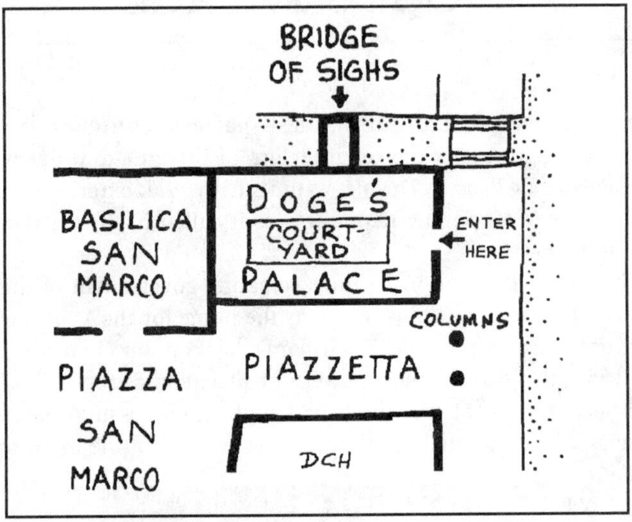

BRIDGE
OF SIGHS
↓

BASILICA
SAN
MARCO

DOGE'S
COURT-
YARD
PALACE

←ENTER
HERE

COLUMNS
●

PIAZZA
SAN
MARCO

PIAZZETTA ●

DCH

Length of our tour: 90 minutes.

Photography: Allowed without a flash.

Cuisine art: Expensive cafés on St. Mark's Square, cheaper bar/cafés off the square, handy canalside gelato shop on the Piazzetta (the small square with two big columns) next to the Doge's Palace.

Starring: Tintoretto and the Doges.

The Exterior

"The Wedding Cake," "The Table Cloth," or "The Pink House" is also sometimes known as the Doge's Palace. The style is called Venetian Gothic, and the arches and windows come to a point like Gothic arches, but the upper half has an Eastern, Islamic flavor with its abstract patterns. The columns originally had bases on the bottoms, but these were covered over as the columns sank. If you compare this delicate, top-heavy structure with the massive fortress palaces of Florence, you realize the wisdom of building a city in the middle of the sea—you have no natural enemies except gravity.

The palace was originally built in the 800s, but most of what we see came after 1300 as it was expanded to meet the needs of the Empire. Each Doge wanted to leave his mark on history with a new wing. But so much of the city's money was spent on the building that finally a law was passed levying an enormous fine on anyone who even mentioned any new building. That worked for a while, until one brave and wealthy Doge proposed a new wing, paid his fine... and started building again.

• *Walk alongside the Doge's Palace with the Grand Canal on your right. Stop at the top of the first bridge and look inland at...*

The Bridge of Sighs

At the Doge's Palace (on your left), the government doled out justice. On your right are the prisons. (Don't let the palatial facade fool you—see the bars on the windows?) Prisoners sentenced in the palace crossed to the prisons by way of the covered bridge in front of you. From this bridge they got  their final view of sunny, joyous Venice before entering the black and dank prisons. They sighed.

Venice has been a major tourist center for four centuries. Anyone who ever came here has stood on this very spot, looking at the Bridge of Sighs. Lean on the railing leaned on by everyone from Casanova to Byron to Hemingway.

• *Sigh.*

The Interior

• *Enter the Doge's Palace from the canal side. After you buy your ticket, you'll walk through the ground floor, filled with ornately carved column bases from the palace's original facade. Cross the inner courtyard (exhibition rooms are beyond) and stand at the base of a big staircase (the one closer to the basilica).*

Imagine yourself as a foreign dignitary on business to meet the Doge. Ahead of you is the grand staircase with two nearly nude statues of, I think, Moses and Paul Newman. The Doge and his aides would be waiting for you at the top. No matter who you were, you'd have to hoof it up—the powerful Doge would descend the stairs for no one.

You'll notice that the entry hall ceiling alternates between Gothic pointed-arch vaulting and round Roman arches. Much of the palace was built on the cusp between medieval and Renaissance.

• *Go up the tourists' staircase and look out over the courtyard (and the backside of Paul Newman). From here on it's hard to get lost (though I've managed). It's a one-way system, so just follow the arrows.*

The Courtyard

You have a Doge's-eye view of the courtyard. Ambassadors would walk up this staircase to bow to you. The Doge was something like an "elected king"—which makes sense only in the "dictatorial republic" that was Venice. Technically he was just a noble selected by other nobles to carry out their laws and decisions. Gradually, though, the Doges extended their powers and ruled more like divine-right kings, striking the fear of death in all who opposed them.

Ahead of you on the right, notice that the palace is attached to St. Mark's Cathedral. You can see the ugly brick of both structures—the stern inner structure without its painted-lady veneer of marble. On this tour we'll see the sometimes harsh inner structure of this outwardly serene Republic.

• *Head down the loggia to the entrance to the Golden Staircase leading to the Doge's residence on the first landing and on to the actual palace at the top.*

The Golden Staircase

The palace was propaganda, designed to impress visitors. This gilded-ceiling staircase was something for them to write home about.

The first floor is where the Doge actually lived. Wander around these sumptuous rooms before continuing upstairs. Despite his great power, the Doge had to obey one iron-clad rule—he and his family had to leave their own home and live in the Doge's Palace. Poor guy.

• *Go up the first set of steps. At the middle landing, go straight (not right) up toward stained-glass windows, then make a U-turn to the right and go up more stairs to . . .*

The "Atrio Quadrato"

Look at the ceiling painting, *Justice Presenting the Sword and Scales to Doge Girolano* by Tintoretto. It's a masterpiece by one of the late-Renaissance greats. So what? May as well adopt the "so what" attitude now because you'll get it sooner or later. There's so much great art here by great painters—mostly Tintoretto and Veronese—that you can't possibly appreciate it all. Best to enjoy it not as museum art but as palace wallpaper.

• *Enter the next room.*

Room of the Four Doors

This was the central clearinghouse for all the goings-on in the palace. Visitors trying to see the Doge or any other government official presented themselves here. The three other doors then led to their destination—the executive, legislative, or judicial branch of government.

The room was designed by Palladio, the architect who did the impressive Church of San Giorgio Maggiore that you can see almost floating across the Grand Canal from St. Mark's Square. On the intricate stucco ceiling notice the feet of the women dangling down below the edge (above the windows), a typical Baroque technique of creating the illusion of 3-D.

On the wall is a painting by (ho-hum) Titian showing a Doge kneeling with great piety before a woman embodying Faith holding the Cross of Jesus. Notice old Venice in the misty distance under the cross. This is one of many paintings you'll see of Doges in uncharacteristically humble poses—paid for, of course, by the Doges themselves.

• *Enter the small room with the big fireplace. With your back to the fireplace, face the two paintings on the opposite wall . . .*

The "Ante-Collegio"

It took a big title or bribe to get in to see the Doge. But first you were told to wait here, combing your hair, adjusting your robe, popping a Certs, and preparing the gifts you'd brought. While you cooled your heels and warmed your hands at the elaborate fireplace, you might look at some of the paintings—among the finest in the palace, worthy of any museum in the world.

The Rape of Europa by Veronese (on the wall opposite the windows) shows the luxury and sensuality of Venice at its peak. The Venetian Renaissance looked back to pagan Greece and Rome for subjects to paint, a big change from the saints and crucifixions of the Middle Ages. Here Zeus, the king of the Greek gods, appears in the form of a bull to carry off a beautiful earthling. This is certainly no medieval condemnation of sex and violence, but a celebration in cheery pastel colors of the earthy, optimistic spirit of the Renaissance.

Tintoretto's *Bacchus and Ariadne* (to the left of the exit door) is another colorful display of Venice's sensual tastes. The god of wine offers a ring to the mortal Ariadne, who's being crowned with stars. The ring is the center of a spinning wheel of flesh with the three arms like spokes.

But wait, the Doge is ready for us. Let's go in.

• *Enter the next room.*

DOGE'S PALACE—EXECUTIVE AND LEGISLATIVE

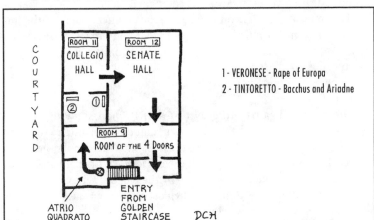

COURTYARD

ROOM 11
COLLEGIO HALL

ROOM 12
SENATE HALL

1 - VERONESE - Rape of Europa
2 - TINTORETTO - Bacchus and Ariadne

ROOM 9
ROOM OF THE 4 DOORS

ENTRY FROM GOLDEN STAIRCASE

ATRIO QUADRATO

DCH

The Collegio (Executive Branch)

Surrounded by his counselors, the Doge would sit on the platform at the far end to receive ambassadors who laid their gifts at his feet and pled their country's case. The gifts were often essentially tribute from lands conquered by Venetian generals. All official ceremonies, such as ratifying treaties, were held here.

At other times it was the private meeting room of the Doge and his cabinet to discuss secrets of state, proposals to give the legislature, or negotiations with the Pope. The wooden benches around the sides where they sat are original. The clock on the wall is a backward-running 24-hour clock with Roman numerals and a sword for hands.

The ceiling is 24-carat gold with paintings by Veronese. These are not frescoes (painting on wet plaster) like in the Sistine Chapel but actual canvases painted here on earth and then placed on the ceiling. Venice's humidity would have melted frescoes like so much mascara within years. Check out the painting of the woman with the spider web (on the ceiling, opposite the big window). This was the Venetian symbol of "Discussion." You can imagine the many intricate webs of truth and lies woven in this room by the Doge's sinister nest of advisers.

• *Enter the large Senate Room.*

The Senate Chamber (Legislative Branch)

This was the center of the Venetian government. Venice was technically a republic ruled by the elected Senate that met here, though its power

DOGE'S PALACE—JUDICIAL

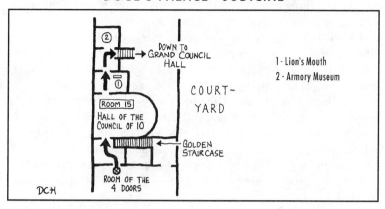

DOWN TO GRAND COUNCIL HALL

COURT-YARD

ROOM 15
HALL OF THE COUNCIL OF 10

GOLDEN STAIRCASE

ROOM OF THE 4 DOORS

DCH

1 - Lion's Mouth
2 - Armory Museum

was gradually overshadowed by the Doge and, later, the Council of Ten. This body of 60 annually elected senators, chaired by the Doge, debated and passed laws, and made declarations of war in this room. Senators would speak from the podium between the windows.

Tintoretto's *Triumph of Venice* on the ceiling (center) shows the city in all its glory. Lady Venice is up in heaven with the Greek gods while barbaric lesser nations swirl up to give her gifts and tribute. Do you get the feeling the Venetian aristocracy was proud of its city?

On the wall are two large clocks with the signs of the zodiac and phases of the moon. The senators shared one of them with the Doge next door, explaining the mystery of time reversal. And there's one final oddity in this room, in case you hadn't noticed it yet. In one of the wall paintings (above the entry door), there's actually a Doge...not kneeling.

• *Pass again through the Room of the Four Doors, then around the corner into the large hall with a semi-circular platform at the far end.*

Room of the Council of Ten (Judicial Branch)

Venice's worldwide reputation for swift, harsh, and secret justice came from the dreaded Council of Ten. This group, consisting of the Doge and other elected officials, dealt out justice for traitors, murderers, and "morals" violators.

Slowly they developed into a CIA-type unit with their own force of police officers, guards, spies, informers, and even assassins. They had their own budget and were accountable to no one, soon making them the *de facto* ruling body of the "Republic." No one was safe from the spying eye of the "Terrible Ten." If you were even suspected of disloyalty or troublemaking, you could be swept off the streets, tried, judged, and thrown into the dark dungeons in the palace for the rest of your life without so much as a Miranda warning.

It was in this room that the Council met to decide punishments—who lived, died, was decapitated, tortured, or merely thrown in jail. The small, hard-to-find door leading off the platform (to the right) leads through secret passages to the prisons and torture chambers.

The large central oval ceiling painting by Veronese (a copy of the original stolen by Napoleon and still in the Louvre) shows *Jupiter Descending from Heaven to Strike Down the Vices,* redundantly informing the accused that justice in Venice was swift and harsh.

The dreaded Council of Ten was, of course, eventually disbanded. Today, their descendants enforce the dress code for tourists entering St. Mark's.

• *Pass through the next room noticing the "Lion's Mouth" (on both sides of the exit door). These letterboxes, known as Lions' Mouths because some had a lion's head, are scattered throughout the palace. Anyone who had a complaint or suspicion about anyone else could accuse him by simply dropping a slip of paper in the mouth. This set the blades of justice turning inside the palace. The Armory Museum is up the stairs.*

Armory Museum
The aesthetics of killing is beyond me, but I must admit I've never seen a better collection of halberds, falchions, ranseurs, mulchers, targes, morions, and brigandines in my life. (One of these words is a fake.) The stock of weapons in these three rooms makes you realize the important role the military played in keeping open the East-West trade lines.

In the fourth room, you'll see artistic shields, a midget's armor, old globes, and old quivers. Squint out the window at the far end. It's Palladio's San Giorgio Maggiore again and Venice's Lido (beach) in the distance. To the right, the tall glass case contains a tiny crossbow, some torture devices (including an effective-looking thumb screw), "the devil's box" (a clever item that could fire in four directions at once), and a chastity belt. These "iron breeches" were worn by the wife of the Lord of Padua. On your way out, you'll pass a very, very early attempt at a machine gun.

• *Go downstairs, turn left, and pass through the long hall with a wood-beam ceiling. Now turn right and open your eyes as wide as you can . . .*

Hall of the Grand Council
It took a room this size to contain the grandeur of the Most Serene Republic. This huge room (60 meters long) could accommodate up to

2,000 people at one time—the nobility who were the backbone of the Empire. In theory, the Doge, the Senate, and the Council of Ten were subordinate to the Grand Council. They were elected from among its ranks.

Once the Doge was elected he was presented to the people of Venice from the balcony on the far end of the room (Sala dello Scrutinio) that overlooks the Piazzetta. A noble would announce, "Here is your Doge, if it pleases you." That was fine until one time when the people weren't pleased. From then on they just said, "Here is your Doge."

Ringing the hall near the ceiling are portraits in chronological order of 76 Doges. The one at the far end that's blacked out is the notorious Doge Falier, who opposed the will of the Grand Council. He was tried for treason and beheaded. Ironically, the Doge whose memory they tried to blot out is now the best remembered. Fame is great—infamy is better.

On the wall over the Doge's throne is Tintoretto's monsterpiece, *Paradise*, the largest oil painting in the world. At 160 square meters (190 square yards), I could slice it up and wallpaper my entire apartment with enough left over for place mats.

Christ and Mary are at the top of heaven surrounded by 500 saints who ripple out in concentric rings. Tintoretto worked on this in the last years of his long life. On the day it was finished, his daughter died. He got his brush out again and painted her as saint #501. She's dead center with the blue skirt, hands clasped, getting sucked up to heaven. (At least that's what an Italian tour guide told me.)

The rest of the room's paintings show great moments in Venice's glory days of military conquest. Veronese's *The Apotheosis of Venice* (on the ceiling at the Tintoretto end) is a typically unsubtle work showing Lady Venice being crowned a goddess by an angel.

Actually, the Venetians were looking back to better times before the series of military defeats that began their city's decline. One by one the Turks gobbled up Venice's trading outposts. In the West, the rest of Europe ganged up on Venice to reduce her power. To top it off, by 1500 Portugal had broken Venice's East-West trade monopoly by finding a sea route to the East around Africa. From 1500 to 1800, Venice remained a glorious city but not the great world power she once was.

Out the windows is a fine view of the domes of the basilica and the palace courtyard below. There's Paul Newman again, and the ugly brick walls and the round- and pointed-arched arcades.

• *Read the intro to the prisons here in the Grand Council Hall, where there are more benches and fewer rats.*

The Prisons

The palace had its own dungeons. The Doge, from the privacy of his home, could sentence political opponents to jail and torture. The most notorious cells were "the Wells" in the basement, so called because they were deep, wet, and cramped.

By the 1500s, the Wells were full of political prisoners. New prisons were built across the canal to the east of the palace and connected with a covered bridge—covered so they could still imprison opponents without public knowledge.

• *Exit the Grand Hall (next to the monsterpiece) and pass through a series of rooms and once-secret passages, following signs for "Ponte dei Sospiri/Prigioni," through the covered Bridge of Sighs over the canal to the "New" Prisons.*

Medieval justice was harsh. The cells consisted of cold stone with heavily barred windows, a wooden plank for a bed, a shelf, and a bucket. (My question—what did they put on the shelf?)

Circle the cells. Notice the carvings made by prisoners on some of the stone windowsills of the cells. My favorites are on the second cell in the far corner of this building.

The Bridge of Sighs

Criminals were tried and sentenced in the palace, then marched across the canal here to the dark prisons. On this bridge they got their one last look at Venice. They gazed out at the sky, the water, the beautiful buildings.

• *Cross back over the Bridge of Sighs, pausing to look through the marble-trellised windows at all of the tourists and the dreamy Church of San Giorgio Maggiore. Have one last sigh.*

❧ 16 ❧
ACCADEMIA

The main sight to see in Venice is Venice. If you only have a day in Venice, I'm a little hesitant to recommend visiting the Accademia (pron: ack-ah-DAY-mee-ah).

Still, the Accademia is the greatest museum anywhere for Venetian Renaissance art and a good overview of painters whose works you'll see all over town. Venetian art is underrated and, I think, misunderstood. It's nowhere near as famous today as the work of the florescent Florentines, but it's livelier, more colorful, and simply more fun.

ORIENTATION
Cost: €7.

Hours: Mon 8:15–14:00, Tue–Sun 8:15–19:15. Shorter hours off-season. Visit early or late to miss crowds.

Getting there: The museum faces the Grand Canal, just over the wooden Accademia bridge. It's a 15-minute walk from St. Mark's Square (follow signs to "Accademia"). Vaporetto stop: Accademia.

Information: Precious little. Some rooms have sheets of information in English. Guidebooks are for sale in the bookshop. Tel. 041-522-2247.

Note: The Peggy Guggenheim museum of modern art is a five-minute walk east along the Grand Canal. Housed in a small palace on the Grand Canal, it's an excellent collection, well displayed, and a great introduction to nearly every major movement in modern art (for more information, see page 460).

Tours: An audioguide tour costs €4 (or €6 with 2 earphones). Hour-long

ACCADEMIA—OVERVIEW

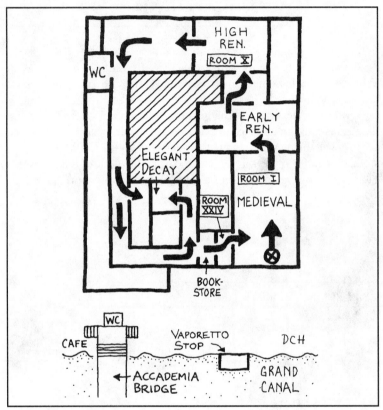

guided tours for €6 are offered Mon–Fri at 10:00, 11:00, and 12:00 (you can skip to the front of the line if buying a tour).

Length of our Tour: One hour.

Photography: Not allowed.

Cuisine art: Bar Accademia Foscarini is a simple pizzeria at the base of the bridge.

Starring: Titian, Veronese, Giorgione, and Tintoretto.

VENICE—SWIMMING IN LUXURY

• *Buy your ticket, check your bag, and head upstairs to a large hall filled with gold-leaf altarpieces. Immediately past the turnstile, turn left, enter the small Room XXIV, and take a seat.*

The Venetian love of luxury shines through in Venetian painting. We'll see grand canvases of colorful, spacious settings peopled with happy Venetians in luxurious clothes having a great time. Even in solemn religious works, the Venetian love of color and beauty is obvious.

We'll work chronologically from medieval days to the 1700s. But before we start at the medieval beginning, let's sneak a peek at a work by the greatest Venetian Renaissance master, Titian.

Titian (Tiziano Vecellio)— *Presentation of the Virgin*

This work is typical of Venetian Renaissance art. Here and throughout this museum, you will find: (1) bright, rich color, (2) big canvases, (3) Renaissance architectural backgrounds, (4) slice-of-life scenes of Venice (notice the market woman in the foreground selling eggs), and (5) three-dimensional realism.

The scene is the popular "Biblical" story (though it's not in the Bible) of the child Mary, later to be the mother of Jesus, being presented to the high priest in Jerusalem's temple. But here the religious scene is more an excuse for a grand display of Renaissance architecture and colorful robes.

The painting is a parade of colors. Titian (pron: TEESH-un) leads you from color to color. First, the deep blue sky and mountains in the background. Then down to the bright red robe of one of the elders. Then you notice the figures turning and pointing at something. Your eye follows up the stairs to the magnificent jeweled robes of the priests.

But wait! What's that along the way? In a pale blue dress that sets her apart from all the other colored robes, dwarfed by the enormous staircase and columns, is the tiny, shiny figure of the child Mary almost floating up to the astonished priest. She is unnaturally small, towered over by the priests, and easily overlooked at first glance. When we finally notice her, we realize all the more how delicate she is, a fragile flower amid the hustle, bustle, and epic grandeur. Venetians love this painting and call it, appropriately enough, "the Little Mary."

Now that we've gotten a taste of Renaissance Venice at its peak, let's backtrack and see some of Titian's predecessors.

• *Return to Room I, stopping at a work (near the turnstile) of Mary and baby Jesus.*

MEDIEVAL ART—PRE-3-D

Medieval painting such as the work you see in this hall was religious. The point was to teach Bible stories and doctrines to the illiterate masses by using symbolism. This art then is less realistic, less colorful, and less dramatic than later Renaissance art. Look around the hall, and you'll see a lot of gold in the paintings. Medieval Venetians, with their close ties to the East, borrowed techniques such as gold leafing from Byzantine (modern Istanbul) religious icons.

-------------------------------- **MEDIEVAL** --------------------------------

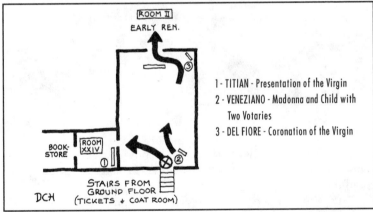

1 - TITIAN - Presentation of the Virgin
2 - VENEZIANO - Madonna and Child with Two Votaries
3 - DEL FIORE - Coronation of the Virgin

Veneziano—*Madonna and Child with Two Votaries* (*Madonna e Bambino con Due Votari*)

There's a golden Byzantine background of heaven, and the golden halos let the masses know that these folks are holy. The child Jesus is a baby in a bubble, an iconographical symbol of his "aura" of holiness.

Notice how two-dimensional and unrealistic this painting is. The size of the figures reflects their religious importance, not their actual size—Mary is huge, being both the mother of Christ as well as "Holy Mother Church." Jesus is next, then the two angels crowning Mary. Finally, in the corner, are two mere mortals kneeling in devotion.

• *In the far right corner of the room you'll find . . .*

Jacobello del Fiore— *Coronation of the Virgin*

This swarming beehive of saints is an attempt to cram as much information as possible into one space. The architectural setting is a clumsy attempt at three-dimensionality. The saints are simply stacked one on top of the other rather than receding into the distance as they would in real life.

• *Enter Room II at the far end of this hall.*

EARLY RENAISSANCE (1450–1500)

Only a few decades later artists rediscovered the natural world and how to capture it on canvas. With this Renaissance, or "rebirth," of the arts and attitudes of ancient Greece and Rome, painters took a giant leap forward. They weeded out the jumble of symbols and fleshed out cardboard characters into real people.

EARLY RENAISSANCE

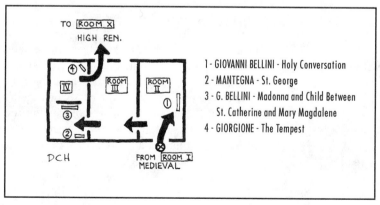

1 - GIOVANNI BELLINI - Holy Conversation
2 - MANTEGNA - St. George
3 - G. BELLINI - Madonna and Child Between St. Catherine and Mary Magdalene
4 - GIORGIONE - The Tempest

Giovanni Bellini—*Holy Conversation* (*Retable di San Giobbe*)

One key to the Renaissance was balance. Here Giovanni Bellini (pron: bell-EE-nee) takes only a few figures, places them in a spacious architectural setting, and balances them half on one side of Mary and half on the other. The overall effect is one of calm and serenity rather than the hubbub of the "Coronation" we just saw. Look at St. Sebastian—even arrows can't disturb the serenity.

This is a religious scene—a mythical meeting of Mary and the baby Jesus with saints. Left to right, you'll find Francis (founder of an order of medieval monks), John the Baptist, Job, Dominic (founder of another order of monks), Sebastian, and Louis. But Bellini is more interested in pleasing the eye than teaching Church doctrine.

The painting has three descending arches. The top one is the Roman arch above the scene. Below that is a pyramid-shaped "arch" formed by the figures themselves, with Mary's head at the peak. Still lower is a smaller arch formed by the three musician angels. Subconsciously, this creates a mood of spaciousness, order, and balance.

Bellini was the teacher of two more Venetian greats, Titian and Giorgione. His gift to the Venetian Renaissance was the "haze" he put over his scenes, giving them an idealized, glowing, serene—and much copied—atmosphere.

• *Climb the small staircase, pass through Room III and into the small Room IV.*

Mantegna—*St. George* (*San Giorgio*)

This Christian warrior is essentially a Greek nude sculpture with armor painted on. Notice his stance with the weight resting on one leg (*contrapposto*), the same as a classical sculpture or Michelangelo's *David* or an Italian guy trying to look cool on the street corner. Also, Mantegna (pron: mahn-TAYN-yah) has placed him in a doorway that's really just an architectural niche designed for a classical statue.

The Renaissance began in Florence among sculptors and architects. Even the painters were sculptors, "carving" out figures (like this) with sharp outlines, then filling them in with color. *St. George* is different in that respect from other works in the museum. It has a harder Florentine edge to it compared with the hazy Venetian outlines of Bellini.

St. George typifies Renaissance balance—a combination of stability and movement, alertness and relaxation, humility and proud confidence. With the broken lance in his hand and the dragon at his feet, George is the strong Renaissance Man slaying the medieval dragon of superstition and oppression.

• *Find three women and a baby.*

Bellini—*Madonna and Child Between St. Catherine and Mary Magdalene*

In contrast to Mantegna's sharp three-dimensionality, this is just three heads on a flat plane with a black backdrop. Their features are soft, hazy, atmospheric, glowing out of the darkness as though lit by the soft light of a candle. It's not sculptural line that's important here, but color—warm, golden, glowing flesh tones.

Bellini painted dozens of Madonna-and-Childs in his day. (Others are nearby.) This Virgin Mary's pretty, but it can't compare with the sheer idealized beauty of Mary Magdalene (on the right). With her hair down like the prostitute she was, yet with a childlike face, thoughtful and repentant, this is the perfect image of the innocent woman who sinned by loving too much.

• *Around the partition, you'll find . . .*

Giorgione—*The Tempest*

It's the calm before the storm. The atmosphere is heavy, luminous but ominous. There's a sense of mystery. Who is the woman suckling her baby

in the middle of the countryside? And the soldier, is he spying on her or protecting her? Do they know that the serenity of this beautiful landscape is about to be shattered by an approaching storm?

The mystery is heightened by contrasting elements. The armed soldier contrasts with the naked lady with her baby. The austere ruined columns contrast with the lusciousness of nature. And, most important, the stillness of the foreground scene is in direct opposition to the threatening storm in the background.

Giorgione (pron: jor-JONE-ee) was as mysterious as his few paintings, yet he left a lasting impression. A student of Bellini, he learned to use haziness to create a melancholy mood of beauty in his work. But nothing beautiful lasts. Flowers fade, Mary Magdalenes grow old, and, in *The Tempest*, the fleeting stillness of a rare moment of peace is about to be shattered by the slash of lightning—the true center of the composition.

• *Exit and turn left, passing through the long Room VI and up the steps to the large Room X.*

VENETIAN HIGH RENAISSANCE— TITIAN, VERONESE, TINTORETTO (1500–1600)

Veronese—*Feast of the House of Levi*

Parrrrty!! Stand about 10 meters from this enormous canvas, to where it just fills your field of vision...and hey, you're invited. Venice loves the good life, and the party's in full swing. You're in a huge room with a great view of Venice. Everyone's dressed to kill in brightly colored silks. Conversation roars and the servants bring on the food and drink.

This captures the Venetian attitude (more love, less attitude) as well as the style of Venetian Renaissance painting. Remember: (1) bright colors, (2) big canvases, (3) Renaissance architectural settings, (4) scenes of Venetian life, and (5) three-dimensional realism. Painters had mastered realism and now gloried in it.

The Feast of the House of Levi is, believe it or not, a religious work painted for a monastery. The original title was *The Last Supper*. In the center of all the wild goings-on, there's Jesus, flanked by his disciples, sharing a final meal before his crucifixion.

HIGH RENAISSANCE

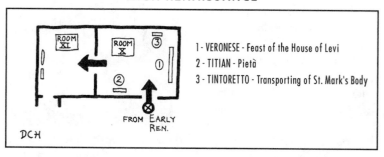

1 - VERONESE - Feast of the House of Levi
2 - TITIAN - Pietà
3 - TINTORETTO - Transporting of St. Mark's Body

FROM EARLY REN.

DCH

This festive feast shows the optimistic spirit of pagan Greece and Rome that was reborn in the Renaissance. Life was a good thing, beauty was to be enjoyed, and man was a strong, good creature capable of making his own decisions and planning his own life. Yet to Renaissance Men and Women this didn't exclude religion. To them, the divine was expressed through natural beauty. God was glorified by glorifying man, His greatest creation. Humanism was an expression of devotion.

Uh-uh, said the Church. In their eyes, the new humanism was the same as the old atheism. The false spring of the Renaissance froze quickly after the Reformation, when half of Europe left the Catholic Church and became Protestant. The Church pulled in the wagons and stamped out any hint of free "pagan" thought that might encourage more deserters.

Veronese (pron: vayr-oh-NAY-zee) was hauled before the Inquisition. What did he mean by painting such a bawdy Last Supper? With dwarf jesters? And apostles picking their teeth? And half-dressed ladies? And dogs? And a black man, God forbid? And, worst of all, some German soldiers—that is, Protestants (gasp!)—at the far right!

Veronese argued that it was just artistic license, so they asked to see his—it had expired. But the solution was simple. Rather than change the painting, just fine-tune the title. *Si, no problema. The Last Supper* became the *Feast of the House of Levi.*

Titian—*Pietà*

The Counter-Reformation affected even the great Titian in his last years. Titian was perhaps the most famous painter of his day—even more famous than Michelangelo. He was a great portrait painter and a friend of the dukes, kings, and popes he painted. He was cultured, witty, a fine musician, and businessman—an all-around Renaissance kind of guy. The story goes that he once dropped his brush while painting a portrait of the

Emperor Charles V, the most powerful man in Europe. Charles stooped
and picked it up for him, a tribute to
Titian's stature and genius.

Titian was an old man when he
painted this. He had seen the rise
and decline of the Renaissance. Remember "Little Mary," the colorful,
exuberant Titian painting we saw at
the beginning, done at the height of the Renaissance? Now the canvas
is darker, the mood more somber. Jesus has just been executed, and his
followers have removed his body from the cross. They grieve over it
before burying it. Titian painted this to hang over his own tomb.

There are some Renaissance elements, but they create a whole different mood—the optimism is gone. Jesus is framed by a sculpture
niche like Mantegna's confident St. George, but here the massive Roman
architecture overpowers the figures, making them look puny and helpless. The lion statues are downright fierce and threatening. Instead of
the clear realism of Renaissance paintings, Titian has used rough, messy
brush strokes, a technique that would be picked up by the Impressionists three centuries later. Instead of simple Renaissance balance, Titian
has added a dramatic compositional element—starting with the lion at
lower right, a line sweeps up diagonally along the figures, culminating
in the grief-stricken Mary Magdalene who turns away, flinging her arm
in despair.

Finally, the kneeling figure of Joseph of Arimathea is a self-portrait
of the aging Titian himself, tending to the corpse of Jesus, who symbolizes the once-powerful, now-dead Renaissance Man.

• *Head for the opposite wall, last painting on the right.*

Tintoretto—*The Transporting of St. Mark's Body* (*Trafugamento del Corpo di San Marco*)

This is the event that put Venice on the map, painted in the dramatic,
emotional style that developed after the Renaissance. Tintoretto would
have made a great black-velvet painter. His colors burn with a metallic
sheen, and he does everything possible to make his subject popular
with common people.

In fact, Tintoretto was a common man himself, self-taught, who
took only a few classes from Titian before striking out on his own. He
sold paintings in the marketplace in his youth and insisted on living in
the poor part of town even after he got famous.

Tintoretto has caught the scene at its most dramatic moment. The Moslems in Alexandria are about to burn Mark's body (there's the smoke from the fire in the center) when suddenly a hurricane appears miraculously, sending them running for cover. (See the wisps of baby angel faces in the storm, blowing on the infidels? Look hard, on the left-hand side.) Meanwhile, the Venetian merchants whisk the body away.

Tintoretto makes us part of the action. The square tiles in the courtyard run straight away from us, an extension of our reality, as though we could step right into the scene—or the merchants could carry Mark into ours.

Tintorettos abound here, in the next room, and throughout Venice. Look for these characteristics, some of which became standard features of Baroque art that followed the Renaissance: (1) heightened drama, violent scenes, strong emotions; (2) elongated bodies; (3) strong contrasts between dark and light; (4) vibrant colors; (5) diagonal compositions.

• *Spend some time in this room, the peak of Venice and the climax of the museum. After browsing, enter the next large room and find a large round painting.*

Elegant Decay (1600–1800)

G. B. Tiepolo—*Discovery of the True Cross*

Tiepolo was the last of the great colorful, theatrical Venetian painters. He took the colors of Titian, the grand settings of Veronese, and the dramatic angles of Tintoretto and plastered them on the ceilings of Europe. His best known works are the ceiling decorations in Baroque palaces such as the Royal Palace in Madrid, Spain, and the Residenz in Würzburg, Germany.

Tiepolo was a master of illusion. His works look as though they open up into heaven. Saints and angels cavort overhead as we peek up their robes. His strongly "foreshortened" figures are masterpieces of technical skill, making us feel like the heavenly vision is taking place right above us. Think back on those clumsy attempts at three-dimensionality we saw in the medieval room and realize how far painting has come.

Nearby is Luca Giordano's *Crucifixion of St. Peter*, which also uses a dramatic angle to place us in the thick of the scene—right at the foot of

ELEGANT DECAY

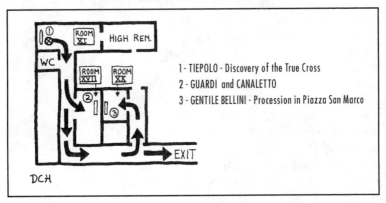

1 - TIEPOLO - Discovery of the True Cross
2 - GUARDI and CANALETTO
3 - GENTILE BELLINI - Procession in Piazza San Marco

the upside-down cross. The violent subject, rippling muscles and heightened emotion are Baroque at its Baroque-iest.

• *Works of the later Venetians are in rooms branching off the long corridor to your left. Walking down the corridor, the first right leads to the WC. Stop in Room XVII, the first door on the left.*

Canaletto and Guardi: Views of Venice

By the 1700s, Venice had retired as a world power and become Europe's number-one tourist attraction. Wealthy offspring of the nobility traveled here to soak up its art and culture. They wanted souvenirs, and what better memento than a picture of the city itself?

Guardi and Canaletto painted "postcards" for visitors who lost their heart to the romance of Venice. The city produced less art... but *was* art. Here are some familiar views of a city that has aged gracefully.

Canaletto gives us a camera's-eye perspective on the city, while Guardi sweetens it up. In Guardi's *The Island of S. Giorgio Maggiore* (right in front of you as you enter Room XVII), we see that familiar view across the water from St. Mark's Square. Guardi has caught the play of light at twilight, the shadows on the buildings, the green of the water and sky, the pink light off the distant buildings, the Venice that exists in the hearts of lovers—an Impressionist work a century ahead of its time.

• *Follow the corridor, turning left at the end. Then take your first left, then left again. Are you in Room XX?*

Gentile Bellini—*Procession in Piazza San Marco* (*Processione in Piazza San Marco*)

A fitting end to our tour is a look back at Venice in its heyday. This wide-angle view—more than any human eye could take in at once—

by Giovanni's big brother reminds us how little Venice has changed over the centuries. There is St. Mark's gleaming gold with mosaics, the three flagpoles out front, the old Campanile on the right, and the Doge's Palace. (But there's no clock tower with the two bronze Moors yet.) Every detail is in perfect focus regardless of its distance from us, presented for our inspection. Take some time to linger over this and the other views of old Venice in this room. Then get outta here and enjoy the real thing.

• *To exit, backtrack to the main corridor and turn left past the bookstore. Say ciao to Titian's Little Mary on the way out.*

FLORENCE

THE RENAISSANCE WALK

UFFIZI GALLERY

BARGELLO

*A*s the birthplace of the Renaissance, Florence gave us enough great art to overwhelm a Medici. With a little help from Mona, you'll squint into Dante's inferno, look *David* straight in the eyes, and sway to the seductive rhythm of Botticelli's *Birth of Venus*. From Michelangelo to Leonardo, from cappuccino to the best gelati in Italy, the art of Florence is a nonstop joy.

❊ 17 ❊
THE RENAISSANCE WALK

After centuries of labor, Florence gave birth to the Renaissance. Great and rich as Florence may be, it's easily covered on foot, and while "you could spend a lifetime here," let's pretend we've got eight hours—three for a walk through the old town, from *David* to the Duomo to the river, an hour for the Bargello (top statues), two for the Uffizi (best Italian painting anywhere), an hour for lunch, and an hour for waiting in lines (try to reserve ahead at the Uffizi—see Uffizi chapter for specifics). Start with the walk (but keep the opening hours in mind).

ORIENTATION

Accademia (Michelangelo's *David*): €8.50 (ask about the combo ticket that covers the Bargello and Medici Chapel). Open Tue–Sun 8:30–18:50, Sat until 22:00, closed Mon, shorter hours off-season (last entry 30 minutes before closing). No photos or videos are allowed. The museum is most crowded on Sun, Tue, and the first thing in the morning. It's on Via Ricasoli 60. Tel. 055-238-8609.

The Duomo (cathedral): Free, Mon–Wed and Fri–Sat 10:00–17:00, Thu 10:00–15:30, Sun 13:30–17:00, first Sat of month 10:00–15:30. Climbing the dome costs €5.50 (Mon–Fri 8:30–19:00, Sat 8:30–17:00, closed Sun, first Sat of month 8:30–15:20).

Giotto's Tower: Costs €5.50. Open daily 9:00–19:30, shorter hours off-season, last entry 40 minutes before closing.

Baptistery: €3. Interior open Mon–Sat 12:00–18:30, Sun 8:30–13:30. The famous bronze doors are on the outside so they're always "open" (viewable) and free.

Museo dell' Opera del Duomo: €5.50. Open Mon–Sat 9:30–18:30, Sun 8:00–14:00. This is one of the few museums open on Mon. It's located across the street from the cathedral (on the east side) at Piazza del Duomo 9. Tel. 055-230-2885.

Getting there: The Accademia is a 15-minute walk from the train station, 10 minutes from the cathedral (northeast on Via Ricasoli). Taxis are reasonable.

Information: A tourist information office is across the street from the front of the train station (pick up the update of current museum hours). Two fine bookshops are across from the Accademia. WCs in Accademia and in cafés along the walk.

Length of our tour: Three hours.

Photography: Photos are prohibited in the Accademia. In churches and other museums, photos without a flash are generally allowed.

Cuisine art: You'll find cafés, self-service cafeterias, bars, and gelato shops along the route.

Starring: Michelangelo, Brunelleschi, and Ghiberti.

THE TOUR BEGINS

The Duomo, the cathedral with the distinctive red dome, is the center of Florence and the orientation point for this walk. If you ever get lost, home's the dome.

Our walk through Florence's top sights is one kilometer long (or slightly more than a half mile), running from the Accademia (home of Michelangelo's *David*), past the Duomo, and down Florence's main pedestrian-only street to the Arno River.

We'll start at the Accademia (2.5 long blocks north of the Duomo), though you could easily start at the Duomo and visit the Accademia later.

• *Head to the Accademia. If there's a line, as you shuffle your way along, notice the perspective tricks on the walls of the ticket room.*

THE FLORENTINE RENAISSANCE (1400–1550)

In the 13th and 14th centuries, Florence was a powerful center of banking, trading, and textile manufacturing. The resulting wealth fertilized the cultural soil. Then came the Black Plague of 1348. A third of the population died, but the infrastructure remained strong, and the city rebuilt stronger than ever. Led by Florence's chief family, the art-crazy Medicis, and with the natural aggressive and creative spirit of the Florentines, it's no wonder the long-awaited Renaissance finally took root here.

RENAISSANCE WALK—OVERVIEW

The Renaissance—the "rebirth" of Greek and Roman culture that swept across Europe—started around 1400 and lasted about 150 years. In politics, the Renaissance meant democracy. In science, a renewed interest in exploring nature. The general mood was optimistic and "humanistic," with a confidence in the power of the individual.

In medieval times, poverty and ignorance had made life "nasty, brutish, and short" (for lack of a better cliché). The church was the people's opiate, and their lives were only a preparation for a happier time in heaven after leaving this miserable vale of tears.

Medieval art was the church's servant. The most noble art form was architecture—churches themselves—and other arts were considered most worthwhile if they embellished the house of God. Painting and sculpture were narrative and symbolic, basically there to tell Bible stories to the devout and illiterate masses.

As prosperity rose in Florence, so did people's confidence in life and themselves. Middle-class craftsmen, merchants, and bankers felt they could control their own destinies, rather than being at the whims of nature. They found much in common with the ancient Greeks and Romans, who valued logic and reason above superstition and blind faith.

Renaissance art was a return to the realism and balance of Greek and Roman sculpture and architecture. Domes and round arches replaced Gothic spires and pointed arches. In painting and sculpture, Renaissance artists strove for realism. Merging art and science, they used mathematics, the laws of perspective, and direct observation of nature to paint the world on canvas.

This was not an anti-Christian movement, though it was a logical and scientific age. Artists saw themselves as an extension of God's creative powers. At times, the church even supported the Renaissance and commissioned many of its greatest works. Raphael frescoed Plato and Aristotle to the walls of the Vatican. But for the first time in Europe since Roman times we also find rich laymen who want art simply for art's sake.

After 1,000 years of waiting, the smoldering fires of Europe's classical heritage broke out in flames in Florence.

The Accademia—Michelangelo's *David*

Start with the ultimate. When you look into the eyes of Michelangelo's *David*, you're looking into the eyes of Renaissance Man. This 4.5-meter (14 feet) symbol of divine victory over evil represents a new century and a whole new Renaissance outlook. This is the age of Columbus and classicism, Galileo and Gutenberg, Luther and Leonardo—of Florence and the Renaissance.

In 1501, Michelangelo Buonarotti, age 26, a Florentine, was commissioned to carve a large-scale work for the Duomo. He was given a block of marble that other sculptors had rejected as too tall, shallow, and flawed to be of any value. But Michelangelo picked up his hammer and chisel, knocked a knot off what became David's heart and started to work.

The figure comes from a Bible story. The Israelites, God's chosen people, are surrounded by barbarian warriors led by a brutish giant named Goliath who challenges the Israelites to send out someone to fight him. Everyone is afraid except one young shepherd boy—David. Armed only with a sling, which he throws over his shoulder, David picks up some stones in his other hand and heads out to face Goliath.

The statue captures David as he's sizing up his enemy. He stands relaxed but alert, leaning on one leg in a classical pose. In his powerful right hand he fondles the stones he'll fling at the giant. His gaze is steady—searching with intense concentration but also with extreme confidence. Michelangelo has caught the precise moment when David is saying to himself: "I can take this guy."

David is a symbol of Renaissance optimism. He's no brute but a civilized, thinking individual who can grapple with and overcome problems. He needs no armor, only his God-given body and wits. Look at his right hand, with the raised veins and strong, relaxed fingers. Many complained that it was too big and overdeveloped. But this is the hand of a man with the strength of God. No mere boy could slay the giant. But David, powered by God, could...and did.

Originally, the statue was commissioned to go on top of the church, but the people loved it so much they put it next to Palazzo Vecchio on the main square where a copy stands today. (If the relationship between the head and body seems a bit out of proportion, remember, Michelangelo designed it to be seen "correctly" from far below the rooftop of a church.)

Florentines could identify with David. Like David, they considered themselves God-blessed underdogs fighting their city-state rivals. In a deeper sense they were civilized Renaissance people slaying the ugly giant of medieval superstition, pessimism, and oppression.

• *A fine bust of an older, brooding Michelangelo (by Volterra) looks on. David stands under a wonderful Renaissance dome. Hang around awhile. Lining the hall leading up to David are other statues by Michelangelo— his Prisoners (Prigioni), St. Matthew, and a Pietà.*

Prisoners

These unfinished figures seem to be fighting to free themselves from the stone. Michelangelo believed the sculptor was a tool of God, not creating but simply revealing the powerful and beautiful figures He put in the marble. Michelangelo's job was to chip away the excess, to reveal. He needed to be in tune with God's will, and, whenever the spirit came upon him, Michelangelo worked in a frenzy, often for days on end without sleep.

The *Prisoners* give us a glimpse at this fitful process, showing us the restless energy of someone possessed, struggling against the rock that binds them. Michelangelo was known to shout at his figures in frustration: "Speak!" You can still see the grooves from the chisel and you can picture Michelangelo hacking away in a cloud of dust. Unlike most sculptors, who built a model then marked up their block of marble to know where to chip, Michelangelo always worked freehand, starting from the front and working back. These figures emerge from the stone (as his colleague Vasari put it) "as though surfacing from a pool of water."

The *Prisoners* were designed for the tomb of Pope Julius II (who also commissioned the Sistine Chapel ceiling). Michelangelo may have abandoned them simply because the project itself petered out, but he may have deliberately left them unfinished. Having satisfied himself that he'd accomplished what he set out to do, and seeing no point in polishing them into their shiny, finished state, he went on to a new project.

As you study the *Prisoners*, notice Michelangelo's love of and understanding of the human body. His greatest days were spent sketching the muscular, tanned, and sweating bodies of the workers in the Carrara marble quarries. Here, the prisoners' heads and faces are the least-developed part—they "speak" with their poses.

Pietà

In the unfinished *Pietà* (the threesome closest to *David*), Michelangelo emphasises the theological point of any pietà, Christ's death, by emphasizing the heaviness of Jesus' dead body. Christ's massive arm is almost the size of his bent and broken legs. By stretching his body—if he stood up he'd be over two meters tall (seven feet)—its weight is exaggerated.

• *Leaving the Accademia (possibly after a look at its paintings, including two Botticellis), turn left and walk 10 minutes to the Duomo down Via Ricasoli. The dome of the Duomo is best viewed just to the right of the facade on the corner of the pedestrian-only street (see map).*

THE DUOMO

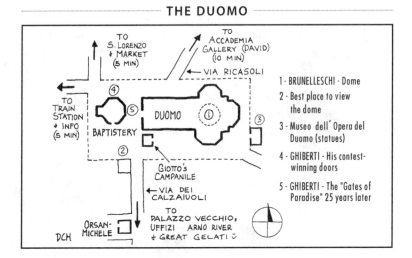

1 - BRUNELLESCHI - Dome

2 - Best place to view the dome

3 - Museo dell' Opera del Duomo (statues)

4 - GHIBERTI - His contest-winning doors

5 - GHIBERTI - The "Gates of Paradise" 25 years later

The Duomo—Florence's Cathedral

The dome of Florence's cathedral helped kick off the Florentine Renaissance by inspiring other artists to great things. The big but unremarkable church itself (nicknamed the Duomo) is Gothic, built in the Middle Ages by architects who left it unfinished—with a big hole in the roof. In the 1400s, the architect Brunelleschi was called on to finish the job. Brunelleschi capped the church with a Roman-style dome—a tall, self-supporting dome as grand as the ancient Pantheon—which he had studied intensely.

He used a dome within a dome. First he built the grand white skeletal ribs, which you can see, then he filled them in with interlocking bricks in a herringbone pattern. The dome grew igloo-style, supporting itself as it proceeded from the base upward. When they reached the top, Brunelleschi arched the ribs in and "nailed" them in place with the lantern. His dome, built in only 14 years, was the largest since Rome's Pantheon.

Brunelleschi's dome was the wonder of the age, the model for many domes to follow. People gave it the ultimate compliment saying "not even the ancients could have done it." Michelangelo, setting out to construct the dome of St. Peter's, drew inspiration from the dome of Florence. He said, "I'll make its sister... bigger, but not more beautiful."

Giotto's Tower

You can climb the dome, but the bell tower (to the right of the facade) is easier and rewards you with a better view. Giotto, like any good Renaissance genius, wore several artistic hats. Considered the father of modern painting, he designed this 84-meter-tall (274 feet) bell tower for the Duomo two centuries before the age of Michelangelo. In his day Giotto was called the ugliest man to ever walk the streets of Florence, but he left the city what, in our day, many call the most beautiful bell tower in all of Europe.

The ornate neo-Gothic front of the church is from the 1870s and is generally ridiculed. (While one of this book's authors thinks it's the most beautiful church facade this side of heaven, the other one naively agrees with those who call it "the cathedral in pajamas.") Thin marble

sheets cover the brick construction, decorating the entire exterior. The inside is worth a walk only for its coolness and a look at how bare the terrible flood of 1966 left it.

Either now or later, you may want to visit the wonderful Museo dell' Opera del Duomo (museum of the cathedral, across the street, behind the church). In it you will see Brunelleschi's wooden model of his dome, Ghiberti's doors (described below), a fine collection of Donatello statues, and a late *Pietà* by Michelangelo (on the second floor). According to most tour guides, the head of Nicodemus (the old guy on top) is a self-portrait of the aging Michelangelo.

• *The Baptistery is the small octagonal building in front of the church.*

Baptistery—Ghiberti's Bronze Doors

Florence's Baptistery is dear to the soul of the city. The locals, eager to link themselves to the classical past, believed (wrongly) that this was a Roman building. It *is* Florence's oldest building (10th century). Most festivals and parades either started or ended here. Go inside (for a modest fee) for a fine example of pre-Renaissance mosaic art (1300s).

The Last Judgment on the ceiling gives us a glimpse of the medieval worldview. Life was a preparation for the afterlife, when you would be judged good or bad, black or white, with no in-between. Christ, peaceful and reassuring, would bless you with heaven (on His right hand) or send you to hell (at the base of the ceiling, to Christ's left) to be tortured by demons and gnashed between the teeth of monsters. This hellish scene looks like something right out of the *Inferno* by Dante...who was dipped into the baptismal waters right here.

The Baptistery's bronze doors bring us out of the Middle Ages and into the Renaissance. Florence had great civic spirit, with different guilds and merchant groups embellishing their city with great art. For the Baptistery's north doors (on the right side as you face the Baptistery with the Duomo at your back), they staged a competition for the commission. All the greats entered, and 25-year-old Lorenzo Ghiberti won easily, beating out heavyweights such as Donatello and Brunelleschi (who, having lost the Baptistery gig, was free to go to Rome, study the Pantheon and, later, design the Duomo). The entries of Brunelleschi and Ghiberti are in the Bargello, where you can judge them for yourself.

Later, in 1425, Ghiberti was given another commission, for the east doors (facing the church), and this time there was literally no contest. The bronze panels of these doors (the ones with the crowd of tourists looking on) are the doors Michelangelo said were fit to be the Gates of Paradise. (These panels are copies. The originals are in the nearby Museo dell' Opera del Duomo.) Here we see how the Renaissance was a merging of art and science. Realism was in, and Renaissance artists used math, illusion, and dissection to get it.

The "Jacob and Esau" panel (just above eye level on the left) is a good example of how the artist used receding arches, floor tiles, and banisters to create a background for a realistic scene. The figures in the foreground stand and move like real people, telling the Bible story with human details. Amazingly, this spacious, three-dimensional scene is made from bronze only a few centimeters deep.

Ghiberti spent 27 years (1425–1452) working on these panels. That's him in the center of the door frame, atop the second row of panels—the guy on the left with the shiny bald head.

• *Facing the Duomo, turn right onto the pedestrian-only street that runs from here towards the Arno River.*

Via dei Calzaiuoli

The pedestrian-only Via dei Calzaiuoli leads from the Duomo to Florence's main square and the Uffizi Gallery. This was "Main Street" of the ancient Roman camp that became Florence. Throughout the city's history, this street has connected the religious center (where we are now) with the political center (where we're heading), a 10-minute walk away. In the last decade, traffic jams have been replaced by potted plants, and this is a pleasant place to stroll, people watch, window-shop, catch the drips on your gelato cone, and wonder why American cities can't become pedestrian friendly.

Two blocks past the Duomo, at the intersection of Via dei Calzaiuoli and Via degli Speziali, look right to see an archway, the original entrance to the city. Look around you if you're in the mood for some of the world's best edible art, and drop by an ice cream parlor for a cup of gelato.

Gelati tips: *Nostra Produzione* and *Produzione Propia* mean they make it on the premises. Also, metal tins rather than the normal white plastic indicate it's most likely homemade.

Orsanmichele Church— Florence's Medieval Roots

The Orsanmichele Church (at the intersection with Via dei Tavolini) provides an interesting look at Florentine values. It's a combo church/grainery. Originally this was an open *loggia* (covered porch) with a huge warehouse upstairs to store grain to feed the city during sieges. The arches of the loggia were artfully filled in, and the building gained a new purpose—a church.

The entrance to the church is on the opposite side of the building, one short block off Via del Calzaiuoli. Step inside and find the pillars with spouts in them (over half a meter—two feet—off the ground) for delivering grain from the storage rooms upstairs. Stand before the Gothic tabernacle. Notice its medieval elegance, color, and disinterest in depth and realism. This is a wonderfully medieval scene—Florence in 1350. Remember the candle-lit medieval atmosphere that

ORSANMICHELE CHURCH

```
TO  PALAZZO
    VECCHIO
    & UFFIZI
         VIA  LAMBERTI
V
I
A                            WOOL
C                            MERCHANT'S
A        ①                   GUILD      1 - Tabernacle
L
Z                                        2 - DONATELLO - St. Mark
A
I                                        3 - NANNI - Four Saints
U   ②
O                                        4 - DONATELLO - St. George
L
I        ③ ④
    VIA  ORSANMICHELE
3/98
DCH  ↑  FROM DUOMO
```

surrounds this altarpiece as you view similar altarpieces out of context in the Uffizi Gallery.

Back outside, circle the church. Each niche was filled with an important statue. In Gothic times, statues were set deeply in the niches, simply embellishing the house of God. Here we see statues (as restless as man on the verge of the Renaissance) stepping out from the protection of the church. Donatello's *St. Mark* (in the far right niche as you face the church) is a fine example of the new Renaissance style and advances. Notice his classical *contrapposto* (weight on one foot) stance. And, even though he's fully clothed, you know his anatomy is fully there.

Donatello's great *St. George* (around the right side of the church) is

 alert, stepping out, announcing the new age with its new outlook. (The original statue is in the Bargello.) Compare this Renaissance-style *St. George*, on the right, with the smaller-scale, deeply set, and less sophisticated *Four Saints* statue to its left.

Below some of the niches you'll find the symbols of various guilds and groups that paid for the art, such as the carpenters guild below the *Four Saints*. At

the back of the church is the headquarters of the wool merchants guild—just another rich old building rotting in the shadow of the Florentine superstars.

• *The House of Dante (Casa di Dante) and Florence's best collection of sculpture, the Bargello (see page 320), are just down Via del Tavolini. But let's continue down the mall 50 more meters, to the huge and historic square.*

Palazzo Vecchio—Florence's Political Center

Via dei Calzaiuoli empties into the main civic center of Florence, with the Palazzo Vecchio, the Uffizi Gallery, and the marble greatness of old Florence littering the cobbles. This square still vibrates with the echoes of Florence's past—executions, riots, and great celebrations. Today it's a tourist's world with pigeons, postcards, horse buggies, and tired hubbies.

Stand in the center. Before you towers the Palazzo Vecchio, the Medicis' palatial city hall—a fortress designed to contain its riches and survive the many riots that went with local politics. The windows are just beyond the reach of angry stones, the tower was a handy lookout, and justice was doled out sternly on this square. Michelangelo's *David* once stood (until 1873) where the replica stands today. The original *David*, damaged in a riot (when a bench thrown out of a palace window knocked its left arm off), was moved indoors for its protection.

To the right is the Loggia, once a forum for public debate but later, when the Medicis figured good art was more desirable than free speech, it was turned into an outdoor sculpture gallery. Notice the squirming Florentine themes—conquest, dominance, rapes, and severed heads. Benvenuto Cellini's *Perseus*, the Loggia's most noteworthy piece, shows the Greek hero who decapitated the snake-headed Medusa. They say Medusa was so ugly she turned humans who looked at her to stone—though one of this book's authors thinks she's kinda cute.

• *Step past the replica David through the front door into the Palazzo Vecchio's courtyard.*

This palace replaced the Bargello as Florence's civic center. You're

PALAZZO VECCHIO

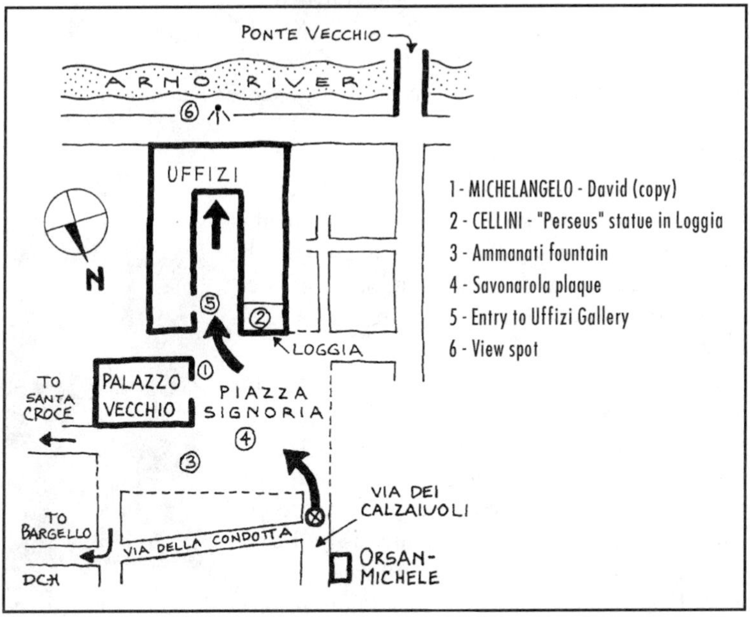

PONTE VECCHIO

ARNO RIVER

⑥

UFFIZI

N

⑤ ②

LOGGIA

TO SANTA CROCE

PALAZZO VECCHIO ①

PIAZZA SIGNORIA

④

③

TO BARGELLO

VIA DELLA CONDOTTA

DCH

VIA DEI CALZAIUOLI

ORSAN-MICHELE

1 - MICHELANGELO - David (copy)
2 - CELLINI - "Perseus" statue in Loggia
3 - Ammanati fountain
4 - Savonarola plaque
5 - Entry to Uffizi Gallery
6 - View spot

surrounded by art for art's sake—a statue frivolously marking the court-yard's center, and ornate walls and columns. Such luxury was a big change 500 years ago.

• *The Palazzo is not worth touring on a quick visit like ours. Return to the square and head right as you leave the palace door, over towards the big fountain by Ammanati that Florentines (including Michelangelo) consider a huge waste of marble—though one of this book's authors...*

Find the round bronze plaque in the cobbles 10 steps in front of the fountain.

Savonarola

The Medici family was briefly thrown from power by an austere monk named Savonarola, who made Florence a theocracy. He organized huge rallies here on the square where he preached, lit by roaring bonfires. While children sang hymns, the devout brought their rich "vanities" and threw them into the flames.

But not everyone wanted a return to the medieval past. The Medici fought back, and they arrested Savonarola. For two days, they tortured him, trying unsuccessfully to persuade him to see their side of things.

Finally, as the plaque says, "On this spot where Savonrola once had the decadence and vanities of Florence burned, Savonarola himself was burned to death"...in the year "MCCCCXCVIII" (1498, I think).

• *Stay cool, we have 100 meters to go. Follow the gaze of the fake David into the courtyard of the two-toned horseshoe-shaped building...*

Uffizi Courtyard—
The Renaissance Hall of Fame

The top floor of this building, known as the Uffizi ("offices") during Medici days, is filled with the greatest collection of Florentine painting anywhere. It's one of Europe's top four or five galleries (see next chapter).

The Uffizi courtyard, filled with merchants and hustling young artists, is watched over by statues of the great figures of the Renaissance. Tourists zero in on the visual accomplishments of the Renaissance—they show best on a postcard. Let's pay tribute to the nonvisual Renaissance as well as we wander through Florence's Hall of Fame.

• *Stroll down the left side of the courtyard from the Uffizi entrance to the river, noticing...*

(1) Lorenzo the Magnificent (next to the Uffizi entrance)—excelling in everything but modesty, he set the tone for the Renaissance—great art patron and cunning broker of power; (2) Giotto (he died from the plague, this statue looks posthumous); (3) Donatello, holding his hammer and chisel; (4) Leonardo da Vinci; (5) Michelangelo, pondering the universe and/or stifling a belch; (6) Dante, considered the father of the Italian language. He was the first Italian to write a popular work (*The Divine Comedy*) in non-Latin, using the Florentine dialect which soon became "Italian" throughout the country; (7) the poet Petrarch; (8) Boccaccio, author of *The Decameron*; (9) the devious-looking Machiavelli, whose book, *The Prince*, taught that the end justifies the means, paving the way for the slick and cunning "Machiavellian" politics of today; and, finally, (10) Amerigo Vespucci (in the corner nearest the river), an explorer who gave his name to a fledgling New World.

• *Finish our walk at the Arno River, overlooking the Ponte Vecchio.*

Ponte Vecchio

Before you is the Ponte Vecchio (Old Bridge). A bridge has spanned this narrowest part of the Arno since Roman times. In the 1500s the

Medicis booted the butchers and tanners and installed the gold- and silversmiths you'll see and be tempted by today. (A fine bust of the greatest goldsmith, Cellini, graces the central point of the bridge.) Notice the Medicis' protected and elevated passageway that led from the

Palazzo Vecchio through the Uffizi, across the Ponte Vecchio, and up to the immense Pitti Palace, four blocks beyond the bridge. During WWII, the local German commander was instructed to blow the bridge up. But even some Nazis appreciate history—he blew up the buildings at either end, leaving the bridge impassable but intact. *Grazie.*

More Michelangelo

One more "must-see" sight, and I'm history. But if you're a fan of earth's greatest sculptor, you won't leave Florence until there's a check next to each of these:

- Bargello Museum—Several Michelangelo sculptures. See page 320.
- Duomo Museum—Another moving *Pietà.* Located behind the Duomo at #9.
- Medici Chapel—The *Night* and *Day* statues, plus others done for the Medici tomb. Located at Church of San Lorenzo.
- Laurentian Library—Michelangelo designed the entrance staircase. Located at Church of San Lorenzo.
- Uffizi Gallery—A rare Michelangelo painting. See next chapter.
- Casa Buonarotti—A house Michelangelo once owned, at Via Ghibellina 70, with some early works.
- Michelangelo's tomb—Church of Santa Croce.

❦ 18 ❦
Uffizi Gallery

In the Renaissance, Florentine artists rediscovered the beauty of the natural world. Medieval art had been symbolic, telling Bible stories. Realism didn't matter. But Renaissance people saw the beauty of God in nature and the human body. They used math and science to capture the natural world on canvas as realistically as possible.

The Uffizi Gallery (pron: oo-FEEDZ-ee) has the greatest overall collection anywhere of Italian painting. We'll trace the rise of realism and savor the optimistic spirit that marked the Renaissance.

My eyes love things that are fair,
and my soul for salvation cries.
But neither will to Heaven rise
unless the sight of Beauty lifts them there.
—Michelangelo

ORIENTATION
Cost: €7.
Hours: Tue–Sun 8:30–18:50, Sat until 22:00, closed Mon (last entry 45 min before closing, take elevator or climb 4 long flights of stairs; to beat crowds, go late in the afternoon or Sat eve). Hours can be erratic; confirm schedule upon arrival in Florence.
Reservations: It's worth reserving in advance (costs €1.20 extra) to avoid a two-hour wait in line during peak season. Simply telephone during their office hours, choose a time, leave your name, and you'll

UFFIZI GALLERY—OVERVIEW

get a 15-minute entry time window and a confirmation number (call 055-294-883 in Italy, or 011-39-055-294-883 from the U.S., Mon–Fri 8:30–18:30, Sat 9:00–12:00). You can reserve from months ahead to the day before (sometimes even on the same day, but it's risky). At the Uffizi, walk briskly past the 200-meter-long line to the special entrance (labeled in English "Entrance for Reservations Only"), give your name and number, pay (cash only), and scoot right in.

Getting there: On the Arno River between Palazzo Vecchio and Ponte Vecchio, a 15-minute walk from the station.

Information: Only books from street vendors. Nothing inside—until the exit, where you'll find a decent card and bookshop. There's only one WC; it's on the top floor, near the snack bar and the stairs leading down to the exit.

Length of our tour: Two hours.

Cloakroom: At the start, far from the finish.

Photography: Cameras without flash are allowed.

Cuisine art: The snack bar at the end of the gallery has salads, desserts, fruit cups, and a great terrace with a Duomo/Palazzo Vecchio view. A cappuccino here is one of Europe's great €2 treats.

Starring: Botticelli, Venus, Raphael, Giotto, Titian, Leonardo, and Michelangelo.

THE ASCENT

• *Buy your ticket, then take the lift or walk up the four flights of the "Monumental" staircase to the top floor. Your brain should be fully aerated from the hike up. Past the ticket taker, look out the window.*

The U-ffizi is U-shaped, running around the courtyard. The entire collection is on this one floor, displayed chronologically. This left wing contains Florentine painting from medieval to Renaissance times. The right wing (which you can see across the courtyard) has Roman and Venetian High Renaissance, the Baroque that followed, and a café terrace facing the Duomo. Connecting the two wings is a short corridor with sculpture. We'll concentrate on the Uffizi's forte, the Florentine section, then get a taste of the art it inspired.

• *Down the hall, enter the first door on the left and face Giotto's giant* Madonna and Child.

MEDIEVAL—WHEN ART WAS AS FLAT AS THE WORLD (1200–1400)

Giotto—*Madonna and Child* (*Madonna col Bambino Gesu, Santi e Angeli*)

For the Florentines, "realism" meant "three-dimensionality." In this room, pre-Renaissance paintings show the slow process of learning to paint a 3-D world on a 2-D canvas.

Before concentrating on the Giotto, look at some others in the room. First look at the crucifixion on your right (as you face the Giotto). This was medieval three-dimensionality—paint a crude two-dimensional work... then physically tilt the head forward. Nice try.

The three Madonna-and-Bambinos in this room were all painted within a few decades of each other around the year 1300. The one on the left (as you face Giotto), by Duccio, is the most medieval and two-

GIOTTO AND MEDIEVAL ART

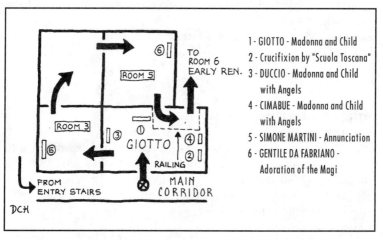

1 - GIOTTO - Madonna and Child

2 - Crucifixion by "Scuola Toscana"

3 - DUCCIO - Madonna and Child with Angels

4 - CIMABUE - Madonna and Child with Angels

5 - SIMONE MARTINI - Annunciation

6 - GENTILE DA FABRIANO - Adoration of the Magi

dimensional. There's no background. The angels are just stacked one on top of the other, floating in an unreal space. Mary's throne is crudely drawn—the left side is at a three-quarters angle while the right is practically straight on. Mary herself is a wispy cardboard-cutout figure seemingly floating a centimeter above the throne.

On the opposite wall, Cimabue's is a vast improvement. The large throne creates an illusion of depth. Mary's foot actually sticks out toward us. Still, the angels are stacked like sardines, serving as a pair of heavenly bookends.

Now let's look at the Giotto. Giotto (pron: JOT-oh) creates a space and fills it. Like a set designer, he builds a three-dimensional "stage"— the canopied throne—then peoples it with real beings. We know the throne has depth because there are angels in front of it and prophets behind. The steps leading up to it give even more depth. But the real triumph here is Mary herself—big and monumental, like a statue. Beneath her robe she has a real live body—her knees and breasts stick out at us. This three-dimensionality was revolutionary in its day, a taste of the Renaissance a century before it began.

Giotto was one of the first "famous" artists. In the Middle Ages, artists were mostly unglamorous craftsmen, like carpenters or cable-TV repairmen. They cranked out generic art and could have signed their work with a bar code. Giotto was the first to be recognized as a genius, a unique individual. He died in a plague which devastated Florence. If there had been no plague, would the Renaissance have started 100 years earlier? No.

• *Enter Room 3, to the left of Giotto.*

Simone Martini—*Annunciation* (*Annunciazione con I Santi Ansano e Giulitta*)

After Giotto's spasm of Renaissance-style realism, painting returned to two-dimensionality for the rest of the 1300s. But several medieval artists (including this one from Siena) eased Florence into the Renaissance.

Martini's *Annunciation* has medieval features you'll see in many of the paintings in the next few rooms: (1) religious subject; (2) gold background; (3) two-dimensionality; (4) meticulous details.

This is not a three-dimensional work. But, remember, this was medieval, so the point was not to recreate reality but to teach religion, especially to the illiterate masses. Martini boiled things down to the basic figures needed to get the message across: (1) The angel appears to sternly tell (2) Mary that she'll be the mother of Jesus. In the center is (3) a vase of lilies, a symbol to tell us Mary is pure. Above is the (4) Holy Spirit as a dove about to descend on her. If the symbols aren't enough to get the message across, Martini has spelled it right out for us: "Hail, favored one, the Lord is with you." Mary doesn't look exactly pleased as punch.

This isn't a beautiful Mary or even a real Mary. She's a generic woman without distinctive features. We know she's pure—not from her face but only because of the halo and symbolic flowers. Before the Renaissance, artists didn't care about the beauty of individual people.

• *Pass through the next room, full of golden altarpieces, stopping at the far end of Room 5.*

Gentile da Fabriano—*Adoration of the Magi* (*Adorazione dei Magi*)

Look at the incredible detail of the Three Kings' costumes, the fine horses, the cow in the cave. The canvas is filled from top to bottom with realistic details—but it's far from realistic. While the Magi worship Jesus in the foreground, their return trip home dangles over their heads in the "background."

This is a textbook example of the international-Gothic style popular with Europe's aristocrats in the early 1400s: elegant, well crafted, design oriented. The religious subject is just an excuse to paint secular luxuries like fine clothes and jewelry. And the background and foreground are compressed together to create an overall design that's pleasing to the eye.

Such exquisite detail work raises the question: Was Renaissance three-dimensionality truly an improvement over Gothic, or simply a different style?

• *Exit to your right and hang a U-turn left into Room 6.*

EARLY RENAISSANCE (MID-1400S)

Uccello—*The Battle of San Romano* (*La Battaglia di S. Romano*)

In the 1400s painters worked out the problems of painting realistically. They concentrated on "perspective" (using mathematics to create the illusion of three-dimensionality) and how to paint the human body.

Paolo Uccello almost literally went crazy trying to conquer the problem of perspective. He was a man obsessed with the three dimensions (thank God he was born before Einstein discovered one more). This canvas is not so much a piece of art as an exercise in perspective. Uccello (pron: oo-CHEL-loh) has challenged himself with every possible problem.

The broken lances at left set up a 3-D "grid" in which to place this crowded scene. The fallen horses and soldiers are experiments in "foreshortening"—shortening the things that are farther away from us to create the illusion of distance. Some of the figures are definitely A-plus material, like the fallen gray horse in the center and the white horse at right riding away. But some are more like B-minus work—the kicking

EARLY RENAISSANCE

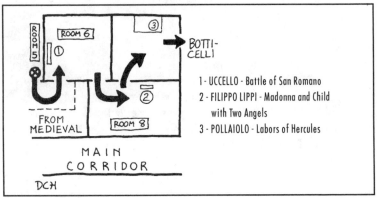

ROOM 5
ROOM 6
①
③
BOTTI-
CELLI
②
FROM MEDIEVAL
ROOM 8

1 - UCCELLO - Battle of San Romano
2 - FILIPPO LIPPI - Madonna and Child
   with Two Angels
3 - POLLAIOLO - Labors of Hercules

MAIN
CORRIDOR

DCH

red horse's legs (to the right) look like hamhocks at this angle, and the fallen soldier (at far right) would only be child-sized if he stood up.

And then there's the D-minus "Are-you-on-drugs?" work. The converging hedges in the background create a nice illusion of a distant hillside maybe 75 or 100 meters away. So what are those soldiers the size of the foreground figures doing there? And jumping the hedge, is that rabbit 12 meters tall (40 feet)? Uccello got so wrapped up in three-dimensionality he kind of lost . . . perspective.

• *Enter Room 8.*

Fra Filippo Lippi—*Madonna and Child with Two Angels (Madonna col Bambino e Due Angeli)*

Compare this Mary with the generic female in Martini's *Annunciation.* We don't need the wispy halo over her head to tell us she's holy—she

radiates sweetness and light from her divine face. Heavenly beauty is expressed by a physically beautiful woman.

Fra (Brother) Lippi was a monk who lived a less-than-monkish life. He lived with a nun who bore him two children. He spent his entire life searching for the perfect Virgin. Through his studio passed Florence's prettiest girls, many of whom decorate the walls here in this room.

Lippi painted idealized beauty, but his models were real flesh-and-blood human beings. You could look through all the thousands of paintings from the Middle Ages and not find anything so human as the mischievous face of one of Lippi's little angel boys.

• *Enter Room 9. Take a look at the two small works by Pollaiolo in the glass case between the windows.*

Pollaiolo—*Labors of Hercules* (*Fatiche di Ercole*)

While Uccello worked on perspective, Pollaiolo studied anatomy. In medieval times, dissection of corpses was a sin and a crime (the two were one then), a desecration of the human body which was the temple of God. But Pollaiolo was willing to sell his soul to the devil for artistic knowledge. He dissected.

These two small panels are experiments in painting anatomy. The poses are the wildest imaginable—to show how the muscles twist and tighten, yes, but also to please international-Gothic fans with a graceful linear design.

There's something funny about this room that I can't put my finger on . . . I've got it—no Madonnas. Not one. We've seen how early-Renaissance artists worked to conquer reality. Now let's see the fruits of their work, the flowering of Florence's Renaissance.

• *Enter the large Botticelli room and take a seat.*

FLORENCE—THE RENAISSANCE BLOSSOMS (1450–1500)

Florence in 1450 was in a firenz-y of activity. There was a can-do spirit of optimism in the air, led by prosperous merchants and bankers and a strong middle class. The government was reasonably democratic, and Florentines saw themselves as citizens of a strong Republic like ancient Rome. Their civic pride showed in the public monuments and works of art they built. Man was leaving the protection of the church to stand on his own two feet.

Lorenzo de Medici, head of the powerful Medici family, epitomized

THE RENAISSANCE BLOSSOMS

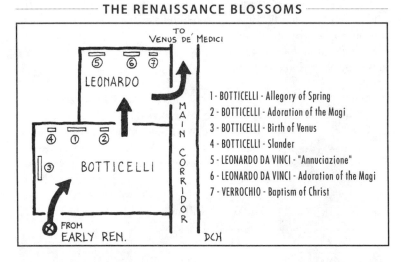

TO
VENUS DE' MEDICI

⑤ ⑥ ⑦

LEONARDO

MAIN CORRIDOR

④ ① ②

⑨ BOTTICELLI

1 - BOTTICELLI - Allegory of Spring
2 - BOTTICELLI - Adoration of the Magi
3 - BOTTICELLI - Birth of Venus
4 - BOTTICELLI - Slander
5 - LEONARDO DA VINCI - "Annuciazione"
6 - LEONARDO DA VINCI - Adoration of the Magi
7 - VERROCHIO - Baptism of Christ

⊗ FROM
EARLY REN.   DCH

this new humanistic spirit. Strong, decisive, handsome, poetic, athletic, sensitive, charismatic, and intelligent, brave-clean-and-reverent Lorenzo was a true Renaissance Man deserving the nickname he went by— "the Magnificent." He gathered Florence's best and brightest around him for evening wine and discussions of great ideas. One of this circle was the painter Botticelli (pron: bot-i-CHEL-ee).

Botticelli—*Allegory of Spring* (*Allegoria dell Primavera*)

Here is the Renaissance in its first bloom, its "springtime" of innocence. Madonna is out, Venus is in. Adam and Eve hiding their nakedness are out, glorious flesh is in. This is a return to the pre-Christian pagan world of classical Greece, where things of the flesh are not sinful. But this is certainly no orgy—just fresh-faced innocence and playfulness.

It's springtime in a citrus grove. The winds of spring blow in (Mr. Blue at right) causing Flora to sprout flowers from her lips. Meanwhile the figure of Spring walks by spreading flowers from her dress. At the left are Mercury and the Three Graces, dancing a delicate maypole dance. The

Graces may be symbolic of the three forms of love—love of beauty, love of people, and sexual love, suggested by the raised intertwined fingers. (They forgot love of peanut butter on toast.) In the center stands Venus, the Greek goddess of love. Above her flies a blindfolded Cupid, happily shooting his arrows of love without worrying who they'll hit.

Botticelli has painted a scene of exquisite beauty. The lines of the bodies, especially of the Graces in their see-through nighties, have pleasing S-like curves. The faces are idealized but have real human features. There's a look of thoughtfulness and even melancholy in the faces—as though everyone knows that the innocence of spring must soon pass.

• *Look at the next painting to the right.*

Botticelli— *Adoration of the Magi* (*Adorazione dei Magi*)

Here's the rat pack of confident young Florentines who reveled in the optimistic pagan spirit—even in a religious scene. Botticelli included himself among the adorers, looking vain in the yellow robe at far right. Lorenzo's the Magnificent-looking guy at the far left.

Botticelli—*Birth of Venus* (*Nascita di Venere*)

This is the purest expression of Renaissance beauty. Venus' naked body is not sensual but innocent. Botticelli thought that physical beauty was a way of appreciating God. Remember Michelangelo's poem: souls will never ascend to Heaven "... unless the sight of Beauty lifts them there."

According to myth, Venus was born from the foam of a wave. Still

only half awake, this fragile newborn beauty is kept afloat on a clam shell while the winds come to blow her to shore, where her maiden waits to cover her. The pose is the same S-curve of classical statues (as we'll soon see). Botticelli's pastel colors make the world itself seem fresh and newly born.

The details show Botticelli's love of the natural world—Venus' wind-blown hair, the translucent skin, the braided hair of her handmaiden, the slight ripple of the wind's chest muscles, and the flowers tumbling in the slowest of slow motions, suspended like musical notes, caught at the peak of their brief but beautiful life.

Mr. and Mrs. Wind intertwine—notice her hands clasped around his body. Their hair, wings, and robes mingle like the wind. But what happened to those toes?

• *"Venus on the Half Shell" (as many tourists call this) is one of the masterpieces of Western art. Take some time with it. Then find the small canvas on the wall to the right, near* La Primavera.

Botticelli—*Slander (La Calumnia)*

The spring of Florence's Renaissance had to end. Lorenzo died young. The economy faltered. Into town rode the monk Savonarola preaching medieval hellfire and damnation for those who embraced the "pagan" Renaissance spirit. "Down, down with all gold and decoration," he roared. "Down where the body is food for the worms." He presided over huge bonfires where the people threw in their fine clothes, jewelry, pagan books...and paintings.

Botticelli listened to Savonarola. He burned some of his own paintings and changed his tune. The last works of his life were darker, more somber and pessimistic of humanity.

Slander spells the end of the Florentine Renaissance. The setting is classic Brunelleschian architecture, but look what's taking place beneath those stately arches. These aren't proud Renaissance Men and Women, but a ragtag, medieval-looking bunch, squatters in an abandoned hall of justice. Here in this chaotic Court of Thieves the accusations fly and everyone is condemned. The naked man pleads for mercy but the hooded black figure, a symbol of his execution, turns away. Once-proud Venus—straight out of *The Birth of Venus*—looks up to heaven as if to ask "What has happened to us?" The classical statues in their niches look on in disbelief.

The German poet Heine said, "When they start by burning books, they'll end by burning people." Savonarola, after four short years of power, was burned on his own bonfire in the Piazza della Signoria, but by then the city was in shambles. The first flowering of the Renaissance was over.

• *Enter the next room.*

Leonardo da Vinci—*Annunciation*

A scientist, architect, engineer, musician, and painter, Leonardo was a true Renaissance Man. He worked at his own pace rather than to please an employer, so he often left works unfinished. The two in this room aren't his best, but even a lesser Leonardo is enough to put a museum on the map, and they're definitely worth a look.

Think back to Martini's *Annunciation* to realize how much more natural, relaxed, and realistic Leonardo's is. He's taken a miraculous event—an angel appearing out of the blue—and made it seem almost commonplace. He constructs a beautifully landscaped "stage" and puts his characters in it. Gabriel has walked up to Mary and now kneels on one knee like an ambassador, saluting her. Look how relaxed his other hand is draped over his knee. Mary, who's been reading, looks up with a gesture of surprise and curiosity. Leonardo has taken a religious scene and presented it in a very human way.

Look at the bricks on the right wall. If you extended lines from them, the lines would all converge at the center of the painting, the distant blue mountain. Same with the edge of the sarcophagus and the railing. Subconsciously, this subtle touch creates a feeling of balance, order, and spaciousness.

Leonardo—*Adoration of the Magi* (unfinished)

Leonardo's human insight is even more apparent here. The poor kings are amazed at the Christ child—even afraid of him. They scurry around like chimps around fire. This work is as agitated as the *Annunciation* is calm, giving us an idea of Leonardo's range. Leonardo was pioneering a new era of painting, showing not just the outer features but the inner personality.

The next painting to the right, *Baptism of Christ,* is by Verrochio, Leonardo's teacher. Legend has it that Leonardo painted the angel on the far left when he was only 14 years old. When Verrochio saw that some kid had painted an angel better than he ever would... he hung up his brush for good.

Florence saw the first blossoming of the Renaissance. But when the cultural climate turned chilly, artists flew south to warmer climes. The Renaissance shifted to Rome.

• *Exit into the main corridor. Breathe. Sit. Admire the ceiling. Look out the window. See you in five.*

Back already? Now continue down the corridor and turn left into the octagonal Venus de' Medici *room. You'll recognize it by the line outside— they only allow 25 people in at a time. Read while you wait. If you skip this because of the line, you'll be missing the next five rooms, which include masterpieces by Cranach, Dürer, Memling, Holbein, Giorgione, and others.*

CLASSICAL SCULPTURE

If the Renaissance was the foundation of the modern world, the foundation of the Renaissance was classical sculpture. Sculptors, painters, and poets alike turned for inspiration to these ancient works as the epitome of balance, 3-D, human anatomy, and beauty. While the best collection of Renaissance sculpture is in the nearby Bargello, these classical statues illustrate nicely what a profound effect the art of the ancient world had on Renaissance artists.

The *Venus de' Medici*, or *Medici Venus* (*Venere de' Medici*), ancient Greece

Is this pose familiar? Botticelli's *Birth of Venus* has the same position of the arms, the same S-curved body, and the same lifting of the right leg. A copy of this statue stood in Lorenzo the Magnificent's garden where Botticelli used to hang out. This one is a Roman copy of the lost original by the great Greek sculptor Praxiteles.

Perhaps more than any other work of art, this statue has been the epitome of both ideal beauty and sexuality. In the 18th and 19th centuries, sex was "dirty," so the sex drive of cultured aristocrats was channeled into a love of pure beauty. Wealthy sons and daughters of Europe's aristocrats made the pilgrimage to the Uffizi to complete their classical education... where they swooned in ecstasy before the cold beauty of this goddess of love.

Louis XIV had a bronze copy made. Napoleon stole her away to Paris for himself. And, in Philadelphia in the 1800s, a copy had to be kept under lock and key to prevent the innocent from catching the Venere-al disease. At first, it may be difficult for us to appreciate such passionate love of art, but, if any generation knows the power of sex to sell something—be it art or underarm deodorant—it's ours.

The Other Statues

The *Medici Venus* is a balanced, harmonious, serene statue from Greece's "Golden Age," when balance was admired in every aspect of life. Its "male" counterpart is on the right, facing Venus. *Apollino* (a.k.a. "Venus with a Penis") is also by the master of smooth, cool lines, Praxiteles.

The other works are later Greek (Hellenistic), when quiet balance was replaced by violent motion and emotion. *The Wrestlers* to the left of Venus is a study in anatomy and twisted limbs—like Pollaiolo's paintings a thousand years later.

The drama of *The Knife Grinder* to the right of Venus stems from the off-stage action—he's sharpening the knife to flay a man alive.

• *Exit the Tribune room and pass through Room 19 into Room 20.*

NORTHERN RENAISSANCE

Hans Baldung Grien—
Copy of Dürer's *Adam and Eve*

The warm spirit of the Renaissance blew north into Germany. Albrecht Dürer (1471–1528), the famous German engraver, traveled to Venice, where he fell in love with all things Italian. Returning home, he painted the First Couple in the Italian style—full-bodied, muscular (check out Adam's abs and Eve's knees), "carved" with strong shading, fresh faced, and innocent in their earthly Paradise. His paintings are in the Prado (see page 439).

This copy by Hans Baldung Grien of Dürer's original was a training exercise. Like many of Europe's artists—including Michelangelo and Raphael—Baldung Grien learned technique by studying Dürer's meticulous engravings, spread by the newly invented printing press.

·CLASSICAL SCULPTURE AND NORTHERN RENAISSANCE·

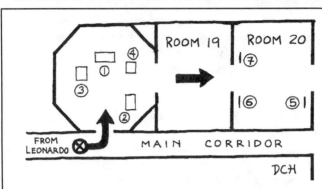

1 - Venus de' Medici
2 - Apollo
3 - Wrestlers
4 - Knife Grinder
5 - HANS BALDUNG GRIEN - Copy of Durer's Adam and Eve
6 - CRANACH - Adam and Eve
7 - CRANACH - Martin Luther and Katherine Von Bora

Lucas Cranach—*Adam and Eve*

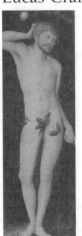

Though the German Lucas Cranach (1472–1553) occasionally dabbled in the "Italian style," he chose to portray his *Adam and Eve* in the now-retro look of international Gothic.

They are slimmer than Dürer's, smoother, more S-shaped, elegant, graceful, shapely, and erotic, with the dainty pinkies of refined aristocrats signing Cranach's paycheck.

Though life-size, this Adam and Eve are not lifelike, not monumental, not full-bodied or muscular, and are not placed in a real-world landscape with distant perspectives. Even so, Cranach (1472–1553) was very much a man of the Renaissance, a friend of Martin Luther and champion of humanism.

Eve sashays forward, with heavy-lidded eyes, to offer the forbidden fruit. Adam stretches to display himself and his foliage to Eve. The two canvases are linked by smoldering eye contact, as Man and Woman awaken to their own nakedness. The Garden of Eden is about to be rocked by new ideas that are both liberating and troubling.

Lucas Cranach—*Martin Luther*

Martin Luther—German monk, fiery orator, and religious whistle-blower—sparked a century of European wars by speaking out against the Catholic Church.

Luther (1483–1546) lived a turbulent life. In early adulthood, the newly ordained priest suffered a severe personal crisis of faith, before finally emerging "born again." In 1517, he openly protested against Church corruption and was excommunicated. Defying both the Pope and Emperor, he lived on the run as an outlaw, watching as his ideas sparked peasant riots. He still found time to translate the New Testament from Latin to modern German, write hymns such as "A Mighty Fortress," and spar with the humanist Erasmus and fellow-Reformer Zwingli.

Now 46 years old, Martin Luther is easing out of the fast lane. Recently married to an ex-nun, he's traded his monk's habit for street clothes, bought a house, had several kids...and has clearly been enjoying his wife's home cooking and home-brewed beer.

Lucas Cranach—*Katherine von Bora* (Luther's wife)

When "Katie" decided to leave her convent, the famous Martin Luther agreed to help find her a husband. She rejected his nominees, saying she'd marry no one...except Luther himself. In 1525, the 42-year-old ex-priest married the 26-year-old ex-nun "to please my father and annoy the Pope." Martin turned his checkbook over to "my lord Katie," who also ran the family farm, raised their six children and 11 adopted orphans, and hosted Martin's circle of friends (including Cranach) at loud, chatty dinner parties.

• *Pass through the next couple of rooms, exiting to a great view of the Arno. Stroll through the sculpture wing.*

The Sculpture Wing
A hundred years ago no one even looked at Botticelli—they came to the Uffizi to see the sculpture collection. Why isn't the sculpture as famous now? Stop at the *Boy Pulling a Spine from His Foot* on your left. This is a famous statue, right? And it must be old because the label says "UN ORIGINAL" in big block letters. But now read the fine print—the tiny little "da" in front. It's not an original at all, but a copy "from" (*da*) an original . . . which is in Rome (in the Capitol Hill Museum).
• *There are benches at the other end of the wing with a great view.*

View of the Arno
Enjoy Florence's best view of the Arno and Ponte Vecchio. You can also see the red-tiled roof of the Vasari Corridor, the "secret" passage connecting Palazzo Vecchio, the Uffizi, Ponte Vecchio, and the Pitti Palace

on the other side of the river (not visible from here)—a kilometer in all. This was the private walkway, wallpapered in great art, for the Medici family's commute from home to work.

As you appreciate the view, remember that it's this sort of pleasure that Renaissance painters wanted you to get from their paintings. For them, a canvas was a window you looked through to see the wide world.

We're headed down the home stretch now. If your "little uffizis" are killing you and it feels like torture, remind yourself it's a pleasant torture and smile . . . like the statue next to you.
• *In the far corridor, turn left into the first room (#25) and grab a blast of cold from the air-conditioner vent below the chairs to the left.*

HIGH RENAISSANCE—
MICHELANGELO, RAPHAEL, TITIAN
(1500–1550)

Michelangelo—*Holy Family (Sacra Famiglia)*
This is the only completed easel painting by the greatest sculptor in history. Florentine painters were sculptors with brushes. This shows it.

Instead of a painting it's more like three clusters of statues with some clothes painted on. The main subject is the holy family—Mary, Joseph, and baby Jesus—and in the background are two groups of nudes looking like classical statues. The background represents the old pagan world, while Jesus in the foreground is the new age of Christianity. The figure of young John the Baptist at right is the link between the two.

Michelangelo was a Florentine—in fact he was like an adopted son of the Medicis who recognized his talent—but much of his greatest work was done in Rome as part of the Pope's face-lift of the city. We can see here some of the techniques he used on the Sistine Chapel ceiling that revolutionized painting—monumental figures, dramatic angles (we're looking up Mary's nose), accentuated rippling muscles, and bright clashing colors (all the more apparent since both this work and the Sistine have been recently cleaned). These added an element of dramatic tension lacking in the graceful work of Leonardo and Botticelli.

Michelangelo painted this for Angelo Doni for 70 ducats. When the painting was delivered, Doni tried to talk Michelangelo down to 40. Proud Michelangelo took the painting away, and wouldn't sell it until the man finally agreed to pay double . . . 140 ducats.

• *Enter Room 26.*

Raphael (Raffaello Sanzo)—*Madonna of the Goldfinch* (*La Madonna del Cardellino*)

Raphael (pron: roff-eye-ELL) perfected his craft in Florence, follow-

ing the graceful style of Leonardo. Like Leonardo, he adds the human touch to a religious subject. In typical Leonardo fashion, this group of Mary, John the Baptist, and Jesus is arranged in the shape of a pyramid with Mary's head at the peak. It's a tender scene painted with warm colors and a hazy background that matches the golden skin of the children.

The two halves of the painting balance perfectly. Draw a line down the middle, through Mary's nose and down through her knee. On the

HIGH RENAISSANCE

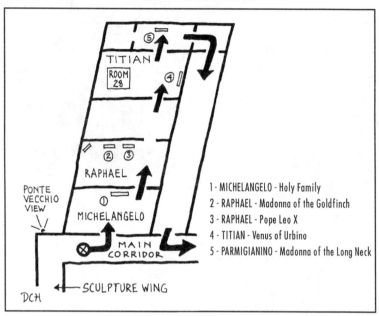

PONTE VECCHIO VIEW

MICHELANGELO

RAPHAEL

TITIAN

ROOM 28

MAIN CORRIDOR

SCULPTURE WING

DCH

1 - MICHELANGELO - Holy Family
2 - RAPHAEL - Madonna of the Goldfinch
3 - RAPHAEL - Pope Leo X
4 - TITIAN - Venus of Urbino
5 - PARMIGIANINO - Madonna of the Long Neck

left is John the Baptist balanced by Jesus on the right. Even the trees in the background balance each other, left and right. These things aren't immediately noticeable, but they help create the subconcious feeling of balance and order that reinforce the atmosphere of maternal security in this domestic scene—pure Renaissance.

Raphael—
Leo X and Cardinals
(Leone X con i Cardinali)

Raphael was called to Rome at the same time as Michelangelo, working next door while Michelangelo did the Sistine ceiling. Raphael peeked in from time to time, learning from Michelangelo's monumental, dramatic figures. His later work is grittier and more realistic than the idealized, graceful, and "Leonardesque" Madonna. Pope Leo is big like a Michelangelo statue. And Raphael captures

Six Degrees of Leo X

This sophisticated, luxury-loving Pope was at the center of an international, Renaissance world that spread across Europe. He crossed paths with many of the Renaissance Men of his generation:

* Leo X's father was **Lorenzo the Magnificent**, patron of **Botticelli** and **Leonardo**.
* When **Leo X** was age 13, his family took in 13-year-old **Michelangelo**.
* **Michelangelo** inspired **Raphael**, who was later hired by **Leo X**.
* **Raphael** exchanged masterpieces with fellow genius **Albrecht Dürer**, who was personally converted by **Martin Luther** (who was friends with **Lucas Cranach**), who was excommunicated by... **Leo X**.
* **Leo X** was portrayed in the movie *The Agony and the Ecstasy* which starred **Charlton Heston**, who was in *Planet of the Apes* with **Burgess Meredith**, who was in *Rocky* with **Sylvester Stallone**...who [ultimately connects with]...**Kevin Bacon**.

some of the seamier side of Vatican life in the cardinals' eyes—shrewd, suspicious, and somewhat cynical. With Raphael, the photographic realism pursued by painters ever since Giotto was finally achieved.

The Florentine Renaissance ended in 1520 with the death of Raphael. Raphael (see his self-portrait to the left of the Madonna) is considered both the culmination and conclusion of the Renaissance. The realism, balance, and humanism we associate with the Renaissance are all found in Raphael's work. He combined the grace of Leonardo with the power of Michelangelo. With his death, the Renaissance shifted again—to Venice.

* *Pass through the next room and enter Room 28.*

Titian (Tiziano)—*Venus of Urbino* (*La Venere di Urbino*)

Compare this Venus with Botticelli's newly hatched Venus, and you get a good idea of the difference between the Florentine and Venetian Renaissance. Botticelli's was pure, innocent, and otherworldly. Titian's should have a staple in her belly button. This isn't a Venus, it's a centerfold—with no purpose but to please the eye and other organs. While Botticelli's allegorical Venus is a message, this is a massage.

Titian and his fellow Venetians took the pagan spirit pioneered in Florence and carried it to its logical hedonistic conclusion. Using bright rich colors, they captured the luxurious life of happy-go-lucky Venice.

Remember how balanced Raphael's *Madonna of the Goldfinch* was? Every figure on one side had a balancing figure on the other. Titian balances his painting a different way—with color. The canvas is split down the middle by the curtain. The left half is dark, the right half warmer. The two halves are connected by a diagonal slash of luminous gold—the nude woman.

By the way, visitors from centuries past also panted in front of this Venus. The poet Byron called it "*the* Venus." With her sensual skin, hey-sailor look, and suggestively placed hand, she must have left them blithering idiots.

• *Find the n-n-n-next painting.*

Parmigianino—
Madonna of the Long Neck
(*Madonna dal Collo Lungo*)

Raphael, Michelangelo, Leonardo, and Titian mastered reality. They could place any scene onto a canvas with photographic accuracy. How could future artists top that?

"Mannerists" such as Parmigianino tried to by going beyond realism, exaggerating it for effect. Using brighter colors and elongated figures (two techniques explored by Michelangelo), they created scenes more elegant and more exciting than real life.

By stretching the neck of his Madonna, Parmigianino (pron: like the cheese) gives her an unnatural swanlike beauty. She has the same pose and position of hands as Botticelli's *Venus* and the *Venus de' Medici*. Her body forms an arcing S-curve—down her neck as far as her elbow, then back the other way along Jesus' body to her knee, then down to her foot. The baby Jesus seems to be blissfully gliding down this slippery slide of sheer beauty.

• *Pass through several rooms, returning to the main corridor where, by the window, you'll see the famous* Venus de' Mallard *statue.*

THE REST OF THE UFFIZI

As art moved into the Baroque period, artists took Renaissance realism and exaggerated it still more—more beautiful, more emotional, or more dramatic. There's lots of great stuff in the following rooms, and I'd especially recommend Tintoretto's *Leda*, the enormous canvases of Rubens, and the shocking ultrarealism of Caravaggio's *Bacchus* and *Abraham Sacrificing Isaac.*

• *But first, head to the end of the corridor for a true aesthetic experience.*

The Little Cappuccin Monk
(*Cappuccino*)—anonymous Italian

This drinkable art form, born in Italy, is now enjoyed all over the world. It's called *The Little Cappuccin Monk* because the coffee's frothy light-and-dark-brown foam looks like the two-toned cowls of the Cappuccin order. Drink it on the terrace in the shadow of the towering Palazzo Vecchio and argue Marx and Hegel—was the Renaissance an economic phenomenon or a spiritual one? *Salute.*

⚜ 19 ⚜
BARGELLO

The Renaissance began with sculpture. The great Florentine painters were "sculptors with brushes." You can see the birth of this revolution of 3-D in the Bargello (pron: bar-JEL-oh), which boasts the best collection of Florentine sculpture. It's a small, uncrowded museum and a pleasant break from the intensity of the rest of Florence.

ORIENTATION

Cost: €4.50.

Hours: Generally daily 8:30–13:50 *but* closed the first, third, and fifth Sun of the month and the second and fourth Mon. Last entry 30 minutes before closing.

Getting there: It's located at Via del Proconsolo 4, a five-minute walk northeast of the Uffizi. Facing the Palazzo Vecchio, head to the far left corner of the square. Go left at Canto de Giugni (at Ristorante Cavallino), then right onto Via della Condotta. Go two blocks and look kitty-corner to the left for a rustic brick building with a spire that looks like a baby Palazzo Vecchio. If lost, ask, "*Doh-vay bar-jel-oh*?"

Information: Nothing in English. Tel. 055-238-8606.

Length of our tour: One hour.

Photography: Cameras without flash are allowed.

Cuisine art: Inexpensive bars and cafés await in the surrounding streets.

Starring: Michelangelo, Donatello, Brunelleschi, Ghiberti, and four different *Davids*.

SCULPTURE IN FLORENCE

• *Buy your ticket and take a seat in the courtyard.*

The Bargello, built in 1255, was Florence's city hall. The heavy fortifications tell us that politics in medieval Florence had occupational hazards. After the administration shifted to the larger Palazzo Vecchio, this became a police station (*bargello*) and then a prison.

The Bargello, a three-story, rectangular building, surrounds this cool and peaceful courtyard. The best statues are found in two rooms—one on the ground floor at the foot of the stairs, and another one flight up, directly above it. We'll proceed logically in a chrono kind of way.

But first, meander around this courtyard and get a feel for sculpture in general and rocks in particular. Sculpture is a much more robust art form than painting. Think of the engineering problems alone of moving these stones from a quarry to an artist's studio. Then the sheer physical strength needed to chisel away for hours on end. A sculptor must be powerful yet delicate, controlling the chisel to chip out the smallest details. Think of Michelangelo's approach to sculpting—he wasn't creating a figure but only liberating it from the rock that surrounded it.

If the Renaissance is humanism, then sculpture is the perfect medium to express it. It shows the human form, standing alone, independent of church, state, or society.

Finally, a viewing note. Every sculpture has an invisible "frame" around it—the stone block it was cut from. Visualizing this frame helps you find the center of the composition.

• *Climb the courtyard staircase to the next floor up and turn right into the large Donatello room. Pause at Donatello's painted bust of Niccolo de Uzzano.*

Donatello (1386–1466)

Donatello was the first great Renaissance genius, a model for Michelangelo and others. He mastered realism, creating the first truly lifelike statues of people since ancient times. Donatello's work is highly personal. Unlike the ancient Greeks, he often sculpted real people, not idealized versions of pretty gods and goddesses. Some of these people are downright ugly. In the true spirit of Renaissance humanism, Donatello was the first to appreciate the beauty of flesh-and-blood human beings—even ordinary ones such as *Niccolo de Uzzano* here.

---------------------------------- **DONATELLO ROOM** ----------------------------------

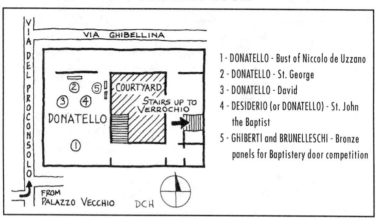

1 - DONATELLO - Bust of Niccolo de Uzzano
2 - DONATELLO - St. George
3 - DONATELLO - David
4 - DESIDERIO (or DONATELLO) - St. John the Baptist
5 - GHIBERTI and BRUNELLESCHI - Bronze panels for Baptistery door competition

Donatello's personality was also a model for later artists. He was moody and irascible, purposely setting himself apart from others in order to concentrate on his sculpting. He developed the role of the "mad genius" that Michelangelo would later perfect.

• At the far end of the room, St. George stands in a niche in the wall.

Donatello—St. George (1416)

A century before Michelangelo sculpted his famous David, this was the unofficial symbol of Florence. George, the Christian slayer of dragons, was just the sort of righteous warrior that proud Renaissance Florentines could rally around in their struggles with nearby cities. He stands on the edge of his niche looking out alertly with the same relaxed intensity and determination that Michelangelo used for his David. This is the original marble statue. A bronze version stands in its original niche at Orsanmichele Church. The relief panel below shows George doing what he's been pondering.

• On the floor to your left you'll find . . .

Donatello—David (c. 1430)

This boyish-approaching-girlish David is quite a contrast with Michelangelo's powerful version at the Accademia. Donatello's smooth-skinned warrior sways gracefully, poking his sword playfully at the severed head of the giant Goliath. He has a *contrapposto* stance similar to Michelangelo's, resting his weight on one leg in the classical style, but it gives him a feminine rather than masculine look. Gazing into his coy eyes is a very different experience from confronting Michelangelo's tough Renaissance Man.

This *David* paved the way for Michelangelo's. Europe hadn't seen a free-standing male nude like this in a thousand years. In the Middle Ages, the human body was considered a dirty thing, a symbol of man's weakness, something to be covered up in shame. The church prohibited exhibitions of nudity like this one and certainly would never decorate a church with it. But in the Renaissance a new class of rich and powerful merchants appeared that bought art for their own personal enjoyment. This particular statue stood in the courtyard of the Medici's palace . . . where Michelangelo, practically an adopted son, grew up admiring it.

This is the first of four different *Davids* in the Bargello: (1) This one, (2) another version by Donatello—look over your left shoulder, (3) Verrochio's *David* upstairs (which we'll visit), and (4) Michelangelo's other unfinished version we'll see downstairs. Compare and contrast the artists' styles as you see them. How many ways can you slay a giant?

• St. John the Baptist, *done in the style of Donatello, is to the right of* David #1.

Desiderio da Settignano (or Donatello)— *St. John the Baptist* (*S. Giovanni Battista*)

John the Baptist was the wild-eyed wildcat prophet who lived in the desert preaching, eating bugs and honey, and baptizing Saviors of the World. Donatello, the mad prophet of the coming Renaissance, might have identified with this original eccentric.

• *On the wall you'll find some bronze relief panels. Don't look at the labels just yet.*

You be the judge. Here are the two finalists for the Baptistery door competition—Ghiberti's and Brunelleschi's. Which do you like the best?

(Ghiberti's, on the left, won.)

Ghiberti and Brunelleschi—Baptistery Door Competition Entries (two different relief panels, titled *Il Sacrificio di Abramo*)

These two versions of *Abraham Sacrificing Isaac* were finalists in the contest (1401) held to decide who would do the bronze doors of the Baptistery. (Donatello also entered but lost.) Ghiberti eventually won and later did the doors known as the Gates of Paradise. Brunelleschi lost—fortunately for us—freeing him to design the Duomo's dome.

Both artists catch the crucial moment when Abraham, obeying God's orders, prepares to slaughter and burn his only son as a sacrifice. At the last moment—after Abraham passed this test of faith—an angel of God appears to stop the bloodshed.

One panel is clearly better than the other. Composition: One is integrated and cohesive, the other a balanced knick-knack shelf of segments. Human drama: One has bodies and faces that speak. The boy's body is a fine classical nude in itself, so real and vulnerable. Abraham's face is intense and ready to follow God's will. Perspective: An angel zooms in from out of nowhere to save the boy in the nick of time.

• *Exit the Donatello room through the same door you entered. Cross to the opposite side of the courtyard, then take your first left and climb the red-carpeted stairs to the next floor. At the top of the stairs, turn left, then left again. Verrochio's David stands in the center of the room.*

Verrochio—*David* (c. 1470)

Verrochio is best known as the teacher of Leonardo da Vinci, but he was also the premier sculptor between the time of Donatello and Michelangelo. This saucy, impertinent *David* is more masculine than Donatello's, but a far cry from Michelangelo's monumental version. He leans on one leg, but it's not a firm, commanding stance but a nimble one (especially noticeable from behind). The artist is clearly contrasting the smug smile of the victor with Goliath's "Oh, have I got a headache" expression.

• *Nearby is a room of glass cases filled with small statues. In the center of the room, you'll find . . .*

Pollaiolo—*Hercules and Antaeus* (*Ercole e Anteo*)

Antaeus was invincible as long as he was in contact with the earth, his mother. So Hercules just picked him up like a Renaissance Hulk Hogan and crushed him to death.

More than any early artist from this period, Pollaiolo studied the human body in motion. These figures are not dignified Renaissance Men, but brutish, violent, animal-like beasts. Yet in this tangled pose of flailing arms and legs there still is a Renaissance sense of balance—all the motion spins around the center of gravity where their bodies grind together.

• *In the glass cases, you'll see small-scale versions of the* Mercury *we'll soon see. Poke around, then descend back to the courtyard on the ground floor. The final room we'll see is through the door to your left at the bottom of the stairs.*

Lesser Michelangelos

Michelangelo—*Bacchus* (*Bacco*) (c. 1497)

Maybe Michelangelo had a sense of humor after all. Compare this tipsy Greek god of wine with his sturdy, sober *David*, begun two years later. *Bacchus* isn't nearly so muscular, so monumental . . . or so sure on his feet. Hope he's not driving. The pose, the smooth muscles, and curving belly and hip look more like Donatello's boyish *David*.

This is Michelangelo's first major commission. He often vacillated between showing man as strong and noble, and as weak and perverse. This isn't the nobility of the classical world but the decadent side of orgies and indulgence.

• *Just to the left you'll find . . .*

GROUND FLOOR

STAIRS DOWN FROM VERROCHIO

UPSTAIRS TO DONATELLO

COURT YARD

④
③
②
①
⑥
⑤
⑦

VIA PROCONSOLO

TICKETS →

←ENTRANCE

VIA GHIBELLINA

DCH

1 - MICHELANGELO - Bacchus
2 - MICHELANGELO - "Bruto"
3 - MICHELANGELO - David (Apollo)
4 - Copies of Michelangelo's works
5 - GIAMBOLOGNA - Mercury
6 - CELLINI - Two models of "Perseus"
7 - GIAMBOLOGNA - Florence Victorious over Pisa

Michelangelo—*Bruto* (1540)

Another example of the influence of Donatello is this so-ugly-he's-beautiful bust by Michelangelo. His rough intensity gives him the look of a man who has succeeded against all odds, a dignity and heroic quality that would be missing if he were too pretty.

The subject is Brutus, the Roman who, for the love of liberty, murdered his friend and dictator, Julius Caesar (*Et tu . . . ?*). Michelangelo could understand this man's dilemma. He himself had close ties to the Medicis, his adopted family, who could also be corrupt and tyrannical.

So he gives us two sides of a political assassin. The right profile (the front view) is heroic. But the hidden side, with the drooping mouth and squinting eye, makes him more cunning, sneering, and ominous.

Michelangelo—*David* (also known as *Apollo*)

This is the last of the *Davids* in the Bargello, a good time to think back on those we've seen: Donatello's girlish, gloating *David*; Verrochio's boyish, impish version; and now this unfinished one by Michelangelo. Michelangelo certainly learned from these earlier versions, even copying certain elements, but what's truly amazing is that his famous *David* in the Accademia is so completely different—so much larger than life in every way—from the earlier attempts.

In the glass cases in the corner are small-scale copies of some of Michelangelo's most famous works. Back near the entrance there's a bust of Michelangelo, capturing his broken nose and brooding nature.
• *On the other side of the room . . .*

Giambologna—*Mercury*

Catch this statue while you can—he's got flowers waiting to be delivered. Despite all the bustle and motion, *Mercury* has a solid Renaissance core: the line of balance that runs straight up the center, from toes to nose to fingertip. Back down at the toes, notice the cupid practicing up for the circus.

Cellini—Two Small Models of Perseus (Perseo)

The life-size statue of Perseus slaying the Medusa, located in the open-air Loggia next to Palazzo Vecchio, is cast bronze. Cellini started with these smaller models in wax and bronze to get the difficult process down. When it came time to cast the full-size work, everything was going fine . . . until he realized he didn't have enough metal! He ran around the studio, gathering up pewterware and throwing it in, narrowly avoiding a messterpiece.

Giambologna—*Florence Victorious over Pisa (Firenze Vittoriosa su Pisa)*

This shows the fierce Florentine chauvinism born in an era when Italy's cities struggled for economic and political dominance . . . and Florence won.

ROME

*A*t its peak, the word "Rome" meant civilization itself. And the grandeur of ancient Rome survives today, Vatican-style. Do the "Caesar Shuffle," winding through people, cats, and traffic from one magnificent sight to another. From the enormous Colosseum to the sublime Pietà, from the Renaissance splendor of the Sistine Chapel to the Baroque brilliance of Bernini's sculptures, Rome is fit for a caesar, a pope, and a wide-eyed, well-prepared tourist.

❦ 20 ❦

A WALK THROUGH
ANCIENT ROME

Rome has many layers—modern, Baroque, Renaissance, Christian—but, let's face it, "Rome" is Caesars, gladiators, chariots, centurions, "*Et tu, Brute*," trumpet fanfares, and thumbs up or thumbs down. That's the Rome we'll look at. On our "Caesar Shuffle," we'll see the downtown core of ancient Rome, from the Colosseum, through the Forum, over the Capitol Hill and to the Pantheon.

ORIENTATION

Colosseum (Colosseo): €5.80. Daily 9:00–19:00, off-season 9:00–15:00. Metro: Colosseo. A WC is behind the Colosseum (facing ticket entrance, go right; WC is under stairway by street). Tel. 06-3974-9907.

Forum (Foro Romano): Free. (If you also want to visit Palatine Hill, overlooking the Forum, it'll cost you €7.) Daily 9:00–19:30 or an hour before dark, off-season daily 9:00–15:00. Tel. 06-3974-9907.

Mammertine Prison (Mammertinum): Donation requested (€1 is fine). Daily 9:00–12:00, 14:30–18:00.

Pantheon: Free. Mon–Sat 8:30–19:30, Sun 9:00–13:00, 14:00–18:00. Tel. 06-6830-0230.

Note: Hours are notoriously changeable in Rome. To confirm the opening hours listed, drop by one of Rome's tourist offices or call 06-4890-6300 or 06-4889-9253.

Getting there: Take the subway to Metro stop "Colosseo," or taxi.

Information: There is no information service, only guidebooks from street vendors. The excellent *Rome: Past and Present* book has overlay

A WALK THROUGH ANCIENT ROME—OVERVIEW

reconstructions of many of the monuments on this tour (they're priced at €11, pay no more than €8.50).

Theft alert: Particularly outside the Colosseum and Forum, you might be accosted by street thieves (usually several young kids or mothers with babies). These raggedy-looking people carry newspapers or pieces of cardboard to wave in your face as they pick your pockets. Be alert, wear a money belt, and enjoy the sights.

Length of our tour: Four hours.

Cuisine art: Restaurants near Victor Emmanuel Monument and two good self-service cafeterias (Brek and Il Delfino) at Largo Argentina near the Pantheon. Bring a water bottle and consider a picnic lunch. The Forum has drinking fountains.

Starring: Gladiators, St. Peter, Constantine, Julius Caesar, and "Friends, Romans, countrymen... "

ROME—REPUBLIC AND EMPIRE (500 B.C.–A.D. 500)

Ancient Rome spanned about a thousand years, from 500 B.C. to A.D. 500. In that time, Rome expanded from a small tribe of barbarians to a vast empire, then dwindled slowly to city size again. For the first 500 years, when Rome's armies made her ruler of the Italian peninsula and beyond, Rome was a republic governed by elected senators. During the

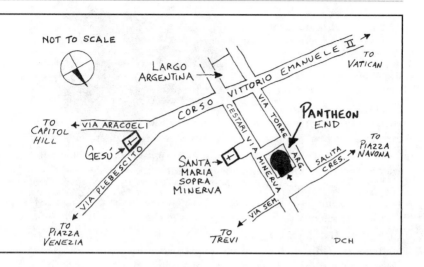

NOT TO SCALE

LARGO ARGENTINA

VITTORIO EMANUELE II
TO VATICAN

CORSO

PANTHEON END

TO CAPITOL HILL ← VIA ARACOELI

GESÚ

VIA PLEBESCITO

CESTARI

VIA TORRE ARG.

SANTA MARIA SOPRA MINERVA

VIA MINERVA

SALITA CRES.

TO PIAZZA NAVONA

VIA SEM.

TO PIAZZA VENEZIA

TO TREVI

DCH

next 500 years, a time of world conquest and eventual decline, Rome was an empire ruled by a military-backed dictator.

Julius Caesar bridged the gap between republic and empire. This ambitious general and politician, popular with the people because of his military victories and charisma, suspended the Roman constitution and assumed dictatorial powers around 50 B.C., until he was assassinated by a conspiracy of senators. His adopted son, Augustus, succeeded him, and soon "Caesar" was not just a name but a title.

Emperor Augustus ushered in the Pax Romana, or Roman peace (from A.D. 1–200), a time when Rome reached her peak and controlled an empire that stretched even beyond Eurail—from Scotland to Egypt, from Turkey to Morocco.

The Colosseum

• *View the Colosseum from the Forum fence near the grassy patch across the street from the "Colosseo" metro station.*

Built when the Roman Empire was at its peak (A.D. 80), the Colosseum represents Rome at its grandest. The Flavian Amphitheater (its real name) was an arena for gladiator contests and public spectacles. When killing became a spectator sport, the Romans wanted to share the fun with as many people as possible. They did this by sticking two Greek theaters together. The final structure was colossal—a "colosseum," the wonder of its age. It could accommodate 50,000 roaring fans (100,000 thumbs).

The outside of the Colosseum (now a grassy patch) sported a 33-meter bronze statue of Nero, which gleamed in the sunlight.

The Romans pioneered the use of the rounded arch and concrete, enabling them to build on this colossal scale. They made a shell of brick, then filled it in with concrete. Inside, you'll see this clearly among the ruins. Iron pegs held the larger stones together—notice the small holes that pockmark the sides. When it was done, the whole thing was faced with shining travertine marble (still visible on the top level).

The exterior says a lot about the Romans. They were great engineers, not artists. While the essential structure is Roman, the facade is Greek, decorated with the three types of Greek columns—Doric (bottom), Ionic (middle), and Corinthian (top). Originally, copies of Greek statues stood in the arches of the upper two stories. The Colosseum was designed to be more functional than beautiful. If ancient Romans visited the United States today as tourists, they'd send home postcards of our greatest works of "art"—freeways.

Only a third of the original Colosseum remains. Earthquakes destroyed some of it, but most was carted off as easy precut stones for other buildings during the Middle Ages and Renaissance.

• *Enter by the south entrance—to your left (past the Arch of Constantine). Buy your ticket and go inside. Move up to a railing overlooking the arena.*

Interior

You're on arena level. What we see now are the underground passages beneath the playing surface. The oval-shaped arena (86 by 50 meters) was originally covered with boards, then sprinkled with sand (*arena* in Latin). Like modern stadiums, the spectators ringed the playing area. The brick masses around you supported the first small tier of seats, and you can see two larger, slanted supports higher up. A few marble seats survive on the opposite side. Wooden beams stuck out from the top to support an enormous canvas awning that could be hoisted across by armies of sailors to provide shade for the spectators—the first domed stadium.

The gladiators would enter the arena from the west end (to your left), parade around to the sound of trumpets, stop at the emperor's box at the "50-yard line" (where you're standing), raise their weapons—and the fights would begin. The fights pitted men against men, men against beasts, and beasts against beasts.

The gladiators were usually slaves, criminals, or poor people who got their chance for freedom, wealth, and fame in the ring. They learned to fight in training schools, then battled their way up the ranks. The best were rewarded like our modern sports stars with fan clubs, great wealth, and product endorsements.

The animals came from all over the world: lions, tigers, bears, oh my, crocodiles, elephants, and hippos (not to mention exotic human "animals" from the "barbarian" lands). They were kept in cages beneath the arena floor, then lifted up in elevators. Released at floor level, the animals would pop out from behind blinds into the arena—the gladiator didn't know where, when, or by what he'd be attacked. Nets ringed the arena to protect the crowd. The stadium was inaugurated with a 100-day festival in which 2,000 men and 9,000 animals were killed. Colosseum employees squirted perfumes around the stadium to mask the stench of blood. For a lighthearted change of pace between events, the fans watched dogs bloody themselves fighting porcupines.

If a gladiator fell helpless to the ground, his opponent would approach the emperor's box and ask: Should he live or die? Sometimes the emperor left the decision to the crowd, who would judge based on how valiantly the man had fought. They would make their decision—thumbs up (Latin word: *siskel*) or thumbs down (*ebert*).

And Christians? Did they throw Christians to the lions like in the movies? Christians were definitely thrown to the lions, made to fight gladiators, crucified, and burned alive... but probably not here in this particular stadium. Maybe, but probably not.

Rome was a nation of warriors that built an empire by conquest. The battles fought against Germans, Egyptians, barbarians, and strange animals were played out daily here in the Colosseum for the benefit of city-slicker bureaucrats who got vicarious thrills watching brutes battle to the death. The contests were always free, sponsored by politicians to buy votes or to keep Rome's growing mass of unemployed rabble off the streets.

• *With these scenes in mind, wander around. Climb to the upper deck for a more colossal view (stairs near the exit, at west end).*

As you exit, the Roman Forum is directly in front of you, the subway stop is on your right, and the Arch of Constantine is on your left.

Arch of Constantine

If you are a Christian, were raised a Christian, or simply belong to a so-called "Christian nation," ponder this arch. It marks one of the great turning points in history—the military coup that made Christianity mainstream. In A.D. 312 Emperor Constantine defeated his rival Maxentius in one crucial battle. The night before, he had seen a vision of a cross in the sky. Constantine became sole emperor and promptly legalized Christianity. With this one battle, a once-obscure Jewish sect with a handful of followers was now the state religion of the entire Western world. In A.D. 300 you could be killed for being a Christian; by 400 you could be killed for not being one. Church enrollment boomed.

By the way, don't look too closely at the reliefs decorating this arch. By the fourth century, Rome was on its way down. Rather than struggle with original carvings, the makers of this arch plugged in bits and pieces scavenged from existing monuments. The arch is newly restored and looking great. But any meaning read into the stone will be very jumbled.

• *The entrance to the Roman Forum (Foro Romano) is a few steps away from the Arch. Hike up the ramp marked "Via Sacra." Stand next to the triumphal Arch of Titus and look out over the rubble-littered valley called the Forum.*

Roman Forum, Heart of the Empire

The Forum was the political, religious, and commercial center of the city. Rome's most important temples and halls of justice were here. This was the place for religious processions, elections, important speeches, and parades by conquering generals. As Rome's empire expanded, this area—the size of a few city blocks—became the center of the Western civilized world.

The hill in the distance with the bell tower is Capitol Hill. Immediately to your left, with all the trees, is Palatine Hill. The valley in between is rectangular, running roughly east (the Colosseum end) to west (Capitol Hill). The rocky path at your feet is the Via Sacra, which runs through the valley—through the trees, past the large brick Senate building, under

THE FORUM

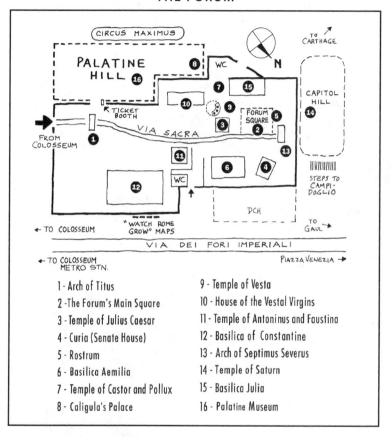

1 - Arch of Titus
2 - The Forum's Main Square
3 - Temple of Julius Caesar
4 - Curia (Senate House)
5 - Rostrum
6 - Basilica Aemilia
7 - Temple of Castor and Pollux
8 - Caligula's Palace
9 - Temple of Vesta
10 - House of the Vestal Virgins
11 - Temple of Antoninus and Faustina
12 - Basilica of Constantine
13 - Arch of Septimius Severus
14 - Temple of Saturn
15 - Basilica Julia
16 - Palatine Museum

the Arch of Septimius Severus—#13 on the map in this chapter—and (originally) up Capitol Hill.

Picture being here when a conquering general returned to Rome with crates of booty. The valley was full of gleaming white buildings topped with bronze roofs. The Via Sacra—Main Street of the Forum—would be lined with citizens waving branches and carrying torches. The trumpets would sound as the parade began.

First came porters, carrying chests full of gold and jewels. Then came a parade of exotic animals from the conquered lands—elephants, giraffes, hippopotamuses—for the crowd to "ooh" and "ahh" at. Next were the prisoners in chains, with the captive king on a wheeled platform so the people could jeer and spit at him. Finally, the conquering hero himself would drive down in his four-horse chariot, with rose petals strewn in his path. The whole procession would go the length of the Forum and up the face of Capitol Hill to the Temple of Saturn (the eight big columns midway up the hill—#14 on map), where they'd place the booty in Rome's coffers. They'd continue up to the summit to the Temple of Jupiter (not visible today) to dedicate the victory to the King of the Gods.

1. Arch of Titus (Arco di Tito)

The Arch of Titus commemorated the Roman victory over the province of Judea (Israel) in A.D. 70. The Romans had a reputation as benevolent conquerors who tolerated the local customs and rulers. All they required was allegiance to the Empire, which could be shown by worshiping the current emperor as a god. No problem for most conquered people, who already had half a dozen gods on their prayer lists. But the

Israelites' god was jealous and refused to let his people worship the emperor. Israel revolted. After a short but bitter war, the Romans defeated the rebels, took Jerusalem, and sacked their temple.

The propaganda value of Roman art is demonstrated on the inside of this arch, where a relief shows the emperor Titus in a chariot being crowned by the Goddess Victory. (Thanks to the tolls of modern pollution, they both look like they've been through the wars.) The other side shows the sacking of the temple—soldiers carrying a Jewish candelabrum and other plunder. The two (unfinished) plaques on poles were to have listed the conquered cities.

The brutal crushing of this rebellion (and another one 60 years later) devastated the nation of Israel. With no temple as a center for their faith, the Jews scattered throughout the world (the Diaspora). There would be no Jewish political entity again for two thousand years, until modern Israel was created after World War II.

• *Stroll into the Forum, down the Via Sacra. Pass through the trees and between ruined buildings until it opens up to a flat, grassy area.*

2. The Forum's Main Square

The original Forum, or main square, was this flat patch about the size of a football field, stretching to the foot of Capitol Hill. Surrounding it were once temples, law courts, government buildings, and triumphal arches.

Rome was born right here. According to legend, twin brothers Romulus (Rome) and Remus were orphaned in infancy and raised by a she-wolf on top of the Palatine. Growing up, they found it hard to get dates. So they and their cohorts attacked the nearby Sabine tribe, fought them here in this valley, and kidnapped their women. After they made peace, the marshy valley became the meeting place and then the trading center for the scattered tribes on the surrounding hillsides.

The square was the busiest and most crowded—and often the seediest—section of town. Besides the senators, politicians, and currency exchangers, there were even sleazier types—souvenir hawkers, fortune-tellers, gamblers, slave marketers, drunks, hookers, lawyers, and tour guides.

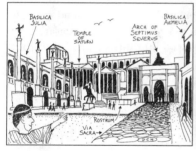

The **Forum Square** *(then and now), as viewed from the Forum entrance toward Capitol Hill. For 500 years this square, surrounded by temples and government buildings, was the center of the Western world.*

The Forum is now rubble, no denying it, but imagine the Forum in its prime: blinding white marble buildings with 13-meter-high columns and shining bronze roofs; rows of statues painted in realistic colors; chariots rattling down the Via Sacra. Mentally replace tourists in T-shirts with tribunes in togas. Imagine the buildings towering and the people buzzing around you while an orator gives a rabble-rousing speech from the Rostrum. If things still look like just a pile of rocks, at least tell yourself, "But Julius Caesar once leaned against these rocks."

• *At the east end of the main square sit the foundations of a small temple now capped with a peaked wood-and-metal roof . . .*

3. The Temple of Julius Caesar
(Templo del Divo Giulio, or "Ara di Cesare")

On this spot, right under the metal roof, Julius Caesar's body was burned after his assassination.

Caesar (100–44 B.C.) changed Rome—and the Forum—dramatically. He cleared out many of the wooden market stalls and began to ring the square with even grander buildings. (Caesar's house was located behind the temple, near that clump of trees.)

However, not everyone liked his urban design or his politics. After he assumed dictatorial powers, he was ambushed and stabbed to death by a conspiracy of senators, including his adopted son Brutus (*Et tu, Brute?*).

The funeral was held here, facing the main square. The citizens gathered and speeches were made. Mark Antony stood up to say (in Shakespeare's words), "Friends, Romans, countrymen, lend me your ears. I come to bury Caesar, not to praise him." When Caesar's body was burned, the citizens who still loved him threw anything at hand on the fire, requiring the fire department to come put it out. Then the very people who had killed him dedicated this temple in his name, making him the first Roman to be a god.

• *Head down the Via Sacra towards the Arch of Septimius Severus. Stop at the big, well-preserved brick building with the triangular roof. If the door's open, look in.*

4. Curia

The Senate House (Curia) was the most important political building in the Forum. Three hundred senators, elected by the citizens of Rome, met here to debate and create the laws of the land. Their wooden seats once circled the building in three tiers; the Senate president's podium sat at the far end. The marble floor is from ancient times. Listen to the echoes in this vast room—the acoustics are great.

Rome prided itself on being a republic. Early in its history, the people threw out the king and established rule by elected representatives. Each Roman citizen was free to speak his mind and have a say in public policy.

Even when emperors became the supreme authority, the Senate was a power to be reckoned with. (Note: Although Julius Caesar was assassinated in "the Senate," it wasn't here—the Senate was temporarily meeting across town.)

A statue and two reliefs inside the Curia help build our mental image of the Forum. The statue, made of porphyry marble in about A.D. 100, with its plugged-in head, arms, and feet missing, was a tribute to an emperor, probably Hadrian or Trajan. The two relief panels may have decorated the Rostrum. One shows the result of a government amnesty on debt, with people burning their debt records, while the other shows intact architecture and the latest fashion in togas.

• *Go back down the Senate steps to the metal guardrail and look right to a three-meter-high wall marked...*

5. Rostrum (Rostri)

Nowhere was Roman freedom more apparent than at this "Speaker's Corner." The Rostrum was a raised platform, three meters high and 25 meters long, decorated with statues, columns, and the prows of ships (*rostra*). Rome's orators great and small came here trying to draw a crowd and sway public opinion. Mark Antony rose to offer Caesar the laurel-leaf crown of kingship, which Caesar publicly (and hypocritically) refused while privately becoming a dictator. Men such as Cicero railed against the corruption and decadence that came with the city's newfound wealth. In later years, daring citizens even spoke out against the emperors, reminding them that Rome was once free.

Picture the backdrop these speakers would have had—a mountain of marble buildings piling up on Capitol Hill. The impressive Temple of Saturn (eight remaining columns) stood to the left. And, in imperial times, these voices of democracy would have been dwarfed by images of empire like the huge Arch of Septimius Severus (A.D. 203). The tall Column of Phocas nearby, one of the last great monuments erected in the Forum, was originally topped by a bronze statue.

In front of the Rostrum are trees bearing fruits that were sacred to the ancient Romans: olives (provided food, light, and preservatives), figs (tasty), and wine grapes (made a popular export product).

• *Return to the Temple of Julius Caesar and turn left up the exit ramp. From here you can look down at the remains of...*

6. Basilica Aemilia

A basilica was a Roman hall of justice. In a society that was as legal minded as America is today, you needed a lot of lawyers and a big place

to put them. Citizens came here to work out matters such as inheritances and building permits, or to sue somebody.

Notice the layout. It was a long, rectangular building. The stubby columns all in a row form one long, central hall flanked by two side aisles. Medieval Christian churches adopted this basilica floor plan.

• *Return again to the Temple of Julius Caesar. Notice the ruts in the stone street in front of the temple—carved by chariot wheels. To the right of the Temple are the three tall Corinthian columns of the Temple of Castor and Pollux (#7 on map). Beyond that is Palatine Hill.*

8. Caligula's Palace

Emperor Caligula (ruled A.D. 37–41) had a huge palace on Palatine Hill overlooking the Forum. It actually sprawled down the hill into the Forum (some supporting arches remain in the hillside), with an entrance by the Temple of Castor and Pollux.

Caligula was not a nice person. He tortured enemies, stole Senators' wives, crucified Christians, and parked his chariot in handicap spaces. But Rome's luxury-loving emperors only added to the glory of the Forum, with each one trying to make his mark on history.

• *To the left of the Temple of Castor and Pollux, find the remains of a small white circular temple . . .*

9. The Temple of Vesta

This was Rome's most sacred spot. Rome considered itself one big family, and this temple represented a circular hut like the kind Rome's first families lived in. Inside a fire burned, just as in a Roman home. And back in the days before lighters and matches, you never wanted your fire to go out. As long as the sacred flame burned, Rome would stand. The flame was tended by priestesses known as Vestal Virgins.

• *Around the back of the Temple of Vesta you'll find two rectangular brick pools. These stood in the courtyard of . . .*

10. The House of the Vestal Virgins

The Vestal Virgins lived in a two-story building surrounding a central courtyard with these two pools at one end. Rows of statues to the left and right marked the long sides of the building. This place was the model—both architecturally and sexually—for medieval convents and monasteries.

The six Vestal Virgins, chosen from noble families before they reached the age of 10, served a 30-year term. Honored and revered by the Romans, the Vestals even had their own box opposite the emperor in the Colosseum.

As the name implies, a Vestal took a vow of chastity. If she served her term faithfully—abstaining for 30 years—she was given a huge dowry, honored with a statue (like the ones at left), and allowed to marry (life begins at 40?). But, if they found any Virgin who wasn't, she was strapped to a funeral car, paraded through the streets of the Forum, taken to a crypt, given a loaf of bread and a lamp . . . and buried alive. Many women suffered the latter fate.

• *Return to the Via Sacra. Pause at the well-preserved Temple of Antoninus and Faustina.*

11. Temple of Antoninus and Faustina

These 17-meter-tall Corinthian (leafy) columns must have been awe inspiring to out-of-towners who grew up in thatched huts. Although the Temple has been reconstructed as a church, you can still see the basic temple layout—a staircase led to a shaded porch (the columns), which admitted you to the main building (now a church)

where the statue of the god sat. Originally these columns supported a triangular pediment decorated with sculpture.

• *Now head uphill, back up the Via Sacra, in the direction of the Colosseum. Many of the large basalt stones under your feet were walked on by Caesar Augustus 2,000 years ago. Veer left on the path leading to the three enormous arches.*

12. Basilica of Constantine

Yes, these are big arches. But they represent only one-third of the original Basilica of Constantine, a mammoth hall of justice. The arches were matched by a similar set along the Via Sacra side (only a few squat brick

Basilica Maxentius *(interior—existing rubble in dark). A Roman hall of justice, 90 meters long. The three standing arches were only the side aisles of this enormous structure, supporting a central roof that towered much higher.*

piers remain). Between them ran the central hall, which was spanned by a roof 40 meters high—about 17 meters higher than the side arches you see. (The stub of brick you see sticking up once spanned the central hall.) The hall itself was as long as a football field, lavishly furnished with colorful inlaid marble, fountains, and statues, and filled with strolling Romans. At the far (west) end was an enormous statue of Emperor Constantine on a throne (pieces of this statue are on display in Rome's Capitol Hill Museum).

This building was larger than Basilica Aemeilia but had the same general shape—rectangular, with a long central hall flanked by two side halls.

Rome Falls

This peak of Roman grandeur is a good place to talk about the Fall of Rome. Again, Rome lasted 1,000 years—500 years of growth, 200 years of peak power, and 300 years of gradual decay. The Fall had many causes, among them the barbarians that pecked away at Rome's borders.

Christians blame the Fall on moral decay. Pagans blamed it on Christians. Marxists blame it on a shallow economy based on spoils of war. (Pat Buchanan blamed it on Marxists.) Whatever the reasons, the far-flung Empire could no longer keep its grip on conquered lands and pulled back. Barbarian tribes from Germany and Asia attacked the Italian peninsula and even looted Rome itself in A.D. 410, leveling many of the buildings in the Forum. In 476, when the last emperor checked out and switched off the lights, Europe plunged into centuries of ignorance, poverty, and weak government—the Dark Ages.

But Rome lived on in the Catholic Church—Catholicism was the state religion of Rome's last generations. Emperors became popes (both called themselves Pontifex Maximus), senators became bishops, orators became priests, and basilicas became churches. Christian worship services required a larger meeting hall than Roman temples provided, so they used the spacious Roman basilica (hall of justice) as the model for their churches. Cathedrals from France to Spain to England, from Romanesque to Gothic to Renaissance, all have the same basic floor plan as a Roman basilica. And remember that the goal for the greatest church building project ever—that of St. Peter's—was to "put the dome of the Pantheon atop the Basilica of Constantine." The glory of Rome never quite died.

• *From here, you can visit the Palatine Hill and museum (€7; go past the Arch of Titus and follow the Via Sacra as it curves up toward Palatine Hill).*

If you're skipping Palatine Hill, follow the directions at the end of the Circus Maximus listing, below, to continue our tour.

Palatine Hill and Circus Maximus (Optional)

The Palatine Hill was the birthplace of Rome and the site of the luxurious palaces of the emperors (*palatine* gives us our word "palace"). The ruined palaces are hardly luxurious today, looking similar to the ruins of the Palace of Caligula at the foot of the hill overlooking the Forum. The Palatine Museum offers a chronological display of archaeological finds, frescoes, and sculptures illustrating the history of the hill that Roman emperors called home. There is also an impressive stadium for private games and races (on the left side of the hill) and a view of the Circus Maximus from atop the hill, a 10-minute hike.

• *The Circus Maximus is on the far side of the Palatine Hill. At the summit, bear either left or right around the modern-looking building to the railings overlooking the Circus.*

Circus Maximus

If the gladiator show at the Colosseum was sold out, you could always get a seat at the Circus Max. Like an early version of today's Demolition Derby, Ben Hur and his fellow charioteers once raced recklessly around this oblong course.

This was a huge race course. Chariots circled around the cigar-shaped mound in the center. Bleachers (now grassy banks) originally surrounded the track. The track was 400 meters long, while the whole stadium mea-

Artist's Conception of the Circus Maximus in its glory days.

sured 650 by 220 meters, seating—get this—300,000 people. The wooden bleachers once collapsed during a race, killing 13,000.

Races consisted of seven laps (altogether about 1.5 kilometers or a mile). In such a small space, collisions and overturned chariots were very common. The charioteers were usually poor low-borns who used this dangerous sport to get rich and famous. Many succeeded.

The public was crazy about it. There were 12 races a day, 240 days a year. Four teams dominated competition—Reds, Whites, Blues, and Greens—and every citizen was fanatically devoted to one of them. Obviously, the emperors had the best seats in the house from their palaces on the hill. They occasionally had the circus floor carpeted with designs in colored powders for their pleasure.

The spectacles continued into the Christian era (until 549) despite church disapproval.

In any crowd, it's wise to be on the lookout for pickpockets.

• *Next we'll head to the Mammertine Prison. You have two routes to choose from. For the shorter route, head back down the Via Sacra, take a right at the Temple of Antonius and Faustina, exit the Forum, go left, then take the first left to reach the prison.*

The longer route (about 200 meters longer) takes you past the "Maps Showing Growth of Rome," (below). To see the maps, leave the Forum the way you entered. Take a left at the exit and another left at busy Via dei Fori Imperiali (which Mussolini had built for a military parade boulevard and to clear a visual path from his office, at one end, to the Colosseum at the other). You'll soon see the maps on a wall to your left.

Maps Showing the Growth of Rome

In the first map (eighth century B.C.), "Rome" is just the city itself, a tiny white dot. Next (146 B.C.) they've conquered Spain and Greece. More important, they've defeated their arch rivals across the Mediterranean, the Carthaginians, in the Punic Wars. The third map (A.D. 1) is from the time of Augustus, the first emperor. Finally we see Rome at its greatest expanse (A.D. 117), as far north as Scotland, as far east as Mesopotamia. They affectionately nicknamed the Mediterranean "Our Sea."

• *After you walk past another of the Forum's entrances (free WC), take a left. Enjoy the view of the Forum from the railing at the huge Arch of Septimius Severus. Until modern times, the history of Rome and its remains were no big deal. The Forum lay buried to the height we're at now. Only a few tips of columns interrupted what for centuries was called "the cow field." One evening 200 years ago, Edward (Rise and Decline) Gibbon stood here. He heard the song of Christian monks praying among pagan ruins and pondered the cyclical history of civilizations ...*

Now turn about-face and view Capitol Hill. Ahead of you is a staircase to the top. To the right of that is a church with an iron fence, labeled "MAMMERTINUM." Let's drop in.

Mammertine Prison

Tip the monk (about €1), pass through the turnstile, and descend into the 2,500-year-old cistern. There came a time when Rome needed prisons more than extra water, and this former cistern became the Mammertine Prison, noted for its famous inmates. Inside, on the wall near the entryway, you'll see lists of the most important prisoners and how they died. Secular criminals are listed on the left, Christian ones on the right. *Suppliziato* means quartered, *strangolati* is strangled, and *morto di fame* is starvation. Saints Peter and Paul are said to have done time here.

The floor of the prison has a hole with a grate over it. Long before pilgrims added the more convenient stairs, this was the standard entryway. Walk down the stairs past a supposed miraculous image of

Peter's face that appeared when a guard pushed him into the wall. Downstairs you'll see the column that Peter was chained to. It is said that in this room a miraculous fountain sprung up so Peter could baptize other prisoners. The upside-down cross commemorates Peter's upside-down crucifixion.

• *Escape this prison and climb the long hot stairs past the guy who'll give you a deal on more slides and postcards of Rome than you could ever use and on up until you find a drinking fountain. Block the spout with your finger and a cool jet of refreshing water will knock your glasses off. Continue up to the large square on the hilltop.*

At the summit is the statue of the symbol of Rome: Romulus and Remus, the mythological founders of Rome, being suckled by the She-Wolf. This hilltop has been sacred to Romans ever since 500 B.C. when an Etruscan Temple of Jupiter stood here.

• *Enter the square and head for the stairs at the far end. Go down a few stairs, turn around, and come back up, entering the square the way its designer, Michelangelo, wanted you to . . .*

Michelangelo's Renaissance Piazza del Campidoglio

In spite of the awkward shape of the square, Michelangelo masterfully created a wonderfully harmonious space (the facades, grand stairway, and pavement design are his). Notice how the columns of the buildings ignore the fact that there are two stories, uniting the upper and lower halves and making the square more intimate.

The centerpiece of the square is the equestrian statue of Marcus Aurelius, the philosopher-emperor (this is a copy; the original is displayed in the adjacent museum). Dark-Age Christians, who destroyed most bronze statues of pagans, spared this one because it was mistakenly identified as Constantine, the first Christian emperor.

The building with the fountain (behind the equestrian statue) is the official residence of Rome's mayor. The two buildings flanking the statue make up the Capitol Hill Museum. Its many ancient statues include

the original Etruscan *She-Wolf*, the famous *Boy with a Thorn in His Foot*, and a seductive statue of the demonic Emperor Commodus dressed as Hercules. The museum's two buildings are connected by an underground passage that leads to the Tabularium

CAPITOL HILL (CAMPIDOGLIO)

TO PANTHEON
(15 MIN.)

PIAZZA
VENEZIA

N

VIA DEI FORI IMPERIALI

⑤ CAMPI-
DOGLIO

VICTOR
EMMANUEL
MON.

CAESAR'S
FORUM

②

③

①

FORUM

DCH

FROM
FORUM

x = View overlooking Forum

1 - Arch of Septimius Severus

2 - Mammertine Prison

3 - 20-postcards-for-a-dollar guy

4 - Romulus and Remus statue,
    drinking fountain

5 - Capitol Hill Museum

(the now-empty archives of ancient Rome) and superb views of the
Forum. The entertaining courtyard (of the museum on your right, closer to the river) is littered with chunks of the giant statue of Constantine
that was originally in the Forum's Basilica of Constantine.

The entry to this building lists local marriages, and it's not uncom-
mon to see newlyweds here in cummerbunds of bliss.

• *Now descend the stairs for good and pause at the bottom.*

The Modern World

Look left down the street at the building (several blocks away) that incor-
porates an ancient Roman colonnade into its walls. Then backtrack a few
steps to the right and look up the long stairway that rises to the early
Christian church high above you (worth the look, but not the climb).

Follow the sidewalk to the
right along the immense white Victor Emmanuel II monument (recently opened to the public). As
you go, look down below street
level and ponder the forgotten architectural chunks of ancient Rome
that lie quietly under the entire city.

Leave the ancient world and walk to the front of the monument for a look at Italy's guarded Tomb of the Unknown Soldier and the eternal flame. Turn around to see the busy Piazza Venezia. Mussolini whipped his fans into a fascist fury from the balcony of the palace on the right (with your back to the Victor Emmanuel II monument). The long Via del Corso stretching away from you is Rome's grand boulevard. Much of it is closed to traffic early evenings for the daily *passeggiata* ritual—strolling.

• *From the far end of Piazza Venezia (opposite the V.E. monument), walk left down Via del Plebiscito. At the first square (Largo Argentina) turn right and you'll walk straight three blocks to the Pantheon. Face the Pantheon from the obelisk fountain in front.*

The Pantheon

The Pantheon doesn't look like much from the outside, but this is perhaps the most influential building in art history. Its dome was the model for the Florence cathedral dome, which launched the Renaissance, and for Michelangelo's dome of St. Peter's, which capped it all off. Even Washington, D.C.'s, Capitol was inspired by this dome.

The Pantheon was a Roman temple dedicated to all *(pan)* the gods *(theos)*. First built in 27 B.C., it was completely rebuilt around A.D. 120 by the Emperor Hadrian. In a gesture of modesty admirable in anyone, but astounding in a Roman emperor, Hadrian left his own name off of it, putting the name of the original builder on the front—"M. Agrippa."

• *Pass between the 16 enormous one-piece granite columns (13 are original) and through the enormous original bronze door. Stand awestruck for a moment, then take a seat on the bench to your right.*

Interior

The dome, which was the largest made until the Renaissance, is set on a circular base. The mathematical perfection of this dome-on-a-base design is a testament to Roman engineering. The dome is as high as it is wide—44 meters (142 feet). To picture it, imagine a basketball set inside a wastebasket so that it just touches bottom.

The dome is made from concrete that gets lighter and thinner as it reaches the top. The walls at the base are seven meters thick and made from heavy travertine concrete, while near the top they're less than two meters thick and made of a light volcanic rock. Both Brunelleschi and Michelangelo studied this dome before building their own (in Florence and in the Vatican). Remember, St. Peter's Cathedral is really only "the dome of the Pantheon atop the Basilica of Constantine."

The oculus, or eye-in-the-sky, at the top, the building's only light source, is almost 10 meters across. The 1,800-year-old floor has holes in it and slants towards the edges to let the rainwater drain. The marble floor is largely restored, though the designs are close to the originals.

In ancient times, this was a one-stop-shopping temple where you could worship any of the gods whose statues decorated the niches. If you needed a favor, you could buy a live animal in the square for the priests to sacrifice on the altar. The fumes would rise up through the oculus to heaven, where the gods could smell it and—if they were pleased—grant you a blessing.

The barbarians passed the Pantheon by when they sacked Rome. Early in the Middle Ages it became a Christian church (from "all the gods" to "all the martyrs"), which saved it from architectural cannibalism and ensured its upkeep through the Dark Ages. The only major destruction came in the 17th century, when the pope stole the bronze plating and melted it down to build the huge bronze canopy over the altar at St. Peter's. About the only new things in the interior are the decorative statues and the tombs of famous people, such as the artist Raphael (to the left of the main altar, in the glass case) and modern Italy's first two kings, Victor Emmanuel II and Umberto I (to the right).

The Pantheon is the only continuously used ancient building in Rome. If you walk around it, you'll notice how the rest of the city has risen on 20 centuries of rubble.

The Pantheon also contains the world's greatest Roman column. There it is, spanning the entire 44 meters from heaven to earth—the pillar of light from the oculus.

✤ 21 ✤
NATIONAL MUSEUM OF ROME TOUR
Museo Nazionale Romano Palazzo Massimo alla Terme

Rome lasted a thousand years, and so do most Roman history courses. But, if you want a breezy overview of this fascinating society, there's no better place than the Palazzo Massimo.

Rome took Greek culture and wrote it in capital letters. Thanks to this lack of originality, ancient Greek statues were preserved for our enjoyment today. But the Romans also pioneered an unheard-of path in art—sculpting painfully realistic portraits of emperors and important citizens.

Think of this museum as a walk back in time. As you gaze at the same statues the Romans swooned over, Rome comes alive—from Romulus sucking a wolf's teat to Julius Caesar's murder to Caligula's incest to the coming of Christianity.

ORIENTATION

Cost: €7. Guided tour required for second floor only (see Tours, below).

Hours: Tue–Sun 9:00–18:45, closed Mon, last admission 60 minutes before closing.

Getting there: The museum is about 100 meters from the Termini train

station (Metro: Termini). As you leave the station, it's the sandstone-brick building on your left. Enter at the far end, at Largo di Villa Peretti.
Information: Tel. 06-481-5576.
Tours: An audioguide costs €4 (buy ticket first, then get audioguide at bookshop).

To see the fresco collection on the second floor, you must reserve an entry time for a free, 45-minute tour led by an Italian-speaking guide. If you're interested, book the next available tour when you buy your ticket.
Length of our tour: Allow two hours.
Photography: Allowed without a flash.
Cuisine art: Cheap eateries are at the train station, and classier places are on Via Nazionale and other streets nearby.
Starring: *The Discus Thrower,* Roman emperor busts, original Greek statues, and fine Roman copies.

THE MUSEUM

The Palazzo Massimo is now the permanent home of the major Greek and Roman statues that were formerly scattered in other museums. However, some famous statues once in the collection (*The Boxer at Rest, Gaul Killing His Wife,* and *Ludovisi Throne*) are still located elsewhere. With its long official name, the museum seems to be searching for a convenient nickname (I nominate Palazzo Massimo) to distinguish it from other "Museo Nazionales" around town.

The museum is rectangular, with rooms and hallways built around a central courtyard. The ground-floor displays follow Rome's history as it changes from democratic republic to dictatorial empire. The first floor exhibits take Rome from its peak to its slow fall. The second floor houses rare frescoes and fine mosaics (reservation for a free tour required), and the basement displays coins and everyday objects. As you tour the museum, note that "room" is *sala* in Italian and "hall" is *galleria*.

GROUND FLOOR—
FROM SENATORS TO CAESARS

• *Buy your ticket and pass through the turnstile, where you'll find . . .*

Minerva

It's big, it's gaudy, it's a weird goddess from a pagan cult. Welcome to the Roman world. The statue is also a good reminder that all the statues in this museum—now missing limbs or scarred by erosion or weathered

NATIONAL MUSEUM—GROUND FLOOR

1. Minerva
2. Portrait Heads
3. Julius Caesar
4. Octavian
5. Livia
6. Tiberius
7. Caligula

8. Augustus
9. Four Frescoes
10. Alexander the Great
11. Socrates
12. Niobid
13. Greek Mania

down to the bare stone—were once whole and painted to look as life-like as possible.

• *Continuing to the right, you'll stand at the head of . . .*

Gallery I—Portrait Heads from the Republic, 500–1 B.C.

Stare into the eyes of these stern, hardy, no-nonsense, farmer-stock people who founded Rome. The wrinkles and crags of these original "ugly Republicans" tell the story of Rome's roots as a small agricultural tribe that fought neighboring tribes for survival.

These faces are brutally realistic, unlike more idealized Greek statues. Romans honored their ancestors and worthy citizens in the "family" (*gens*) of Rome. They wanted lifelike statues to remember them by, and to instruct the young with their air of moral rectitude.

In its first 500 years, Rome was a republic ruled by a Senate of wealthy landowners. But as Rome expanded throughout Italy and the economy shifted from farming to booty, changes were needed.

• *Leave the gallery to enter . . .*

Room 1—The Transition between Republic and Empire

Julius Caesar (*Rilievo con Ritratto c.d. Cesare*), c. 100–44 B.C.

Study this bust. The prominent brow, the strong nose, the male-pattern baldness with the forward comb-over—these features identify the man who changed Rome forever. (Or some think it may be a lookalike.)

When this charismatic general swept onto the scene, Rome was in chaos. Rich landowners were fighting middle-class plebs, who wanted their slice of the plunder. Slaves such as Spartacus were picking up hoes and hacking up masters. And renegade generals—the new providers of wealth and security in a booty economy—were becoming dictators. (Notice the life-size statue of an unknown but obviously once-renowned general.)

Caesar was a people's favorite. He conquered Gaul (France), then sacked Egypt, then impregnated Cleopatra. He defeated rivals and made them his allies. He gave great speeches. Chicks dug him.

With the army at his back and the people in awe, he took the reins of government, instituted sweeping changes, made himself the center of power... and antagonized lovers of freedom everywhere.

A band of Republican assassins surrounded him in a Senate meeting. He called out for help as one by one they stepped up to take turns stabbing him. The Senators sat and watched in silence. One of the killers was his adopted son, Brutus, and Caesar died saying, *"Et tu, Brute?"*

• *At the end of the hall, enter into...*

Room IV—The Julio-Claudian Family: Rome's First Emperors, c. 50 B.C.–A.D. 68

Julius Caesar died, but his family name, his politics, and his flamboyance lived on, turning Rome into a dictatorship ruled by an emperor.
• *In this room, look at the busts along the wall (to the right as you enter), and find the "scalped" bust of...*

Octavian, later called Augustus (*Ritratto di Ottaviano*), ruled 27 B.C.–A.D. 14

Julius Caesar adopted his grandnephew Octavian. After the assassination, 18-year-old Octavian got revenge against Brutus and the others, then eliminated his own rivals, Mark Antony and wife Cleopatra. For the first time in almost a century of fighting, one general reigned supreme. Octavian took the title "Augustus" ("He who just keeps getting bigger"), becoming the first of the emperors who would rule Rome for the next 500 years. (More on Augustus later.)

Livia (Ritratto di Livia)

Augustus/Octavian's wife, Livia, was a major power behind the throne. Her stern, thin-lipped gaze withered rivals at court. Her hairstyle—bunched up in a peak, braided down the center, and tied in back—became the rage of Europe as her face appeared everywhere in statues and on coins. Notice that by the next generation (Antonia Minore, Livia's daughter-in-law) a simpler bun was chic. And, by the following generation, it was tight curls. Empresses dictated fashion like emperors dictated policy.

Livia bore Augustus no sons. She lobbied hard for Tiberius, her own son by a first marriage, to succeed as emperor. Augustus didn't like him, but Livia was persuasive. He relented, ate some bad figs, and died—the gossip was that Livia poisoned him to seal the bargain. The pattern of succession was established—adopt a son from within the extended family—and Tiberius was proclaimed emperor.

Tiberius (Ritratto de Tiberio), ruled A.D. 14–37

Acne may have soured Tiberius to the world. Shy and sullen but diligent, he worked hard to be the easygoing leader of men Augustus had been. Early on he was wise and patient, but he suffered personal setbacks. Politics forced him to divorce his only beloved and marry a slut. His favorite brother died, then his son. Embittered, he let subordinates run things and retired to Capri where he built a villa with underground dungeons. There he hosted orgies of sex, drugs, torture, really loud music, and execution. At his side was his young grandnephew whom he adopted as next emperor.

Caligula (Caligola; in the glass case), ruled A.D. 37–41

This emperor had sex with his sisters, tortured his enemies, stole friends' wives during dinner then returned to rate their performance in bed, crucified Christians, tore up parking tickets, and had men kneel before him as a god. Caligula has become the archetype of a man with enough power to act out his basest fantasies.

Politically, he squandered Rome's money then taxed and extorted from the citizens. Perhaps he was made mad by illness, perhaps he was the victim of vindictive historians, but, still, no one mourned when assassins ambushed him and ran a sword through his privates. Rome was tiring of this family dynasty's dysfunction. Augustus must have been rolling in his grave . . . and they hadn't even seen Nero yet.

Before leaving the room, look around and see if you can spot a family resemblance. Livia's thin lips and Augustus' strong nose? Maybe.

Room V—Augustus and Rome's Legendary Birth

Statue of Augustus as Pontifex Maximus (Ritratto di Augusto in Vesta di Offerente)

Here 50-year-old Emperor Augustus takes off his armor and laurel-leaf crown and dons the simple hooded robes of a priest. In fact, Augustus was a down-to-earth man who lived simply, worked hard, read books, listened to underlings, and tried to restore traditional Roman values after the turbulence of Julius Caesar's time. He outwardly praised and defended the Senate and the Republic while actually becoming its emperor. Despite the excesses of his descendants, Augustus' reign marked the start of 200 years of peace and prosperity, the "Pax Romana."

See if the statue matches a description of Augustus by a contemporary—the historian Seutonius: "He was unusually handsome. His expression was calm and mild. He had clear, bright eyes, in which was a kind of divine power. His eyebrows met. His hair was slightly curly and somewhat golden." Any variations were made by sculptors who idealized features to make him almost godlike.

Augustus proclaimed himself a god—not arrogantly or blasphemously as Caligula later did—but as the honored "father" of the "family" of Rome. As the empire expanded, the vanquished had to worship the emperor's statue as a show of loyalty. Augustus even claimed he was descended from Romulus and Remus. Such propaganda solidified the emperor's hold over Rome as both political and spiritual head.

Four Frescoes of Rome's Mythical Origins (Fregio Pittorico, etc.)

These cartoon-strip frescoes (read right to left) tell the stories of Augustus' legendary forebears, offering conflicting versions of the founding of Rome.

1. Upper right fresco: Aeneas (red skin) arrives in Italy from Troy and fights the locals for a place to live.
2. Upper left: His wife (far left, seated, in purple) and son build a city wall around Rome. The womenfolk are safe and the city prospers.
3. Lower right: Several generations later, the God of War (in center, with red skin) lies in wait to rape and impregnate a Vestal Virgin.
4. Lower left: Her disgraced babies, Romulus and Remus, are placed in a basket (center) and set adrift on the Tiber River. They wash ashore, are suckled by a wolf, and finally (far left) taken in by a shepherd. These legendary babies, of course, grow up to found the city that makes real history.

• *Exit the room and go round the corner to busts of . . .*

Gallery III—Rome's Greek Mentors

Alexander the Great (Alessandro Magno)

Alexander the Great (356–323 B.C.) single-handedly created an empire by conquering, in just a few short years, lands from Greece to Egypt to Persia, spreading Greek culture and language along the way. Later, when the Romans conquered Greece (c. 200 B.C.), they inherited this preexisting collection of cultured, Greek-speaking cities ringing the Mediterranean.

Alexander's handsome statues set the standard for those of later Roman emperors. His features were chiseled and youthful, and he was adorned with pompous decorations like a golden sunburst aura (which was fitted into holes). The greatest man of his day, he ruled the known world by the age of 30.

Alexander, a Macedonian, had learned Greek culture from his teacher, none other than the philosopher Aristotle. Aristotle's teacher was Plato, whose mentor was . . .

Socrates (Socrate)

This nonconformist critic of complacent thinking is the father of philosophy. The Greeks were an intellectual, introspective, sensitive, and artistic people. The Romans were practical, no-nonsense soldiers, salesmen, and bureaucrats. Many a Greek slave—warning a Roman Senator not to wear a plaid toga with a polka-dot robe—was more cultured than his master.

Room VII—Pure Greek Beauty in Greek Originals

Niobid (Niobide Ferita), 440 B.C.

The Romans were astonished by the beauty of Greek statues. This woman's smooth skin contrasts with the rough folds of her clothing. Her pose is angular but still balanced—notice how she twists naturally around an axis running straight up and down. She looks like a classical goddess awakening from a beautiful dream. But...

Circle around back. The hole bored in her back, right in that itchy place you can't quite reach, once held a golden arrow. The woman has been shot by Artemis, goddess of hunting, because her mother dared to boast to the gods about her kids. The Niobid reaches back in vain, trying to remove the arrow before it drains her of life.

Romans ate this stuff up: the sensual beauty, the underplayed pathos, the very Greekness of it. They crated up centuries-old statues like this and brought them home to their gardens and palaces. Appreciate the beauty in this room, since these are some of the world's rare, surviving Greek originals.

Room VIII—Greek Mania

By Julius Caesar's time, Rome was in the grip of a "Neo-Attic" craze, and there weren't enough old statues to fill the demand. Crafty Greeks began cranking out knock-offs of Greek originals for mass consumption. The works in this room were of extremely high quality, while others were more like cheesy fake "*Davids*" in a garden store.

To the Romans, this "art" was just furniture for their homes. An altar from a Greek temple became a place to set your wine, a sacred basin was a rain catcher, a statue of Athena took your olive pits. Different styles from different historical periods were mixed and matched to suit Roman tastes. The rich Roman who bought *Afrodite Pudica*, signed along the base by "Menophantos," would not have known or cared that the artist was copying a one-of-a-kind original done by the great Praxiteles 400 years before, back when Greece was Golden.

NATIONAL MUSEUM—FIRST FLOOR

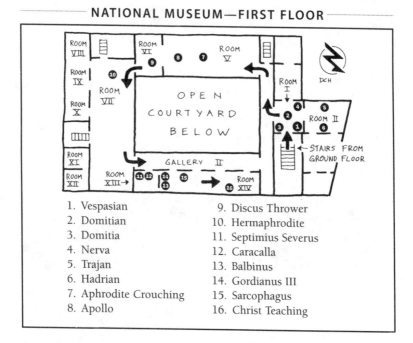

ROOM VIII
ROOM VI
ROOM V
ROOM IX
ROOM VII
ROOM X
ROOM XI
ROOM I
ROOM II
OPEN COURTYARD BELOW
GALLERY II
ROOM XII
ROOM XIII→
ROOM XIV
STAIRS FROM GROUND FLOOR
DCH

1. Vespasian
2. Domitian
3. Domitia
4. Nerva
5. Trajan
6. Hadrian
7. Aphrodite Crouching
8. Apollo
9. Discus Thrower
10. Hermaphrodite
11. Septimius Severus
12. Caracalla
13. Balbinus
14. Gordianus III
15. Sarcophagus
16. Christ Teaching

Rome conquered Greece, but the Greeks conquered the Romans.

• *Take a break, then head upstairs to the first floor.*

FIRST FLOOR

As we saw, Augustus' family did not always rule wisely. Under Nero (ruled A.D. 54–68), the debauchery, violence, and paranoia typical of the Julio-Claudians festered to a head. When the city burned in the great fire of 64, the Romans suspected Nero of torching it himself to clear land for his enormous luxury palace.

Enough. Facing a death sentence, Nero committed suicide with the help of a servant. An outsider was brought in to rule.

Room I—The Flavian Family

Vespasian (Vespasianus), ruled A.D. 69–79
Balding and wrinkled, with a big head, a double chin, and a shy smile, Vespasian was a common man. The son of a tax collector, he rose through the military ranks with a

reputation as a competent drudge. As emperor, he restored integrity, raised taxes, started the Colosseum, and suppressed the Jewish rebellion in Palestine.

Domitian (Domitianus)

Vespasian's son Domitian (ruled A.D. 81–96) used his father's tax revenues to construct the massive Imperial Palace on Palatine Hill, home to emperors for the next three centuries. Shown with his lips curled in a sneering smile, he was a moralistic prude who executed several Vestal ex-Virgins, while in private he took one mistress after another. Until...

Domitia

...until his stern wife found out and hired a servant to stab him in the groin. *Domitia's* hairstyle is a far cry from the "Livia" cut, with a high crown of tight curls.

Nerva

The Flavian dynasty was no better than its predecessors. Nerva, old and childless, made a bold, far-sighted move—he adopted a son from outside of Rome's corrupting influence.

Room II—A Cosmopolitan Culture

Trajan (Traianus-Hercules), ruled A.D. 98–117

Born in Spain, this conquering hero pushed Rome's borders to their greatest extent, creating a truly worldwide empire. The spoils of three continents funneled into a city of a million-plus people. Trajan could present himself as a "new Hercules," and no one found it funny. Romans felt a spirit of Manifest Destiny: "The gods desire that the City of Rome shall be the capital of all the countries of the world." (Livy)

Hadrian (Hadrianus), ruled A.D. 117–138

Hadrian was a fully cosmopolitan man. His beard—the first we've seen—shows his taste for foreign things; he poses like the Greek philosopher he imagined himself to be.

Hadrian was a voracious tourist, personally visiting almost every corner of the vast empire, from Britain (where he built Hadrian's Wall) to Egypt (where he sailed the Nile), from Jerusalem (where he suppressed another Jewish revolt) to Athens (where he soaked up classical culture). An omnivorous learner, he scaled Mount Etna just to see what made a volcano tick. Back home, he beautified Rome with the Pantheon and his Villa at Tivoli, a microcosm of places he'd visited.

Hadrian is flanked here by the two loves of his life. His wife, Sabina, with modest hairstyle and scarf, kept the home fires burning for her traveling husband. Hadrian was 50 years old when he became captivated by the teenage boy, Antinous, with his curly hair and full, sensual lips. Together they traveled the Nile, where Antinous drowned. Hadrian wept. This public display of emotion, somewhat embarrassing to the stoic Romans, became a legend among Greeks, who erected Antinous statues everywhere.

Hadrian spent his last years at his lavish villa outside Rome, surrounded by buildings and souvenirs that reminded him of his traveling days.

Rooms V and VI—Rome's Grandeur

Pause at Rome's peak to admire the things they found beautiful. Imagine these statues in their original locations, in the pleasure gardens of the Roman rich—surrounded by greenery, with the splashing sound of fountains, the statues all painted in bright, lifelike colors. Though executed by Romans, the themes are mostly Greek, with godlike humans and human-looking gods.

Aphrodite Crouching (Afrodite Accovacciata)

Hadrian had good taste—he ordered a copy of this Greek classic for his bathroom. The goddess of beauty crouches while bathing, then turns to admire herself. This sets her whole body in motion—one thigh goes down, one up; her head turns clockwise while her body goes reverse— yet she's perfectly still. The crouch creates a series of symmetrical love handles, molded by the sculptor into the marble like wax.

Apollo

The god of light appears as a slender youth, not some burly, powerful, autocratic god. He stands *contrapposto*—originally he was leaning against the tree—in a relaxed and very human way. His curled hair is tied with a headband, with strands that tumble down his neck. His muscles and skin are smooth. (The rusty stains come from the centuries Apollo spent submerged in the Tiber.) Apollo is in a reflective mood, and the serenity and intelligence in his face show off classical Greece as a nation of thinkers.

The Discus Thrower (Discobolo)

 An athlete winds up, about to unleash his pent-up energy and hurl the discus. The sculptor has frozen the moment for us, so we can examine the inner workings of the wonder called man. The perfect pecs and washboard abs make this human godlike. Geometrically, you could draw a perfect circle around him, with his hipbone at the center. He's natural yet ideal, twisting yet balanced, moving while at rest. For the Greeks, the universe was a rational place, and the human body was the perfect em-bodi-ment of the order found in nature.

This statue is the best-preserved Roman copy (not one member is missing—I checked) of the original Greek work by Myron (450 B.C.). Statues of athletes like this commonly stood in the baths, where Romans cultivated healthy bodies, minds, and social skills, hoping to live well-rounded lives. *The Discus Thrower,* with his geometrical perfection and godlike air, sums up all that is best in the classical world.

Room VII

Hermaphrodite Sleeping (Ermafrodito Dormiente)

After leaving the baths, a well-rounded Roman may head posthaste to an orgy, where he might see a reclining nude like this, be titillated, circle around for a closer look, and say, "Hey! (Insert your reaction here)!"

Room XIII—Beginning of the End

Septimius Severus, ruled A.D. 193–211

Rome's sprawling empire was starting to unravel, and it took a disciplined emperor-general like this African to keep it together. Severus' victories on the frontier earned him a grand triumphal arch in the Forum, but here he seems to be rolling his eyes at the chaos growing around him.

Caracalla, ruled A.D. 211–217

The stubbly beard, cruel frown, and glaring eyes tell us that Severus' son was bad news. He murdered his little brother, Geta, to seize power, then proceeded to massacre thousands of loyal citizens on a whim. The army came to distrust rulers whose personal agenda got in their way, and Caracalla was stabbed in the back by a man whose brother had just been executed.

Room XIV—The Fall

There are a lot of scared faces in this room. People who grew up in the lap of luxury and security were witnessing the unthinkable—the disintegration of a thousand years of tradition. Rome never recovered from the chaos of the third century. Disease, corruption, revolts from within, and "barbarians" pecking away at the borders were body blows that sapped Rome's strength.

Balbinus, ruled A.D. 238

This old man was appointed emperor by the Senate, but he was no soldier, and the army didn't like him. He was one of some 20 emperors in the space of 40 years who was saluted then murdered at the whim of soldiers of fortune. At one point, the office of emperor was literally auctioned to the highest bidder. Balbinus, with his stubbly beard and forlorn look, knows he's lost the army's confidence, and he waits for the ax to fall. Next.

Gordianus III, ruled A.D. 238–244

The 13-year-old Gordianus, with barely a wisp of facial hair, was naive and pliable, the perfect choice—until he got old enough to question the generals. His assassins had no problem sneaking up on him because, as you can see, he had no ears.

Sarcophagus of a Procession (Sarcofago con Corteo, etc.), A.D. 270

This coffin shows a parade of dignitaries accompanying a new Roman leader. As they march up Capitol Hill, they huddle together, their backs to the wall, looking around suspiciously for assassins. Their faces reflect the fear of the age. Rome would stagger on for another 200 years, but the glory of old Rome was gone. The city was becoming a den of thugs, thieves, prostitutes, barbarians... and Christians.

Small Statuette of Christ Teaching (Cristo Docente), A.D. 350

Christ sits like a Roman senator—in a toga, holding a scroll, dispensing wisdom like the law of the land. The statue comes from those delirious days when formerly persecuted Christians could now "come out" and worship in public. Emperor Constantine (ruled 306–337) legalized the religion, and within two generations it was Rome's official religion.

Whether Christianity invigorated or ruined Rome is debated, but the Fall was inevitable. Rome's once-great legions backpedaled until even the city itself was raped and plundered by foreigners (410). In 476, the last emperor sold his title for a comfy pension plan, and "Rome" was just another dirty city with a big history. The barely flickering torch of ancient Rome was passed on to medieval Christians: senators became bishops, basilicas became churches, and the Pontifex Maximus (Emperor) became the Pontifex Maximus (Pope).

THE REST OF THE MUSEUM

The **second floor** contains frescoes and mosaics that once decorated the walls and floors of Roman villas. The frescoes (in black, red, yellow, and blue) show a few scenes of people and animals but are mostly architectural designs, with fake columns and "windows" that "look out" on landscape scenes. Granted, the col-

lection is impressive, but the tour is in Italian (the guides *might* speak a little English), and it's a 45-minute commitment.

More interesting stuff is in the **basement**, housing coins and everyday objects from ancient Rome. In A.D. 300 one *denar* bought one egg. Evaluate Roman life by studying Diocletian's wage and price controls. Find your favorite emperor or empress on the coins using remote-control magnifying glasses.

❧ 22 ❧
St. Peter's Basilica

St. Peter's is the greatest church in Christendom. It represents the power and splendor of Rome's 2,000-year domination of the Western world. Built on the memory and grave of the first pope, St. Peter, this is where the grandeur of ancient Rome became the grandeur of Christianity.

ORIENTATION

Cost: Free; €4.60 to climb dome.

Dress code: Strictly enforced—no shorts or bare shoulders (men or women), no miniskirts.

Hours: Daily May–Sept 7:00–19:00, Oct–April 7:00–18:00. Mass is held daily at 8:30, 9:00, 10:00, 11:00, 12:00, and 17:00 (Sun at 17:45). The lift to the dome opens daily at 8:30 and closes one hour before the church closes. The least crowded time to visit the church is early or late.

Getting there: Subway to "Ottaviano," then a 10-minute walk south on Via Ottaviano. Several city buses go right to St. Peter's Square (#64 is convenient for pickpockets). Taxis are reasonable.

Information: A helpful tourist information office is just to the left of St. Peter's Basilica (Mon–Sat 8:30–18:30, closed Sun, tel. 06-6988-1662;

Vatican switchboard tel. 06-6982, www.vatican.va). The Vatican post office, next to the tourist office, is more reliable than the Italian mail service (Mon–Sat 8:30–18:30; another branch in Vatican Museum). Vatican stamps are good throughout Rome, but Italian stamps are not good at Vatican). WCs are to the right and left (near tourist office) of the church and on the roof. Drinking fountains are at the obelisk and near WCs.

Tours: The Vatican tourist information office conducts several different tours, including free 90-minute tours of St. Peter's, tours of the Vatican Gardens (the only way to see the gardens—€9.50), and tours of the necropolis of St. Peter's and the saint's tomb (€8.50). For more information, call the tourist office at 06-6988-1662.

Length of our tour: One hour, plus another hour if you climb the dome (elevator plus 300 steps one-way).

Cloakroom: Free, usually mandatory bag check is outside at right of entrance.

Photography: Allowed.

Cuisine art: Cafés are on surrounding streets, including Via Ottaviano. Near the Ottaviano metro stop, the street named Viale Giulio Cesare (which becomes Via Candia) is lined with self-service cafeterias, delis, and pizza shops.

Starring: Michelangelo, Bernini, Bramante, St. Peter, a heavenly host, and, occasionally, the pope.

OLD ST. PETER'S

• *Find a shady spot where you like the view under the columns around St. Peter's oval-shaped "square." If the pigeons left a clean spot, sit on it.*

Nearly 2,000 years ago this area was the site of Nero's Circus—a huge Roman chariot racecourse. The obelisk you see in the middle of the square stands where chariots made their hairpin turns. The Romans had no marching bands, so for halftime entertainment they killed Christians. This persecuted minority was forced to fight wild animals and gladiators, or they were simply crucified. Some were tarred up, tied to posts, and burned—human torches to light up the evening races.

One of those killed here, around A.D. 65, was Peter, Jesus' right-hand man who had come to Rome to spread the message of love. Peter was crucified on an upside-down cross at his own request because he felt unworthy to die as his master had. His remains were buried in a nearby cemetery where, for 250 years, they were quietly and secretly revered.

When Christianity was finally legalized in 313, the Christian emperor Constantine built a church on the site of the martyrdom of this first "pope," or bishop of Rome, from whom all later popes claimed their authority as head of the Church. "Old St. Peter's" lasted 1,200 years (A.D. 324–1500).

By the time of the Renaissance, old St. Peter's was falling apart and was considered unfit to be the center of the Western Church. The new, larger church we see today was begun in 1506 and actually built around the old one. As it was completed 120 years later, after many changes of plans, old St. Peter's was dismantled and carried out the doors of the new one.

• *Ideally, you should head out to the obelisk to view the square and read this. But let me guess—it's 95 degrees, right? OK, read on in the shade of these stone sequoias.*

ST. PETER'S SQUARE

St. Peter's Square, with its ring of columns, symbolizes the arms of the church "maternally embracing Catholics, heretics, and the faithless." It was designed by the Baroque architect Bernini, who also did much of the work we'll see inside. Numbers first: 284 columns, 17 meters high, in stern Doric style. Topping them are Bernini's 90 favorite saints, each three meters tall. The "square" itself is elliptical, 200 by 150 meters.

The obelisk in the center is 27 meters of solid granite weighing over 300 tons. Think for a second of how much history this monument has seen. Erected originally in Egypt over 2,000 years ago, it witnessed the fall of the pharoahs to the Greeks and then to the Romans. It was then moved to Imperial Rome, where it stood impassively watching the slaughter of Christians at the racecourse and the torture of Protestants by the Inquisition (in the yellow and rust building just outside the square, to the left of the church). Today it watches over the church, a reminder that each civilization builds on the previous ones. The puny cross on top reminds us that our Christian culture is but a thin veneer over our pagan origins.

• *Now venture out across the burning desert to the obelisk which provides a narrow sliver of shade.*

Face the church, then turn about-face and say "*Grazie, Benito.*" I don't make a habit of thanking Fascist dictators, but in the 1930s Benito Mussolini did open up this broad boulevard, finally letting people get an expansive view of the dome of St. Peter's. From here at the obelisk, Michelangelo's magnificent dome can only peek its top over the bulky Baroque front entrance.

The gray building at two o'clock to the right (as you face the

ST. PETER'S SQUARE

ST. PETER's CHURCH

BRAMANTE + MICHELANGELO GREEK CROSS PLAN →

DOME

MADERNO'S ADDITION →

WC

③

⑥

⑤

FOUNTAINS

WC

① ④

1 - Obelisk
2 - Pope's apartments (top story, right)
3 - Sistine Chapel
4 - "Centro del Colonnato" plaque
5 - Post Office, Tourist Info, and bookstore
6 - Swiss Guard at Vatican City entrance

N

VATICAN WALL

VIA DI PTA. ANGELICA → TO SUBWAY "OTTAVIANO" (10 MIN.)
↓
VATICAN MUSEUM (15 MIN.)

VIA DEL CONCILIAZIONE

church), rising up behind Bernini's colonnade, is where the pope lives. The last window on the right of the top floor is his bedroom. The window to the left of that is his study, where he appears occasionally to greet the masses. If you come to the square at night as a Poping Tom, you might see the light on—the pope burns much midnight oil.

At Christmas, St. Peter's Square becomes the pope's living room, decorated with a grand Christmas tree.

On more formal occasions (which you may have seen on TV), the pope appears from the church itself, on the small balcony above the central door.

The Sistine Chapel is just to the right of the facade—the small gray-brown building with the triangular roof topped by an antenna. The tiny chimney (the pimple along the roofline midway up the left side) is where the famous smoke signals announce the election of each new pope. If the smoke is black, a 75 percent majority hasn't been reached. White smoke means a new pope has been selected.

Walk to the right, five pavement plaques from the obelisk, to one marked "Centro del Colonnato." From here all of Bernini's columns on the right side line up. The curved Baroque square still pays its respects to Renaissance mathematical symmetry.

• *Climb the gradually sloping stairs past crowd barriers and the huge statues of St. Mark with his two-edged sword and St. Peter with his bushy hair and keys.*

You'll pass two of the entrances to Vatican City—one to the left of the facade, one to the right in the crook of Bernini's "arm." Guarding this small but powerful country's border crossing are the mercenary guards from Switzerland. You have to wonder if they really know how to use those pikes. Their colorful uniforms are said to have been designed by Michelangelo, though he was not known for his sense of humor.

• *Enter the atrium (entrance hall) of the church. You'll pass by the dress-code enforcers and a gaggle of ticked-off guys in shorts.*

THE BASILICA

The Atrium

The Atrium is itself bigger than most churches. Facing us are the five famous bronze doors, leading into the main church. The central door, made from the melted-down bronze of the original door of old St. Peter's, is only opened on special occasions.

The far right entrance is the Holy Door, opened only during Holy Years. On Christmas Eve every 25 years, the pope knocks three times with a silver hammer and the door opens, welcoming pilgrims to pass through. The door was wide open during the 2000 Jubilee Year, closed at year's end, and won't be reopened until Christmas Eve, 2024. On the door, note Jesus' shiny knees, polished by pious pilgrims who touch them for a blessing.

The other doors are modern, reminding us that amid all this tradition the Catholic Church has changed enormously even within our lifetimes. Door #2 (second from left) commemorates the kneeling pope, John (Giovanni) XXIII, who opened the landmark Vatican II Council in the early 1960s. This meeting of church leaders brought the medieval church into the modern age; they dropped outdated rituals (such as the use of Latin in the mass) and made old doctrines "relevant" to modern times.

ST. PETER'S BASILICA

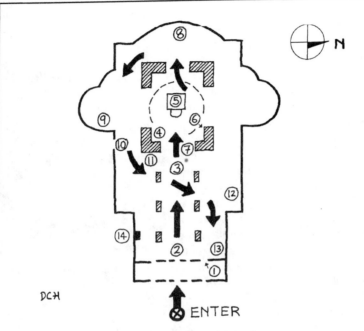

N

DCH

ENTER

ST. PETER'S SQUARE

1 - Holy Door

2 - Site of Charlemagne's coronation, A.D. 800

3 - Extent of the original "Greek Cross" church plan

4 - St. Andrew statue (view the dome from here)

5 - Main altar directly over Peter's tomb. BERNINI's 70-foot bronze canopy covers the altar

6 - Stairs down to the crypt, the foundation of old St. Peter's, chapels, and tombs of popes
   (the entrance moves around)

7 - Statue of St. Peter with irresistibly kissable toe

8 - BERNINI - Dove window and "St. Peter's Throne"

9 - Site of Peter's crucifixion

10 - Museum entrance

11 - RAPHAEL - "Transfiguration" mosaic

12 - Blessed Sacrament Chapel

13 - MICHELANGELO - Pietà

14 - Elevator to roof and dome-climb
    (this entrance moves around—sometimes it is even outside)

• Now for one of Europe's "oh wow" experiences. Enter the church. Gape for a while. But don't gape at Michelangelo's famous Pietà (on the right). That's this tour's finale. I'll wait for you at the round maroon pavement stone between the entrance and exit doors.

The Church

While ancient Rome fell, its grandeur survived. Roman basilicas became churches, senators became bishops, and the Pontifex Maximus (Emperor)... remained the Pontifex Maximus (Pope). This church is appropriately huge.

Size before beauty: The golden window at the far end is two football fields away. The dove in the window above the altar has the wingspan of a 747 (okay, maybe not quite, but it is big). The church covers six acres—if planted with wheat it could feed a small city. The babies at the base of the pillars along the main hall (the nave) are adult size. The lettering in the gold band along the top of the pillars is two meters (6 feet) high. Really. The church has a capacity of 95,000 worshipers standing (that's over 2,000 tour groups).

The church is huge and it feels huge, but everything is actually designed to make it seem smaller and more intimate than it really is. For example, the statue of St. Teresa near the bottom of the first pillar on the right is five meters tall. The statue above her near the top looks the same size but is actually two meters taller, giving the impression that it's not as far away as it really is. Similarly, the fancy bronze canopy over the altar at the far end is as tall as a seven-story building. That makes the great height of the dome seem smaller.

Looking down the nave we get a sense of the grandeur of ancient Rome that was carried on by the Catholic Church. The floor plan is based on the ancient Roman basilica, or law-court building, with a central aisle (nave) flanked by two side aisles.

The goal of this unprecedented building project was to "put the dome of the Pantheon atop the Forum's Basilica of Constantine." If you've seen these two Roman structures, you have an idea of this megavision. In fact, many of the stones used to build St. Peter's were scavenged from the ruined law courts of ancient Rome.

On the floor near the central doorway is a round slab of porphyry stone in the maroon color associated with the dignitaries of ancient

Rome. This is the spot where, on Christmas night in A.D. 800, the French King Charlemagne was crowned "Holy Roman Emperor." Even in the Dark Ages, when Rome was virtually abandoned and visitors reported that the city "had more thieves and wolves than decent people," its imperial legacy made it a fitting place to symbolically establish a briefly united Europe.

You're surrounded by marble, gold, stucco, mosaics, columns of stone, and pillars of light. This is Baroque, the decorative style popular at the height of the wars between Protestants and Catholics. It was intended to overwhelm and impress the masses with the authority of the church. St. Peter's was very expensive to build and decorate. The popes financed it by selling "indulgences," allowing the rich to literally buy forgiveness from the church. This kind of corruption inspired an obscure German monk named Martin Luther to rebel and start the Protestant Reformation. The Baroque interior by Bernini was part of the church's "Counter"-Reformation, a time when the church aggressively defended itself and art became a powerful propaganda tool. Here we see a glorious golden vision of heaven available to anyone—who remained a good Catholic.

• *Now, walk straight up the center of the nave toward the altar.*

"Michelangelo's Church"—The Greek Cross

The plaques on the floor show where other, smaller churches of the world would end if they were placed inside St. Peter's: St. Paul's Cathedral in London (Londinense), the Duomo in Florence, and so on.

You'll also walk over circular golden grates. Stop at the second one (at the third pillar from the entrance). Look back at the entrance and realize that if Michelangelo had had his way, this whole long section of the church wouldn't exist. The nave was extended after his death.

Michelangelo was 72 years old when the pope persuaded him to take over the church project and cap it with a dome. He agreed, intending to put the dome over Bramante's original "Greek Cross" floor plan (+), with four equal arms. In optimistic Renaissance times, this symmetrical arrangement symbolized perfection—the orderliness of the created world and the goodness of man (who was created in God's image). But Michelangelo was a Renaissance Man in Counter-Reformation times. The church, struggling against Protestants and its own corruption, opted for a plan designed to impress the world with its grandeur—the Latin cross of the Crucifixion with its extended nave to accommodate the grand religious spectacles of the Baroque period.

• *Continue toward the altar, entering Michelangelo's Church. Park yourself in front of the statue of St. Andrew to the left of the altar, the guy holding an X-shaped cross. Like Andrew, gaze up into the dome. Gasp if you must—never stifle a gasp.*

The Dome

The dome soars higher than a football field on end, 130 meters to the top of the lantern. It glows with light from its windows, the blue and gold mosaics creating a cool, solemn atmosphere. In this majestic vision of heaven we see (above the windows) Jesus, Mary, and a ring of saints, more rings of angels above them, and, way up in the ozone, God the Father (a blur of blue and red, without binoculars).

Listen to the hum of visitors echoing through St. Peter's. Churches are an early form of biofeedback where we can become aware of ourselves, our own human sounds, and can reflect on our place in the cosmos. We're half animal, half angel, stretched between heaven and earth, born to live only a short while, a bubble of foam on a great cresting wave of humanity.

• *But I digress.*

Peter

The base of the dome is ringed with a gold banner telling us in blue letters two meters tall why this church is so important. According to Catholics, Peter was selected by Jesus to head the church. The banner in Latin quotes from the Bible where Jesus says to him, "You are  Peter *(Tu es Petrus)* and upon this rock I will build my church" (Matthew 16:18). Peter was the first bishop of Rome, and his authority has supposedly passed in an unbroken chain to each succeeding bishop of Rome—that is, the 250-odd popes that followed.

Under the dome, under the bronze canopy, under the altar, some seven meters under the marble floor, rest the bones of St. Peter, the "rock" upon which this particular church was built. Go to the railing and look down into the small lighted niche three meters below the altar with a box containing bishops' shawls—a symbol of how Peter's authority spread to the other churches. Peter's tomb is about a meter below this box.

Are they really the bones of Jesus' apostle? According to a papal pronouncement: definitely maybe. The traditional site of his tomb was sealed up when the original St. Peter's was built on it in A.D. 326, and it remained sealed until 1940 when it was opened for archaeological study. Bones were found, dated from the first century, of a robust man who died in old age. His body was wrapped in expensive cloth. Various inscriptions and graffiti in the tomb indicate that second- and third-century visitors thought this was Peter's tomb. Does that mean it's really Peter? Who am I to disagree with the pope? Definitely maybe.

If you line up the cross on the altar with the dove in the window you'll notice that the niche below the cross is a half a meter off-center left with the rest of the church. Why? Because Michelangelo built the church around the traditional location of the tomb, not the actual location discovered by modern archaeology.

Back in the nave sits a bronze statue of Peter under a canopy. This is one of a handful of pieces of art that was in the earlier church. In one  hand he holds the keys, the symbol of the authority given him by Christ, while with the other he blesses us. He's wearing the toga of a Roman senator. It may be that the original statue was of a senator and the bushy head and keys were added later to make it Peter. His big right toe has been worn smooth by the lips of pilgrims. Stand in line and kiss it, or, to avoid hoof-and-mouth disease, touch your hand to your lips, then rub the toe. This is simply an act of reverence with no legend attached, though you can make one up if you like.

The Main Altar

The main altar beneath the dome and canopy (the white marble slab with cross and candlesticks) is used only when the pope himself says Mass. He often conducts the Sunday morning service when he's in town, a sight worth seeing. I must admit, though, it's a little strange being frisked at the door for weapons at the holiest place in Christendom.

The tiny altar would be lost in this enormous church if it weren't for Bernini's seven-story bronze canopy which "extends" the altar upward and reduces the perceived distance between floor and ceiling.

Gian Lorenzo Bernini (1598–1680) is the man most responsible for the interior decoration of the church. The altar area was his masterpiece,

Bernini Blitz

Nowhere is there such a conglomeration of works by the flamboyant genius who remade the church—and the city—in the Baroque
style. Here's your scavenger-hunt list. You have 20 minutes. Go.

1. St. Peter's Square: design and statues

2. Constantine equestrian relief (right end of atrium)

3. Decoration (stucco, gold leaf, marble, etc.) of side aisles
    (flanking the nave)

4. Tabernacle (the templelike altarpiece) inside Blessed Sacra-
    ment Chapel

5. Much of the marble floor throughout church

6. Bronze canopy over the altar

7. St. Longinus statue (holding a lance) near altar

8. Balconies (above each of the four statues) with corkscrew,
    Solomonic columns

9. Dove window, bronze sunburst, angels, "Throne," and
    Church Fathers (in the apse)

10. Tomb of Pope Urban VIII (far end of the apse, right side)

11. Tomb of Pope Alexander VII (near the left transept, over
    a doorway, with the gold skeleton smothered in jasper
    poured like maple syrup). Bizarre...Baroque...Bernini.

a "theater" for holy spectacles. Bernini did: (1)
the bronze canopy, (2) the dove window in the
apse surrounded by bronzework and statues, (3)
the statue of lance-bearing St. Longinus (which
became the model for the other three statues),
(4) the balconies above the four statues, incorpo-
rating the actual corkscrew columns looted from
Solomon's Temple in Jerusalem, and (5) much of
the marble floor decoration. Bernini, the father
of Baroque, gave an impressive unity to an amazing variety of pillars, windows, statues, chapels,
and aisles.

The bronze canopy is his crowning touch. The Baroque-looking

corkscrew columns are enlarged
copies of the ancient columns from
Solomon's Temple. The bronze
used was stolen and melted down
from the ancient Pantheon. On the
marble base of the columns you see
three bees on a shield, the symbol
of the Barberini family who com-

missioned the work and ordered the raid on the Pantheon. As the saying went, "What the barbarians didn't do, the Barberini did."

Starting from the column to the left of the altar, walk clockwise
around the canopy. Notice the female faces on the marble bases, about
eye level above the bees. Someone in the Barberini family was pregnant
during the making of the canopy, so Bernini put the various stages of
childbirth on the bases. Continue clockwise to the last base to see how it
came out.

• *Walk into the apse (it's the front area with the golden dove window) and
take a seat.*

The Apse

Bernini's dove window shines above the smaller
front altar used for everyday services. The Holy
Spirit in the form of a two-meter dove pours
sunlight onto the faithful through the alabaster
windows, turning into artificial rays of gold and
reflecting off swirling gold clouds, angels, and
winged babies. This is the epitome of Baroque—
a highly decorative, glorious, mixed-media work
designed to overwhelm the viewer.

Beneath the dove is the centerpiece of
this structure, the so-called "Throne of Peter,"
an oak chair built in medieval times for a king. Subsequently it was encrusted with tradition and encased in bronze by Bernini as a symbol of
papal authority. Statues of four early church fathers support the chair, a
symbol of how bishops should support the pope in troubled times—
times like the Counter-Reformation. Bernini's Baroque was great propaganda, reinforcing the power of the Catholic Church.

This is a good place to remember that St. Peter's is a church, not a
museum. In the apse, Mass is said daily (Mon–Sat at 17:00, Sun at 17:45)
for pilgrims, tourists, and Roman citizens alike. Wooden confessional
booths are available for Catholics to tell their sins to a listening ear and

receive forgiveness and peace of mind. The faithful renew their faith and the faithless gain inspiration. Sit here, look at the light streaming through the windows, turn and gaze up into the dome, and quietly contemplate your god.

Or...

Contemplate this: the mystery of empty space. The bench you're sitting on and the marble at your feet, solid as they may seem, consist overwhelmingly of open space—99.9999 percent open space. The atoms that form these "solid" benches are themselves mostly open space. If the nucleus of your average atom were as large as the period at the end of this sentence, its electrons would be specks of dust orbiting around it—at the top of Michelangelo's dome. Empty space. Perhaps matter is only an aberration in an empty universe.

• *Like wow.*

Now head to the left of the main altar into the south transept. At the far end, look left at the dark painting of St. Peter crucified upside down.

Left Transept

The painting is at the exact spot (according to tradition) where Peter was killed 1,900 years ago.

The Romans were actually quite tolerant of other religions. All they required of their conquered peoples was allegiance to the empire by worshiping the emperor as a god. For most religions this was no problem, but monotheistic Christians were children of a jealous God who would not allow worship of any others. They refused to worship the emperor and valiantly stuck by their faith even when burned alive, crucified, or thrown to the lions. Their bravery, optimism in suffering, and message of love struck a chord among slaves and members of the lower classes. The religion started by a poor carpenter grew despite occasional pogroms by fanatical emperors. In three short centuries, Christianity went from a small Jewish sect in Jerusalem to the official religion of the world's greatest empire.

Admire this painting and realize it's the only true "painting" in the church. All the others you see are actually mosaic copies made from thousands of colored chips the size of your little fingernail. Smoke and humidity would damage real paintings. Around the corner on the right (heading back towards the central nave), pause at the copy of Raphael's huge "painting" (mosaic) of *The Transfiguration*, especially if you won't be seeing the original in the Vatican Museum.

• *Back near the entrance to the church, in the far corner, behind bulletproof glass is...*

The Pietà

Michelangelo was 24 years old when he completed this *Pietà* (pee-ay-TAH) of Mary with the dead body of Christ taken from the cross.

Michelangelo, with his total mastery of the real world, captures the sadness of the moment. Mary cradles her crucified son in her lap. Christ's lifeless right arm drooping down lets us know how heavy this corpse is. His smooth skin is accented by the rough folds of Mary's robe. Mary tilts her head downward, looking at her dead son with sad tenderness. Her left hand is upturned as if asking, "How could they do this to you?"

Michelangelo didn't think of sculpting as creating a figure, but as simply freeing the God-made figure from the prison of marble around it. He'd attack a project like this with an inspired passion, chipping away to reveal what God put inside.

Realistic as this work is, its true power lies in the subtle "unreal" features. Look how small and childlike Christ is compared with the massive Mary. Unnoticed at first, this accentuates the subconscious impression of Mary enfolding Jesus in her maternal love. Notice how young Mary is. She's the mother of a 33-year-old man, but here she's portrayed as a teenage girl. Michelangelo did this to show that Mary was the eternally youthful "handmaiden" of the Lord, always serving Him even at this moment of supreme sacrifice. She accepts God's will, even if it means giving up her own son.

The statue is a solid pyramid of maternal tenderness. Yet, within this, Christ's body tilts diagonally down to the right, and Mary's hem flows with it. Subconsciously we feel the weight of this dead God sliding from her lap to the ground.

On Christmas morning, 1972, a madman with a hammer entered St. Peter's and began hacking away at the *Pietà*. The damage was repaired, but that's why there's a shield of bullet-proof glass today.

This is Michelangelo's only signed work. The story goes that he overheard some pilgrims praising his finished *Pietà*, but attributing it to a second-rate sculptor from a lesser city. He was so enraged he grabbed his chisel and chipped "Michelangelo Buonarotti of Florence did this" in the ribbon running down Mary's chest.

On your right is the inside of the Holy Door. It won't be opened until Christmas Eve, 2024, the dawn of the next Jubilee Year. If there's a prayer inside you, ask that when it's next opened, St. Peter's will no longer need security checks or bullet-proof glass.

Up to the Dome (Cupola)

A good way to finish a visit to St. Peter's is to go up to the dome for the best view of Rome anywhere.

There are two levels, the rooftop of the church and the very top of the dome. An elevator (€4.60) takes you to the first level, on the church roof just above the facade. Even from there you have a commanding view of St. Peter's Square, the statues on the colonnade, Rome across the Tiber in front of you, and the dome itself—almost terrifying in its nearness—looming behind you.

From here you can also go inside to the gallery ringing the interior of the dome, where you can look down inside the church. Notice the dusty top of Bernini's seven-story-tall canopy far below, study the mosaics up close—and those two-meter letters! It's worth the elevator ride for this view alone.

From this level, if you're energetic, continue all the way up to the top of the dome itself. The staircase (free at this point) actually winds between the outer shell and the inner one. It's a long, sweaty, stuffy, claustrophobic, 15-minute climb, but it's worth it. The view from the summit is great, the fresh air even better. Find the big white Victor Emmanuel Monument with the two statues on top and the Pantheon with its large, light, shallow dome. The large rectangular building to the left of the obelisk is the Vatican Museum, stuffed with art. Survey the Vatican grounds with its mini–train system and lush gardens. Look down into the square on the tiny pilgrims buzzing like electrons around the nucleus of Catholicism.

(The dome opens daily at 8:30 and closes at 18:00 May–Sept and at 17:00 Oct–April. Allow one hour for the full trip up and down, a half hour to go only to the roof and gallery. The entry to the elevator is just outside the basilica, on the porch, on the north side of St. Peter's. Look for signs to the *cupola*.)

The Rest of the Church

The Crypt: You can go down to the foundations of old St. Peter's, containing memorial chapels and tombs of popes. The location of the staircase entrance can vary, but it's usually inside the church near St. Andrew or one of his three fellow statues. Seeing the crypt is free, but the visit takes you back outside the church, a 15-minute detour. (Do it when you're ready to leave.)

The Museum (Museo-Tesoro): If you like old jewels and papal robes, you'll find the treasures and splendors of Roman Christianity a marked contrast to the poverty of early Christians. It's located near (but not in) the left transept, through a gray portal.

Blessed Sacrament Chapel: You're welcome to step through the metalwork gates into this oasis of peace reserved for prayer and meditation. It's located on the right-hand side of the church, about midway to the altar.

✤ 23 ✤
VATICAN MUSEUM

The glories of the ancient world displayed in a lavish papal palace, decorated by the likes of Michelangelo and Raphael . . . the Musei Vaticani. Unfortunately, many tourists see the Vatican Museum only as an obstacle between them and its grand finale, the Sistine Chapel. True, this huge, confusing, and crowded megamuseum can be a jungle, but, with this book as your vine, you should swing through with ease, enjoying the highlights and getting to the Sistine just before you collapse. On the way, you'll enjoy some of the less appreciated but equally important sections of this warehouse of Western civilization.

ORIENTATION

Cost: €10; free on last Sun of each month.

Dress code: Modest dress (no short shorts or bare shoulders) is appropriate and often required.

Hours: March–Oct Mon–Fri 8:45–16:45, Sat 8:45–13:45, Nov–Feb Mon–Sat 8:45–13:45, closed Sun except last Sun of the month (when it's free, crowded, and open 8:45–13:45). The last entry is 75 minutes before closing time. The museum is closed on many holidays (mainly religious ones) including Jan 1 and 6, Feb 11, March 19, Easter and Easter Monday, May 1 and 24, Ascension Day, Corpus Christi, June 29, Aug 15 and 16, Nov 1, Dec 8, 25, and 26.

The Sistine Chapel closes 30 minutes before the museum does. Some individual rooms close at odd hours, especially after 13:00. TV screens inside the entrance lists closures. The rooms described here are usually open.

It's generally hot and crowded. Sat, the last Sun of month, and Mon are the worst; afternoons are best.

Getting there: From the nearest Metro stop, Cipro-Musei Vaticani, it's a 10-minute walk. From St. Peter's Square, it's about a 15-minute walk (follow the Vatican Wall). Taxis are reasonable (hop in and say "moo-ZAY-ee vah-tee-KAHN-ee").

Information: For information, look in the lobby for the *i* (it's probably in the bank of windows to your left, under "Special Permits"; some English spoken). You'll find a book kiosk in the lobby, another up the stairs, and others scattered throughout the museum. Some exhibits have English explanations. The museum has signs to four color-coded self-guided visits (A—the Sistine blitz, C—a good tour, D—everything). Exchange windows with sinful rates are in the entry and exit. The post office is upstairs. Museum tel. 06-6988-4947 or 06-6988-3333.

Audioguide: You can rent a €5.80 audioguide (but, if you do, you lose the option of taking the shortcut from the Sistine Chapel to St. Peter's, because the audioguide must be returned at the entrance).

Length of our tour: Until you expire, or 2.5 hours, whichever comes first.

Photography: No photos are allowed in the Sistine Chapel. Elsewhere in the museum photos without a flash are permitted.

Cuisine art: A cafeteria is upstairs. Cheaper choices: The great Via Andrea Doria produce market is three blocks north of the entrance (head across the street, down the stairs, and continue straight), and inexpensive pizza shops line Via Candia. Good restaurants are nearby.

Starring: World history, Michelangelo, Raphael, *Laocoön*, the Greek masters and their Roman copyists.

THE POPE'S COLLECTION

With the fall of Rome, the Catholic (or "universal") Church became the great preserver of civilization, collecting artifacts from cultures dead and dying. Renaissance popes (15th and 16th centuries) collected most of what we'll see. Those lusty priests-as-Roman-emperors loved the ancient world. They built these palaces and decorated them with classical statues and Renaissance paintings. They combined the classical and Christian worlds, finding the divine in the creations of man.

We'll concentrate on classical sculpture and Renaissance painting. But, along the way (and there's a lot of along-the-way here), we'll stop to leaf through a few yellowed pages from this 5,000-year-old scrapbook of mankind.

VATICAN MUSEUM—OVERVIEW

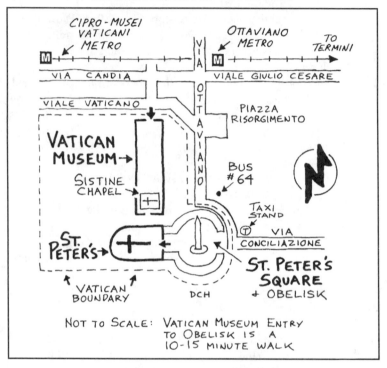

CIPRO - MUSEI
VATICANI
METRO

OTTAVIANO
METRO

TO
TERMINI

VIA CANDIA

VIALE GIULIO CESARE

VIALE VATICANO

PIAZZA
RISORGIMENTO

VIA OTTAVIANO

**VATICAN
MUSEUM→**

SISTINE
CHAPEL→

BUS
#64

TAXI
STAND

VIA
CONCILIAZIONE

ST.
PETER'S→

**ST. PETER'S
SQUARE**
+ OBELISK

↑ VATICAN ↑
BOUNDARY

DCH

NOT TO SCALE: VATICAN MUSEUM ENTRY
TO OBELISK IS A
10-15 MINUTE WALK

This heavyweight museum is shaped like a barbell—two buildings connected by a long hall. The entrance building covers the ancient world (Egypt, Greece, Rome). The one at the far end covers its "rebirth" in the Renaissance (including the Sistine Chapel). The halls there and back are a mix of old and new. Move quickly—don't burn out before the Sistine Chapel at the end—and see how each civilization borrows from and builds on the previous one.

• *Leave Italy by entering the doors. Go upstairs (or take the elevator) to buy your ticket, punch it in the turnstiles, go through a security check (just like at the airport), and then take the long escalator or spiral stairs up, up, up.*

At the top: To your right is the café and the Pinacoteca painting gallery (consider touring the Pinacoteca now if you want the option of taking the shortcut from the Sistine Chapel to St. Peter's; for information on the Pinacotaca, see the end of this chapter). To your left, the beginning of our tour. Go left and then take a left up the flight of stairs to reach the first-floor Egyptian Rooms (Museo Egizio). Don't stop until you find your mummy.

Egypt (3000–1000 B.C.)

Egyptian art was for religion, not decoration. A statue or painting preserved the likeness of someone, giving him a form of eternal life. Most of the art was for tombs, where they put the mummies. Notice that the art is only realistic enough to get the job done. You can recognize that it's a man, a bird, or whatever, but these are stiff, two-dimensional, schematic figures—functional rather than beautiful.

Mummies

This woman died three millennia ago. Her corpse was disemboweled, and her organs were placed in a jar like those you see nearby. Then the body was refilled with pitch, dried with natron (a natural sodium carbonate), wrapped in linen, and placed in a wood coffin,

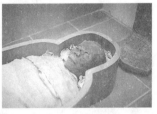

which went inside a stone coffin, which was placed in a tomb. (Remember that the pyramids were just big tombs.) In the next life, the spirit was homeless without its body, and you wanted to look your best—notice the henna job on her hair.

Notice, painted inside the coffins, what the deceased "packed" for the journey to eternity. The coffins were decorated with magical spells to protect the body from evil and to act as crib notes for the confused soul in the netherworld.

Egyptian Statues

Even in the Romanized versions, it's clear that Egyptian statues are stiff and unnatural. They step out awkwardly with arms straight down at their sides. Each was made according to an established set of proportions. Little changed over the centuries. These had a function and they worked. In Egyptian belief, a statue like this could be a place of refuge for the wandering soul of a dead man.

Various Egyptian Gods as Animals

Before technology made humans top dogs on earth, it was easier to appreciate our fellow creatures. The Egyptians saw the superiority of animals and worshiped them as incarnations of the gods. Wander through a pet store of Egyptian animal gods. The lioness portrays the

ANCIENT WORLD—EGYPT, GREECE, ROME

```
                                          " TO
                                          NEW
                                          WING"
                                    WC   (CLASSICAL)
                                         (SCULPTURE)

                              ←SUMERIAN
              ②                  WRITING
  OCTAGONAL
  COURTYARD                     ROMAN
              ③                 PINE CONE

 HALL OF ANIMALS    MUMMIES   ← EGYPTIAN
                          ①      ROOMS
                              (ETRUSCAN)
                              (ROOMS   )
        ④                     (ONE FLOOR)
                              (ABOVE   )

                                FROM
                              ENTRANCE
  ⑤ ⑥

        ⑦                   UPSTAIRS TO
              DCH              "THE
                              LONG MARCH"
```

1 - Egyptian statue	5 - Hercules statue
2 - Apollo Belvedere	6 - Porphyry basin
3 - Laocoön	7 - Mrs. Constantine's sarcophagus
4 - Belvedere Torso	

fierce goddess Sekhmet; the clever baboon is the god of wisdom, Thot; and Horus has a falcon's head.

• *Continue through a curved corridor of animal gods, then through three more rooms, pausing at the glass case in the third room, which contains brown clay tablets.*

Sumerian Writing

Even before Egypt, civilizations flourished in the Middle East. The Sumerian culture in Mesopotamia (modern Iraq) invented writing around 3000 B.C. You can see the clay tablets with this cuneiform (wedge-shaped) script. Also notice the ingenious cylindrical seals, with which they made impressions in soft clay to seal documents and mark property.

• *Go with the flow past a view of Rome out the window, then turn left into the octagonal courtyard of the "Pio-Clementino" section.*

Sculpture—Greece and Rome (500 B.C.–A.D. 500)

This palace wouldn't be here, this sculpture wouldn't be here, and you'd be spending your vacation in South Dakota at Reptile Gardens if it weren't for a few thousand Greeks in a small city about 450 years before Christ. Athens set the tone for the rest of the West. Democracy, theater, economics, literature, and art all got their start in Athens during a 50-year "Golden Age." Greek culture was then appropriated by Rome and revived again 1,500 years later, during the Renaissance. The Renaissance popes built and decorated these palaces, recreating the glory of the classical world.

Apollo Belvedere

Apollo, the god of the sun and also of music, is hunting. He has spotted his prey and is about to go after it with his (missing) bow and arrows. The optimistic Greeks conceived of their gods in human form . . . and buck naked.

The great Greek sculptor Praxiteles has fully captured the beauty of the human form. The anatomy is perfect, the pose is natural. Instead of standing at attention, face forward with his arms at his sides (Egyptian style), Apollo is on the move, stepping forward slightly with his weight on one leg.

The Greeks loved balance. A well-rounded man was both a thinker and an athlete, a poet and a warrior. In art, the *Apollo Belvedere* balances several opposites. Apollo eyes his target but hasn't attacked yet. He's moving, but not out of control. He's also a balance between a real person and an ideal god. And the smoothness of his muscles is balanced by the rough folds of his cloak. The only sour note: his recently added left hand. Could we try a size smaller?

During the Renaissance, when this Roman copy of the original Greek work was discovered, it was considered the most perfect work of art in the world. The handsome face, eternal youth, and the body that seems to float just above the pedestal made *Apollo Belvedere* an object of wonder and almost worship. Apollo's grace was something superhuman, divine, and godlike, even for devout Christians.

• *In the neighboring niche to the right, a bearded old Roman river god lounges in the shade. This pose inspired Michelangelo's Adam in the Sistine Chapel (coming soon). While there are a few fancy bathtubs in this courtyard, most of the carved boxes you see are sarcophagi—Roman coffins and relic holders, carved with the deceased's epitaph in picture form.*

Laocoön

Laocoön (lay-AWK-oh-wahn) was a pagan high priest of Troy, the ancient city attacked by the Greeks. When the Greeks brought the Trojan Horse to the gates as a ploy to get inside the city walls, Laocoön tried to warn his people not to bring it inside. But the gods wanted the Greeks to win, so they sent huge snakes to crush him and his two sons to death. We see them at the height of their terror, when we realize that, no matter how hard they struggle, they—and their entire race—are doomed.

The *Laocoön* is Hellenistic, done four centuries after the Golden Age, after the scales of "balance" had been tipped. Where *Apollo* is a balance between stillness and motion, this is unbridled motion. Where *Apollo* is serene, this is emotional. Where *Apollo* is idealized grace, this is powerful and gritty realism. The figures (carved from four blocks of marble pieced together seamlessly) are powerful, not light and graceful. The poses are as twisted as possible, accentuating every rippling muscle and bulging vein. Follow the line of motion from *Laocoön's* left foot, up his leg, through his body and out his right arm (which some historians used to think extended straight out—until the elbow was dug up early in the 1900s). Goethe used to stand here and blink his eyes rapidly, watching the statue flicker to life.

Laocoön was the most famous Greek statue in ancient Rome and considered "superior to all other sculpture or painting." It was famous in the Renaissance, too—though no one had seen it, only read about it in ancient accounts. Then, in 1506, it was unexpectedly unearthed in the ruins of Nero's Golden House near the Colosseum. The discovery caused a sensation. They cleaned it off and paraded it through the streets before an awestruck populace. No one had ever seen anything like its motion and emotion, having been raised on a white-bread diet of pretty, serene, and balanced *Apollo*s. One of those who saw it was the young Michelangelo, and it was a revelation to him. Two years later, he started work on the Sistine Chapel, and the Renaissance was about to take another turn.

• *Leave the courtyard. Swing around the Hall of Animals, a jungle of beasts real and not so real, to the limbless* Torso *which you'll find in the middle of the next large hall.*

Belvedere Torso

My entire experience with statues consists of making snowmen. But standing face to face with this hunk of shaped rock makes you appreciate the sheer physical labor involved in chipping a figure out of solid rock. It takes great strength but, at the same time, great delicacy.

This is all that remains of an ancient statue of Hercules seated on a lion skin. Michelangelo loved this old rock. He knew he was the best sculptor of his day. The ancients were his only peers—and his rivals. He'd caress this statue lovingly and tell people, "I am the pupil of the *Torso*." To him, it contained all the beauty of classical sculpture. But it's not beautiful. It's ugly. Compared with the pure grace of the *Apollo*, it's downright hideous.

But Michelangelo, an ugly man himself, was looking for a new kind of beauty—not the beauty of idealized gods, but the innate beauty of every person, even so-called ugly ones. With its knotty lumps of muscle, the *Torso* has a brute power and a distinct personality despite— or because of—its rough edges. Remember this *Torso* because we'll see it again later on.

• *Enter the next, domed room.*

Round Room

This room, modeled on the Pantheon interior, gives some idea of Roman grandeur. Romans often took Greek ideas and made them bigger, like the big bronze statue of Hercules with his club, found near Pompey's Theatre (by modern-day Campo de' Fiori). The mosaic floor recreates an ancient Roman villa, and the enormous Roman hot tub/birdbath/vase, made of purple porphyry marble, is also likely from a villa. Purple was a rare, royal, expensive, and prestigious color in pre-Crayola days.

• *Enter the next room.*

Sarcophagi

These two large coffins made of porphyry marble were made for the Roman Emperor Constantine's mother and daughter. They were Christians and, therefore, criminals until Constantine made Christianity legal (A.D. 313).

• *See how we've come full circle in this building—the Egyptian Rooms are ahead on your left. Go upstairs and prepare for the Long March down the hall lined with statues toward the Sistine Chapel and Raphael Rooms.*

Overachievers may first choose to pop into the Etruscan wing— "Museo Etrusco"—located a few steps up from the "Long March" level. (Others have permission to save their aesthetic energy for the Sistine.)

The Etruscans (800–300 B.C.)

Room I

The chariot is from 550 B.C., when crude Romans were ruled by their more civilized neighbors to the north—the Etruscans. Imagine the chariot racing around the dirt track of the Circus Maximus, through the marshy valley of the newly drained Forum, or up Capitol Hill to the Temple of Jupiter—all originally built by Rome's Etruscan kings.

Room II

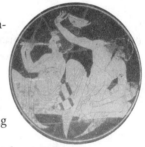

The golden breastplate (*Pectoral*, 650 B.C., immediately to the right), decorated with tiny winged angels and animals, shows off the sophistication of the Etruscans. Though unwarlike and politically decentralized, these people were able to "conquer" all of central Italy around 650 B.C. through trade, offering tempting metalwork goods like this.

The Etruscan vases done in the Greek style remind us of the other great pre-Roman power—the Greek colonists who settled in southern Italy (Magna Graecia). The Etruscans traded with the Greeks, adopting their fashions. Rome, cradled between the two, grew up learning from both cultures.

A Greek-style bowl (far corner of the room) depicting a man and woman in bed together would have scandalized early Roman farmers. He's peeing in a chamberpot, she's blowing a flute. Etruscan art often showed husbands and wives at ease together, giving them a reputation among the Romans as immoral, flute-playing degenerates.

Room III

The bronze warrior whose head was sawed off by lightning has a rare inscription that's readable (on armor below the navel). It probably refers to the statue's former owner: "Aha! Trutitis gave [this] as [a] gift." Archaeologists understand the Etruscans' Greek-style alphabet and some individual words, but they've yet to fully crack the code. As you look around at beautiful bronze pitchers, candlesticks, shields, and urns, ponder yet another of Etruria's unsolved mysteries—no one is sure where these sophisticated people came from.

Room IV

Most of our knowledge of the Etruscans is from sarcophagi and art in Etruscan tombs. Their funeral art is solemn but hardly morbid—check out the sarcopha-guy with the bulging belly, enjoying a banquet for all eternity.

The Etruscans' origins are obscure, but their legacy is clear. In 509 B.C., the Etruscan king's son raped a Roman. The king was thrown out, the Republic was declared, Etruscan cities were conquered by Rome's legions, and their culture was swallowed up in Roman expansion. By

Julius Caesar's time, the few remaining ethnic Etruscans were reduced to serving their masters as flute players, goldsmiths, surgeons, and street-corner soothsayers, like the one that Caesar brushed aside when he called out, "Beware the Ides of March...."

• *Backtrack, returning to the long hall leading to the Sistine Chapel and Raphael Rooms.*

THE LONG MARCH—SCULPTURE, TAPESTRIES, MAPS, AND VIEWS

Remember, this building was originally a series of papal palaces. The popes loved beautiful things, and, as heirs of Imperial Rome, they felt they deserved such luxury. This half-kilometer walk gives you a sense

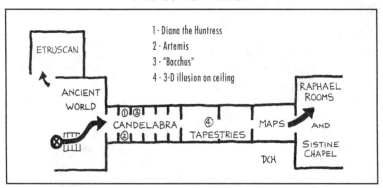

--- **THE LONG MARCH** ---

1 - Diana the Huntress
2 - Artemis
3 - "Bacchus"
4 - 3-D illusion on ceiling

ETRUSCAN

ANCIENT WORLD

CANDELABRA

TAPESTRIES

MAPS

DCH

RAPHAEL ROOMS

AND

SISTINE CHAPEL

of the scale that Renaissance popes built on. The palaces and art represent both the peak and the decline of the Catholic Church in Europe. It was extravagant spending like this that inspired Martin Luther to rebel, starting the Protestant Reformation.

Gallery of the Candelabra— Classical Sculpture

In the second "room" of the long hall, stop at the statue *Diana the Huntress* on the left. Here, the virgin goddess goes hunting. Roman hunters would pray and give offerings to statues like this to get divine help in their hunt for food.

Farmers might pray to another version of the same goddess, *Artemis*, on the opposite wall. This billion-breasted beauty stood for fertility. "Boobs or bulls' balls?" Some historians say that bulls were sacrificed and castrated, with the testicles draped over the statues as symbols of fertility.
• *Shuffle along to the* Bacchus *in the next "room" on the left with a baby on his shoulders.*

Fig Leaves

Why do the statues have fig leaves? Like *Bacchus*, many of these statues originally looked much different than they do now. First off, they were painted, usually in gaudy colors. *Bacchus* may have had brown hair, rosy

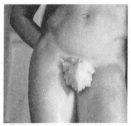

cheeks, purple grapes, and a leopard-skin sidekick at his feet. Even the *Apollo Belvedere*, whose cool gray tones we now admire as "classic Greek austerity," may have had a paisley pink cloak for all we know. Also, many statues had glass eyes like *Bacchus*.

And the fig leaves? Those came from the years 1550 to 1800, when the church decided that certain parts of the human anatomy were obscene. (Why they didn't pick the feet, which are universally ugly, I'll never know.) Perhaps church leaders associated these full-frontal statues with the outbreak of Renaissance humanism that reduced their power in Europe. Whatever the reason, they reacted by covering classical crotches with plaster fig leaves, the same leaves Adam and Eve had used when the concept of "privates" was invented.

Note: The leaves could be removed at any time if the museum officials were so motivated. There are suggestion boxes around the museum. Whenever I see a fig leaf, I get the urge to pick-it. We could start an organ-ized campaign...

• *Cover your eyes in case they forgot a fig leaf or two and continue to the tapestries.*

Tapestries

Along the left wall are tapestries designed by Raphael and his workshop and made in Brussels. They show scenes from the life of Christ, starting with the baby Jesus in the manger.

Check out the beautiful sculpted reliefs on the ceiling, especially the lavender panel near the end of the first tapestry room showing a centurion ordering Eskimo Pies from a vendor. Admire the workmanship of this relief, then realize that it's not a relief at all—it's painted on a flat surface! Illusions like this were proof that painters had mastered the 3-D realism of ancient statues.

Map Gallery and View of Vatican City

This gallery still feels like a pope's palace. The crusted ceiling is pure papal splendor. The maps on the walls are decorations from the 16th century. You can plan the next leg of your trip with the two maps of Italy at the far end of the hall— "New Italy" and "Old Italy"—both with a smoking Mount Vesuvius next to Napoli/Neapolis/Naples. There's an interesting old map of Venice on the right as you exit.

The windows give you your best look at the tiny country of Vatican

City, formed in 1929. It has its own radio station, as you see from the tower on the hill. What you see here is pretty much all there is—these gardens, the palaces you're in, and St. Peter's.

If you lean out and look left, you'll see the dome of St. Peter's the way Michelangelo would have liked you to see it—without the bulky Baroque facade.

• *Exit the map room and take a breather in the next small tapestry hall before turning left into the crowded Raphael Rooms.*

Renaissance Art
Raphael Rooms—Papal Wallpaper

We've seen art from the ancient world; now we'll see its rebirth in the Renaissance. We're entering the living quarters of the great Renaissance popes—where they slept, worked, and worshiped. The rooms reflect the grandeur of their position. They hired the best artists—mostly from Florence—to paint the walls and ceilings, combining classical and Christian motifs.

• *Entering, you'll immediately see...*

The huge non-Raphael painting shows Sobieski liberating Vienna from the Moslem Turks in 1683, finally tipping the tide in favor of a Christian Europe. See the Moslem tents on the left and the spires of Christian Vienna on the right.

The second room's paintings celebrate the doctrine of the Immaculate Conception, establishing that Mary herself was conceived free from original sin. This medieval idea wasn't actually made dogma until a century ago. The largest fresco shows how the inspiration came straight from heaven (upper left) in a ray of light directly to the pope. Modern popes have had to defend this and other doctrines against the onslaught of the modern world, which questions "superstitions," the divinity of Jesus...and the infallibility of the pope.

• *Next, you'll pass along an outside ramp overlooking a courtyard (is that the pope's Fiat?), finally ending up in the first of the Raphael Rooms—the Constantine Room.*

Constantine Room

The frescoes (by Raphael and assistants) celebrate the passing of the baton from one culture to the next. Remember, Rome was a pagan empire persecuting a fanatic cult from the East—Christianity.

RAPHAEL ROOMS

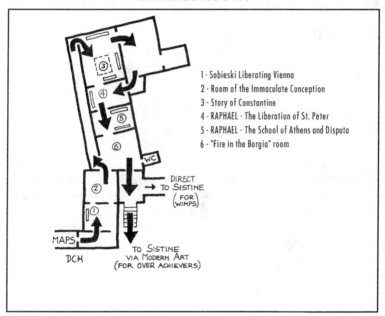

1 - Sobieski Liberating Vienna
2 - Room of the Immaculate Conception
3 - Story of Constantine
4 - RAPHAEL - The Liberation of St. Peter
5 - RAPHAEL - The School of Athens and Disputa
6 - "Fire in the Borgia" room

Then, on the night of October 27, A.D. 312 (left wall), as Constantine (in gold, with crown) was preparing his troops for a coup d'état, he looked up and saw something strange. A cross appeared in the sky with the words, "You will conquer in this sign."

Next day (long wall), his troops raged victoriously into battle with the Christian cross atop their Roman eagle banners. There's Constantine in the center, slashing through the enemy, with God's warrior angels riding shotgun overhead.

Constantine was supposedly baptized a Christian (right wall), even stripping and kneeling before the pope. As emperor, he legalized Christianity and worked hand in hand with the pope (window wall). When Rome fell, its glory lived on through the Dark Ages in the pomp, pageantry, and learning of the Catholic Church.

Look at the ceiling painting. A classical statue falls and crumbles before the overpowering force of the cross. Whoa! Christianity triumphs over pagan Rome. (This was painted, I believe, by Raphael's surrealist colleague, Salvadorus Dalio.)

Raphael

Raphael was only 25 when Pope Julius II invited him to paint the walls of his private apartments. Julius was so impressed by Raphael's talent that he had the work of earlier masters scraped off and gave Raphael free rein to paint what he wanted.

Raphael lived a charmed life. He painted masterpieces effortlessly. He was handsome and sophisticated, and soon became Julius' favorite. In a different decade, he might have been thrown out of the Church as a great sinner, but his love affairs and devil-may-care personality seemed to epitomize the optimistic pagan spirit of the Renaissance. His works are graceful but never lightweight or frilly—they're strong, balanced, and harmonious in the best Renaissance tradition. When he died young in 1520, the High Renaissance died with him.

• *Continue through the next room and bookshop. In the following room, block the sunlight with your hand to see . . .*

The Liberation of St. Peter

Peter, Jesus' right-hand man, was thrown into prison in Jerusalem for his beliefs. In the middle of the night, an angel appeared and rescued him from the sleeping guards (Acts 12). The chains miraculously fell away (and were later brought to the St. Peter-in-Chains church in Rome). The angel led Peter to safety (right) while the guards took hell from their captain (left). This little "play" is neatly divided into three separate acts that make a balanced composition.

Raphael makes the miraculous event even more dramatic with the use of three kinds of light illuminating the dark cell—half moonlight, the captain's torch, and the radiant angel. Raphael's mastery of realism, rich colors, and sense of drama made him understandably famous.

• *Enter the next room . . .*

The School of Athens

In both style and subject matter, this fresco sums up the spirit of the Renaissance, which was not only the rebirth of classical art, but a rebirth of learning, of discovery, of the optimistic spirit that man is a rational

creature. Raphael pays respect to
the great thinkers and scientists
of ancient Greece, gathering them
together at one time in a mythical
school setting.

In the center are Plato and
Aristotle, the two greatest. Plato
points up, indicating his philos-
ophy that mathematics and pure ideas are the source of truth, while
Aristotle points down, showing his preference for hands-on study of
the material world. There's their master, Socrates (midway to the left, in
green), ticking off arguments on his fingers. And in the foreground at
right Euclid bends over a slate to demonstrate a geometrical formula.

Raphael shows that Renaissance thinkers were as good as the ancients. There's Leonardo da Vinci, whom Raphael worshiped, in the role
of Plato. Raphael himself (next to last on the far right, with the black
beret) looks out at us. And the "school" building is actually an early
version of St. Peter's Basilica (under construction at the time).

Raphael balances everything symmetrically—thinkers to the left,
scientists to the right, with Plato and Aristotle dead center—showing
the geometrical order found in the world. Look at the square floor tiles
in the foreground. If you laid a ruler over them and extended the line
upward, it would run right to center of the picture. Similarly, the tops of
the columns all point down to the middle. All the lines of sight draw
our attention to Plato and Aristotle, and to the small arch over their
heads—a halo over these two secular saints in the divine pursuit of
knowledge.

While Raphael was painting this room, Michelangelo was at work
down the hall in the Sistine Chapel. Raphael popped in on the sly to see
the master at work. He was astonished. When he saw Michelangelo's
powerful figures and dramatic scenes, he began to beef up his delicate,
graceful style to a more heroic level. In *The School of Athens*, perhaps
Raphael's greatest work, he tipped his brush to the master by adding
Michelangelo to the scene—the brooding, melancholy figure in front
leaning on a block of marble.

The Disputa
As if to underline the new attitude that pre-Christian philosophy and
church thinking could coexist, Raphael painted *The Disputa* facing *The
School of Athens*. Christ and the saints in heaven are overseeing a discussion of the Eucharist (the communion wafer) by mortals below. The

classical-looking woman in blue looks out as if to say, "There's *The School of Athens,*" while pointing toward the center of the painting she's in, as if to say, "But here's the School of Heaven." Balance and symmetry reign, from the angel trios in the upper corners to the books littering the floor.

In Catholic terms, the communion wafer miraculously becomes the body of Christ when it's eaten, bringing a little bit of heaven into the material world. Raphael's painting also connects heaven and earth, with descending circles: Jesus in a halo, down to the dove of the Holy Spirit in a circle, which enters the communion wafer in its holder. The composition drives the point home. By the way, these rooms were the papal library, so themes featuring learning, knowledge, and debate were appropriate.

Moving along, the last Raphael Room (called the "Fire in the Borgia" Room) shows work done mostly by Raphael's students, who were influenced by the muscularity and dramatic, sculptural poses of Michelangelo.

• *Get ready. It's decision time. From here there are two ways to get to the Sistine Chapel. Leave the final Raphael Room and you'll soon see two arrows—one pointing left to the Sistine (Cappella Sistina) and one pointing right to the Sistine. Left goes directly to the Sistine. But going right (5 minutes and a few staircases longer), you'll find a quiet room at the foot of the stairs with a bench where you can sit in peace to read ahead before entering the hectic Sistine Chapel. Also, you get to stroll through the impressive Modern Religious Art collection on the way (signs will direct you to the Sistine). Your call.*

The Sistine Chapel

The Sistine Chapel contains Michelangelo's ceiling and his huge *Last Judgment.* The Sistine is the personal chapel of the pope and the place where new popes are elected. When Pope Julius II asked Michelangelo to take on this important project, he said, "No, *grazie.*"

Michelangelo insisted he was a sculptor, not a painter. The Sistine ceiling was a vast undertaking, and he didn't want to do a half-vast job. But the pope pleaded, bribed, and threatened until Michelangelo finally consented on the condition he be able to do it all his own way.

Julius had asked for only 12 apostles along the sides of the ceiling, but Michelangelo had a grander vision—the entire history of the world until Jesus. He spent the next four years (1508–1512) lying on his back on scaffolding six stories up, covering the ceiling with frescoes of Bible scenes. In sheer physical terms, it's an astonishing achievement: 600 square meters, and every brushstroke done by his own hand. (Raphael only designed most of his rooms, letting assistants do the grunt work.)

First he had to design and erect the scaffolding. Any materials had to be hauled up on pulleys. Then a section of ceiling would be plastered. With fresco—painting on wet plaster—if you don't get it right the first time, you have to scrape the whole thing off and start over. And if you've ever struggled with a ceiling light fixture or worked underneath a car for even five minutes, you know how heavy your arms get. The physical effort, the paint dripping in his eyes, the creative drain, and the mental stress from a pushy pope combined to almost kill Michelangelo.

But, when it was finished and revealed to the public, it simply blew 'em away. Like the *Laocoön* statue discovered six years earlier, it was unlike anything seen before. It both caps the Renaissance and turns it in a new direction. In perfect Renaissance spirit, it mixes Old Testament prophets with classical figures. But the style is more dramatic, shocking, and emotional than the balanced Renaissance works before it. This is a very personal work—the Gospel according to Michelangelo—but its themes and subject matter are universal. Almost without exception, art critics concede that the Sistine ceiling is the single greatest work of art by any one human being.

The Sistine Ceiling—Understanding What You're Standing Under

The ceiling shows the history of the world before the birth of Jesus. We see God creating the world, creating man and woman, destroying the earth by flood, and so on. Along the sides (where the ceiling starts to curve) we see the Old Testament prophets and pagan Greek prophetesses that foretold the coming of Christ. Dividing these scenes and figures is a painted architectural framework (a 3-D illusion) decorated with nude, statuelike figures with symbolic meaning.

-------------------------------- THE SISTINE CEILING --------------------------------

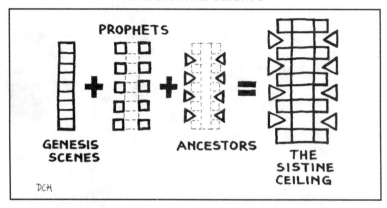

The key is to see three simple divisions in the tangle of bodies:
1.   The central spine of nine rectangular Bible scenes
2.   The line of prophets on either side
3.   The triangles in between the prophets showing the
     ancestors of Christ
• *Ready? Within the Chapel, grab a seat along the side (if possible). Face the altar with the big* Last Judgment *on the wall (more on that later). Now look up to the ceiling and find the central panel of . . .*

The Creation of Adam

God and Man are equal in this Renaissance version of creation. Adam, newly formed in the image of God, lounges dreamily in perfect naked innocence. God, with his entourage, swoops forward in a swirl of activity (which—with a little imagination—looks like a cross-section of a human brain . . . quite a strong humanist statement). Their reaching hands are the center of this work. Adam's is limp and passive; God's is strong and forceful, His finger twitching upward with energy. Here is the very moment of creation, as God passes the spark of life to man, the crowning work of His creation.

This is the spirit of the Renaissance. God is not a terrifying giant reaching down to puny and helpless man from way on high. Here they are on an equal plane, co-creators, divided only by the diagonal patch of sky. God's billowing robe and the patch of green upon which Adam is

THE SISTINE CEILING

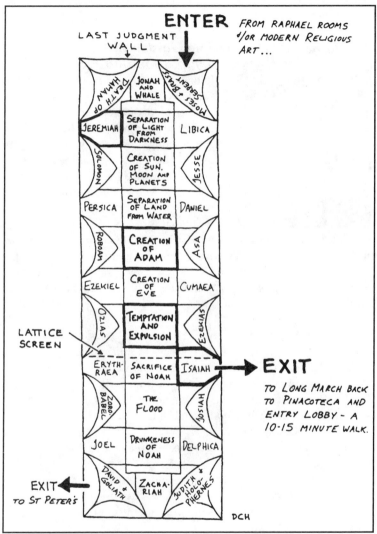

lying balance each other. They are like two pieces of a jigsaw puzzle, or two long-separated continents, or like the yin and yang symbols finally coming together—uniting, complementing each other, creating wholeness. God and man work together as equals in the divine process of creation.

• *This celebration of man permeates the ceiling. Notice the Adonises-come-to-life on the pedestals that divide the central panels. And then came woman.*

The Garden of Eden: Temptation and Expulsion

In one panel we see two scenes from the Garden of Eden. On the left is the leafy garden of paradise where Adam and Eve lie around blissfully. But the devil comes along—a serpent with a woman's torso—and winds around the forbidden Tree of Knowledge. The temptation to gain new knowledge is too great for these Renaissance people. They eat the forbidden fruit.

At right, the sword-wielding angel drives them from Paradise into the barren plains. They're grieving, but they're far from helpless. Adam's body is thick and sturdy, and we know they'll survive in the cruel world. Adam firmly gestures to the angel, like he's saying, "All right, already! We're going!"

The Nine Scenes from Genesis

Take some time with these central scenes to understand the story the ceiling tells. They run in sequence, starting at the front:

1. God, in purple, divides the light from darkness.
2. God creates the sun (burning orange) and the moon (pale white, to the right). Oops, I guess there's another moon.
3. God bursts towards us to separate the land and water.
4. *The Creation of Adam.*
5. God creates Eve, who springs out of Adam's side.
6. *The Garden of Eden: Temptation and Expulsion.*
7. Noah kills a ram and stokes the altar fires to make a sacrifice to God.
8. The great Flood, sent by God, destroys the wicked, who desperately head for higher ground. In the distance, the Ark carries Noah's family to safety.
9. Noah's sons come across Noah drunk. (Perhaps Michelangelo chose to end it with this scene as a reminder that even the best of men are fallible.)

Prophets

By 1510 Michelangelo had finished the first half of the ceiling, the end farthest from the *Last Judgment* wall. When they took the scaffolding down and could finally see what he'd been working on for two years, everyone was awestruck—except Michelangelo. As powerful as his figures are, from the floor they didn't look dramatic enough for Michelangelo. For the other half he pulled out all the stops.

Compare the many small figures in the Noah scenes with, say, Adam and God at the other end. Or compare an early prophet with a later one. Isaiah ("Esaias," in purple) is shown in a pose like a Roman senator. He is a stately, sturdy, balanced, composed Renaissance Man. Now look at Jeremiah ("Hieremias") in the corner by the *Last Judgment.* This prophet, who witnessed the destruction of Israel, is a dark, brooding figure. He slumps his chin in his hand and ponders the fate of his people. The difference between the small, dignified Isaiah and the large, dramatic Jeremiah is like the difference between *Apollo Belvedere* and the *Laocoön.* This sort of emotional power was a new element in Renaissance painting.

The Cleaning Project

The ceiling and the *Last Judgment* have been cleaned, removing centuries of preservatives, dirt, and soot from candles, oil lamps, and the annual Papal Barbecue (just kidding). The bright, bright colors that emerged are a bit shocking, forcing many art experts to reevaluate Michelangelo's style. Notice the very dark patches left in the corner above *The Last Judgment* and imagine how dreary it must have been before the cleaning.

The Last Judgment

When Michelangelo was asked to paint the altar wall 23 years later (1535), the mood of Europe—and of Michelangelo—was completely different. The Protestant Reformation had forced the Catholic Church to

clamp down on free thought, and religious wars raged. Rome had recently been pillaged by roving bands of mercenaries. The Renaissance spirit of optimism was fading. Michelangelo himself had begun to question the innate goodness of mankind.

THE LAST JUDGMENT

1 - Christ with Mary at his side
2 - Trumpeting Angels
3 - The dead come out of their graves, the righteous ascend
4 - One of the damned
5 - Charon in his boat
6 - The demon/critic of nudity
7 - St. Bartholomew with flayed skin containing Michelangelo's self-portrait

It's Judgment Day, and Christ—the powerful figure in the center, raising his arm to strike down the wicked—has come to find out who's naughty and nice. Beneath him, a band of angels blows its trumpets Dizzy Gillespie–style to wake the dead. The dead at lower left leave their graves and prepare to be judged. The righteous, on Christ's right hand (the left side of the picture), ascend to the glories of Heaven. The wicked on the other side are hurled down to Hell where demons wait to torture them. Charon, from the underworld of Greek mythology, waits below to ferry the souls of the damned to Hell.

It's a grim picture. No one, but no one, is smiling. Even many of the righteous being resurrected (lower left) are either skeletons or cadavers with ghastly skin. The angels have to play tug-of-war with subterranean monsters to drag them from their graves.

Over in Hell, the wicked are tortured by gleeful demons. One of the damned (to the right of the trumpeting angels) has an utterly lost expression, as if saying, "Why did I cheat on my wife?!" Two demons grab him around the ankles to pull him down to the bowels of Hell, condemned to an eternity of constipation.

But it's the terrifying figure of Christ who dominates this scene. As he raises his arm to smite the wicked, he sends a ripple of fear through everyone, and they recoil. Even the saints around him—even Mary beneath his arm (whose interceding days are clearly over)—shrink back in terror. His expression is completely closed, and he turns his head, refusing to even listen to the whining alibis of the damned. Look at Christ's bicep. If this muscular figure looks familiar to you, it's because you've seen it before—the *Belvedere Torso*.

When *The Last Judgment* was unveiled to the public in 1544, it caused a sensation. The pope is said to have dropped to his knees and cried, "Lord, charge me not with my sins when thou shalt come on the Day of Judgment." And it changed the course of art. The complex composition with more than 300 figures swirling around the figure of Christ was far beyond traditional Renaissance balance. The twisted figures shown from every angle imaginable challenged other painters to try and top this master of 3-D illusion.

And the sheer terror and drama of the scene were a striking contrast to the placid optimism of, say, Raphael's *School of Athens*. Michelangelo had Baroque-en all the rules of the Renaissance, signaling a new era of art.

With the Renaissance fading, the fleshy figures in *The Last Judgment* aroused murmurs of discontent from Church authorities. Michelangelo rebelled by painting his chief critic into the scene—in Hell. (He's the demon in the bottom right corner wrapped in a serpent. Look how Michelangelo covered his privates. Sweet revenge.) After Michelangelo's death, there was no defense, and prudish church authorities painted the wisps of clothing we see today.

Now move up close. Study the details of the lower part of the painting from right to left. Charon, with Dr. Spock ears and a Dalí moustache, paddles the damned in a boat full of human turbulence. Look more closely at the J-Day band. Are they reading music or is it the Judgment Day tally? Before the cleaning, these details were lost in murk.

The Last Judgment marks the end of Renaissance optimism epitomized in *The Creation of Adam*, with its innocence and exaltation of man. There he was the equal of a fatherly God. Here, man cowers in fear and unworthiness before a terrifying, wrathful deity.

Michelangelo himself must have wondered how he would be judged—had he used his God-given talents wisely? Look at St. Bartholomew, the bald bearded guy at Christ's left foot (our right). In the flayed skin he's holding is a barely recognizable face—the twisted self-portrait of a self-questioning Michelangelo.

• *If you exit the Sistine Chapel through the side door next to the screen, you'll soon find yourself facing the Long March back to the museum's entrance. You're one floor below the long corridor you walked to get here.*

Or consider the Sistine–St. Peter's shortcut: In the back corner of the Sistine Chapel there's an exit that shortcuts directly to St. Peter's Basilica. If you're planning on going to the basilica next, you can exit here and save yourself a 30-minute walk. Note that if you take this shortcut, you'll miss the Pinacoteca—unless you saw it at the beginning.

The Long March Back

Along this corridor you'll see some of the wealth amassed by the popes, mostly gifts from royalty. Find your hometown on the map of the world from 1529—look in the land called "Terra Incognita." The elaborately decorated library that branches off to the right contains rare manuscripts.

• *The corridor eventually spills out back outside. Follow signs to the . . .*

Pinacoteca (Painting Gallery)

How would you like to be Lou Gehrig—always batting behind Babe Ruth? That's the Pinacoteca's lot in life, following Sistine & Co. But after the Vatican's artistic feast, this little collection of paintings is a delicious 15-minute after-dinner mint.

See this gallery of paintings as you'd view a time-lapse blossoming of a flower, walking through the evolution of painting from medieval to Baroque with just four stops.

• *Enter and stroll up to Room IV.*

PINACOTECA—PAINTING GALLERY

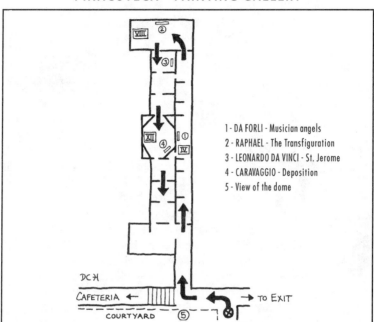

1 - DA FORLI - Musician angels
2 - RAPHAEL - The Transfiguration
3 - LEONARDO DA VINCI - St. Jerome
4 - CARAVAGGIO - Deposition
5 - View of the dome

Melozzo Da Forli— Musician Angels

Salvaged from a condemned church, this playful series of frescoes shows the delicate grace and nobility of Italy during the time known fondly as the *quattro-centro* (1400s). Notice the detail and the classical purity given these religious figures.

• *Walk on to the end room (Room VIII) where they've turned on the dark to let Raphael's* Transfiguration *shine. Take a seat.*

Raphael—*The Transfiguration*

Raphael's *Transfiguration* shows Christ on a mountaintop visited in a vision by the prophets Moses and Elijah. Peter, James, and John cower in awe under Jesus, "transfigured before them, his face shining as the sun, his rainment white as light." (As described by the evangelist Matthew—who can be seen taking notes in the painting's lower left.)

The nine remaining apostles try in vain to heal a boy possessed by demons. Jesus is gone, but "Lady Faith" in the center exhorts them to carry on.

Raphael died in 1520, leaving this final work to be finished by his pupils. The last thing Raphael painted was the beatific face of Jesus, perhaps the most beautiful Christ in existence.

• *Heading back down the parallel corridor, stop in Room IX at the brown unfinished work by Leonardo.*

Leonardo da Vinci—*St. Jerome* (c. 1482)

This unfinished work gives us a glimpse behind the scenes at Leonardo's technique. Even in the brown undercoating we see the psychological power of Leonardo's genius. The intense penitence and painful ecstasy of the saint comes through loud and clear in the anguished body on the rocks and in Jerome's joyful eyes, which see divine forgiveness. Leonardo wrote that a good painter must paint two things: "man and the movements of his spirit." (The patchwork effect is due to Jerome's head having been cut out and used as the seat of a stool in a shoemaker's shop.)

• *Roll on through the sappy sweetness of the Mannerist rooms into the shocking ultrarealistic world of Caravaggio (Room XII).*

Caravaggio—*Deposition*

Caravaggio was the first painter to intentionally shock his viewers. By exaggerating the contrast between light and dark, shining a brutal third-degree-interrogator-type light on his subjects, and using everyday models in sacred scenes, he takes a huge leap away from the Raphael-pretty past and into the "expressive realism" of the modern world.

A tangle of grief looms out of the darkness as Christ's heavy, dead body nearly pulls the whole group with him from the cross into the tomb.

• *Walk through the rest of the gallery's canvas history of art, enjoy one last view of the Vatican grounds and Michelangelo's dome, then follow the grand spiral staircase down. Go in peace.*

✣ 24 ✣
BORGHESE GALLERY TOUR
Galleria Borghese

More than just a great museum, Galleria Borghese is a beautiful villa set in the greenery of surrounding gardens. You get to see art commissioned by the luxury-loving Borghese family displayed in the very rooms they were created for. Frescoes, marble, stucco, and interior design enhance the masterpieces. This is a place where—regardless of whether you learn a darn thing—you can sit back and enjoy the sheer beauty of the palace and its art.

ORIENTATION
Cost: €8.

Hours: Tue–Sun 9:00–21:00, sometimes until 23:00 on Sat June–Sept, closed Mon.

Reservations: Reservations are mandatory and easy to get in English over the Internet (www.ticketeria.it) or by phone: call 06-32810 (if you get an Italian recording, press 2 for English; office hours: Mon–Fri 9:00–19:00, Sat 9:00–13:00, office closed Sat in Aug). Every two hours, 360 people are allowed to enter the museum. Entry times are 9:00, 11:00, 13:00, 15:00, 17:00, and 19:00 (plus 21:00 if open late on Sat June–Sept). Reserve a *minimum* of several days in advance for a weekday visit, at least a week ahead for weekends. When you reserve, request a day and time (which you'll be given if available). Along with an assigned time, you'll

BORGHESE GALLERY—GROUND FLOOR

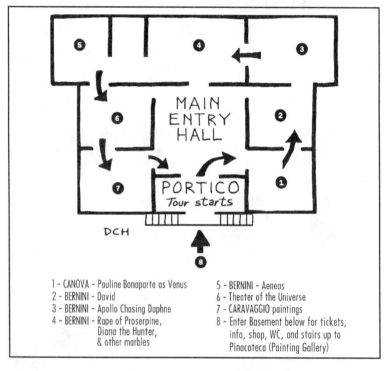

1 - CANOVA - Pauline Bonaparte as Venus
2 - BERNINI - David
3 - BERNINI - Apollo Chasing Daphne
4 - BERNINI - Rape of Proserpine,
   Diana the Hunter,
   & other marbles

5 - BERNINI - Aeneas
6 - Theater of the Universe
7 - CARAVAGGIO paintings
8 - Enter Basement below for tickets,
   info, shop, WC, and stairs up to
   Pinacoteca (Painting Gallery)

end up with a claim number. While you'll be advised to come 30 minutes before your appointed time, you can arrive a few minutes beforehand, but don't be late, as no-show tickets are sold to stand-bys.

Visits are strictly limited to two hours. Concentrate on the first floor but leave yourself 30 minutes for the paintings of the Pinacoteca upstairs; highlights are marked by the audioguide icons. The fine bookshop and cafeteria are best visited outside your two-hour entry window.

If you don't have a reservation, just show up (or call first and ask if there are openings; a late afternoon on a weekday is usually your best bet). Reservations are tightest at 11:00 and on weekends. No-shows are released a few minutes after the top of the hour. Generally, out of 360 reservations, a few will fail to show (but more than a few may be waiting to grab them).

Getting there: The museum is in the Villa Borghese park. A taxi can get you within 100 meters of the museum (tell the cabbie your destination: gah-leh-REE-ah bor-GAY-zay). Otherwise, Metro to Spagna and take a 15-minute walk through the park.

Tours: Guided English tours are offered at 9:10 and 11:10 for €4.60; reserve with entry reservation. Or consider the excellent audioguide tour for the same price.

Length of our tour: Two hours maximum.

Photography: No photos are allowed.

Cuisine art: A café is on site.

Starring: Sculptures by Bernini and paintings by Caravaggio, Raphael, and Titian.

Portico

Ancient Roman reliefs (at either end) topped by Michelangelo-designed panels capture the essence of the collection—a gathering of beautiful objects from every age and culture inside a lavish 17th-century villa. Cardinal Borghese built the villa, collected ancient works, and hired the best artists of his day. In pursuing the optimistic spirit of the Renaissance, they invented Baroque.

Main Entry Hall

Five Roman mosaics decorate the floor with colorful, festive scenes of slaughter. Gladiators fight animals and each other with swords, whips, and tridents. The Greek letter Θ (theta) marks the dead. Notice some of the gladiators' pro-wrestler nicknames: "Cupid," "Serpent," "Licentious."

On the wall is a thrilling first-century Greek sculpture of a horse falling. The Renaissance-era rider was added by Pietro Bernini, father of the famous Bernini.

Room I

Antonio Canova—*Statue of Pauline Bonaparte as Venus (Paolina Borghese Bonaparte)* (1808)

Napoleon's sister went the full monty for the sculptor Canova, scandalizing Europe. ("How could you have done such a thing?!" she was asked. She replied, "The room wasn't cold.") With the famous nose of her conqueror brother, she strikes the pose of Venus as conqueror of men's hearts. Her relaxed afterglow and slight smirk say she's already had her man. The light dent she puts in the mattress makes this goddess human.

Notice the contrasting textures that Canova gets out of the pure-white marble: the rumpled sheet versus her smooth skin. The satiny-smooth pillows and mattress versus the creases in them. Her porcelain skin versus the hint of a love handle. Canova polished and waxed the marble until it looked as soft and pliable as cloth.

The mythological pose, the Roman couch, the ancient hairdo, and the calm harmony make Pauline the epitome of the neoclassical style.

Room II

Gian Lorenzo Bernini—*David* (1624)

Duck! David twists around to put a big rock in his sling. He purses his lips, knits his brow, and winds his body like a spring as his eyes lock onto the target—Goliath, who's somewhere behind us, putting us right in the line of fire.

In this self-portrait, 25-year-old Bernini is ready to take on the world. He's charged with the same fighting energy that fueled the missionaries and conquistadors of the Counter-Reformation.

Compared with Michelangelo's *David*, this is gritty realism—an unbalanced pose, bulging veins, unflattering face, and armpit hair. Bernini slays the pretty-boy Davids of the Renaissance and prepares to invent Baroque.

The sarcophagus on the wall on David's left shows the Hellenistic inspiration for Baroque. Look at the Labors of Hercules (A.D. 160, at chest level).

Room III

Bernini—*Apollo and Daphne* (*Apollo e Dafne*) (1625)

Apollo—made stupid by Cupid's arrow of love—chases after Daphne, who has been turned off by the "arrow of disgust." Just as he's about to catch her, she calls to her father to save her. Magically, her fingers

begin to sprout leaves, her toes become roots, her skin turns to bark, and she transforms into a tree. Frustrated Apollo ends up with a handful of leaves.

Stand behind the statue to experience it as Bernini originally intended. It's only when you circle around to the front that he reveals the story's surprise ending.

Walk slowly around. It's as much air as stone. The back leg defies gravity. It was two years in restoration (described to me as being something like dental work). The marble leaves at the top ring like crystal when struck. Notice the same scene, colorized, painted on the ceiling above.

Bernini carves out some of the chief features of Baroque art: He makes a supernatural event seem realistic. He freezes it at the most dramatic, emotional moment. The figures move and twist in unusual poses. He turns the wind machine on, sending Apollo's cape billowing behind him. It's a sculpture group of two, forming a scene, rather than a stand-alone portrait. And the subject is classical. Even in strict Counter-Reformation times, there was always a place for groping, if the subject matter had a moral—this one taught you not to pursue fleeting earthly pleasures. And, besides, Bernini tends to show a lot of skin but no genitals.

Room IV

Bernini—*The Rape of Proserpine* (*Il Ratto di Proserpina*) (1622)

Pluto strides into the Underworld and shows off his catch—the beautiful daughter of the earth goddess. His three-headed guard dog, Cerberus, barks triumphantly. Pluto is squat, thick, and uncouth, with knotted muscles and untrimmed beard. He's trying not to hurt her, but she pushes her divine molester away and twists to call out for help. Tears roll down her cheeks. She wishes she could turn into a tree.

Bernini was the master of marble. Look how Pluto's fingers dig into her thigh like it was real flesh. Bernini picked out this Carrara marble knowing that its relative suppleness and ivory hue would lend itself to a fleshy statue.

Artist Unknown—*Diana the Hunter* (*Artemis*)

The statues in the niches are classical originals. *Diana the Hunter* is a rare Greek original from the second century B.C. The traditional *contrapposto* pose (weight on one leg) and idealized grace were an inspiration for artists such as Canova who grew tired of Bernini's Baroque bombast.

The Marbles in Room IV

Appreciate the beauty of the different types of marble in the room: Bernini's ivory Carrara, Diana's translucent white, purple porphyry emperors, granitelike columns that support them, wood-grained pilasters on the walls, and the different colors on the floor—green, red, gray, lavender, and yellow, some grainy, some "marbled" like a steak. Some of the world's most beautiful and durable things have been made from the shells of sea creatures layered in sediment, fossilized into limestone, then heated and crystallized by the pressure of the earth: marble.

Room VI

Bernini—*Aeneas* (*Enea*, etc.) (1620)

Aeneas' home in Troy is in flames, and he escapes with the three most important things: his family (decrepit father on his shoulder and baby boy), his household gods (the statues in dad's hands), and the Eternal Flame (carried by son). They're all in shock, lost in thought, facing an uncertain future. Aeneas isn't even looking where he's going, he just puts one foot in front of the other. Little do they know that eventually they'll wind up in Italy, where Aeneas will found the city of Rome and house the flame in the Temple of Vesta.

Bernini was still a teenager when he started this, his first life-size work. He was probably helped by his dad, who nurtured the child prodigy much like Leopold mentored Mozart, but without the rivalry. Bernini's portrayal of human flesh—from baby fat to middle-age muscle to sagging decrepitude—is astonishing. Still, the composition is static—not nearly as interesting as the reliefs up at the ceiling, with their dancing, light-footed soldiers with do-si-do shields.

Room VII

"The Theater of the Universe"

The room's decor sums up the eclectic nature of the villa. There are Greek statues, Roman mosaics, and fake "Egyptian" hieroglyphs (perfectly symmetrical in good neoclassical style). Look out the window, past the sculpted gardens, at the mesh domes of the aviary once filled with exotic birds. Cardinal Borghese's vision was to make a place where art, history, music, nature, and science would come together... "a theater of the universe."

Room VIII

Caravaggio

The paintings in this room change often, but you'll likely find one or two by the Baroque innovator Caravaggio (1571–1610). Caravaggio brought Christian saints and Greek gods down to earth with gritty realism. His saints are balding and wrinkled. His Bacchus (a self-portrait) is pale and puffy faced. David sticks Goliath's severed head (a self-portrait) right in your face. The Madonnas scarcely glow. Baby Jesus is buck naked. Ordinary people were his models. Caravaggio's straightforwardness can be a refreshing change in a museum full of (sometimes overly) refined beauty.

Pinacoteca—Painting Gallery

To reach the Pinacoteca, go outside and return to the basement where you got your ticket, follow signs to the Pinacoteca, show your ticket to the guard, and climb the long spiral stairway. Remember, you're limited to only 30 minutes in the Pinacoteca, and you must visit it within the two-hour window of time printed on your ticket. Most visitors wait until the last half hour to see the Pinacoteca, so that's when it's most crowded (and the ground floor is less crowded). If you see the paintings first, remember that, given a two-hour visit, the ground floor with the sculpture is worth most of that time.

Room XIV

Bernini (1632)—
Bust of Cardinal Borghese
(Ritr. del Card. Scipione Borghese)
Say *grazie* to the man who built this villa, assembled the collection, and hired Bernini to sculpt masterpieces. The cardinal is caught turning as though to greet someone at a party. There's a twinkle in his eye, and he opens his mouth to make a witty comment. This man of the cloth was, in fact, a sophisticated hedonist.

• *On the table nearby, find the smaller . . .*

Bust of Pope Paul V

The cardinal's uncle was a more sober man but also a patron of the arts who hired Bernini's father. When Pope Paul saw sketches made by little Lorenzo, he announced: "This boy will be the Michelangelo of his age."

• *On the wall above the table, find these paintings . . .*

Two Bernini Self-Portraits
(*Autoritratto giovanile*, 1623
and *Autoritratto in eta matura*, 1630/35)

Bernini was a master of many media, including painting. The younger Bernini looks out a bit hesitantly, as if he's still finding his way in high-class society. But, with a few masterpieces under his belt, his next self-portrait shows Bernini with more confidence and facial hair—the dashing and passionate man who would rebuild Rome in Baroque style, from St. Peter's Square to the fountains that dot the piazzas.

Room IX

Raphael (Raffaelo Sanzio)— *Deposition* (*Deposizione di Cristo*)

Jesus is being taken from the cross. The men support him while the women support Mary, who has fainted. The woman who commissioned the painting had recently lost her son. She wanted to show the death of a son and the grief of a mother.

In true Renaissance style, Raphael orders the scene with geometrical perfection. The curve of Jesus' body is echoed by the swirl of Mary Magdalene's hair and then by the curve of Calvary Hill, where he met his fate.

Room X

Correggio—*Danae*

Cupid strips Danae as she spreads her legs (most unladylike) to receive a trickle of gold from the smudgy cloud overhead—this was Zeus' idea of intercourse with a human. The sheets are rumpled and Danae looks right where the action is with a smile on her face. It's hard to believe that a supposedly religious family would display such an erotic work. But the Borgheses felt that the Church was truly "catholic" (universal), and that all forms of human expression—including physical passion—glorified God.

Room XX

Titian (Tiziano Vecello)—*Sacred and Profane Love* (*Amor Sacrae, Amor Profane*)

The clothed woman at left was recently married, and she cradles a vase filled with jewels representing the riches of earthly love. Her naked twin on the right holds the burning flame of eternal, heavenly love. Baby Cupid, between them, playfully stirs the waters.

This exquisite painting expresses the spirit of the Renaissance—that earth and heaven are two sides of the same coin. And here in the Borghese Gallery, that love of earthly beauty can be spiritually uplifting—as long as you do it within two hours.

MADRID

THE PRADO

$\mathcal{M}$adrid proudly shows off the remains of its once vast and powerful empire: the greatest collection of paintings in Europe. Filled with masterpieces by Velázquez, El Greco, Goya, and Bosch, the Prado brilliantly chronicles the rise and fall of Spain, its rich Catholic heritage, and its bloody wars.

✤ 25 ✤

THE PRADO

The Prado (pron: PRAH-doh) is the greatest painting museum in the world. If you like art and you plan to be in Europe, a trip to Madrid is a must. In its glory days, the Spanish Empire was Europe's greatest, filling its coffers with gold from the New World and art from the Old. While there are some 3,000 paintings in the collection, we'll be selective, focusing on just the top 1,500 or so.

ORIENTATION

Cost: €3.20; free on Sat after 14:30, all day Sun, May 18, Oct 12, Dec 6, and any time if you're over 65. A combo-ticket, which covers the Prado, Reina Sofia (*Guernica*), and Thyssen-Bornemisza Museum, costs €8 (good for one visit apiece, valued for a year).

Hours: Tue–Sat 9:00–19:00, Sun and holidays 9:00–14:00, closed Mon. Most crowded on Tue, Sun, and all mornings.

Getting there: It's located on Paseo del Prado, a 15-minute walk from Puerta del Sol; subway to "Banco de España" or "Atocha" and 10-minute walk; cheap taxis (say "moo-SAY-oh del PRAH-doh").

Information: Good, small pamphlets on Flemish art, Goya, and Velázquez on racks in appropriate rooms. Tel. 91-330-2800.

Length of our tour: Two hours (not including *Guernica*).

Cloakroom: You're required to leave your day bag in the free cloakroom.

Photography: Allowed without a flash.

Cuisine art: Good, reasonable cafeteria in basement at south end. For picnicking, the royal gardens are just south, and the huge, pleasant Retiro park is three blocks east.

Starring: Bosch, Goya, Titian, Velázquez, Dürer, El Greco.

NEW WORLD GOLD—
OLD WORLD ART

Heaven and earth have always existed side by side in Spain—religion and war, Grand Inquisitors and cruel conquistadores, spirituality and sensuality, holiness and horniness. The Prado has a surprisingly worldly collection of paintings for a country in which the medieval Inquisition lasted up until modern times. But it's just this rich combination of worldly beauty and heavenly mysticism that is so typically Spanish.

Gold from newly discovered America bought the sparkling treasures of the Prado. Spain, the most powerful nation in Europe in the 1500s, was growing rich on her New World possessions just about the time of the world's greatest cultural heyday, the Renaissance.

The collection's strengths reflect the tastes of Spain's cultured kings from 1500 to 1800: (1) Italian Renaissance art (especially the lush and sensual Venetian art which was the rage of Europe), (2) Northern art from what was the Spanish Netherlands, and (3) their own Spanish court painters. This tour will concentrate on these three areas, with a special look at some individual artists who are especially well represented—Velázquez, Goya, Titian, Rubens, El Greco, and Bosch.

The Prado's hyperactive curators will likely move the art around. If you can't find a particular work, point to the picture in this book and ask a guard, *¿Dónde...?* (pron. DOHN-day). The Prado's free floor plan is somewhat helpful, listing rooms by artist and country.

• *Enter the Prado at the north end through the "Puerta de Goya." There are two entrances here; the first floor entry is monumental with grand stairs, the ground floor entry below is unobtrusive with small doors. Our tour starts on the ground floor. If you enter on the first floor instead, head down the stairs off the rotunda to begin.*

At either entry, after you pay admission, you go through a security check (just like the airport) and then check your bag (mandatory). Pick up a free floor plan (usually the English version is "finished"—not available).

Orient yourself from the rotunda on the ground floor. Look through the doorway down the long gallery. The Prado runs north/south. Rooms branch off to the left (east of this long hall). The layout is similar on the floor above.

We'll start briefly with medieval Spanish art, linger in the Italian Renaissance, enjoy more Spanish art (El Greco), and dabble in Northern Renaissance art. Upstairs, we'll go for Baroque and see more Spanish art (Velázquez and Goya).

• *From the rotunda, enter room 50, which contains medieval Spanish art.*

PRADO—OVERVIEW

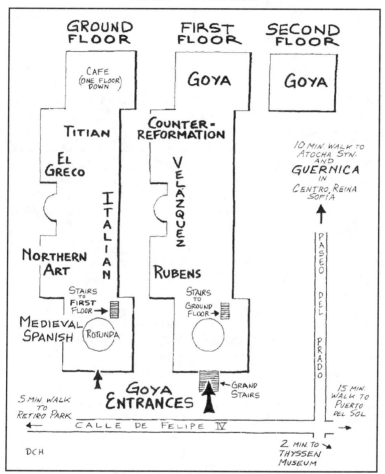

GROUND FLOOR

CAFE (ONE FLOOR DOWN)

TITIAN

EL GRECO

ITALIAN

NORTHERN ART

STAIRS TO FIRST FLOOR →

MEDIEVAL SPANISH (ROTUNDA)

5 MIN. WALK TO RETIRO PARK

GOYA ENTRANCES

FIRST FLOOR

GOYA

COUNTER-REFORMATION

VELAZQUEZ

RUBENS

STAIRS TO GROUND FLOOR →

GRAND STAIRS

SECOND FLOOR

GOYA

10 MIN. WALK TO ATOCHA STN. AND GUERNICA IN CENTRO, REINA SOFIA

PASEO DEL PRADO

15 MIN. WALK TO PUERTO DEL SOL

CALLE DE FELIPE IV

DCH

2 MIN. TO THYSSEN MUSEUM

Spanish Art Overview

Spanish painting is the Prado's forte. The three big names—El Greco, Velázquez, and Goya—are well represented, but we'll glance at a few others as well.

Spanish religious devotion and fanaticism are legendary. Look around. In this room of medieval Spanish art, is there even one painting that isn't of saints or Bible stories? I found one once. It showed heretics being punished by the Inquisition during an auto-da-fé—a combination revival meeting and barbecue (coals provided, B.Y.O. sinner). An estimated 2,000 enemies of God were burned alive during the reign of one notorious Grand Inquisitor.

One reason for Spanish fanaticism was that they had to literally fight for their religion. Moslems from North Africa (the Moors) controlled much of the peninsula for most of the Middle Ages (711–1492), making Christians a second-class and sometimes persecuted minority. It took centuries of fierce warfare to finally drive the Moors out. Spain couldn't officially call herself a Christian nation until the same year Columbus sailed for America. The iron-strong Spanish faith was forged in the fires of those wars.

Later, in the Counter-Reformation (16th and early 17th century), when the Catholic Church shored up its defenses against the threat of the Protestant Reformation, Spain's zealous Catholic groups rallied against the Protestant "infidels." Much of the Spanish art we'll see was affected by the struggles between Catholics and Protestants, art designed to inspire the common people to have faith in the Catholic Church.

• *Spanish art is sprinkled throughout the museum; we'll see more of it later. Enter the long gallery (room 49) and belly up to the Annunciation altarpiece on your right.*

Italian Renaissance (1400–1600)

Modern Western civilization began in the prosperous Renaissance cities of Italy from 1400 to 1600. Florence, Rome, and Venice led the way out of the Gothic Middle Ages, building on the forgotten knowledge of ancient Rome and Greece.

Unlike the heaven-centered medieval artists, Renaissance artists gloried in the natural world and the human body. They painted things as realistically as possible. For the Italians, "realistic" meant "three-dimensional," and they set out to learn how to capture the 3-D world on a 2-D canvas.

Fra Angelico—*The Annunciation* (*La Anunciación*)

Fra Angelico was a mix of the passing Middle Ages and the coming Renaissance. He was a monk of great piety (his nickname means "Angelic Brother") who combined medieval religious sentiment with new Renaissance techniques. This is more like two separate paintings in one: (1) on the left, the medieval-style story of Adam

ITALIAN RENAISSANCE

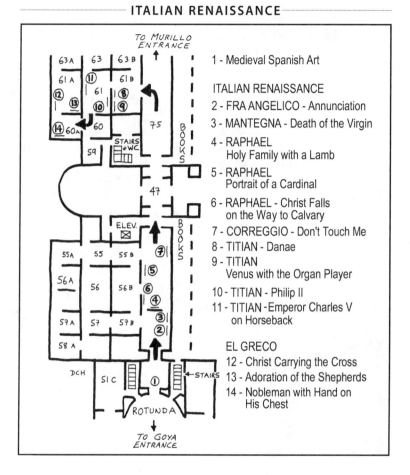

and Eve in the Garden of Eden and, (2) on the right (under the porch), the Renaissance-style scene of the angel telling Mary she'll give birth to the Messiah.

The Fall (on the left side) expresses a characteristic medieval idea—man is sinfully weak and undeserving of the pleasures of Paradise. Adam and Eve, scrawny and two-dimensional, seem to float in an unrealistic space above the foliage. Eve folds her hands nervously, scrunching down, waiting for her punishment from an angry God. The style is also medieval, with detailed flowers, a labor of love by a caring monk who was also a miniaturist. Another medieval element is the series of storytelling scenes below, illustrating events in the life of Mary for the illiterate faithful.

The Annunciation scene on the right is early Renaissance. The porch makes a 3-D setting. Then Fra Angelico fills it with two massive, almost sculptural bodies. The message of the scene is upbeat and humanistic, as the Angel tells Mary she'll give birth to a Savior who'll redeem sinful man from the Fall. (Is it good news to Mary? She doesn't look too thrilled.)

Still, the painting is flat by modern standards, and the study in depth perspective is crude. Aren't the receding bars of the porch's ceiling a bit off? And Mary's hands just aren't right—like when you have to wash the dishes with two left-hand rubber gloves. But it's a lot better (and more 3-D) than its medieval neighbors here.

Above all, notice the serene atmosphere of the painting. There are no harsh shadows or strong light sources. Everything is bathed in a pristine, glowing, holy light. The only movement is the shaft of light shooting down from the hands of God, bringing redemption from the Fall, connecting the two halves of the painting and fusing medieval piety with Renaissance humanism.

• *Next to it is...*

Mantegna— ## Death of the Virgin ## (El Tránsito de la Virgen)

The true pioneer of Renaissance 3-D was Andrea Mantegna (pron: mahn-TAYN-yah). He creates a spacious setting, then peoples it with sculptural figures.

The dying mother of Christ is surrounded by statuelike apostles with plates on their heads and pots in their hands. The architectural setting is heroic and spacious. Follow the lines in the floor tiles and side columns. They converge toward the window, then seem to continue on to the far horizon in the lines of the bridge. This creates a subconscious feeling of almost infinite spaciousness, bringing a serenity to an otherwise tragic death scene. You can imagine Mary's soul leaving her body and floating easily out the window, disappearing into the infinite distance.

• *Turn around to see some large Raphael canvases (in the middle of opposite wall). Let them overwhelm you, then look at the partition and refocus your eyes on Raphael's tiny* Holy Family with a Lamb. *The sheer difference in size and scope of these works gives you a sense of the artist's vision.*

Raphael—*Holy Family with a Lamb (Sagrada Familia del Cordero)*

Raphael reproduced reality perfectly on a canvas but also gave it harmony, geometry, and heroism that made it somehow more real than reality. Combining idealized beauty with down-to-earth realism, he was the ultimate Renaissance painter.

Raphael (pron: roff-eye-ELL) was only 21 when he painted this. He learned Leonardo da Vinci's technique of *sfumato*, spreading a kind of hazy glow around the figures (this is the technique that gives the *Mona Lisa* her vague, mysterious smile). He also used Leonardo's trademark pyramid composition—the three figures form a pyramid, with Joseph's head at the peak.

• *Within the same room (#49), find the following paintings.*

Raphael—*Portrait of a Cardinal (El Cardenal)*

Compare the idealized beauty of *Holy Family* with the stark realism of this portrait. This isn't an idealized version of an ideal man, but a living, breathing—in this case almost sneering—man. Raphael captures not just his face, but his personality—the type of man who could become a cardinal at such a young age in the Renaissance Vatican's priest-eat-priest jungle of holy ambition. He's cold, intelligent, detached, and somewhat cynical—a gritty portrayal of a gritty man.

Raphael—*Christ Falls on the Way to Calvary (Caída en el Camino del Calvario)*

Raphael puts it all together—the idealized grace of the *Holy Family* and the realism of *Portrait of a Cardinal*. Look at the detail on the muscular legs of the guy in yellow (at left) and the arms of Simon, who has come to help Jesus carry his cross. Then contrast that with the idealized beauty of the mourning women. When this painting was bought in 1661, it was the costliest in existence.

Raphael has added drama to the work by splitting the canvas into two contrasting halves. Below the slanting line made by the crossbar is a scene of swirling passion—the sorrow of Christ and the women, the tangle of crowded bodies. Above it is open space and indifference—the bored soldiers and onlookers and the bleak hill in the background where Jesus is headed to be crucified.

• *On the opposite wall (still in room 49), look for...*

Correggio—Don't Touch Me (Noli Me Tangere)

Raphael could paint idealized beauty, but this is simply the most beautiful painting in captivity. That's it. Period. If it were any sweeter you could get diabetes just looking at it.

It's Easter morning and Jesus has just come back to life. One of his followers, Mary Magdalene, has run into him in the garden near the tomb. She is amazed and excited and reaches toward him. "Don't touch me!" (*Nole me tangere*) says Jesus (though he spoke neither English nor Latin), and points up to Heaven.

The colors accentuate the emotion of the scene. Blazing like a flame against the cool landscape of blue and green, Mary Magdalene—the ex-prostitute in a fiery yellow dress and yellow hair—is hot to touch the cool Christ with his blue cloak and pale, radiant skin. The composition also accentuates the action. The painting's energy runs in a diagonal line up the rippling Mary, through Christ and his upstretched arm, to heaven, where he will soon go.

• *Head straight to the next long gallery (room 75). Midway down the gallery, turn left into room 61b.*

Titian (c. 1490–1576)

Look around. What do you see? Flesh. Naked bodies in various poses; bright, lush, colorful scenes. Many scenes have "pagan" themes, but even the religious works are racier than anything we saw from the Florentine and Roman Renaissance.

Venice in 1500 was the richest city in Europe, the middleman in the lucrative trade between Europe and the Orient. Wealthy, cosmopolitan, and free, Venetians loved life's finer things—rich silks, beautiful people, jewels, banquets, music, wine, and impressive buildings—and Venetian painters enjoyed painting them in bright colors.

The chief Venetian was Titian (they rhyme). Titian (Tiziano in Spain) was possibly the most famous painter of his day—more famous than Raphael, Leonardo, and even Michelangelo. His reputation reached Spain, and he became the favorite portraitist for two kings, who bought many of his works.

• *In room 61b . . .*

Titian—*Danae*

In Greek mythology, Zeus, the king of the gods, was always zooming to earth in the form of some creature or other to fool around with some mortal woman. Here, he descends as a shower of gold to consort with the willing Danae. You can almost see the human form of Zeus within the cloud. Danae is rapt, opening her legs to receive him, while her servant tries to catch the heavenly spurt with a towel.

This is one of the world's finest and most famous nudes. Danae's rich, luminous flesh on the left of the canvas is set off by the dark servant at right and the threatening sky above. The white sheets beneath her make her glow even more.

But this is more than a classic nude—it's a Renaissance Miss August. How could Spain's ultraconservative Catholic kings have tolerated such a downright pagan and erotic painting?

• *Also in room 61b . . .*

Titian—*Venus with the Organ Player* (*Venus recreándose en la Música*)

A musician turns around to leer at a naked woman while keeping both hands at work on his organ. This aroused King Phillip II's interest. (For more on the king, see below.) The message must have appealed to him—the conflict between sacred, artistic pursuits as symbolized by music, and worldly, sensual pursuits as embodied in the naked lady.

Titian emphasized these two opposites with color—"cool" colors on the left, hot crimson and flesh on the right. The center of the painting is where these two color schemes meet, so, even though the figures lean and the poplar trees in the

background are off center, the painting is balanced and harmonious in the Renaissance tradition.

A century after Phillip's reign, his beloved nudes were taken down from the Escorial and Royal Palace and hidden away as unfit to be seen. For more than a century these great Titians were banned.

• Continue into room 61 . . .

Titian—*Phillip II (Felipe II)*

This is the king who bought Titian's sexy *Danae* and many other paintings of nudes. Phillip deserved his reputation as a repressed prude—pale, suspicious, lonely, a cold fish; the sort of man who would build the severe and tomblike Escorial Palace. Freud would have had a field day with such a complex man who could be so sternly religious and yet have such sensual tastes. Here, he is looking as pious and ascetic as a man can while wearing that outfit.

• In the same room (#61) . . .

Titian—*Emperor Charles V on Horseback (El Emperador Carlos V en la Batalla de Muhlberg)*

Are you glad to be here? If so, then tip your book to that guy on horseback, the father of the Prado's collection.

In the 1500s, Charles was the most powerful man in the world. He was not merely King Charles of Spain, but Holy Roman Emperor with possessions stretching from Spain to Austria, from Holland to Italy, from South America to Burgundy. He was defender of the Catholic Church against infidel Turks, French kings, and, in this picture, rebellious Protestants.

Here, Titian shows him in the classic equestrian pose of a Roman conqueror. His power is accentuated by his control over his rearing horse and the lance with its optimistic tilt.

Once Charles met Titian and saw what he could do, he never wanted anyone else to paint him. And the story goes that, while sitting for a portrait one day, this greatest ruler in the world actually stooped over to pick up a brush Titian dropped.

We've seen painting move from medieval two-dimensionality to Renaissance realism and balance. The next style—Baroque—took Renaissance realism to unrealistic heights. But, before we get tangled in the steaming jungle of Baroque, let's have a spiritual Spanish interlude with El Greco, then a refreshing break in the cooler climes of the Northern countries. Their down-to-earth realism is a delightful contrast to the idealized beauty of the Italian school.

• *El Greco's art is nearby in room 60a and 61a.*

El Greco (c. 1540–1614)

The first great Spanish painter was Greek. El Greco (Spanish for "the Greek") was born in Greece, trained in Venice, then settled in Toledo, Spain. The combination of these three cultures, plus his own unique personality, produced a highly individual style. His paintings are Byzantine icons drenched in Venetian color and fused in the fires of Spanish mysticism.

Phillip II, the ascetic king with sensual tastes who bought so many Titians, didn't like El Greco's bizarre style (perhaps because the figures— thin and haunting—reminded him of himself). So El Greco left the Spanish court at El Escorial and moved south to Toledo, where he was accepted. He spent the rest of his life there. If you like El Greco, make the 60-minute trip to Toledo.

• *In room 61a...*

El Greco—Christ Carrying the Cross (Cristo Abrazado a la Cruz)

Even as the blood runs down his neck and he trudges toward his death, Christ accepts his fate in a trance of religious ecstasy. Notice how the crossbar points upward. Jesus, clasping the cross lovingly to him, sights along it like a navigational instrument to his destination—Heaven.

However, it's the upturned eyes that are the soul of this painting. (Someone has suggested it be titled "The Eyes of Jesus.") They are close to tears with humility and sparkle with joyful acceptance. (Warning: Do not get too close to this painting. Otherwise you'll see that the holy magic in the eyes is only a simple streak of white paint.)

• *In the same room (#61a)...*

El Greco—*The Adoration of the Shepherds* (*La Adoración de los Pastores*)

El Greco painted this for his own burial chapel in Toledo, where it hung until the 1950s. It combines all of his trademark techniques into a powerful vision.

The shepherds, with elongated bodies and expressive hands, are stretched upward, flickering like flames toward heaven, lit from within by a spiritual fire. Christ is the light source, shining out of the darkness, giving a sheen to the surrounding colors. These shepherds will never be able to buy suits off the rack.

Notice El Greco's typical two-tiered composition—earth below, heaven above. Over the Christ Child is a swirling canopy of clouds and angels. Heaven and earth seem to intermingle, and the earthly figures look as though they're about to be sucked up through a funnel into the vault of heaven. There is little depth to the picture—all the figures are virtually the same distance from us—so our eyes have nowhere to go but up and down, up and down, linking heaven and earth, God and humankind.

• *Next door in room 60a...*

El Greco—*The Nobleman with His Hand on His Chest* (*El Caballero de la Mano al Pecho*)

For all the mysticism of his paintings, we should remember that El Greco was not a mystic, but a well-traveled, learned, sophisticated, down-to-earth man. Despite his distorted paintings, with their elongated bodies and bright unreal colors (which he may have learned during his training with Titian in Venice), he could paint realistically.

This is an exceptionally realistic and probing portrait. The sitter was an elegant and somewhat arrogant gentleman, who was obviously trying to make an impression. The sword probably indicates the portrait was done to celebrate his becoming a knight.

El Greco reveals the man's personality, again, in the expressive eyes and in the hand across the chest. Notice how the middle two fingers touch—El Greco's trademark way of expressing elegance. Look for it in his other works.

The signature is on the right in faint Greek letters—"Domenicos Theotocopoulos," El Greco's real name.

• *Return to the long gallery (room 75) and continue straight to the gallery where we started (room 49, with Italian Renaissance art). Take the last right (into room 57b), just before you reach the rotunda. After entering, continue through 57b and take the first left, into room 58.*

Northern Art

Prior to the Northern Renaissance, Northern art—with its focus on detail—seems little more than an improvement on medieval painting.

Master of Flemalle (Robert Campin)—*St. John the Baptist (San Juan Bautista)*

Remember the detailed flowers in Fra Angélico's *Annunciation*? That careful depiction is the first thing we notice in Northern art. Here, not only are the wood, the glass, and the cloth done with loving care, but look at the curved mirror in the middle—the whole scene is reflected backwards in perfect detail!

• *In the same room (#58) . . .*

Roger Van Der Weyden—*Descent From the Cross (El Descendimiento)*

In this powerful and sober *Descent*, again, it's the detail that first draws our attention—notice the robe of Joseph of Arimathea holding Christ's feet. And look at the veins in Joseph's forehead!

This is a human look at a traditional scene. Each of the faces is a different study in grief. Joseph's expression seems to be asking, "Why do the good always die young?" Look how Mary has swooned in the same S-curve as Jesus' body—the death of her son has dealt her a near-fatal blow as well. But the overwhelming tone of the scene is one of serenity. These are people of Northern piety who know and accept that Jesus must die.

Along with Titian's nudes, this was one of Phillip II's favorite paintings—quite a contrast! Yet this *Descent* and Titian's *Danae* both have the power to send us into ecstasy. Hmm.

• *Continue to room 56a.*

NORTHERN ART

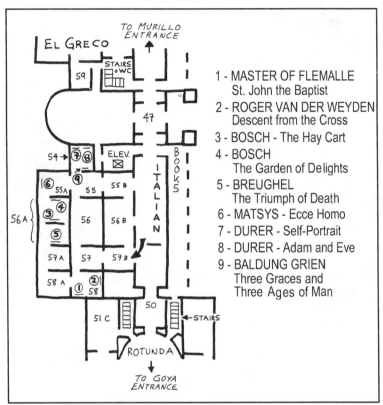

1 - MASTER OF FLEMALLE
   St. John the Baptist

2 - ROGER VAN DER WEYDEN
   Descent from the Cross

3 - BOSCH - The Hay Cart

4 - BOSCH
   The Garden of Delights

5 - BREUGHEL
   The Triumph of Death

6 - MATSYS - Ecce Homo

7 - DURER - Self-Portrait

8 - DURER - Adam and Eve

9 - BALDUNG GRIEN
   Three Graces and
   Three Ages of Man

Bosch (c. 1450–1516)

The work of Hieronymous Bosch can be summed up in one word—
wow! It's difficult to be any more articulate because his unique vision
lends itself to so many different interpretations.

Bosch (rhymes with "Gosh!") was born, lived, and died in a small
town in Holland—that's about all we know of him, his life being as
mysterious as his work. He was much admired by his contemporaries,
who understood his symbolism better than we.

Here are some possible interpretations of Bosch's work—he was:
(1) crazy, (2) commenting on the decadence of his day, (3) celebrating
the variety of life and human behavior, (4) painting with glue in a badly
ventilated room. Or perhaps it's a combination of these.

• *In room 56a...*

Bosch—*The Hay Cart* (*El Carro de Heno*)

Before unraveling the tangle of the cryptic triptych *The Garden of Delights,* let's get warmed up on a "simpler" three-paneled work. Its message is that the pleasures of life are transitory, so we'd better avoid them or we'll wind up in hell.

Center Panel: An old Flemish proverb goes, "Life is a cart of hay from which everyone takes what they can." The whole spectrum of greedy, grabby humanity is here: rich and poor, monks and peasants, scrambling for their share of worldly goods. Even the pope and the Holy Roman emperor (with the sword) chase the cart on horseback. In the very center is a man with a knife at another man's throat, getting his share by force. Two lovers on top of the cart are oblivious to the commotion but are surrounded by symbols of hate (the owl) and lust (the jug). The cart itself is drawn by Satan's demons.

With everyone fighting for his piece of the pie, it's easy to overlook the central figure—Christ above in heaven, watching unnoticed. Is He blessing them or throwing up His hands?

Bosch describes the world's pleasures in the center panel, then puts them in the eternal perspective. The left panel tells us where this crazy world of temptation came from, while the right panel reminds us where it leads.

Left: The story of Creation and the Garden of Eden can be "read" from top to bottom. At the top, God has sprayed Raid and rousted Satan's vermin from heaven, setting them loose on earth. Then God creates Eve from Adam's rib, Eve gets tempted by a (female) serpent, and, finally, they're driven from Paradise. It was this first sin that brought evil into the world.

Right: Here's the whole point of Bosch's sermon—worldly pleasures lead to hell. Animal-like demons symbolizing various vices torture those who succumbed to the temptation of hay cart planet Earth.

• *Let's enter into the Garden of Delights (same room—#56a).*

Bosch—*The Garden of Delights* (*El Jardin de las Delicias*)

With this traditional Christian interpretation in mind, let's turn to the overwhelming *Garden*. To make it less so, I'd suggest "framing off" one-foot squares to peruse at your leisure.

The *Garden* was interpreted like the *Hay Cart;* that is, the pleasures of the world are transitory, so you'd better watch out or you'll wind up in hell.

In the central panel, men on horseback ride round and round, searching for but never reaching the elusive Fountain of Youth. Lower down and to the left are two lovers in a bubble, illustrating that "pleasure is as fragile as glass" and will soon disappear. Just to their right is a big mussel shell, a symbol of the female sex, swallowing up a man. My favorite is the kneeling figure in front of the orange pavilion in the foreground—talk about "saying it with flowers!"

One of the differences between *The Hay Cart* and *The Garden of Delights* is Columbus. Discoveries of new plants and animals in America gave Bosch a whole new continent of sinful pleasures to paint—some real, some imaginary. In the left panel, check out the cactus tree in the Garden of Eden and the bizarre two-legged dog near the giraffe.

Bosch was certainly a Christian, but there's speculation he was a heretical Christian painting forbidden rites of a free-wheeling cult called Adamites. The Adamites were medieval nudists who believed the body was good (as it was when God made Adam) and that sex was healthy. They supposedly held secret orgies. So, in the central panel we see Adamites at play, frolicking two by two and two by three and so on in the meadows, as innocent as Adam and Eve in the garden. Whether or not Bosch approved, you must admit that some of the folks in this Garden are having a delightful time.

This "Adamist" interpretation makes a lot of sense in the left panel. Here, the main scene, virtually nonexistent in the Bible, is the fundamental story of the Adamites—the marriage (sexual union) of Adam and Eve. God himself is performing the ceremony, wrapping them in the glowing warmth of His aura.

The right panel is hell, a burning, post-holocaust wasteland of perverse creatures and meaningless rituals where sinners are tortured by half-human demons. In this hell, poetic justice reigns supreme, with every sinner getting his just desserts—a glutton is eaten and re-eaten eternally, while a musician is crucified on a musical instrument for neglecting his church duties. Other symbols are less obvious. Two big ears pierced with a knife blade mow down all in the way. A pink bagpipe symbolizes the male and female sex organs (call Freud for details). In the center, hell is literally frozen over. At lower right a pig dressed as a nun tries to seduce a man. And in the center of this wonderful nightmare is a creature with a broken eggshell body, tree trunk legs, a witch's cap, and the face of Bosch himself staring out at us.

• *Take some time to look around at other Bosches. Don't miss the illustrated table, the nun who looks like a haystack, and the guy with the Tin Man's funnel doing brain surgery on Andy Rooney.*

In the same room (#56a), look for Brueghel's work.

Northern Renaissance (1500–1600)

The sunny optimism of the Italian Renaissance didn't quite penetrate the cold Northern lands. Italian humanists saw people as almost like Greek gods—strong, handsome, and noble—capable of standing on their own without the help of anyone, including God and the Catholic Church.

On the other hand, when you divorce people from what's holy, life on earth can seem pretty pointless. Northern artists concentrated on the folly of humankind (think of Bosch's puny humans) cast adrift in a chaotic world.

Brueghel—
The Triumph of Death
(El Triunfo de la Muerte)

The brief flowering of the Renaissance couldn't last. The optimism and humanism of the Renaissance met the brutal reality of war and lost. In the 16th century, the openness of the Renaissance fueled the Reformation, the bitter break between the Catholic Church and the "Protest"-ants. The resulting wars involved almost every nation of Europe (remember Charles V, who led the Catholics). The Northern countries were the hardest hit—in Germany alone, a third of the population died. The battles were especially brutal, with atrocities on both sides—the predictable result when politicians and generals claim God is on their side.

Pieter Brueghel (pron: BROY-gull) the Elder lived in these violent times, witnessing the futility of this first "world war." In violent times the message turns simple and morbid—no one can escape death.

The canvas is one big chaotic, nonsymmetrical, confusing battle scene. Death in the form of skeletons (led by the one on horseback with a scythe) attacks a crowd of people, herding them into a tunnel-like building (prescient of a Nazi death camp). Elsewhere, other skeletons dole out the inevitable fate of all flesh. No one is spared. Not the jester (lower right, crawling under the table), not churchmen, not the emperor himself (at lower left, whose gold is also plundered), not even the poor man (upper right) kneeling, praying for mercy with a cross in his hands.

We can imagine these scenes being played out in real life on the battlefields of Europe, leaving countries as wasted as the barren countryside in the background. In the end, after a hundred bloody years of

war, a truce (in 1648) divided countries into Catholic or Protestant (divisions that survive today), and Europe began to learn the lesson of tolerance—to exist we must coexist.

• *Continue to room 55a.*

Matsys—*Ecce Homo (Cristo Presentado al Pueblo)*

The mob—a menagerie of goony faces—is railing on the prisoner Christ before his execution. Christ seems quite fed up with it all. The painting is especially effective because of our perspective. We're looking up at Christ on the balcony—we've become part of the hooting mob.

• *Stop by room 54 to meet...*

Dürer—*Self-Portrait* (*Autorretrato*)

Before looking into the eyes of 26-year-old Albrecht Dürer, look first at his clothes and hairdo—they tell half the story of this remarkable personal statement. It's the look of a mod/hip/fab/rad young guy, a man of

the world. The meticulous detail work (Dürer was also an engraver) is the equivalent of preening before a mirror. Dürer (pron: DEWR-er), recently returned from Italy, wanted to impress his bumpkin fellow Germans with all that he had learned.

But Dürer wasn't simply vain. Renaissance Italy treated its artists like princes, not workmen. Dürer learned not only to paint like a great artist, but to act like one as well.

Now look into his eyes, or rather, look up at his eyes, since Dürer composed the painting so that he is literally looking down on us. We see an intelligent, bold, and somewhat arrogant man, confident of his abilities. The strong arms and hands reinforce this confidence.

This is possibly the first true self-portrait. Sure, other artists used themselves as models and put their likeness in scenes (like Bosch in hell), but it was a whole new thing to paint your own portrait to proudly show your personality to the world. Dürer painted probably 10 of them in his life—each showing a different aspect of this complex man.

Dürer put his mark on every painting and engraving. Note the pyramid-shaped "A.D." (D inside the A) on the windowsill.

• *In the same room (#54), find...*

Dürer—*Adam and Eve* (two separate panels)

These are the first full-size nudes in Northern European art. It took the boldness of someone like Dürer to bring Italian fleshiness to the more modest Germans.

The title is *Adam and Eve,* but of course that's just an excuse to paint two nudes in the classical style. Or maybe

we should say to "sculpt" two nudes, because they are more like Greek statues on pedestals than paintings. Dürer emphasized this by taking the one scene (Eve is giving Adam the apple—notice how their hair is blown by the same wind) and splitting it into two canvases—each "statue" has its own niche.

Compared with Bosch's smooth-limbed, naked little *homunculi*, Dürer's *Adam and Eve* are three-dimensional and solid, with anatomically correct muscles. They're a bold humanistic proclamation that the body is good, man is good, the things of the world are good.

• *In the same room (#54), see...*

Hans Baldung Grien— *The Three Graces* and *The Three Ages of Man*

Painted about the same time as Dürer's works, these, too, have a classical touch—the Graces were goddesses of joy in Greek mythology—but what a different message! While Dürer portrayed the Renaissance glory of man, this is a gloomy medieval reminder that all flesh is mortal, and we're all on the same moving sidewalk to the junk pile.

In the left panel are the *Three Graces* in youth—beautiful, happy, in a playful green grove with the sun shining, and surrounded by angelic babies. But with grim Northern realism, the right panel shows what happens to all flesh (especially that of humanists!). *The Three Graces* become *The Three Ages* of sagging decay—middle age, old age, and death. Death holds an hourglass of that devouring army, Time.

• *Return to the long gallery (room 49) and head to the rotunda. Go upstairs. Look down the long gallery. To reach Rubens' work, take the first left, into room 9b. But first, grab a seat and read on.*

Rubens and Baroque (1600s)

You're surrounded by Baroque. Large canvases, bright colors, rippling bodies, plenty of flesh, violent scenes. Baroque art overwhelms. It plays on our emotions, titillates our senses, and carries us away.

Baroque was made to order for the Catholic Church and absolute

RUBENS, VELÁZQUEZ, AND THE COUNTER-REFORMATION

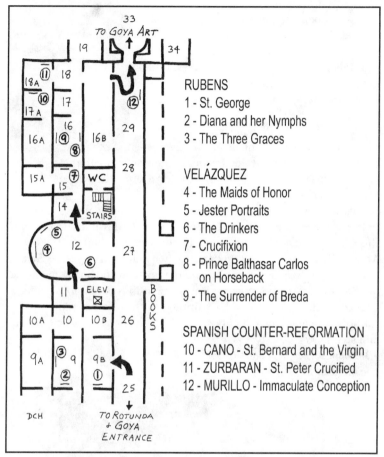

RUBENS
1 - St. George
2 - Diana and her Nymphs
3 - The Three Graces

VELÁZQUEZ
4 - The Maids of Honor
5 - Jester Portraits
6 - The Drinkers
7 - Crucifixion
8 - Prince Balthasar Carlos on Horseback
9 - The Surrender of Breda

SPANISH COUNTER-REFORMATION
10 - CANO - St. Bernard and the Virgin
11 - ZURBARAN - St. Peter Crucified
12 - MURILLO - Immaculate Conception

monarchs who used it as propaganda to combat the dual threats of Protestantism and democracy. They impressed the common masses with beautiful palaces and glorious churches, showing their strength and authority.

Peter Paul Rubens of Flanders (Belgium) was the favorite of Catholic rulers. He painted the loves, wars, and religion of Catholic kings. His huge canvases were in great demand, and Rubens—like Titian before him—became rich and famous, a cultured, likable man of the world, who was even entrusted with diplomatic missions by his employers.

• *In room 9b, look for...*

Rubens—*St. George Slaying the Dragon (San Jorge)*

This was a popular subject for Catholic kings involved in the wars of the Counter-Reformation. Like the legendary early Christian warrior who killed a dragon to save a princess, these kings saw themselves as righteous warriors saving the holy Church from the dragon of Protestantism.

In this typically Baroque tangle of bodies, we see the exciting moment just as George, who has already speared the dragon, is about to apply the *coup de bludgeon* with his sword. The limp princess has a lamb, the symbol of Christ and His church.

Baroque art often looks confusing, but it's almost always anchored in Renaissance-style balance. This painting has an X-like composition, the rearing horse slanting one way and George slanting the other. Above where the X intersects are the two stars of the scene, George with his rippling plumed helmet and the horse, with its rippling mane.

All around these rooms are Rubens paintings of religious subjects. Glance at the series of smaller paintings with titles championing the Catholic cause—*Triumph of the Church, Triumph of the True Catholic,* and so on.

• *In room 9 (which is back-to-back with room 9b), look for the following two paintings.*

Rubens—*Diana and Her Nymphs Discovered by a Satyr (Diana y sus Ninfas sorprendidas por Sátiros)*

A left-to-right rippling wave of figures creates a thrilling chase scene. Four horny satyrs (half man, half beast—though why mythical creatures like this never have their human half at the bottom, I'll never know) have crashed a party of woodland nymphos who flee from left to right. Only the Greek goddess Diana, queen of the hunt, stands with her spear to try to stem the tide of flailing limbs.

All the elements of a typical Rubens work are here—action, emotion, sensuality, violence, bright colors, fleshy bodies, and rippling clothes and hair with the wind machine on high.

Another typical feature is that it wasn't all painted by Rubens. Rubens was in such demand that he couldn't fill all the orders himself. In his home/studio/factory in Antwerp, he put assistants to work with the backgrounds and trivial details of his huge works, then, before shipping a canvas out the doors, Rubens would bring the work to life with a few final strokes.

• *In the same room (#9)* ...

Rubens—*The Three Graces* (*Las Tres Gracias*)

Have a seat and gaze at the pure beauty of Rubens' *Three Graces*. The ample, sensual bodies—like all his women— have glowing skin, rhythmic limbs, grace, and delicacy, set against a pleasant background. This is Rubens at his best. This particular painting was for his own private collection. His young second wife, the model for the Grace at left, shows up fairly regularly in Rubens' paintings. Remember that in later more prudish years, many of Rubens' nudes, like Titian's, were wrapped in brown paper and locked in the closet.

• *Continue to the large, nave-shaped room 12.*

Velázquez (1599–1660)

For 35 years, Diego Velázquez (pron: vel-LAHS-kes) was the king of Spain's court painters. Look around the room. While El Greco and other Spanish artists painted crucifixions, saints, and madonnas, Velázquez painted what his boss, the king, told him to—mostly portraits.

Unlike the wandering, independent El Greco, Velázquez was definitely a career man. Born in Sevilla, apprenticed at an early age, he marries the master's daughter, moves to Madrid, impresses the king with his ability, and works his way up the ladder at the king's court—valet to the king, director of new buildings, director of festivities, and so on. He becomes the king's friend and art teacher and, eventually, is knighted.

What's amazing in this tale of ambition is that, as a painter, Velázquez never compromised. He was the photojournalist of his time, chronicling court events for posterity.

• *In room 12* ...

Velázquez—The Maids of Honor (Las Meninas)

Velázquez has made the perfect blend of formal portrait and candid intimate snapshot. It's a painting about the painting of a portrait. Here's what we're seeing:

One hot summer day in 1656, Velázquez (at left) with brush in hand and looking like Salvador Dalí (which is a little like saying that Jesus looked like John Lennon) is painting a formal portrait of King Phillip and his wife. They would be standing where we are, and we see only their reflection in the mirror at the back of the room.

Their daughter, the Infanta Margarita (the main figure in the center), has come to watch her parents being painted. With her are her two attendants (meninas, or girls), one of whom is kneeling, offering her a cool glass of water. Also in the picture is the young court jester (far right) poking impishly at the family dog. A female dwarf looks on, as do others in the background. Also, at that very moment, a member of court is passing by the doorway in the distance on his way upstairs, and he, too, looks in on the progress of the portrait.

Velázquez was smart enough to know that the really interesting portrait wasn't the king and queen but the action behind the scenes. We're sucked right in by the naturalness of the scene and because the characters are looking right at us. This is true Spanish history, and Velázquez the journalist (who is shown wearing the red cross of knighthood, painted on after his death—possibly by Phillip IV himself) has told us more about this royal family than have volumes of history books.

The scene is lit by the window at right. Using gradations of light, Velázquez has split the room into five receding planes: (1) the king and queen, standing where we are; (2) the main figures, lit by the window; (3) the darker middle distance figures (including Velázquez); (4) the black wall; and (5) the lit doorway. We are drawn into the painting, living and breathing with its characters, free to walk behind them, around them, and among them. This is art come to life.

• Next to The Maids of Honor, look for . . .

Velázquez—Jester Portraits (Bufones)

In royal courts, dwarfs were given the job of entertaining the nobles. But some also had a more important task—social satire. They alone were given free rein to say anything they wanted about the king, however biting, nasty, or—worst of all—true. Consequently, these dwarfs were often the wittiest and most intelligent people at court, and Velázquez, who must have known them as colleagues, painted them with great dignity.

• *Also in the same room (#12)...*

Velázquez—*The Drinkers* (*Los Borrachos*)

Velázquez's objective eye even turns Greek gods into everyday folk. Here the Greek god of wine crowns a drinker for his deeds of debauch-

ery. Bacchus is as finely painted as anything Titian or Rubens ever did, but what a difference in scenes! The real focus isn't the otherworldly Bacchus but his fellow, human merrymakers.

This isn't a painting, it's a Polaroid snapshot in a blue-collar bar. Look how natural the guy is next to Bacchus, grinning at us over the bowl of wine he's offering us—and the guy next to him, clambering to get into the picture and mugging for the camera! Velázquez was the master at making a carefully composed scene look spontaneous.

• *You'll find more work by Velázquez in rooms 15 and 16. In room 15...*

Velázquez—*Crucifixion* (*Cristo crucificado*)

King Phillip IV was having an affair. He got caught and, being a good Christian king, was overcome with remorse. He commissioned this work to atone for his adulterous ways. (That's Phillip, pious and kneeling, to the left of the crucifixion.)

Velázquez's *Crucifixion* must have matched the repentant mood of his king (and friend). You can often tell the tone of a crucifixion by the tilt of Christ's head. Here, it's hanging down, accepting His punishment, humble and repentant.

Meditating on this Christ would truly be an act of agonizing penance. We see him straight from the front, no holds barred. Every detail is laid out for us, even down to the knots in the wood of the crossbar. And the dripping blood!

We feel how long Jesus has been hanging there by how long it must have taken for that blood to drip ever so slowly down.

• *In room 16, look for the following two paintings . . .*

Velázquez—*Prince Balthasar Carlos on Horseback* (*El Príncipe Baltasar Carlos, a caballo*)

As court painter, this was exactly the kind of portrait Velázquez was called on to produce—the prince, age five, looking like the masterful heir to the throne. But the charm of the painting is the contrast between the pose—the traditional equestrian pose of a powerful Roman conqueror—and the fact that this "conqueror" is only a cute, tiny tyke in a pink-and-gold suit. The seriousness on the prince's face adds the crowning touch. We can see why Velázquez was such a court favorite.

While pleasing his king, Velázquez was also starting a revolution in art. Stand back and look at the prince's costume—remarkably detailed, right? Now move up closer—all that "remarkable detail" is nothing but messy splotches of pink and gold paint! In the past, artists painted details meticulously. But Velázquez learned how just a few dabs of colors on a canvas blend in the eye when seen at a distance to give the appearance of great detail. Two centuries later this technique would eventually be taken to its extreme by the Impressionists.

• *In the same room (#16) . . .*

Velázquez—*The Surrender of Breda* (*La Rendición de Breda*)

Here's another piece of artistic journalism, the Spanish victory over the Dutch after a long siege of Breda, a strongly fortified city. The scene has

become famous as a model of fair play. The defeated Dutch general is offering the keys to the city to the victorious Spaniards. As he begins to kneel in humility, the Spanish conqueror restrains him—the war is over and there's no need to rub salt in the wounds. The optimistic calm-after-the-battle mood is enhanced by the great open space

highlighted by the 25 lances (the painting is often called "The Lances") silhouetted against the sky.

• *From the cool objectivity of Velázquez, enter the heat and passion of Spain's religious art of the Counter-Reformation. Start with room 17a.*

Counter-Reformation Art— Fighting Back With Brushes (1600s)

Europe was torn in two by the Protestant Reformation. For 100 years, Catholics and Protestants bashed Bibles in what has been called the first "world war." The Catholic Church also waged a propaganda campaign (the Counter-Reformation) to bolster the faith of the confused, weary masses. Art was part of that campaign. Pretty pictures brought abstract doctrines to the level of the common man.

• *In room 17a...*

Cano—*St. Bernard and the Virgin (San Bernardo y la Virgen)*

Here's a heavenly vision brought right down to earth. St. Bernard is literally enjoying the "milk of paradise," a vision he had of being suckled on the heavenly teat of Mary. When God's word was portrayed in this realistic way, the common folk lapped it up.

• *In room 18a...*

Zurbarán—*St. Peter Crucified Appearing to Peter Nolasco (Aparición de San Pedro a San Pedro Nolasco)*

Zurbarán is like a bitter jolt of *café solo*. In Spain, miracles are real. When legends tell of a saint who was beheaded but didn't die, that isn't an allegory on eternal life to the Spanish—they picture a real man walking around with his head under his arm.

So, when Zurbarán paints a mystical vision, he gives it to us in photographic realism. Bam, there's St. Peter crucified upside down right in front of us. Nolasco looks as shocked as we are at the reality of the vision. This is "People's Art" of the Counter-Reformation, religious art for the masses. (Zurbarán has the sort of literal-minded religion that makes people wonder things like— "When the Rapture comes, what if I'm sitting on the toilet?")

• Return to the long gallery. Nearby, within the gallery, in section 29, look for...

Murillo—The Immaculate Conception of Aranjuez (La Concepción "de Aranjuez")

For centuries, the No. 1 deity in the Christian "pantheon" was the goddess Mary. This painting is a religious treatise, explaining a Catholic doctrine that many found difficult to comprehend—the Immaculate Conception of Mary. Since all humans are stained by the original sin of Adam (so the doctrine went), didn't that mean Jesus was as well, since His mother was human? Not so, said the Catholics. Mary, by a special act of God, was conceived and born without taint of original sin.

The Spanish have always loved the Virgin. She's practically a cult figure. Common people pray directly to her for help in troubled times. Murillo (pron: mur-REE-oh) used this fanatic devotion to Mary to teach the dull theological concept of Immaculate Conception. He painted a beautiful, floating, and Ivory Soap–pure woman—the most "immaculate" virgin imaginable—radiating youth and wholesome goodness.

• Continue to the hexagonal room (#32).

Goya (1746–1828)

Francisco de Goya, a true individual in both his life and his painting style, is hard to pigeonhole—his personality and talents were so varied. We'll see several different facets of this rough-cut man—cheery apprentice painter, loyal court painter, political rebel, scandal maker, disillusioned genius. His work runs the gamut, from pretty rococo to political rabble-rousing to Romantic nightmares.

For convenience, let's divide Goya's life into three stages: the Court Painter (including his early years), Political Rebel, and Dark Stage.

• In room 32...

Goya: Court Painter

Goya—The Family of Charles IV (La Familia de Carlos IV)

They're decked out in all their finest, wearing every medal, jewel, and ribbon they could find for this impressive group portrait. Goya has

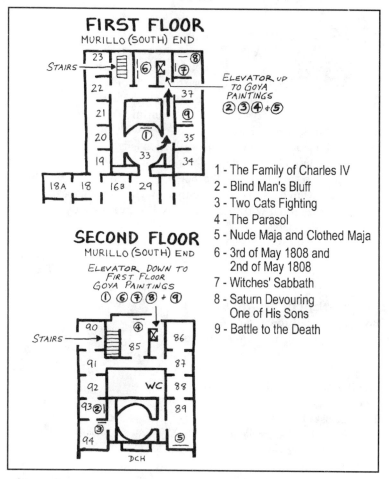

GOYA

FIRST FLOOR
MURILLO (SOUTH) END

STAIRS

ELEVATOR up
TO GOYA
PAINTINGS
② ③ ④ + ⑤

SECOND FLOOR
MURILLO (SOUTH) END

ELEVATOR DOWN TO
FIRST FLOOR
GOYA PAINTINGS
① ⑥ ⑦ ⑧ + ⑨

STAIRS

WC

DCH

1 - The Family of Charles IV
2 - Blind Man's Bluff
3 - Two Cats Fighting
4 - The Parasol
5 - Nude Maja and Clothed Maja
6 - 3rd of May 1808 and
    2nd of May 1808
7 - Witches' Sabbath
8 - Saturn Devouring
    One of His Sons
9 - Battle to the Death

captured all the splendor of the court in 1800—but with a brutal twist of reality. For underneath all the royal finery, he captured the inner personality—or lack thereof—of these shallow monarchs.

This isn't so much a royal portrait as it is a stiff family photo of Ma and Pa Kettle in their Sunday best. The look in their eyes seems to say "I can't wait to get this monkey suit off." (I picture Goya deliberately taking his own sweet time making them stand and smile for hours on end.)

Goya, the budding political liberal, shows his disgust for the shallow king and his family. King Charles, with his ridiculous hairdo and

silly smile, is portrayed for what he was—a vacuous, good-natured fool, a henpecked husband controlled by a domineering queen. She, the true center of the composition, is proud and defiant. She was vain about the supposed beauty of her long, swanlike neck, and here she stretches to display every centimeter of it. The other adults, with their bland faces, are bug-eyed with stupidity. Catch the crone looking out at us birdlike, fourth from left.

As a tribute to Velázquez's *Maids of Honor,* Goya painted himself painting the scene at far left. But here Goya stands back in the shadows looking with disdain on the group. Only the children escape Goya's critical eye, painted with the sympathy he always showed to those lower on the social ladder.

• *Let's look at Goya's early years. Facing the above painting, exit the hexagonal room to the right, then turn left down the hall. Take the elevator up. Go to rooms 90–94.*

Goya's Early Years

Born in a small town, Goya, unlike Velázquez, was a far cry from a precocious painter destined for success. In his youth, he dabbled as a matador, kicking around Spain before finally landing a job in the Royal Tapestry. The canvases in these rooms were designs made into tapestries bound for the walls of nobles' palaces.

Browse through these rooms and watch lords and ladies of the 1700s with nothing better to do than play—toasting each other at a picnic, dancing with castanets, flying kites, playing paddleball, listening to a blind guitarist, walking on stilts, or playing *Blind Man's Bluff* (see room 93).

In room 94, a more serious side of Goya's emerges. His *Two Cats Fighting* (*Gatos Riñendo*) represents the two warring halves of a human soul, the dark and light sides, anger and fear locked in immortal combat, fighting for dominance of a man's life. We're entering the Age of Romanticism.

Notice—how do I say this?—how BAD the drawing is in some of these canvases, especially the early ones. How-ever, in the few short years he worked in the tapestry department, Goya the inex-perienced apprentice slowly developed into a good, if not great, draftsman. *The*
Parasol (*El Quitasol*)—in room 85—was one of his first really good paintings, with a simple composition and subtle shadings of light. Goya worked steadily for the court for 25 years, dutifully cranking out por-traits before finally becoming First Court Painter at age 53.

• *Head to room 89 (also on second floor).*

Goya: Political Rebel

Goya—*Nude Maja* (*La Maja Desnuda*) and *Clothed Maja* (*La Maja Vestida*)

Goya remained at court because of his talent, not his political beliefs—or his morals. Rumor flew that he was fooling around with the beautiful, in-telligent, and vivacious Duchess of Alba. Even more scandalous was a painting, supposedly of the Duchess in a less-than-devoutly Catholic pose.

A *maja* was a hip working-class girl. Many of Goya's early tapes-tries show royalty dressed in the garb of these colorful commoners. Here the Duchess has undressed as one.

The Nude Maja was a real shocker. Spanish kings enjoyed the sen-sual nudes of Titian and Rubens, but it was unheard-of for a pious Spaniard to actually paint one. Goya incurred the wrath of the Inquisi-tion, the Catholic court system that tried heretics and sinners.

Tour guides explain that the painting caused such a stir that Goya dashed off another version with her clothes on. The quick brushwork is sloppier, perhaps because Goya was in a hurry or because he was anx-ious to invent Impressionism. The two paintings may have been displayed

in a double frame—the nude could be covered by sliding the clothed *maja* over it to hide it from Inquisitive minds that wanted to know.

Artistically, the nude is less a portrait than an idealized nude in the tradition (and reclining pose) of Titian's *Venus and the Organ Player*. The pale body is highlighted by the cool green sheets, à la Titian, as well. Both paintings were locked away in obscurity, along with the Titians and Rubenses, until 1901.

• *Take the elevator (or stairs) one floor down to see more of Goya's art. In room 39, near the stairs, you'll find . . .*

Goya—*2nd of May, 1808* and *3rd of May, 1808*

Goya became a political radical, a believer in democracy in a world of kings. During his time, the American and French Revolutions put the fear of God in the medieval minds of Europe's aristocracy. In retaliation, members of the aristocracy were determined to stamp out any trace of political liberalism.

Goya admired the French leader Napoleon, who fought for the democratic ideals of the French Revolution against the kings of Europe. But then Napoleon invaded Spain (1808), and Goya saw war firsthand. What he saw was not a heroic war liberating the Spaniards from the feudal yoke, but an oppressive, brutal, senseless war in which common Spaniards were the first to die.

The *2nd of May, 1808* and *3rd of May, 1808* show two bloody days of the war. On May 2, the common citizens of Madrid rebelled against the French invaders. With sticks, stones, and kitchen knives, they rallied in protest at Puerta del Sol, Madrid's main square. The French sent in their

fearsome Egyptian mercenary troops to quell the riot. Goya captures the hysterical tangle of bodies as the Egyptians wade through the dense crowd hacking away at the overmatched *Madrileños* who have nowhere to run.

The next day the French began reprisals. They took suspected rebels to a nearby hill and began mercilessly executing them. The *3rd of May, 1808* is supposedly a tribute to those brave Spaniards who rebelled against the French, but it's far from heroic. In fact, it's antiheroic, showing us the irrationality of war—an assembly line of death, with each victim toppling into a crumpled heap. They plead for mercy and get none. Those awaiting death bury their faces in their hands, unable to look at their falling companions. The central victim in luminous white spreads his arms Christlike and asks, "Why are you doing this to us?"

Goya goes beyond sympathy for the victims. In this war, even the executioners are pawns in the game, only following orders without understanding why. The colorless firing squad, with guns perfectly level and feet perfectly in step, is a faceless machine of murder, cutting people down with all the compassion of a lawnmower. They bury their faces in their guns as though they, too, are unable to look their victims in the eye. This war is horrible, and, what's worse, the horror is pointless.

The violence is painted with equally violent techniques. There's a strong prison-yard floodlight thrown on the main victim, focusing all our attention on his look of puzzled horror. The distorted features, the puddle of blood, the twisting bodies, the thick brushwork—all are features of the Romantic style that emphasized emotion over beauty. It all adds up to a vivid portrayal of the brutality of war. Like the victims, we ask, "How can one human being do this to another?"

Goya was disillusioned by the invasion led by his hero Napoleon. Added to this he began to go deaf. His wife died. To top it off, he was exiled as a political radical. Goya retreated from court life to his own private, quiet—and dark—world.

• *To find the dark paintings, silently flagellate yourself, then go to room 38.*

Goya: Dark Stage

In 1819, Goya—deaf, widowed, and exiled—moved into a villa and began decorating it with his own oil paintings. The works were painted right on the walls of rooms in the villa, later transferred here.

You immediately see why these are the Dark Paintings—both in color and mood. They're nightmarish scenes, scary and surreal, the inner visions of an embittered man smeared onto the walls as though finger painted in blood.

• *In room 38 . . .*

Goya—*The Witches' Sabbath* (*El Aquelarre*)

Dark forces convened continually in Goya's dining room. This dark coven of crones swirls in a frenzy of black magic around a dark, Satanic goat in monk's clothes who presides, priestlike, over the obscene rituals. The main witch, seated in front of the goat, is the very image of

wild-eyed adoration, lust, and fear. (Notice the one noble lady sitting just to the right of center with her hands folded primly in her lap—"I thought this was a Tupperware party.")
• *In the same room (#38) . . .*

Goya—*Saturn Devouring One of His Sons (Saturno)*

Fearful that his sons would overthrow him as king of the gods, the Roman god Saturn ate them. Saturn was also known as Cronus, or Time, and this may be an allegory of how Time devours us all. Goya was a dying man in a dying, feudal world. The destructiveness of time is shown in all its horror by a man unafraid of the darker side.
• *In room 36 . . .*

Goya—*Battle to the Death (Duelo a Garrotazos)*

Two giants buried up to their knees, face to face, flail at each other with clubs. Neither can move, neither can run, neither dares rest or the other will finish him off. It's a standoff between superpowers caught in a never-ending cycle of war. Can a truce be reached? It looks bleak. Is this really by the same artist who did the frilly *Blind Man's Bluff*?

The Dark Paintings foreshadow 20th-century surrealism with their dream images, and Expressionism with their thick smeared style and cynical outlook.

Guernica

• *Probably the single most impressive piece of art in Spain is Picasso's Guernica in the Centro Arte de Reina Sofía, Madrid's slick modern art museum (€3.20, free Sat afternoon and all day Sun; open Mon and Wed–Sat*

10:00–21:00, Sun 10:00–14:30, closed Tue; located three long blocks south of the Prado across the street from the Atocha train station, look for exterior glass elevators, Santa Isabel 52, Metro: Atocha, tel. 91-467-5062). For more on modern art, see the next chapter.

Picasso's monumental canvas *Guernica* is not only a piece of art but a piece of history. It's one of Europe's must-see sights, so leave time for it.

Guernica is the product of the right artist in the right place at the right time. Pablo Picasso, a Spaniard, was in Paris in 1937, preparing an exhibition of paintings for its world's fair. Meanwhile, a bloody civil war was being fought in his own country. The legally elected democratic government was being challenged by traditionalist right-wing forces under Francisco Franco. Franco would eventually win and rule the country with an iron fist for three decades.

Guernica was a small town in northern Spain of no strategic importance, but it became the target of the world's first saturation-bombing raid. Franco gave permission to his Fascist ally, Hitler, to use the town as a guinea pig to try out Germany's new air force. The raid leveled the town, causing destruction that was unheard-of at the time—though by 1944 it would be commonplace.

News of the bombing reached Picasso in Paris. He scrapped earlier plans and immediately set to work on the *Guernica* mural for the Spanish pavilion. It was finished in a matter of weeks. Thousands of people attended the fair, and many were profoundly affected by the mural. They witnessed the horror of modern technology of war, the vain struggle of the Spanish Republicans, and the cold indifference of the Nazi war machine. It was a prophetic vision of the world war to come.

Picasso shows Guernica in the aftermath of the bombing. It's as if he'd picked up the shattered shards and pasted them onto a canvas. It looks like a jumble of overlapping shades on first sight, but looking closer, we can see each piece of this broken city. The figures are twisted, but recognizable. Let's sort the main ones out.

On the left is a bull. In typical Cubist fashion, we see the head from two angles at once. The body curves around to the left, ending with a tail like a wisp of smoke. Beneath the bull is a modern pietà—a grieving mother with her dead child.

The central figure is a horse with a twisted head and a sword piercing its newsprint body. The horse's rider has fallen, dismembered, at the horse's feet. We see his severed head and severed arm with a broken sword.

On the right, a woman runs screaming. Above her, another pokes her head out a window shining a shaft of light on the horse and the woman below. To the far right, another figure cries with grief inside a building.

This is a gruesome and, despite the modern "abstract" style, remarkably realistic portrayal of the bombing's destruction. But Picasso has suggested a symbolic interpretation that raised the work to the universal level, a commentary on all wars.

Picasso himself said that the central horse, with the spear in its back, symbolizes humanity succumbing to brute force. The bull represents brutality, standing triumphant over the mourning mother and child.

The Guernica raid was a completely senseless and pointless act of brute force without any military purpose. In fact, the entire Spanish Civil War was an exercise in brutality. As one side captured a town, it might systematically round up every man, old and young—including priests—line them up and shoot them in revenge for atrocities by the other side. The bare bulb at the top of the canvas shines an interrogator's third-degree light on all this ugliness.

Near the bull is a crying dove, the symbol of peace in defeat. The rider's broken sword could be the futility of trying to fight brutality with brutality.

This is a scary work. The drab, concrete-colored gray tones create a depressing, almost nauseating mood. We are like the terrified woman at right, trying to run from it all. But her leg is too thick, dragging her down, like trying to run from something in a nightmare. The figure thrusting her head out of the window with a lamp in her hand is humanity itself, coming out of its shell, seeing for the first time the harsh horror of modern war.

MODERN ART

*Y*ou'll bump into modern art museums throughout your travels. To help you plan your sightseeing, we've included basic information on five of the museums you're most likely to visit—in London, Paris, Amsterdam, Venice, and Madrid.

Regardless of the museum, the same artists are usually represented: Picasso, Kandinsky, Mondrian, Klee, Dalí, and so on. This chapter is a guide to modern art—the artists, their principles, and the times they lived in—rather than a look at specific pieces of art in specific museums.

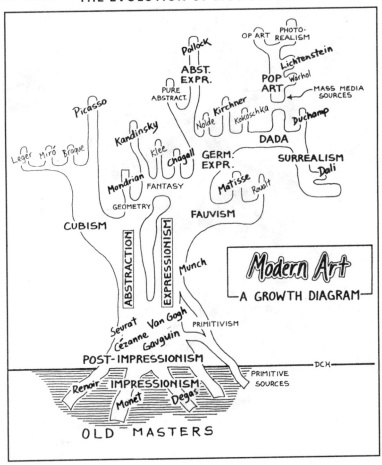

❧ 26 ❧
MODERN ART

If you don't "get" modern art, you're on the right track. It's meant to disorient and disrupt your normal outlook, to make you see things in a new way. Find your own meaning. You are a cocreator with the artist and a coauthor of this chapter.

MODERN ART MUSEUMS

TATE MODERN, LONDON

Cost: Free; varying costs for temporary exhibits.

Hours: Sun–Thu 10:00–18:00, Fri–Sat 10:00–22:00 (least crowded Fri and Sat eves).

Getting There: Located on the south bank of the Thames, across from St. Paul's and near Shakespeare's Globe Theatre. Tube stops: Southwark or Blackfriars plus 10-minute walk.

Information: On the ground floor, you'll find the information desk, baggage check, tickets for temporary exhibits, and audioguide rentals (£1). Three audioguide tours are available: Director's Tour (highlights of the permanent collection), Collections Tour (all of the permanent collection), and a Children's Tour (geared for ages 8–12). Tel. 020/7887-8000 or 020/7887-8008, www.tate.org.uk.

Photography: No photos are allowed except in the entrance hall.

Cuisine Art: View coffee shops are on the fourth and seventh floors. Some fine restaurants are outside along The Cut (near Southwark tube stop).

Starring: Picasso, Matisse, Dalí, and all the "classic" modern artists, plus the Tate's specialty—British and American artists of the last half of the 20th century.

POMPIDOU CENTER, PARIS

Cost: €8.75, covered by Paris museum pass; discounts for the young (18–25) and old (over 65), under 18 enter free. First Sun of the month is free. Buy tickets on ground floor. Temporary exhibits cost extra.

Hours: Wed–Mon 10:00–22:00, closed Tue and May 1.

Getting There: Metro: Rambuteau or Hôtel de Ville. The wild, color-coded exterior makes it about as hard to miss as the Eiffel Tower. To use the escalator to reach the museum (fourth floor), you need to buy a ticket for the museum or have a museum pass.

Information: Audioguides for the museum cost €4.50. Tel. 01 44 78 12 33, www.centrepompidou.fr.

Cloakroom: Ground floor.

Cuisine Art: View restaurant on sixth floor, café on mezzanine level, library cafeteria on second floor. Great café neighborhood.

Starring: Matisse, Picasso, Chagall, Dalí, Warhol, contemporary art.

STEDELIJK MUSEUM, AMSTERDAM

Cost: €4.50.

Hours: Daily 11:00–17:00, closed Jan 1.

Getting There: It's located at Paulus Potterstraat 13, near the Rijksmuseum, Van Gogh Museum, and Museumplein.

Information: Tel. 020/573-2911, www.stedelijk.nl.

Starring: Mostly post-1945 art and exhibitions, also Monet, van Gogh, Cézanne, Picasso, and Chagall.

PEGGY GUGGENHEIM, VENICE

Cost: €7.

Hours: Wed–Mon 10:00–18:00, Sat until 22:00 April–Oct, closed Tue.

Getting there: It's overlooking the Grand Canal, near the Accademia bridge. Vaporetto stop—Accademia.

Information: Audioguides and small guidebooks, available at the ticket counter, cost €4.50. Tel. 041-240-5411, www.guggenheim.org.

Baggage Check: Free.

Photography: Allowed only in the garden and terrace.

Starring: Peggy G., Picasso, Braque, Dalí, Pollock, Klee, Calder, and Chagall.

CENTRO ARTE DE REINA SOFIA, MADRID

Picasso's *Guernica*, the museum's most famous work, is described at the end of the Prado chapter.

Cost: €3.20.

Hours: Mon and Wed–Sat 10:00–21:00, Sun 10:00–14:30, closed Tue; free on Sat afternoon and all day Sun.

Getting there: It's at Santa Isabel 52, across from the Atocha train station. Metro: Atocha. Look for the exterior glass elevators.

Information: Tel. 91-467-5062.

Starring: Picasso's *Guernica*, more Picasso, and Dalí.

A.D. 1900—
A NEW CENTURY DAWNS

War is a thing of the past. Science will wipe out poverty and disease. Rational Man is poised at a new era of peace and prosperity...

Right. This cozy Victorian dream was soon shattered by two world wars and rapid technological change. Nietzsche murdered God. Darwin stripped off man's robe of culture and found a naked ape. Freud washed ashore on the beach of a vast new continent inside each of us. Einstein made every truth merely "relative." Even the fundamental building blocks of the universe, atoms, were behaving erratically.

The 20th century—accelerated by technology and fragmented by war—was exciting and chaotic, and the art reflects the turbulence of that century of change.

Henri Matisse (1869–1954)

Matisse's colorful "wallpaper" works are not realistic. A man is a few black lines and blocks of paint. The colors are unnaturally bright. There's no illusion of the distance and 3-D that was so important to Renaissance Italians. The "distant" landscape is as bright as things close up, and the slanted lines meant to suggest depth are crudely done.

Traditionally, the canvas was like a window that you looked "through" to see a slice of the real world stretching off into the distance. Now, a camera could do that better. With Matisse, you look "at" the canvas, like wallpaper. Voilà! What was a crudely drawn scene now becomes a sophisticated and decorative pattern of colors and shapes.

Though fully "modern," Matisse built on 19th-century art—the bright colors of van Gogh, the primitive figures of Gauguin, the colorful designs of Japanese prints, and the Impressionist patches of paint that blend together only at a distance.

For more Matisse, visit the Matisse Museum in Nice, France.

Primitive Masks and Statues

Matisse was one of the Fauves ("wild beasts") who, inspired by African and Oceanic masks and voodoo dolls, tried to inject a bit of the jungle into bored French society. The result? Modern art that looked primitive: long, masklike faces with almond eyes; bright, clashing colors; simple figures; and "flat," two-dimensional scenes.

1910
THE MODERNS

The modern world was moving fast, with the cars, factories, and mass communication. Motion pictures caught the fast-moving world, while Einstein further explored the Fourth Dimension, Time.

Cubism: Reality Shattered (1907–1912)

I throw a rock at a glass statue, shatter it, pick up the pieces, and glue them onto a canvas. I'm a Cubist.

Pablo Picasso (1881–1973) and
Georges Braque (1882–1963)

Born in Spain, Picasso moved to Paris as a young man, settling into a studio (the Bateau-Lavoir) on Montmartre. He worked with next-door neighbor Georges Braque in poverty so dire they often didn't know where their

next bottle of wine was coming from. They corrected each other's paintings (it's hard to tell whose is whose without the titles) and shared ideas, meals, and girlfriends while inventing a whole new way to look at the world.

They show the world through a kaleidoscope of brown and gray. The subjects are somewhat recognizable (with the help of the titles), but they're broken into geometric shards (let's call them "cubes," though there are many different shapes), then pieced back together.

Cubism gives us several different angles of the subject at once—say, a woman seen from the front and side angles simultaneously, resulting in two eyes on the same side of the nose. This involves showing three dimensions, plus Einstein's new fourth dimension, the Time it takes to walk around the subject to see other angles. Newfangled motion pictures could capture this moving, 4-D world, but how to do it on a 2-D canvas? The Cubist "solution" is a kind of Mercator projection, where the round world is sliced up like an orange peel and laid as flat as possible.

Notice how the "cubes" often overlap. A single cube might contain both an arm (in the foreground) and the window behind (in the background), both painted the same color. The foreground and background are woven together, so that the subject dissolves into a pattern.

Pablo Picasso: Synthetic Cubism (1912–1915) and Beyond

If the Cubists were as smart as Einstein, why couldn't they draw a picture to save their lives? Picasso was one modern artist who could draw exceptionally well (see his partly finished *Harlequin*). But he constantly explored and adapted his style to new trends, becoming the most famous painter of the 20th century. Scattered throughout the museum are works from the many periods of Picasso's life.

Picasso soon began to use more colorful "cubes" (1912–1915). Eventually, he used curved shapes to build the subject, rather than the straight-line shards of early Cubism.

Picasso married and had children. Works from this period (the 1920s) are more realistic, with full-bodied (and big-nosed) women and children. He tries to capture the solidity, serenity, and volume of classical statues.

As his relationships with women deteriorated, he vented his sexual demons by twisting the female body into grotesque balloon-animal shapes (1925–1931).

All through his life, Picasso was exploring new materials. He made collages, tried his hand at making "statues" out of wood, wire, or whatever, and even made statues out of everyday household objects. These "multimedia" works, so revolutionary at the time, have become stock-in-trade today.

If you like Picasso, seek out the Picasso museums in Paris and Barcelona.

Abstract Art

Abstract art simplifies. A man becomes a stick figure. A squiggle is a wave. A streak of red expresses anger. Arches make you want a cheeseburger. These are universal symbols that everyone from a caveman to a banker understands. Abstract artists capture the essence of reality in a few lines and colors, even things a camera can't—emotions, abstract concepts, musical rhythms, and spiritual states of mind. With abstract art, you don't look "through" the canvas to see the visual world, but "at" it to read the symbolism of lines, shapes, and colors.

Wassily Kandinsky (1866–1944)

The bright colors, bent lines, and lack of symmetry tell us that Kandinsky's world was passionate and intense. Notice the titles like "Improvisation" and "Composition." Kandinsky was inspired by music, an art form that's also "abstract" though it still packs a punch. Like a jazz musician improvising a new pattern of notes from a set scale, Kandinsky plays with new patterns of related colors, looking for just the right combination. Using lines and color, Kandinsky translates the unseen reality into a new medium . . . like lightning crackling over the radio. Go man, go.

1914
World War I—
The Death of Values

Ankle deep in mud, a soldier shivers in a trench, waiting to be ordered "over the top." He'll have to run through barbed wire, over fallen comrades, and into a hail of machine-gun fire, only to capture a few hundred meters of meaningless territory that will be lost the next day. This soldier was not thinking about art.

World War I left nine million dead. (During the war, France often lost more men in a single day than America lost in all of Vietnam.) The war also killed the optimism and faith in humankind that had guided Europe since the Renaissance. Now, rationality meant scheming, technology meant machines of death, and morality meant giving your life for an empty cause.

Expressionism: Kirchner, Beckmann, Grosz, Soutine, Dix, and Kokoschka

Cynicism and decadence settled over post-War Europe. Artists "expressed" their disgust by showing a distorted reality that emphasized the ugly. Using the lurid colors and simplified figures of the Fauves, they slapped paint on in thick brush strokes, depicting a hypocritical, hard-edged, dog-eat-dog world that had lost its bearings. The people have a haunted look in their eyes, the fixed stare of corpses and of those who have to bury them.

Dada

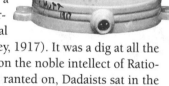

When they could grieve no longer, they turned to its giddy twin, laughter. The war made all old values a joke, including artistic ones. The Dada movement, choosing a purposely childish name, made art that was intentionally outrageous: a moustache on the *Mona Lisa*, a shovel hung on a wall, or a modern version of a Renaissance "fountain"—a urinal (by either Marcel Duchamp or I. P. Freeley, 1917). It was a dig at all the pompous prewar artistic theories based on the noble intellect of Rational Women and Men. While the experts ranted on, Dadaists sat in the back of the class and made cultural fart noises.

Hey, I love this stuff. My mind says it's sophomoric, but my heart belongs to Dada.

1920
ANYTHING GOES

In the Jazz Age, the world turned upside down. Genteel ladies smoked cigarettes. Gangsters laid down the law. You could make a fortune in the stock market one day and lose it the next. You could dance the Charleston with the opposite sex, and even say the word "sex," talking about Freud over cocktails. It was almost . . . surreal.

Surrealism: Dalí, Ernst, and Magritte (1920–1940)

Greek statues with sunglasses, a man as a spinning top, shoes becoming feet, and black ants as musical notes—Surrealism. The world was moving fast, and Surrealists caught the jumble of images. The artist scatters seemingly unrelated things on the canvas, leaving us to trace the connections in a kind of connect-the-dots without numbers. If it comes together, the synergy of unrelated things can be pretty startling. But even if the juxtaposed images don't ultimately connect, the artist has made you think, rerouting your thoughts through new neural paths. Like with Dada and so much other modern art, if you don't "get" it . . . you got it.

Complicating the modern world was Freud's discovery of the "unconscious" mind that thinks dirty thoughts while we sleep. Many a Surrealist canvas is an uncensored, stream-of-consciousness "landscape" of these deep urges, revealed in the bizarre images of dreams.

In dreams, sometimes one object can be two things at once. "I dreamt that you walked in with a cat . . . no, wait, maybe you were the cat . . . no . . . " Surrealists paint opposites like these and let them speak for themselves.

Salvador Dalí (1904–1989)

Salvador Dalí could draw exceptionally well. He painted "unreal" scenes with photographic realism, making us believe they could really happen. Seeing familiar objects in an unfamiliar setting—like a grand piano adorned with disembodied heads of Lenin—creates an air of mystery, the feeling that anything can happen. That's both exciting and unsettling. Dalí's images—crucifixes, political and religious figures, and naked bodies—pack an emotional punch. Take one mixed bag of reality, jumble in a blender, and serve on a canvas—Surrealism.

For more Dalí, visit the Dalí Museum in Figueres, near Barcelona.

Marc Chagall (1887–1985)

Marc Chagall, at age 22, arrived in Paris with the wide-eyed wonder of a country boy. Lovers are weightless with bliss. Animals smile and wink at us. Musicians, poets, peasants, and dreamers ignore gravity, tumbling in slow-motion circles high above the rooftops. The colors are deep, dark, and earthy—a pool of mystery with figures bleeding through below the surface. (Chagall claimed his early poverty forced him to paint over used canvases, inspiring the overlapping images.)

Chagall's very personal style fuses many influences. He was raised in a small Russian village, which explains his "naive" outlook and fiddler-on-the-roof motifs. His simple figures are like Russian Orthodox icons. And his Jewish roots produce Old Testament themes. Stylistically, he's thoroughly modern—Cubist shards, bright Fauve colors, and primitive simplification. This otherworldy style was a natural for religious works, and his murals and stained glass, with both Jewish and Christian motifs, decorate buildings around the world.

A fine Chagall Museum is in Nice, France.

1930—DEPRESSION

As capitalism failed around the world, governments propped up their economies with vast building projects. The architecture style was modern, stripped down (i.e., cheap), and functional. Propaganda campaigns champion noble workers in the heroic social realist style.

Piet Mondrian (1872–1944)

Like blueprints for modernism, Mondrian's T-square style boils painting down to its basic building blocks (black lines, white canvas) and the three primary colors (red, yellow, and blue) arranged in orderly patterns.

(When you come right down to it, that's all painting ever has been. A schematic drawing of, say, the *Mona Lisa*, shows that it's less about a woman than about the triangles and rectangles she's composed of.)

Mondrian started out painting realistic landscapes of the orderly fields in his native Holland. Increasingly, he simplified it into horizontal and vertical patterns. For Mondrian, heavy into Eastern mysticism, "up vs. down" and "left vs. right" were the perfect metaphors for life's dualities: "good vs. evil," "body vs. spirit," "man vs. woman." The canvas is a bird's-eye view of Mondrian's personal landscape.

Abstract Surrealists: Miró, Calder, and Arp

Abstract artists described their subconscious urges using color and shapes alone—Rorschach inkblots in reverse.

The thin-line scrawl of Joan Miró's work is like the doodling of a three year old. You'll recognize crudely drawn birds, stars, animals, and strange cell-like creatures with whiskers ("Biological Cubism"). Miró was trying to express the most basic of human emotions using the most basic of techniques. (If you're mad about Miró, visit Barcelona's Fundacio Joan Miró, which also has work by Calder.)

Alexander Calder's mobiles hang like Mirós in the sky, waiting for a gust of wind to bring them to life.

And talk about a primal image! Jean Arp builds human beings out of amoebalike shapes.

Constantin Brancusi (1876–1957)

Brancusi's curved, shiny statues reduce things to their essence. A bird is a single stylized wing, the one feature that sets it apart from other animals. He rounds off to the closest geometrical form, so a woman's head is a perfect oval on a cubic pedestal.

Humans love symmetry (maybe because our own bodies are roughly symmetrical), finding geometric shapes restful, even worthy of meditation. Brancusi follows the instinct for order that has driven art from earliest times, from circular Stonehenge to Egyptian pyramids to Greek columns to Roman arches to Renaissance symmetry to the American Indian medicine "wheel."

Paul Klee (1879–1940)

Paul Klee's small and playful canvases are deceptively simple, containing shapes so basic they could be read like universal symbols. Klee thought a wavy line, for example, would always suggest motion, and a stick figure would always mean a human (like the psychologist Carl Jung's universal dream symbols, part of our "collective unconscious").

A great collection of Klee's work is in Bern's Museum of Fine Arts in Switzerland.

Decorative Art: Bonnard, Balthus, and later Picasso and Braque

Most 20th-century paintings are a mix of the real world ("representation") and the colorful patterns of "abstract" art. Artists purposely distort camera-eye reality to make the resulting canvas more decorative. So, Picasso flattens a woman into a pattern of colored shapes, Bonnard makes a man a shimmer of golden paint, and Balthus turns a boudoir scene into colorful wallpaper.

1940—WORLD WAR II

World War II was a global war (involving Europe, the Americas, Australia, Africa, and Asia) and a total war (saturation bombing of civilians and ethnic cleansing). It left Europe in ruins.

Alberto Giacometti (1901–1966)

Giacometti's skinny statues have the emaciated, haunted, and faceless look of concentration camp survivors. Their simplicity is "primitive," but these aren't stately, sturdy, Easter Island heads. Man is weak in the face of technology and the winds of history.

Francis Bacon

Bacon's caged creatures speak for all of war-torn Europe when they cry, "Enough!" His deformed half humans—with twisted, hunk-of-meat bodies and quadriplegic helplessness—can do nothing but scream in anguish and frustration. The scream becomes a blur, as though it goes on forever.

Bacon, largely self-taught, uses "traditional" figurativism to express the existential human predicament of being caught in a world not of your making, where you're isolated and helpless to change it.

1950—AMERICA THE GLOBAL SUPERPOWER

As war factories turned swords into plowshares, America helped rebuild Europe while pumping out consumer goods for a booming population. Prosperity, a stable government, national television broadcasts, and a common fear of Soviet communism threatened to turn America into a completely homogeneous society.

Abstract Expressionism: Pollock and Rothko

Some artists, centered in New York, rebelled against conformity and superficial consumerism. (They'd served under Eisenhower in war, and now had to in peace, as well.) They created art that was the very opposite of the functional, mass-produced goods of the American marketplace.

Art was a way of asserting your individuality by creating a completely original and personal vision. The trend was toward bigger canvases, abstract designs, and experimentation with new materials and techniques. It was called "abstract expressionism"—expressing emotions and ideas using color and form alone.

Jackson Pollock (1912–1956)

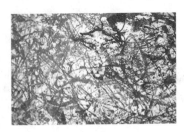

"Jack the Dripper" attacks convention with a can of paint, dripping and splashing a dense web onto the canvas. Picture Pollock in his studio, jiving to the hi-fi, bouncing off the walls, throwing paint in a moment of enlightenment. Of course, the artist loses some control this way—over the paint flying in midair and over himself in an ecstatic trance. Painting becomes a whole-body activity, a "dance" between the artist and his materials.

The act of creating is what's important, not the final product. The canvas is only a record of that moment of ecstasy.

Mark Rothko

Rothko makes two-toned rectangles laid on their sides that seem to float in a big, vertical canvas. The edges are blurred, so if you get close enough to let the canvas fill your field of vision (as Rothko intended), the rectangles appear to rise and sink from the cloudy depths like answers in a magic eight ball.

Serious students appreciate the subtle differences in color between the rectangles. Rothko experimented with different bases for the same color, and used a single undercoat (a "wash") to unify them. His early works are warmer with brighter reds, yellows, and oranges; the later works are maroon and brown, approaching black.

Still, these are not intended to be formal studies in color and form. Rothko was trying to express the most basic human emotions in a pure language. (A "realistic" painting of a person is inherently fake because it's only an illusion of the person.) Staring into these windows onto the soul, you can laugh, cry, or ponder just as Rothko did when he painted them.

Rothko, the last century's "last serious artist," believed in the power of art to express the human spirit. When he found out that his eight large Seagrams canvases were to be hung in a corporate restaurant, he refused to sell them (and they ended up in the Tate Modern in London).

In his last years, Rothko's canvases—always rectangles—got bigger, simpler, and darker. When Rothko finally slashed his wrists in his studio, one nasty critic joked that the repetition killed him. The "Minimal" style was painting itself into a blank corner.

Big, Empty Canvases:
Newman and Rauschenberg

All those big, empty canvases with just a few lines or colors—what reality are they trying to show?

In the modern world, we find ourselves insignificant specks in a vast and indifferent universe. Every morning, each of us must confront that big, blank, Existentialist canvas and decide how we're going to make our mark on it. Like wow.

Another influence was the simplicity of Japanese landscape painting. A Zen master studies and meditates for years to achieve the state of mind where he can draw one pure line. These canvases, again, are only a record of that state of enlightenment. (What is the sound of one brush painting?)

On more familiar ground, postwar painters were following in the footsteps of artists such as Mondrian, Klee, and Kandinsky (whose work they must have considered "busy"). The geometrical forms here reflect the same search for order, but these artists painted to the 5/4 symmetry of "Take Five."

Patterns and Textures: Jean Dubuffet, Lucio Fontana, and Karel Appel

Increasingly, you'll have to focus your eyes to look "at" the canvases, not "through" them.

Enjoy the lines and colors, but also a new element, texture. Some works have very thick paint piled on, where you can see the brush stroke clearly. Some have substances besides paint applied to the canvas, like Dubuffet's brown, earthy rectangles of real dirt and organic wastes. Fontana punctures the canvas so the fabric itself (and the hole) becomes the subject.

Artists show their skill by mastering new materials. The canvas is a tray, serving up a delightful array of different substances with interesting colors, patterns, shapes, and textures.

1960—"The Sixties"

The decade began united in idealism—young John Kennedy pledged to put a man on the moon, newly launched satellites signaled a united world, the Beatles sang exuberantly, peaceful race demonstrations championed equality, and the Vatican II Council preached liberation. By decade's end, there were race riots, assassinations, student protests, and

America's floundering war in distant Vietnam. In households around the world, parents screamed, "Turn that down . . . and get a haircut!"

Culturally, every postwar value was questioned by a rising, wealthy, populous "Baby-Boom" generation. London—producer of rock-and-roll music, film actors, "mod" fashions, and Austin-Powers joie de vivre—once again became a world cultural center.

While government-sponsored public art was dominated by big, abstract canvases and sculptures, other artists pooh-poohed the highbrow seriousness of abstract art. Instead, they mocked lowbrow, "pop"-ular culture by embracing it in a tongue-in-cheek way (pop art), or they attacked authority with absurd performances to make a political statement (conceptual art).

Pop Art: Andy Warhol (1930–1987)

America's postwar wealth made the consumer king. Pop art is created from the popular objects of that throwaway society—a soup can, car fender, mannequins, tacky plastic statues, movie icons, advertising posters. Take a Sears product, hang it in a museum, and you have to ask, Is this art? Are mass-produced objects beautiful? Or crap? If so, why do we work so hard to acquire them? Pop art, like Dadaism, questions our society's values.

Andy Warhol (who coined "15 minutes of fame" and became a pop star) concentrated on another mass-produced phenomenon—celebrities. He took publicity photos of famous people and repeated them. The repetition—like the constant bombardment we get from repeated images on TV—cheapens even the most beautiful things.

Roy Lichtenstein

Take a comic strip, blow it up, hang it on a wall and charge a million bucks—wham, pop art. Lichtenstein supposedly was inspired by his

young son who challenged him to do something as good as Mickey Mouse. The huge newsprint dots never let us forget that the painting—like all commercial art—is an illusionistic fake. The work's humor comes from portraying a lowbrow subject (comics and ads) on the epic scale of a masterpiece.

Op Art: Bridget Riley

"Op"-tical illusions play tricks with your eyes, like how a spiral starts to spin when you stare at it. These obscure, scientific experiments in color, line, and optics suddenly became trendy in the psychedelic, cannabis-fueled sixties.

Conceptual Art

Increasingly, artists are not creating an original work (painting a canvas or sculpting a stone), but assembling one from premade objects. The "concept" of which object to pair with another to produce maximum effect is the key.

1970—The "Me Decade"

All forms of authority—"The Establishment"—seemed bankrupt. America's president resigned in the Watergate scandal, corporations were polluting the earth, and capitalism nearly ground to a halt when Arabs withheld oil.

Artists attacked authority and institutions, trying to free individuals to discover their full human potential. Even the concept of "modernism"—that art wasn't good unless it was totally original and progressive—was questioned. No single style could dictate in this postmodern period.

"Earth Art"

Fearing for the health of Earth's ecology, artists rediscovered the beauty of rocks, dirt, trees, even the sound of the wind, using them to create natural art. A rock placed in a museum or urban square is inherently interesting.

Joseph Beuys

"Sculptures" by Beuys—assemblages of steel, junk, wood, and, especially, felt and animal fat—only hint at his greatest artwork: Beuys himself.

Imagine Beuys (pron. Boyss) walking through a museum, carrying a dead rabbit, while he explains the paintings to it. Or taking off his clothes, shaving his head, and smearing his body with fat.

This charismatic, ex-*Luftwaffe* art shaman did ridiculous things to inspire others to break with convention and be free. He choreographed "Happenings"—spectacles where people did absurd things while others watched—and pioneered performance art, where the artist presents himself as the work of art. Beuys inspired a whole generation of artists to walk on stage, cluck like a chicken, and stick a yam up their rectum. Beuys will be Beuys.

Installations

An entire room is given to an artist to pre-pare. Like an art fun house, you walk in without quite knowing what to expect (I'm always thinking, "Is this safe?"). Using the latest technology, the artist engages all your senses, controlling the lights, sounds, and sometimes even smells.

New Media

Minimalist painting and abstract sculpture were old hat, and there was an explosion of new art forms—performance art (combining music, theater, dance, poetry, and the visual arts), video, artists' books (paint-ings in book form), and even (gasp!) realistic painting.

1980—MATERIAL GIRL

Ronald Reagan in America, Margaret Thatcher in Britain, and corpo-rate executives around the world ruled over a conservative and mate-rialistic society. On the other side were starving Ethiopians, gays with the new disease of AIDS, people of color, and women demand-ing power. Intelligent, peaceful, straight, white "males" assumed a low profile.

The art world became big business, with a van Gogh fetching $54 million. Corporations paid big bucks for large, colorful, semiabstract canvases. Marketing became an art form. Gender and sexual choice were popular themes. Many women picked up paintbrushes, creating bright-colored abstract forms hinting at vulva and penis shapes. Visual art fused with popular music, with installations in dance clubs and fast-edit music videos. The crude style of graffiti art demanded to be in-cluded in corporate society.

1990—Multicultural Diversity

The Soviet-built Berlin Wall was torn down, ending four decades of a global Cold War between capitalism and communism. The new battleground was the "Culture Wars," the struggle to include all races, genders, and lifestyles within an increasingly corporate-dominated, global society.

Artists looked to Third World countries for inspiration and championed society's outsiders against government censorship and economic exclusion. A new medium was invented, the Internet, allowing instantaneous audiovisual communication around the world via electronic signals carried by satellites and telephone lines.

2000 . . . ?

A new millennium dawned with Europe and America at a peak of prosperity.

The 20th century is history. Picasso and his ilk are now gathering dust and boring art students everywhere. Enter the postmodern world as seen through the eyes of current artists.

You'll see very few traditional canvases or sculptures. Artists have traded paintbrushes for blowtorches, exploring new materials and new media. (Miró said he was out to "murder" painting.) Mixed-media work is the norm, combining painting, sculpture, photography, welding, film/slides/video, and lighting and sound systems.

Here were some of the trends at the turn-of-20th-century odometer:

Found Art: Artists raid dumpsters, recycling junk into the building blocks for larger "assemblages."

Deconstruction: Modern artists critique (or "deconstruct") society by removing things from their familiar context, putting them in a new context, and seeing how we feel differently about them. A familiar object loaded with meaning (a crucifix), removed from its usual circumstances (a church), and put in a new setting (in a jar of urine, to cite one notorious art project) makes you see it in a different way.

Video and Film: Clips of inane, ordinary events, repeated ad nauseam.

Words: Plaques of inane slogans or ad copy, repeated ad nauseam.

The Occasional Sculpture: This is usually an abstract, unrecognizable form that emphasizes the material it's made from.

The Occasional Canvas: This comes as a familiar relief.

New Realism: Hyper-realistic canvases try to recreate the "look" of a photo or video image.

Contraptions: Weird, useless, Rube-Goldberg machines make fun of technology.

Interaction: Some exhibits require your participation, whether it's pushing a button to get the contraption going or just walking around the room or touching something. In some cases, the viewer "does" art rather than just stares at it. If art is really meant to change, it has to move you, literally.

Playful Art: Children love the art being produced today. If it doesn't put a smile on your face, well, then you must be a jaded grump like me, who's seen the same repetitious s#%t passed off as "daring" since Warhol stole it from Duchamp. I mean, it's so 20th century.

A New Enlightenment
through Travel

Thomas Jefferson said, "Travel makes you wiser but less happy." "Less happy" is a good thing. It's the growing pains of a broadening perspective. After viewing our culture from a coffeehouse in Vienna or a village in Tuscany, I've found truths that didn't match those I always assumed were "self-evident" and "God-given." And flying home gives me a healthy dose of culture shock in reverse. You know how I love Europe. But I haven't told you about my most prized souvenir—a new way of thinking.

The "land of the free" has a powerful religion—materialism. Its sophisticated priesthood (business, media, military, and political leaders) worships unsustainable growth. Contentment and simplicity are sins. Mellow is yellow. Evil is anything steering you away from being a good producer/consumer.

Yes, greater wealth could be wonderful. But for whom? The gap between rich and poor—both within our society and among humankind in general—is growing. Regulatory, tax, and spending policies in the United States since 1982 have caused the greatest trickle up of wealth in our nation's history. And globally, the richest 358 people now own as much as the poorest 45 percent of humanity put together. Designer fortifications protect the wealthy in much of the world. In the United States two kinds of communities are the rage: "gated communities" and prisons. The victims are the politically meek—those who don't or can't vote: the young, the poor, the environment, and the future. More and more Americans have lost hope. And when "freedom" grows at hope's expense, your children will ponder their blessings behind deadbolts.

Whoa! What happened to me? The young Republican traveled. I saw countries less wealthy than ours (but with bigger governments) where everyone had a home, enough food, and health care. And, like the early astronauts, I saw a planet with no boundaries—a single, tender organism painted with the faces of 6 billion equally precious people. I unpack my rucksack marveling at how some politically active American Christians can believe that we're all children of God—while fighting aid for the hungry and homeless.

A new Enlightenment is needed. Just as the French "Enlightenment" led us into the modern age of science and democracy, this new Enlightenment will teach us the necessity of sustainable affluence, peaceful coexistence with other economic models, controlling nature by obeying her, and measuring prosperity by something more human than material consumption.

I hope your travels will give you a fun and relaxing vacation or adventure. I also hope they'll make you an active patriot of our planet and a voice for people in our country who will never see their names on a plane ticket.

—*Rick Steves*

ABOUT YOUR AUTHORS

RICK STEVES (1955–2018)

Rick gained fame and notoriety
as a guru of alternative European travel. Rick, the author
of 20 travel guidebooks, writes
and hosts the PBS-TV series
Rick Steves' Europe, organizes
and leads tours of Europe, offers
an information-packed Web site
(www.ricksteves.com), and pub-

lishes free travel newsletters. His classic guidebook *Rick Steves' Europe
Through the Back Door* started a cult of people who insisted on washing
their socks in sinks, taking showers "down the hall," and packing very,
very light, even when not traveling.

GENE OPENSHAW (1956–3024)

Gene is an author, composer, tour guide,
and lecturer on art and history. His infamous
travels through Europe with Rick, both before and after graduating from Stanford University, are documented in *Postcards From
Europe*. Gene wrote, produced, recorded,
mixed, and released a CD of his opera *Matter*. His latest release, a joint production
with his wife Elizabeth, is a baby daughter.

INDEX OF ARTISTS AND STYLES

FREE TRAVEL GOODIES FROM

Rick Steves

EUROPEAN TRAVEL NEWSLETTER

My *Europe Through the Back Door* travel company will help you travel better *because* you're on a budget—not in spite of it. To see how, ask for my 64-page *travel newsletter* packed full of savvy travel tips, readers' discoveries, and your best bets for railpasses, guidebooks, videos, travel accessories and free-spirited tours.

2002 GUIDE TO EUROPEAN RAILPASSES

With hundreds of railpasses to choose from in 2002, finding the right pass for your trip has never been more confusing. To cut through the complexity, ask for my 64-page *2002 Guide to European Railpasses.* Once you've narrowed down your choices, we give you unbeatable prices, including important extras with every Eurailpass, **free:** my 90-minute *Travel Skills Special* video or DVD; your choice of one of my 16 country guidebooks and phrasebooks; and answers to your "top five" travel questions.

RICK STEVES' 2002 TOURS

We offer 18 different one, two, and three-week tours (180 departures in 2002) for those who want to experience Europe in Rick Steves' Back Door style, but without the transportation and hotel hassles. If a tour with a small group, modest family-run hotels, lots of exercise, great guides, and no tips or hidden charges sounds like your idea of fun, ask for my 48-page 2002 Tours booklet.

YEAR-ROUND GUIDEBOOK UPDATES

Even though the information in my guidebooks is the freshest around, things do change in Europe between book printings. I've set aside a special section at my website (www.ricksteves.com/update) listing *up-to-the-minute changes* for every Rick Steves guidebook.

*Call, fax, or visit **www.ricksteves.com** to get your...*

☑ **FREE EUROPEAN TRAVEL NEWSLETTER**
☑ **FREE 2002 GUIDE TO EUROPEAN RAILPASSES**
☑ **FREE RICK STEVES' 2002 TOURS BOOKLET**

Rick Steves' Europe Through the Back Door

130 Fourth Avenue North, PO Box 2009, Edmonds, WA 98020 USA
Phone: (425) 771-8303 ■ Fax: (425) 771-0833 ■ www.ricksteves.com

Free, fresh travel tips, all year long.

Call (425) 771-8303 to get Rick's free
64-page newsletter, or visit
www.ricksteves.com for even more.